PRAISE FOR ERICK WADSWORTH

"I heartily endorse this book and the years of dedicated research of Erick Wadsworth."

— GARY HARLO CLAYTON (GREAT-GREAT GRANDSON OF WILLIAM CLAYTON) DONIPHAN, NE. SEMI-RETIRED SALES CAREER. FOREVER A STUDENT OF THE TRAILS

"Wadsworth brings solidly documented clarity and understanding to this period."

— HARLAN SEYFER-TRAIL BOSS, NEBRASKA CHAPTER OF THE OREGON-CALIFORNIA TRAILS ASSOCIATION

"Erick Wadsworth stands virtually alone in this visually and meticulously written reference work."

— R. VAL RASMUSSEN, NEBRASKA MORMON TRAILS ASSOCIATION (NMTA) EDUCATIONAL CHAIRMAN, CACHE JCT. UTAH

THE MISSISSIPPI SAINTS

THE
MISSISSIPPI
SAINTS

A HISTORY OF THE MORMON SPRINGS PIONEERS AND THEIR JOURNEY WEST

ERICK L. WADSWORTH

Trail Publishing

THE MISSISSIPPI SAINTS

Copyright © 2026 Marilyn Wadsworth

Edited and Indexed by Marilyn Wadsworth

Publishing Services provided by Edits by Stacey LLC, Print to Pro

Cover Photo taken by Erick and Marilyn Wadsworth.

Published Posthumously by Erick Wadsworth

For permission requests, write the publisher at marilynrwadsworth@msn.com

Library of Congress Control Number: 2026907725

Paperback: 978-1-7334717-0-1

eBook: 978-1-7334717-2-5

CONTENTS

FOREWORD

BY MARILYN WADSWORTH

This book is lovingly presented to its readers, a product of extensive research and dedication by the author, Erick L. Wadsworth. As his final work of historical accounts, Erick aimed to immortalize the stories of people from the past whom he believed deserved to be remembered. He sought to narrate their life stories and ensure their legacy endured for generations. These were people of faith and hard work, whose paths have shaped their descendants' journeys.

Erick's passion for history and its protagonists began in his youth. At the age of 60, he pursued an M.A. in history from the University of Nebraska Kearney, embarking on a mission to document the resilient pioneers who traversed the Nebraska Territory and the Great Plains on their trek to Zion. His particular interest lay in the history of the LDS Church.

His most recent project focused on the Mississippi Company, which embarked on its westward journey in 1846. Initiating this endeavor in 2021, Erick traveled to numerous locations, including Mississippi, Florence, Santa Fe, Pueblo, Laramie, UC Berkeley, Astoria, Baker City, Grafton, St. George, Salt Lake City, and Bent's Fort. Throughout these travels, he engaged with researchers and historians, delving into all relevant materials for this manuscript.

Erick cherished the journey and the connections he made along the way.

Eager to complete this book, Erick once remarked, "If anything should happen to me, it needs to be indexed and completed." Tragically, after submitting the final draft to his editor, Erick fell ill and passed away suddenly on January 14, 2025. This book is the culmination of four years of unwavering dedication. I hope you read it with the same understanding and love for its subjects that Erick had.

His loving wife,
Marilyn

A PREFACE

In 2019, I published a book entitled *The Last Outfitting Station on the Missouri River, 1864 to 1866: Wyoming, NT, and the Nebraska City Cut-Off Trail.* This book covered establishing a town in Nebraska Territory, which stood about forty miles south of Florence, Nebraska. In addition, the volume details the three years the LDS Church used a little-known trail to cross Nebraska between 1864 and 1866. I wrote it in 2019 for the same reason as this book. It was an extension of my master's thesis, written while I attended the University of Nebraska Kearny from 2010 to my graduation in 2014. Before I wrote the aforementioned book, I found no fully researched volumes written about church migrations during the mid-1860s. I am an active member of The Church of Jesus Christ of Latter-day Saints. My father and brother were baptized in 1956, while the family lived in central Florida. I have made every effort to present the information contained in this book in an unbiased manner. However, my membership in the church may make total objectivity difficult. This book covers the lives of average, everyday people who happened to live in the southern United States. When these individuals heard missionaries from a church that began in the state of New York, they accepted the teachings and were baptized. Soon after joining this new religion, they left the South and headed west. These men, women, and enslaved persons settled several areas in the western United States, and their accomplishments should be remembered. They left everything for an unknown destination in the west.

About five years ago, I discovered a story about a small group of people from Mississippi and Alabama who joined the church I belong to. Shortly after joining this new religion, this group headed west. I began searching for information about this uniqueband, but other than a few articles, I found only small amounts of material about them. Unable to locate a book written about this them, I began considering writing one. I initiated my research by traveling to Monroe County, Mississippi, and Pueblo, Colorado, in 2021. I undertook another trip to Independence, Missouri, in 2023. I completed most of my library research online. In the beginning, this was due to the COVID crisis, but following that, I determined to continue exploring from home. I am currently seventy-two years of age, and my research is conducted alone. With that said, I am pleased to produce this book about an overlooked band of southern believers from the early days of church history.

INTRODUCTION

Many notable researchers and historians have written about the establishment of The Church of Jesus Christ of Latter-day Saints, the years of struggle to locate a place to settle, and the forced exoduses from Kirtland, Ohio; Missouri; and finally Nauvoo, Illinois, in the winter of 1846. Publications in distinguished magazines, lessons taught in seminary, and presentations in various church meetings constitute an important aspect of the culture within the LDS Church. The vast majority of the accounts focus on the early years, from the vanguard wagon train led by Brigham Young in 1847 to the ill-fated Martin and Willie handcart journeys of 1856. The accounts of these early migrations keep the sacrifice and dedication of these daring women and men within our reach, and now, with so many accounts available online, the opportunity to discover their stories is literally at our fingertips.

This book focuses on a forgotten journey that began in northeastern Mississippi in April 1846. They traveled west at the recommendation of Brigham Young and expected to meet with other Latter-day Saint pioneers on the trail at Grand Island in present-day Nebraska. Unfortunately, due to the horrible conditions on the trails from Nauvoo to Iowa and the church's limited finances, the migration west ground to a halt in 1846. The creation of the Mormon Battalion provided desperately needed money to the cash-strapped church. The pioneers of 1846 were forced to stop their western migration on the western banks of the Missouri River at a location named Winter Quarters in the current town of Florence, Nebraska. In the early 1840s, missionaries called to work in the areas of northeastern Mississippi and northwestern Alabama discovered a group of people who accepted their preaching as they represented a church less than fifteen years old. Those who accepted baptism and joined the new religion were a mixture of plantation owners, enslavers, overseers for the plantations, and farmers with little money. This eclectic group, along with other family members from Illinois, not only accepted baptism but also gave up everything they owned to move to an unidentified location in the West.

My original plan for this book focused on the relationship of the Mississippi Saints with the Mormon Battalion, and I originally wrote several chapters about that connection. However, after becoming acquainted with several resolute women and men whose research and writing focused on the Mormon Battalion, I determined my limited knowledge of the Battalion would not benefit others. As you will see, one portion of a chapter in this book concerns the Mormon Battalion and their winter in Pueblo in 1846 to 1847. I am of the opinion the meeting of members of the Mormon Battalion and the six men who traveled east from Pueblo in September 1846 with John D. Lee was not a coincidence. The six men were returning to their homes in the South and had no knowledge of the formation of the Mormon Battalion, much less their march on the Santa Fe Trail at that time. The result of this meeting on the trail was a resting place for several members of the Battalion, their wives, and their children at Pueblo, which likely saved lives. Thus, information about the Mormon Battalion is limited in this book. One of the best places to learn more about the Mormon Battalion and its history is their website at mormonbattalion.com.

The study of this unique group of Saints (Church members) from the South provided an opportunity to learn more about the history of slavery, its introduction in the South, and how the culture of these individuals impacted both the government in the early Utah Territory and the church's ban on Black men receiving the priesthood. This ban denied Black men, of African descent, the right to hold leadership positions and access to temple ordinances, which constitute key components of church values. The Utah Territorial Legislature created a form of slavery in the Utah Territory in 1852, which led to an overall priesthood ban against Black male members of the church years later—even though Elijah Able, a Black church member, received the Melchizedek priesthood in 1835. This book is not intended to be an examination of slavery in Utah Territory or of the priesthood ban that developed over the years. Nevertheless, several Southern enslavers brought their enslaved people to Utah Territory and kept them enslaved until the federal government outlawed all slavery in United States territories in 1862. The lifting of the priesthood ban came by revelation 1 June 1978 to the president of the church at the time, Spencer W. Kimball. Since that time, all "worthy male members of the church" are eligible to receive the priesthood, which offers opportunities for additional service in the church—including participation in temple ordinances. Unfortunately, a form of slavery in Utah Territory and the priesthood ban are a difficult part of the church's history. Two chapters in this book are about the specific experiences of Black men and women who came west, along with their accomplishments and challenges.

The church members that constituted the company known as the Mississippi Saints were not saints. They were everyday people who embraced a new faith with their whole hearts. Their accomplishments are legendary. Members of this group helped found Holladay, Utah. Others traveled to San Bernardino to assist in creating a vibrant settlement in Southern California—until being called back in 1857. Several traveled to the gold fields in Northern California and participated in several settlements there. These men and women built hotels, planted crops, and established orchards. These Mississippi Saints became citizens who were respected by their peers. Mississippi Saints also participated in the establishment and growth of the Cotton

Mission established by Brigham Young. These adults, who had previously lived in the lush green surroundings of the South, experienced the hot, barren climate of southern Utah Territory, constant struggles with the Indigenous people of the area, and continual flooding of the Virgin and other rivers.

On a personal note, one of the stories contained in this book centers on George Washington Gibson, who lived and died while serving in the Cotton Mission. One of his sons, Robert Pulaski Gibson, joined him there. During his short time at Grafton, Utah Territory, a daughter, Laura Jane Gibson, was born 16 June 1864. Many years later, Laura Jane Gibson married Robert Story Henderson Watson, and they settled in a small town in eastern Idaho named Menan. Laura Jane Gibson Watson helped raise my mother, Roba Jean Watson Wadsworth, during the 1920s and 1930s. Mother continually talked about the deep love she held for her Grandmother Watson and how much she treasured the time she spent in her grandmother's home during her childhood. One reason Laura Jane helped raise my mother was due to the divorce of my mother's parents. After the divorce of Roba Jean's parents, she spent many years living under the influence of her maternal grandmother and always remembered the love she felt while in her grandmother's home.

1

EARLY YEARS OF THE CHURCH OF JESUS CHRIST OF LATTER-DAY SAINTS: 1830-1844

The Church of Jesus Christ of Latter-day Saints was formally established 6 April 1830 under the direction of Joseph Smith. The formal organization took place at Fayette, Seneca, New York. The name used to first denote the church on this day was "The Church of Christ." During this first meeting of the new church, Joseph Smith was told he would be known as a seer, translator, prophet, apostle, and an elder of the church.

Oliver Cowdery was one of the two presiding elders in the new church, second in authority to Joseph Smith. Cowdery used the title of "second elder" when signing ministerial licenses. It was Cowdery who preached the first public discourse on Sunday, 11 April 1830, at Fayette, Seneca, New York.[1] The result of this first public sermon, held in the home of Peter Whitmer Sr., was the baptism of five individuals. On 18 April 1830, seven more people were baptized into the newly formed church. Oliver Cowdery baptized all the candidates.[2]

---

1. "Revelation, 6 April 1830 [D&C 21]," p. 28, The Joseph Smith Papers, <accessed May 26, 2021> https://beta.josephsmithpapers.org/paper-summary/revelation-6-april-1830-dc-21/1,

2. Joseph Smith, *History of the Church of Jesus Christ of Latter-day Saints,* 7 Volumes, (Salt Lake City: The Deseret Book Company, 1973), 1:81

This sanctioned religious organization occurred some ten years after the vision of God the Father and Jesus Christ to a young Joseph Smith. It followed the publication of the *Book of Mormon* in 1829, which created another book of scripture for those who believed their new prophet.[3]

KIRTLAND, OHIO: 1831-1838

From the earliest days of the church, a physical gathering to a central geographic location constituted a crucial component of the church's policies. Kirtland, Ohio, became the first gathering location. A preacher named Sidney Rigdon was taught by four missionaries of the newly organized church in October 1830 in northeastern Ohio. Rigdon's popularity as a preacher and his influence on those around him served as a conversion catalyst for others living in Ohio. Those four missionaries—Oliver Cowdery, Peter Whitmer Jr., Parley P. Pratt and Ziba Peterson—baptized approximately 130 individuals from the area into the new gospel in just over a month. Thus, twice as many converts were baptized in the Ohio area as were converted during the first six months of the church's history.

When Joseph Smith and his wife, Emma, arrived in Kirtland on 1 February 1831, the town consisted of roughly 100 members.[4] Settlers living in towns near Kirtland seemed primed to hear the message shared by these four missionaries. One group of about fifty individuals belonged to the Reformed Baptist movement, living on a farm owned by Isaac Morley. They all joined the church. Historian Milton Backman concluded, "More members of this religious movement were attracted to the restored gospel in 1830 than emerged from any other society."[5]

Even though residents in the Kirtland area joined the church,

---

3. Ibid, 5-6, 71
4. Milton Vaughn Backman Jr. (1972) "The Quest for a Restoration: The Birth of Mormonism in Ohio," BYU Studies Quarterly: Vol. 12 : Iss. 4 , Article 3. 346-347, Available at: https://scholarsarchive.byu.edu/byusq/vol12/iss4/3 , <accessed 8 June 2021>
5. Ibid, 351

others held animosity toward those who belonged to this new religion. George Albert Smith recorded the following account in his journal:

> In the spring of 1835, a majority of the inhabitants of Kirtland combined together and warned all the Saints to leave the town. This was done to prevent any of our people from becoming a town charge in the case of poverty. They then bought up all the grain that was for sale in the country around, and refused to sell a particle of it to our people. Mr. Lyman, a Presbyterian owning the Kirtland Mills was at the head of the movement, he accumulated several thousand bushels of grain in his mill and refused to sell the least portion of it to any of the Saints. This arrangement was brought about by a combination of all religious sects in the community.[6]

Fortunately, Joseph Smith learned of the plan, and members living in the area provided funds to purchase wheat from nearby Portage County.[7]

The early missionary successes in Kirtland formed the genesis of significant proselyting activity centering in and around that village. In the month of June 1831, twenty-eight missionaries received their call to journey to Missouri. They were to travel in pairs, and each group was to take different routes, allowing them to reach more locations. Missionaries often took circuitous routes as these new ambassadors headed out to preach in different towns and villages on their circuits.[8] During the Kirtland years, from 1831 to 1837, the state of Ohio was saturated with missionaries. Often, elders would serve short missions. For example, Hyrum Smith, the older brother of Joseph Smith, left on

---

6. George Albert Smith, 1817-1875. George A. Smith autobiography , image 70/657 https://catalog.churchofjesuschrist.org/assets/55f72e1f-bfa2-466c-8cec-c5d4a3009405/0/69?lang=eng, <accessed 8 January 2023>
7. Ibid
8. Davis Bitton, (1971) "Kirtland as a Center of Missionary Activity, 1830-1838," BYU Studies Quarterly: Vol. 11 : Iss. 4 , Article 10. 498-499, Available at: https://scholarsarchive.byu.edu/byusq/vol11/iss4/10, <accessed 10 June 2021>

a mission with Reynolds Cahoon in December 1831. He returned in time to fulfill another mission on 14 January 1832. During his time away, Hyrum and Reynolds preached in Poncort, Leroy, Thompson, Rome, Bloomfield, Furnessytown, Hiram, and Wethersfield—all in Ohio. Others would serve for longer periods of time. Lorenzo Barnes was baptized on 16 June 1833 at the age of twenty-one. Less than one month later, he was ordained an elder in the church and sent on his first mission. He served during the months of August and September, then went back to Kirtland to work on the new temple and teach school. In the spring of 1834, Lorenzo traveled with Joseph Smith to Missouri in an unsuccessful bid to ease tensions in that state. He was home less than a month before leaving on another mission for five-and-a-half months. Barnes briefly returned to Kirtland before leaving on another mission.[9]

During this time of extensive missionary efforts and the building of a House of the Lord, or temple, the church also assumed large contracts for purchasing land in and around Kirtland.[10] Most members of the church were not wealthy, so the ability to support the church through contributions fell woefully short. A different approach was needed to keep the church from going further into debt, and some type of banking system seemed the best solution. An attempt to obtain a charter from the state legislature failed, so the founders pursued an alternative form of "banking" to generate cash and provide credit. Calling it the Kirtland Safety Society Anti-Banking Company, Joseph Smith, Sidney Rigdon, and two others formally organized the bank on 2 November 1836.[11] Although

---

9. Ibid, 499-500

10. Scott H. Partridge, (1972) "The Failure of the Kirtland Safety Society," BYU Studies Quarterly: Vol. 12 : Iss. 4 , Article 8. 439, Available at: https://scholarsarchive.byu.edu/byusq/vol12/iss4/8, <accessed 10 June 2021>

11. *Constitution of the Kirtland Safety Society Bank,* Kirtland Township, *Geauga Co., OH, 2 Nov. 1836. Featured version printed [ca. Dec. 1836] as an extra of* Latter Day Saints' Messenger and Advocate, *Dec. 1836; endorsed by unidentified scribe; one page; CHL.* Available at https://www.josephsmithpapers.org/paper-summary/constitution-of-the-kirtland-safety-society-bank-2-november-1836/1#ft-source-note, <accessed 14 June 2021>

moderately successful for a brief period, the end came quickly, and the doors were closed in the summer of 1837.[12] One reason for the collapse of the institution was the inflated appraisals of real estate used to establish the high face values of shares offered by the Anti-Bank. Unfortunately, the financial condition of the country—and the state—placed tremendous pressure on *all* banks. The bank's failure caused widespread discontent toward Joseph Smith and apostasy among many members of the church, including high-ranking leadership.[13]

Building a House of the Lord became a primary focus of the members of the church who lived in Kirtland. At a conference on 4 May 1833, a new committee began seeking subscriptions, meaning cash, to build a House of the Lord. As noted earlier, the church's financial situation was on shaky ground, and building a structure of significant proportions seemed a daunting task. Nevertheless, against overwhelming odds, these devoted members moved ahead. The first work on the temple began on 5 June 1833 as George A. Smith hauled the first load of stone. At the same time, Hyrum Smith and Reynolds Cahoon began to dig the trench for the foundation. Many residents of Kirtland assisted in the work of building the temple, and after many months of volunteering, the building was completed. It was to be a house unto the Lord, a house of prayer and fasting, and a temple to His name.[14] The physical proportions of this building were significant. The structure was constructed of stone, eighty feet long and sixty feet wide, with a tower 110 feet from the ground. A special meeting called a Solemn Assembly took place on 27 March 1836. During the Solemn Assembly, a dedicatory prayer was offered. Many within the building stated they witnessed angels and the "sound of a

---

12. Paul D. Sampson and Larry T. Wimmer, (1972) "The Kirtland Safety Society: The Stock Ledger Book and The Bank Failure," BYU Studies Quarterly: Vol. 12 : Iss. 4 , Article 7, 429. Available at: https://scholarsarchive.byu.edu/byusq/vol12/iss4/7, <accessed 15 June 2021>

13. Ibid, 430

14. Joseph Fielding Smith, *Essentials in Church History*, (Deseret Book Company for the Church of Jesus Christ of Latter-day Saints, 1979), 128-129

mighty rushing wind" filling the house. Many people in the neighbor-hood came rushing to the building, having heard a strange sound and witnessed a bright light resting on the newly constructed temple.[15]

Lucy Mack Smith, Joseph Smith's mother, described how building the temple began.

> After the close of the meeting, Joseph took the brethren with him for the purpose of selecting a spot for the building to stand up on. The place they made the choice of was situated in the northwest corner of a field of wheat, which was sown by my sons the fall previous, on the farm upon which we were then living. In a few minutes, the fence was removed, and the standing grain was leveled, in order to prepare a place for the building and Hyrum commenced digging a trench for the wall, he having declared that he would strike the first blow.[16]

Joseph's mother also noted that at the time the temple was under construction, "not thirty families of Saints now remained in Kirtland; and they never suffered the work to stop until it was accomplished." She further stated that there was much opposition to the building of the temple, and workers were "compelled to keep a guard around the walls much of the time until they were completed."[17] Lucy Mack Smith concluded her personal recollection of building the temple by stating how often she gave up every bed in her home to accommodate those who were working on the temple and needed a place to sleep. She often placed a single blanket on the floor for herself, her husband, her son Joseph, and his wife, Emma, "with nothing but their cloaks for both bed and bedding."[18] Eventually, the completed temple stood as a testament to the resolve of the Saints who lived in the Kirtland area. Even while enduring the bank fiasco, apostasy within the church, anger against Joseph Smith, never-ending lawsuits, and intense feel-

---

15. Ibid, 158-159
16. Lucy Mack Smith, *The history of Joseph Smith by his Mother,* (American Fork: Covenent Communications, Inc., 2000), 212-213
17. Ibid, 212
18. Ibid.

ings against the Saints held by others living in the area, these loyal members completed a beautiful "House to the Lord." The Kirtland experience abruptly ended during the night of 12 January 1838, when Joseph Smith and Sidney Rigdon fled Kirtland on horseback and did not stop for sixty miles. Concerning their flight west, Joseph recorded that their enemies "continued their pursuit of us more than 200 miles from Kirtland, armed with pistols and guns, seeking our lives."[19] Their next stop, and the next location for the gathering, would be Missouri.

MISSOURI (1831-1839)

The Louisiana Purchase in 1803 created a vast region, consisting of millions of acres, within the United States. The territory of Missouri, established in 1812, would eventually enter the Union as a slave state in 1821. By 1836, the population stood at about 240,000 people. Joseph Smith received a revelation 20 July 1831 designating Missouri as the "land of Zion," and the location for the "city of Zion." Members of The Church of Jesus Christ of Latter-day Saints began immigrating to Jackson County, Missouri, in the summer of 1831. Many early settlers in Missouri came from the southern states, while most church members hailed from the northeastern states.[20] Joseph Smith made a personal visit to Missouri in 1831. He left Kirtland 19 June 1831 with Sidney Rigdon, Martin Harris, Edward Partridge, William W. Phelps, Joseph Coe, Algernon S. Gilbert, and his wife, Emma. Using wagons, canal boats, stages, and steamboats, and walking many miles, Joseph traveled to Independence, Missouri, arriving "about the middle of July." The balance of Joseph's group arrived a few days later. A number of church members from the Colesville branch, in the state of New York, had settled in the area shortly before the arrival of Joseph Smith. On the second day of August 1831, Joseph Smith helped lay the first log for a house "as a foundation of Zion in Kaw township," which

---

19. Smith, *History of the Church of Jesus Christ of Latter-day Saints*, 3: 2-3
20. "Missouri," The Joseph Smith Papers, Available at: https://www.josephsmithpapers. org/place/missouri?highlight=missouri, <accessed 21 June 2021>

stood about twelve miles west of Independence, Missouri. Simultaneously, Sidney Rigdon "consecrated and dedicated" the land of Zion for the "gathering of the Saints." Joseph Smith dedicated a spot for a temple on 3 August 1831, at a location just west of Independence. By 9 August 1831, Joseph Smith and a group of traveling companions headed back to Kirtland.[21]

During the trip to Missouri, Joseph Smith declared the need to raise money to purchase land in Missouri. He tasked Newell Whitney and Oliver Cowdery with raising needed cash from various branches of the church. A brief, embellished description of the lands in Missouri to be purchased reads as follows:

This land being situated in the center of the continent on which we dwell, with an exceeding fertile soil and ready cleared for the hand of the cultivator bespeaks the goodness of our God in providing so goodly a heritage and its climate suited persons from every quarter of this continent whether east, west, north, or south—yea I think I may say for all constitutions from every part of the world and its productions nearly all varieties of both grain and vegetables which are common in this country together with all means for clothing. In addition to this, it abounds with fountains of pure water, the soil climate, and surface all adapted to health indeed I may say that the whole properties of the country invite the Saints to come and partake their blessings. But what more need I say about a country which our heavenly Father holds in his own hands, for if it were unhealthy, he could make it healthy, and if barren, he could make it fruitful. Such is the land which God has provided for us in these last days for an inheritance, and truly it is a goodly land and none other so well suited for all the Saints as this and all those who have faith and confidence in God. Who has ever seen this land will bear the same testimony.[22]

---

21. Smith, *History of the Church of Jesus Christ of Latter-day Saints*, 1:188-206
22. Richard L. Anderson, (1974) "New Data for Revising the Missouri "Documentary History"," BYU Studies Quarterly: Vol. 14 : Iss. 4 , Article 7. 495-496, Available at: https://scholarsarchive.byu.edu/byusq/vol14/iss4/7, <accessed 21 June 2021>

Armed with this glowing description of Missouri, church members from the East began flocking to the state. The first location the Saints attempted to settle in was Jackson County. Soon after their arrival, they experienced trouble with settlers already living in the area. Church members purchased land, established a settlement, and began building a gathering place called Zion. The attitude of the local settlers grew from disgusted to violent in the spring of 1833. By November of that year, church members fled Jackson County for Clay County, across the Missouri River.[23]

Church members settled in Clay County from November 1833 to July 1836, and for a brief period experienced relative peace. During their time in Clay County, church members sought the return of their property in Jackson County. They unsuccessfully implored both the governor of Missouri and the president of the United States. The feelings of Governor Daniel Dunklin of Missouri toward church members became evident in a letter written by him 15 August 1834. "I have no regard for the Mormons, as a separate people; and have an utter contempt for them as a religious sect; while upon the other hand I have much regard for the people of Jackson County, both personally and politically: they are, many of them, my personal friends, and nearly all of them are very staunch [sic] democrats." At the time the governor wrote his letter, the "Mormon question" was quiet. Regarding the governor's words, one distinguished historian noted, "He obviously had no desire at all to uphold Mormon rights to the confiscated Jackson County lands or as citizens of Missouri."[24]

Caldwell County originated from an uninhabited portion of Ray County. By December 1836, settlers were building communities there, including Far West. For the better part of two years, the Saints enjoyed peace. After being compelled to leave Kirtland, Joseph Smith moved church headquarters from Kirtland to Far West in March 1838. Less than six months later, an election took place in nearby

---

23. Stanley B. Kimball, (1974) "Missouri Mormon Manuscripts: Sources In Selected Societies," BYU Studies Quarterly: Vol. 14 : Iss. 4 , 460, Article 6. Available at: https://scholarsarchive.byu.edu/byusq/vol14/iss4/6, <accessed 23 June 2021>
24. Ibid, 460-461

Gallatin, Daviess County, that led to the so-called Mormon War of 1838-1839. Residents denied members of the church the right to vote, and a fight broke out between church members and other settlers. Joseph Smith and others traveled from Far West to Gallatin to protect their friends and protest the unlawful actions. The feelings of many citizens of Missouri were expressed by an unknown writer on 5 November 1838, from St. Louis, Missouri. "These deluded fanatics have been for some years collecting in one or two of the frontier counties of this state and so concentrating their property and forces as to become sufficiently emboldened of late to set the civil law at defiance."[25]

Some fair-minded people understood the illegality of what took place in the winter of 1838-1839. Another letter written from St. Louis, Missouri, expressed outrage at the events that were unfolding in the state. Although the writer noted church members were "victims of a most shameful and debasing posture," he also strongly defended their civil liberties, saying, "I could tell you a long story of the disgraceful Civil War that has but recently terminated in a consummation of foul disgrace to our state. Think of an order from the Executive of a State to a Military Commander to *expel or exterminate* a portion of its citizens." In 1838, Lilburn W. Boggs, governor of Missouri, issued an executive order to either drive church members out of Missouri, or destroy them. The writer concluded the indictment of Governor Lilburn W. Boggs's treatment of the Saints with this powerful statement, "But our sapient governor has ordered that the poor infatuated Mormons shall be stripped of their lives and property, and themselves be expatriated from our Democratic State."[26] The influx of church members to Missouri was significant. One group that left Kirtland formed a wagon train one mile long with 500 Saints. They left Kirtland on 6 July 1838 and headed to Daviess County. Caldwell and Daviess counties became home to approxi-

---

25. Ibid, 461 - 464
26. Ibid, 468

mately 10,000 church members by the fall of 1838.[27] Sadly, the Saints' expulsion from Missouri forced them to flee to Illinois.

The Saints' time in Missouri came to a dramatic end during the fall and winter of 1838-1839. On 30 October 1838, a group of state militia approached Far West and camped for the night about a mile outside of town. On 31 October 1838, a flag of truce was presented by the militia to the citizens of Far West. Unfortunately, George M. Hinkle met with the members of the militia and deceived members of the church by making a separate agreement with the state militia. He agreed to give up church leaders to local authorities and make appropriations for the cost of the militia's conflict against church members. Furthermore, the Saints would leave the state, and all firearms would be turned over to the soldiers. That very evening, Joseph Smith, Sidney Rigdon, and others were taken to the militia camp and subsequently imprisoned for several months. In short order, members of the church turned over all firearms.[28] Estimates place the value of property destroyed in Missouri at about $2,000,000 from the time the Saints first settled in the state until the expulsion. Roughly 1,200 members of the church were driven from Jackson County in 1833, and their property was lost to them.[29] Under sanction of an unlawful pronouncement, an estimated 8,000 members of The Church of Jesus Christ of Latter-day Saints were forcibly driven from their homes—at the same time their prophet-leader was incarcerated in prison.[30] The people driven from the state suffered hunger, pain, and afflictions of every kind. In 1842, Joseph Smith wrote his feelings about the forced exodus.

---

27. Jeffrey N. Walker, (2008) "Mormon Land Rights in Caldwell and Daviess Counties and the Mormon Conflict of 1838: New Findings and New Understandings," BYU Studies Quarterly: Vol. 47 : Iss. 1 , 27-28, Article 1. Available at: https://scholarsarchive.byu.edu/byusq/vol47/iss1/1, <accessed 23 June 2021>

28. Smith, *History of the Church of Jesus Christ of Latter-day Saints*, 3: 187 - 189

29. Smith, *Essentials in Church History,* 209-210

30. Karen Lynn Davidson, David J. Whittaker, Mark Ashurst-McGee, Richard L. Jensen, editors, *The Joseph Smith Papers, Histories, Volume 1: Joseph Smith Histories, 1832-1844,* (Salt Lake City: The Church Historians Press, 2012), 498fn25

Many sickened and died, in consequence of the cold and hardships they had to endure; many wives were left widows, and children orphans, and destitute. It would take more time than allotted to me here to describe the injustice, the wrongs, the murders, the bloodshed, the theft, misery and woe that has been caused by the barbarous, inhuman, and lawless, proceedings of the state of Missouri.

Following their expulsion from Missouri, the Saints traveled east until they arrived at the state of Illinois in 1839. Soon, the city of Nauvoo, Illinois, would rise out of the ashes of tribulation.[31]

NAUVOO (1839-1844)

As the Saints continued to flee Missouri, the residents of Quincy, Illinois, welcomed them with open arms. Perhaps many of the Saints who were fleeing Missouri believed they would make their way back to former settlements in Ohio. However, the warm reception by the citizens of western Illinois caused them to remain at Quincy. Many in Quincy helped and provided employment for the beleaguered travelers.[32] The town of Nauvoo, Illinois, received its charter from the state of Illinois on 16 December 1840. For the next four years, events in that town shaped the future of the still-young church. In early 1841, Joseph received a revelation regarding the construction of a temple in Nauvoo. In March of that year, responsibilities for the Quorum of the Twelve Apostles expanded with the instruction, "to stand in their place next to the First Presidency." November 1841 witnessed the first proxy baptisms for deceased persons in the Nauvoo temple font. In the spring of 1842, Joseph Smith organized the Female Relief Society of Nauvoo. He selected his wife, Emma, as the first president. In early May 1842, Joseph Smith introduced "sacred ceremonies and instructions," known as endowment, to Hyrum Smith, Brigham Young, and others in the upper room of his red brick store in Nauvoo. In July

---

31. Ibid, 498
32. Smith, *Essentials in Church History*, 218-219

1843, the revelation on plural wives and eternal marriage was recorded.[33]

The revelation on plural wives brought instant condemnation from both outside and within the church, and it was one of the factors that led to the eventual murder of the Prophet Joseph Smith and his brother, Hyrum. Another significant issue was Nauvoo's growing military and political power. Neighbors in the surrounding area were now convinced that the solution was to force the Saints out of Nauvoo. The doctrine of plural marriage caused one high-ranking church leader, William Law, to break from the church, legally charge Joseph Smith with adultery, and publish a malicious editorial against Joseph Smith and polygamy in a Nauvoo newspaper named the *Nauvoo Expositor*. Before his break with the church, William Law served in the First Presidency of the church, and he was a close confidant of Joseph. In response, the Nauvoo City Council declared the establishment and the paper a nuisance and ordered the marshal to destroy the press. Under the directive of the city council, the town marshal seized the press, materials, and paper, which he tossed out on the street and destroyed with fire.[34] Events quickly followed that led to the slaughter of Joseph and Hyrum Smith in a small jail in Carthage, Illinois, on 27 June 1844.[35]

THE EXODUS WEST: 1846-1847

The death of Joseph Smith shocked church members and created a crisis in church leadership. The Quorum of the Twelve Apostles had received private instruction on the mode of succession in the church. However, the general membership of the church knew almost nothing

---

33. Karen Lynn Davidson, David J. Whittaker, Mark Ashurst-McGee, Richard L. Jensen, editors, *The Joseph Smith Papers, Histories, Volume 2: Joseph Smith Histories, 1832-1844,* (Salt Lake City: The Church Historians Press, 2012), 300-302

34. Erick L. Wadsworth, *The Last Outfitting Station on the Missouri River, 1864 to 1866: Wyoming, NT, and the Nebraska City Cut-off Trail,* (self-published,[Amazon Digital Services], 2019), 13

35. *The Joseph Smith Papers, Histories,* 2: 303

about church succession, as there was nothing in print. One historian noted that between 1834 and 1844, Joseph Smith had, by "word or action," established eight possible methods of succession: 1) by a counselor in the First Presidency, 2) by special appointment, 3) through the office of Associate President, 4) by the Presiding Patriarch, 5) by the Council of Fifty, 6) by the Quorum of the Twelve Apostles, 7) by three priesthood councils, and 8) by a descendant of Joseph Smith Jr. In time, seven of the eight possibilities dissipated due to personal circumstances or the lack of credibility of their assertions.[36] In early August 1844, a general meeting for all members took place at Nauvoo. Before this meeting, Sidney Rigdon had put forward his claim as Joseph's successor. Following Rigdon's remarks, Brigham Young forcefully declared the authority to lead the church rested with the Quorum of the Twelve. Therefore, the stability in church leadership relied on "established authorities" rather than appointing new ones.[37] Many outsiders hoped the death of Joseph Smith would bring an end to the new church. With the succession crisis averted, leadership in the church could focus on existing challenges both within and outside the church. Many Saints living outside of Nauvoo were driven from their homes, which were burned. Animosity toward church members continued to escalate until the decision to vacate Nauvoo and move west. The decision was made to prepare to move west, and by 1 May 1846, most people had departed Nauvoo for a yet undetermined gathering place somewhere in the sparsely populated West.[38]

Relocation to another state was not possible. Three states had already turned their backs on the members of the church. During the move west, roughly 15,000 members of the church fled Nauvoo and the surrounding areas. The overwhelming task of preparing thousands of people to travel west began. Church members constructed thousands of wagons, located food needed for the long journey, and began preparing for a spring departure. The final decision to begin

---

36. D. Michael Quinn, "The Mormon Succession Crisis of 1844," BYU Studies Quarterly, Vol. 16: No. 2 (1976), 187
37. Ibid, 211
38. Smith, *Essentials in Church History*, 330

vacating Nauvoo took place 2 February 1846, and two days later, the first group crossed the Mississippi River to Iowa. By the end of 1846, Nauvoo stood virtually empty of church members.[39] Brigham Young, as president of the Quorum of the Twelve Apostles, was deeply involved with the planning and implementation of the move west. By the end of 1846, estimates indicate roughly 5,000 Saints were at Winter Quarters (the newly created town on the west bank of the Missouri River). Another 7,500 were scattered across Iowa and at the Ponca camp above Winter Quarters, and an additional 1,500 were in St. Louis or other locations along the Mississippi River. An estimated 2,000 inhabitants of Nauvoo opted not to go west, but most left the Nauvoo area for their own safety.[40]

Two extraordinary chapters of the western migration for members of The Church of Jesus Christ of Latter-day Saints were about to unfold. The first unique occurrence was the raising of the Mormon Battalion. Even though the expelled Saints were escaping west because of religious persecution, the government of the United States sought and obtained 500 volunteers to form the Mormon Battalion to help in the war with Mexico. One significant reason Brigham Young helped raise the Battalion was to bring needed capital to the impoverished Saints spread out across Nebraska and Iowa. During their long arduous trek to San Diego, California, three detachments left the Battalion to winter near current-day Pueblo, Colorado.[41] The second remarkable event is the western movement of a group known as the Mississippi Company, which left their homes in northeastern Mississippi and northwestern Alabama in April 1846. This wagon train was composed of members of the church from the Southern United States, and they were to intersect with other Saints somewhere along the trail. However, that integration never materialized because in 1846, the rest of the Saints were spread out across the

---

39. William Hartley, Glenn Rawson, Dennis Lyman, and Bryant Bush, editors, *History of the Saints: The Great Mormon Exodus and the Establishment of Zion,* (China: Covenant Communications, 2012), 18-19
40. Ibid, 29
41. Ibid, 36

Nebraska and Iowa Territories.[42] This Mississippi Company originally consisted of fourteen families and was under the leadership of William Crosby and John Brown. After reaching Fort Laramie and realizing no other Saints were on the trail, they headed south and settled in Pueblo for the winter.[43]

---

42. B. H. Roberts, *A Comprehensive History of the Church of Jesus Christ of Latter-day Saints*, (Provo, Utah: Published by the church, 19650), 193
43. Ibid, 225, fn2

2

HISTORICAL SETTING OF MISSISSIPPI

As noted in the previous chapter, most of those who traveled in the Mississippi Company wagon train resided in northeastern Mississippi and northwestern Alabama. An examination of Mississippi's historical background and culture offers insight into the uniqueness of those who made up this group. The settlement of the South differed drastically from the settlement in New England. Variances in climate and soil were two significant disparities. New England experienced a shorter growing season than the South, which limited the crops that could grow in the north. This led in part to the development of more industry. The soil in the South, particularly Mississippi and Alabama, seemed perfect for growing cotton and other warm weather crops, which resulted in the expansion of an agricultural society.

Perhaps the two most glaring disparities came in the form of human slavery and the expulsion of Indian tribes from Mississippi to points west of the Mississippi River. The first importation of slaves to Mississippi from Africa took place in 1720. Thus, early on enslavement became a part of the fabric of Southern society.[1] The framers of the Constitution, particularly those from the northern states, sought the eventual prohibition of the slave trade by 1808. However, the total number of enslaved in the North paled in comparison to the numbers in the South. For example, Vermont in the 1790 Federal Census showed only seventeen enslaved individuals in the entire state, while Mississippi in the same census declared upward of 3,400 enslaved.[2] The gradual prohibition of the slave trade by 1808 required no great sacrifice for the North.

FORCED EXPULSION OF CHOCTAW AND CHICKASAW TRIBES

The forced removal of the Choctaw and Chickasaw confederacies from their homeland in central and northern Mississippi in the early 1830s opened some of the country's most productive farmland to settlers.[3] The invention of Eli Whitney's cotton gin, the discovery of gold, and unapologetic racism led to this expulsion. In 1830, the Mississippi legislature passed a bill that extended its control over both the Choctaw and Chickasaw territories within the state. That same year, the US Congress passed the Indian Removal Act, which created the opportunity for Andrew Jackson to negotiate with the affected tribes for their deportation. The Choctaws accepted their fate first with the acceptance of the Treaty of Dancing Rabbit Creek in September 1830. The Choctaws began their migration during the winter of 1830 to Indian Territory, now Oklahoma, along the dreaded Trail of Tears. They had three years to leave the state.[4]

---

1. Ruth B. Hawes, "Slavery in Mississippi." *The Sewanee Review*, 21, no.2 (1913): 224. <Accessed July 14, 2021>. http://www.jstor.org/stable/27532618.
2. Ibid, 225
3. Max Grivno, "Antebellum Mississippi," *Mississippi History Now*, <accessed 14 July 2021>, http://www.mshistorynow.mdah.ms.gov/articles/395/antebellum-mississippi,
4. Greg O'Brien, "Mushulatubbee and Choctaw Removal: Chiefs Confront a Changing World," *Mississippi History Now*, An online publication of the Mississippi Historical Society, http://www.mshistorynow.mdah.ms.gov/articles/12/mushulatubbee-and-choctaw-removal-chiefs-confront-a-changing-world, <accessed 7 August 2021>

The Chickasaws lived in northern Mississippi between the head-waters of the Yazoo and Tombigbee Rivers. During the eighteenth century, estimates place their population between 2,000 and 5,000 people. The Chickasaw and Choctaw nations had much in common. Both spoke similar languages and were organized matrilineally (ancestry traced through the mother's line). Their political makeup was decentralized, with a separate chief for each village. Both cultures viewed the sun as the source of all life on the earth. One crucial differ-ence between the two tribes centered on the ability of the Chickasaws to maintain their independence from other tribes and the Europeans. Military proficiency was a key component of the Chickasaw people, and they continually warred against the Choctaws, the Creeks, the Cherokees, and the French. Many contemporaries believed the Chickasaws to be the "fiercest warriors in all of the southeast."[5] Chickasaw boys were trained in martial arts and were taught to "withstand pain and deprivation without complaint."

During the winter of 1540 - 1541, the Chickasaws encountered Hernando de Soto's expedition and drove them to the west side of the Mississippi River. Later, the Europeans founded an English colony in Carolina in 1670. The Carolinians traded guns and other products with the Chickasaw for deerskins and Indian captives. In the 1690s, the Chickasaw, armed with guns, raided their neighbors to the south —the Choctaw. During this warfare, approximately 2,000 Choctaw were killed, and another 2,000 were sold as slaves to the Carolinians, who in turn sold their captives as slaves to the sugar plantations of the Caribbean islands. For generations, the Chickasaw maintained their way of life with a fierce warrior stance and excellent negotiation skills. In a treaty signed 31 August 1831, the Chickasaw agreed to cede their land east of the Mississippi River for an equal amount of land in the west. This treaty was voided due to the inability to locate suitable land. By 1832, another treaty was signed that required the

____

5. Greg O'Brien, "Chickasaws: The Unconquerable People," *Mississippi History Now*, An online publication of the Mississippi Historical Society, http://www.mshistorynow. mdah.ms.gov/articles/8/chickasaws-the-unconquerable-people, <accessed 7 August 2021>

Chickasaw to sell their land in Mississippi to the US government. Finally, in 1837, a treaty was signed at Doaksville, Indian Territory, in which the Choctaw sold a portion of their land to the Chickasaw. However, it was not until 1854 and 1855 that the final settlement was made between the two Indian nations.[6] The forced removal of Indians from their ancestral homes to mostly less desirable locations continued unabated for many years.

EARLY SETTLEMENT OF THE MISSISSIPPI TERRITORY

Thousands of Americans moved west following the Revolutionary War in a resettlement process historians refer to as the "Great Migration." Mississippi was a part of that great expansion west. In 1798, Congress organized the Mississippi Territory, which included Alabama until 1817. Few settlers lived in Mississippi when it first became a territory. Approximately 5,750 people, including those who were enslaved, lived in the Mississippi Territory settlements in 1800. For the most part, the colonizers lived in two distinct areas within the Mississippi Territory. Roughly 4,500 people lived in the Natchez area, while the remainder resided in Tombigbee settlements along the river of the same name. The American Indians populated the rest of the territory.[7]

Two primary factors influenced the resettlement of Mississippi from other southern agricultural states. One historian points out that generations of "ruinous agricultural practices" in other areas in the South had, by the year 1800, sapped the ground of the old plantations, which created a need for the rich soil found in Mississippi. Another reason for the influx of settlers centered on the decreased European demand for tobacco and rice, combined with Europe's increased need

---

6. Ibid.

7. Charles Lowery, "The Great Migration of the Mississippi Territory, 1798-1819," *Mississippi History Now, an online publication of the Mississippi Historical Society*, http://www.mshistorynow.mdah.ms.gov/articles/169/the-great-migration-to-the-missis sippi-territory-1798-1819; <accessed 14 August 2021>

for cotton. The rich, uncultivated soil in Mississippi and higher prices for cotton, combined with the invention of the cotton gin in the 1790s, provided a justification for people to leave their homes to settle in Mississippi.[8] Bolstered by the promise of soils that produce "noble crops," immigrants settled in Mississippi by the thousands. One settler from Maryland wrote to his family, "The crops [here] are certain… and abundance spreads the table of the poor man and contentment smiles on every countenance." Unfortunately, the promise of serenity made by this unknown author only materialized for a few white Americans. Poor itinerant farmers and enslaved people found no settings at the table of the American dream.[9]

This Great Migration can be divided into two distinct waves. The first began with the creation of the territory and subsided with the War of 1812. The second wave took place following the war and peaked in the years 1818-1819. The national economic "Panic of 1819" reduced the flow of settlers into the territory. By 1811, five new counties in the Mississippi Territory reached a total population of 31,306, with 14,706 of those being enslaved. In other words, 47 percent of the population of these counties was under the bondage of slavery. Following the conclusion of the War of 1812, the migration into Mississippi and Alabama resumed vigorously. By 1820, 99,198 whites and 47,665 enslaved people were living in Alabama Territory, for a total of 137,817 people. Again, the enslaved population stood at slightly less than 50 percent of the entire population. Free white settlers found excellent ground for growing cotton, and Mississippi quickly became a top producing state in the South. By the mid-1800s, Mississippi became one of the wealthiest states in the country due to the growth and marketing of cotton.[10]

---

8. Ibid, 2
9. Ibid, 3
10. Ibid, 4

ENSLAVEMENT

Slavery was present in Mississippi decades before the territory was created. In January 1699, Pierre LeMoyne, Sieur d'Urberville arrived on a group of ships sponsored by the French government and anchored off Ship Island, near the coast of Mississippi. After exploring the area for several days, Iberville selected a location to build a fort, which he named Fort Maurepas in honor of the French Minister of Marine and Colonies. Fort Maurepas only existed for a short time, but it was the first European settlement in Mississippi and the first capital of French Louisiana. This obscure, short-lived settlement in Biloxi, Mississippi, was relocated in 1701 to Mobile, Alabama. By 1722, the colonial capital was moved to New Orleans. Although the settlement was moved west to New Orleans, the French continued to seek opportunities to remain in the Mississippi Gulf Coast area.[11] The site of Natchez, which overlooked the Mississippi River, became a new settlement in 1716. A fort named Rosalie was constructed there, with hopes of developing a successful community near the fort. Unfortunately, desired prosperity never materialized, and by 1721, efforts by France to establish permanent settlements in the Gulf Coast began to evaporate like a fog disappearing under the rays of a hot sun. The French tried several tactics to bring immigrants to Mississippi, and for a brief period, settlers flocked to the area in hopes of finding a better life. However, the steady influx of immigrants was short-lived, and as word spread about the colony's poor history, immigration slowed to a crawl. The French failed to settle successfully in Mississippi.[12]

Possibly the most appalling incident during the French years in

---

11. Michael Bunn and Clay Williams, "A Failed Enterprise: The French Colonial Period in Mississippi," *Mississippi History Now, an online publication of the Mississippi Historical Society,* http://www.mshistorynow.mdah.ms.gov/articles/35/french-colonial-period-in-mississippi, <accessed 28 August 2021>
12. Ibid

Mississippi was the importation of slaves, which began in 1720.[13] When Iberville first founded the colony, he was instructed to breed buffalo, produce silk, find pearls, make timber for ship-building, and look for mines. Not a word was said about planting crops. While serving as governor of the colony, Iberville began looking to the rich soil as a solution for the colony to succeed. "But it was impossible to make the French work, and many of the Indians whom they had subjected deserted to their own villages. He proposed to send Indians to the West Indies and exchange them for slaves. This the minister pronounced impracticable and recommended a direct importation from Africa. This is the first suggestion of African slavery in the history of the territory."[14] From this point, enslavement became a part of the fabric of both the southern and northern settlements. The South endorsed the importation and subjugation of slaves, while the North provided many of the ships and crews that captured and transported those who were formerly free to a life of bondage.

The expansion of slavery in Mississippi increased dramatically in the 1830s. During those years, the number of those who were enslaved and lived in the state exploded from 65,659 to 195,211, an increase of nearly 200 percent.[15] What precipitated this extraordinary rise in the number of enslaved people in Mississippi? Simply put, the growth and harvesting of cotton. Mississippi's cotton production soared from roughly twenty million to seventy million pounds between 1820 and 1833. By 1839, following the opening of Choctaw and Chickasaw land to mostly white settlers, that number skyrocketed to approximately 193.2 million pounds. Just before the start of the Civil War, Mississippi's plantations produced the most cotton of any state in the Union. Most of the enslaved people who were being moved within the United States came to Mississippi from Maryland and Virginia, where years of tobacco growth and stagnant sales began to eat away at the institution of slavery in the older coastal

---

13. Ruth B. Hawes, "Slavery in Mississippi," *The Sewanee Review*, Apr., 1913, Vol. 21. No.2 (Apr., 1913), 224
14. Ibid. 223
15. Max Grivno, "Antebellum Mississippi,"

states such as Georgia and North Carolina. Some of the enslaved who were sent to Mississippi traveled along the Eastern Seaboard to New Orleans and Natchez or were forced to walk overland to slave markets, where the suffering planters hoped to take advantage of the booming cotton and slave market in Mississippi. One early historian estimates that more than 100,000 enslaved individuals came to Mississippi from the north during the 1830s.[16]

Cotton not only created a total dependence of Southerners on slavery, but northern states also benefited financially. During the 1830s, when the Choctaw and Chickasaw lands in Mississippi became available, the two largest buyers of that property were the American Land Company and the New York Land Company. Investors in these two enterprises came from New York, Boston, and other New England areas. By 1860, cotton catapulted New York City into the financial center of the country. Estimates indicate that New York City received 40 percent of all cotton revenue through insurance, transportation, and financing. Businesses from New York also sold products to Southern plantation owners. The results were astounding. One estimate puts the revenue generated at $200,000,000 annually. Another avenue for profit pursued by New Yorkers in the 1850s was the financing of New York-based slave ships that sailed to West Africa, captured slaves, and then transported them to Cuba and Brazil to sell them. Several northern states denied voting rights to the free Black individuals who lived there. New York State enacted property ownership requirements on free Black residents, while white residents had no such prerequisite. Connecticut voters overwhelmingly voted to deny voting rights to free Black residents. Other northern states, such as Indiana, Ohio, and Illinois, dismissed the rights of free Black citizens while actively pursuing the immigration of white Europeans. One notable historian concludes, "White America, not just white Southerners, helped determine that the destiny of Black America would be in the cotton fields of the South for many decades

---

16. Ibid.

to come."[17] Mississippi's reliance on cotton and slavery brought much pain and suffering for residents and enslaved people during the Civil War.

EARLY MISSIONARY WORK IN THE SOUTH

The Church of Jesus Christ of Latter-day Saints originated in New England, with most early church leaders possessing Northern heritage. Initial missionary efforts centered, for the most part, in the northern United States. With the introduction of Missouri as a location for church members to settle, missionary work in the South slowly materialized. The first proselyting in the South resulted from the efforts of several companionships leaving from Kirtland, Ohio, to travel to Jackson County, Missouri, in June 1831. Samuel Smith and Reynolds Cahoon left Kirtland on 8 June 1831 and entered Kentucky after crossing the Ohio River. These two missionaries only traveled about twenty miles in Kentucky as they headed west for Missouri; however, with this brief sojourn in Kentucky, these two became the first known missionaries to labor in a southern state. Joseph Smith left Kirtland for Missouri on 18 June 1831. He and his companions landed at Louisville, Kentucky, where they spent three days waiting for a boat to take them to St. Louis, Missouri. Certainly, Joseph Smith and his companions shared the gospel news with the citizens of Louisville and the surrounding area, but nothing was recorded about their activities while in that city. If any converts were made during this first fledgling missionary effort in the South, nothing was recorded.[18]

During the years 1832 to 1834, missionaries began finding some

---

17. Eugene R. Dattel, "Cotton in a Global Economy: Mississippi (1800-1860)," *Mississippi History Now, an Online Publication of the Mississippi Historical Society,* http://www.mshistorynow.mdah.ms.gov/articles/161/cotton-in-a-global-economy-mississippi-1800-1860; <accessed 24 August 2021>

18. LaMar C. Berrett, "History of the Southern States Mission, 1831-1861" (1960). *Thesis and Dissertations.* 4525. 47-49.https://scholarsarchive.byu.edu/cgi/viewcontent.cgi?article=5524&context=etd, <accessed 11 September 2021>

success in Kentucky and Tennessee. By 1839, these efforts expanded into the states of Virginia, Arkansas, North and South Carolina, and northeastern Mississippi.[19] During the early years of missionary service in the South, those who served there were, for the most part, greeted with hospitality and generosity from Southern residents. Locals often shared their homes, provided food and shelter, and at times offered a place to preach. These early missionaries went without purse or scrip and carried all their possessions in a suitcase or satchel. Once a missionary located a friendly family or home, he would establish a base of operation and seek out others who might have an interest in the message, often within a day's travel of the home.[20] Lysander M. Davis noted in 1839 that he had spent six months in the South, "extending from the Mississippi to the Atlantic," and that the Lord never left him without a place to sleep or without sufficient food. An early companionship, Joshua and Jedidiah Grant, wrote that they had "generally been treated with kindness and hospitality by most of the people: more so than ever were in the north."[21] Not all missionaries experienced Southern hospitality. In 1836, Wilford Woodruff, who later became the fourth president of the church, wrote about his experiences while serving as a young missionary in Tennessee. On 31 July 1836, Elder Woodruff noted he was concerned that "a mob was intending to come against us on Saturday and Sunday." He later wrote in his journal that the animal he had ridden for a year while on his mission died from poisoning. "Thus ended the life of Jude, a beast who had carried me thousands of miles to preach the gospel of Jesus Christ. Also hath carried other elders many miles on the same errand."[22]

---

19. Leonard J. Arrington, "Mormon Beginnings in the American South," Task Papers in LDS History, No. 9 (Salt Lake City: Historical Department of the Church of Jesus Christ of Latter-day Saints, 1976)

20. Ibid, 2

21. Ibid, 3

22. Wilford Woodruff journals and papers, 1828-1898; Wilford Woodruff Journals, 1833-1898; Wilford Woodruff journal, 1833 December-1838 January; Church History Library, image 97/201

Expanding Missionary Efforts in the South

During the first years of church missionary efforts, those who labored had no specific time established for their service. The length of a mission varied from six months to a year or two. Usually, a missionary was ordained to the office of elder before leaving on a mission. There were times when a deacon, teacher, or priest filled missions for the church. For the most part, these missionaries traveled on foot. When river travel was possible, they could travel on a steamer or other watercraft. Appointments were typically arranged for 2:00 p.m., 4:00 p.m., or "candlelight." At times, missionaries would preach outside, but when possible, they taught in a log cabin, a small church, a courthouse, or a small school.[23] Missionaries preached about the restoration of the gospel and the *Book of Mormon* and sold subscriptions. Before returning home from his year-and-a-half mission to the Tennessee Conference, Wilford Woodruff received donations from church members to help him on his trip back to Kirtland, Ohio. David W. Patton and Thomas B. Marsh called on the members to aid with Woodruff's return, and on 4 September 1836, Wilford Woodruff recorded the names of each person who contributed and the amount they freely offered in his journal. Twenty-three members provided $76.35. The smallest donation was twenty-five cents, and the largest contribution came to ten dollars.[24]

While serving in New Orleans in March 1841, Elder Harrison Sagers met with limited success. In a letter written to those living in Nauvoo on 8 June 1841, Elder Sagers noted that shortly after arriving and beginning to preach in that city, antagonistic locals began hurling eggs at him in an effort to stop his discourse. He was then attacked by men seeking to tar and feather him, but he evaded them. The crowd

---

https://catalog.churchofjesuschrist.org/assets/14079217-b2a7-4eff-8b53-1be6c1e9bea5/0/96 <accessed: September 11, 2021>

23. LaMar C. Berrett, "History of the Southern States Mission, 1831-1861" 41

24. Wilford Woodruff journals and papers, 1828-1898; Wilford Woodruff Journals, 1833-1898, image 104/201, https://catalog.churchofjesuschrist.org/assets/14079217-b2a7-4eff-8b53-1be6c1e9bea5/0/103, <accessed 11 September 2021>

became so angry that they threw the benches through the windows of the house they were preaching in and set the fixtures on fire. Sagers further noted he understood that two men who spoke in support of his preaching were beaten by the crowd. At the end of his letter, after stressing the negative events that took place, Elder Sagers wrote that he preached three or four times a week while in the city, during which time eight people "embraced the gospel, and many more [were] believing."[25] John D. Lee experienced success in Rutherford County, Tennessee, as he "baptized upwards of thirty" in that area and held five debates with various ministers.[26] Joshua Grant wrote in September 1841 that several persons were baptized in Smyth County, Virginia. He also mentioned that the church in the area held twenty-five members, "all in good standing," and many were believing. Grant wrote, "prospects in North Carolina, also, were good when I was there last."[27] Although somewhat slower than in other areas of the country, missionary work in the South began to take root.

In early 1838, Elders J. D. Hunter and Benjamin L. Clapp traveled into the county of McNairy, Tennessee, where they participated in more than twenty-five meetings and baptized fourteen individuals. Shortly thereafter, they ventured into northeastern Mississippi, where six people were baptized. Elder Hunter then returned home, which left Elder Clapp alone. When Elder Hunter reported his missionary labors on 26 December 1839, he noted Elder Clapp was still preaching in Mississippi, and more missionaries were needed.[28] One of the first missionary tracts came from the southern states and was written by Francis Gladden Bishop. The tract was about the persecution of the Saints in Missouri. Many who served in the southern states as missionaries later became leaders of the church. Included in the

---

25. Historical Department journal history of the Church, 1830-2008; 1840-1849; 1841; Church History Library, image 68-70/327, https://catalog.churchofjesuschrist.org/assets/2285a7c4-f5e3-4559-9bb5-4be6524033c1/0/67, <accessed: September 11, 2021>
26. Ibid, image 101/327
27. Ibid, image 222-223/327
28. LaMar C.Berrett, "History of the Southern States Mission, 1831-1861" 168

number of those who served a Southern mission were Wilford Woodruff and Lorenzo Snow, who later served as presidents of the church. David W. Patton, Orson Pratt, Charles C. Rich, Erastus Snow, and George Albert Smith all served as missionaries in the southern states, which helped prepare them for heavy assignments later in life.[29]

John Brown's Successful Missionary Efforts in Mississippi

John Brown brought the message of the restored gospel to an area in northeastern Mississippi and northwestern Alabama that greatly impacted the lives of those who believed the message he presented. Many who accepted his message in 1843 left their homes in 1846 for an unknown destination in the West. John Brown was born in Sumner County, Tennessee, on 23 October 1820 to John and Martha Chapman Brown. John was one of fourteen children born into the family. In 1829, John's father moved the family to Perry County, Illinois, where he bought 640 acres of land. John's father and two sisters died within seven years of arriving in Illinois, and the other children married, leaving John and his mother at home. John was baptized into The Church of Jesus Christ of Latter-day Saints in 1841 by Elder George P. Dykes.[30] Shortly after John joined the church, the school where he taught burned to the ground, so he was no longer employed. He traveled to Nauvoo with Robert Crow and Samuel Williams. Upon arriving, John saw Joseph Smith, Hyrum Smith, Brigham Young, Heber C. Kimball, and other members of the Quorum of the Twelve Apostles. Hyrum Smith pronounced a Patriarchal Blessing to John in October 1841, and Hyrum also ordained John an elder 9 February 1842.[31]

John Brown left Nauvoo on his mission to the South on 20 May

---

29. Ibid, 169-170

30. John Zimmerman Brown, *Autobiography of Pioneer John Brown, 1820-1896*, (Stevens & Wallis, Inc. Salt Lake City, Utah 1941) 15

31. Ibid, 33 -34

1843. His companion was H.W. Church. Their first stop was Paducah, Kentucky, on the confluence of the Tennessee and Ohio Rivers in southeastern Kentucky. The two missionaries traveled to John's birthplace in Sumner County, Tennessee. There, they held several public meetings. John Brown also spent time with family members and friends. Elder Church did not show up one day, so John crossed the Tennessee River by himself into Tuscumbia, Alabama. Brown continued working in various small branches in Alabama, where he baptized, instructed new members, and ordained several to the priesthood. Elder Brown was able to reconnect with Elder Church on 31 August. On 18 December 1843, Brown reached Monroe County, Mississippi, where he found a small branch of sixteen newly-baptized members.[32] James Brown and Peter Haws had organized this branch before they returned to Nauvoo. At the time of Elder Brown's arrival in Monroe County, William Crosby served as the presiding elder of this fledgling branch, which they named Buttahatchy [sic]. Elder Brown wrote that on 21 December, he met a young lady named Elizabeth Crosby, who would soon become his wife. Elizabeth Crosby, her sister, Ann, and Mrs. Mary Sparks were baptized six days after John first met Elizabeth.[33] The preaching of the gospel found fertile soil among those living in and around Monroe County, Mississippi, and northwestern Alabama. Elder Brown describes in his own words how the work moved forward.

We now had numerous calls to preach. We preached in almost every neighborhood for several miles around, also in some of the towns and villages in the adjoining counties. It was the season of the year in which the rains fall so profusely and often in this climate. The little streams were impassable, except by ferries, most of the winter. We often had to wade in water up to the waist and cross the main streams

---

32. Ibid, 42-44

33. John Brown reminiscences and journals, 1843-1896; Volume 1, 1843 May-1860 April; Church History Library,
    https://catalog.churchofjesuschrist.org/assets/d8284095-dc09-4b4d-a9b4-92e62c18bf30/0/26; <accessed: September 15, 2021>

and deep water in canoes through the woods and brush to get to our appointment. But notwithstanding all this, we were handsomely rewarded. The Lord was with us and blessed our labors.[34]

John Brown, and those who collaborated with him, taught and baptized many while working in the northeastern Mississippi area. On one occasion, he wrote that he baptized "two Black men, Allen and Green, belonging to brother Flake." Their baptism took place on 7 April 1844. Just three years later, Green Flake entered the Salt Lake Valley as a slave but also as a part of the vanguard wagon train under the direction of Brigham Young. Years later, after receiving his freedom, Green lived in Salt Lake County, Utah, before moving to Idaho Falls, Idaho. Mr. Flake died on 20 October 1903, and his remains were returned to Union, Utah, for burial.[35] During the month of April 1844, Clapp and Brown found themselves in Monroe County, where nine persons were baptized into the church. An important conference was held at Cypry, Tuscaloosa County, Alabama, under the direction of Elder Benjamin L. Clapp. John Brown was appointed clerk of the conference. Seven branches were represented at this meeting, along with 192 members, twelve elders, five priests, four teachers, and two deacons. According to the record, all members were "in good standing."[36] On 18 May 1844, John Brown and Charles Johnson ordained G. W. Gibson (likely the George Washington Gibson who later was part of the Mississippi Saints) a priest.[37] The success of Elder Brown and other missionaries in this area of the South was truly remarkable and would later lead to one of the most unique western migrations of the nineteenth century.

---

34. ibid.

35. John Zimmerman Brown, Autobiography of Pioneer John Brown, 1820-1896, 46

36. "History, 1838–1856, volume E-1 [1 July 1843–30 April 1844]," p. 2009, The Joseph Smith Papers, https://www.josephsmithpapers.org/paper-summary/history-1838-1856-volume-e-1-1-july-1843-30-april-1844/381, <accessed 20 September 2021>

37. John Brown reminiscences and journals, 1843-1896; Volume 1, 1843 May-1860 April; Church History Library, https://catalog.churchofjesuschrist.org/assets/d8284095-dc09-4b4d-a9b4-92e62c18bf30/0/33?lang=eng, <accessed: May 11, 2023>

3

1844 TO 1846

John Brown married Elizabeth Crosby 21 May 1844, just five months after first seeing her. The couple were married in the parlor of the plantation owned by Elizabeth Crosby. Brown was now a part of an extended family that stretched across northwestern Alabama and northeastern Mississippi.[1] Shortly after their wedding, John Brown began visiting the branches where he had previously preached. On 1 June 1844, he and a companion began visiting "all the branches under which I had been laboring." The first branch they visited was in Noxubee County, Mississippi. Brown briefly returned to Monroe County before heading back out again. During the month of July 1844, Brown visited Neshoba, Newton, Madison, and Holmes counties in central and eastern Mississippi. While traveling, Brown heard rumors of the murders of his church leaders, but he did not believe the stories. However, when he reached Holmes County, he became convinced the story about the death of the prophet and patri-

---

1. Charmaine Lay Kohler, *Southern Grace, A Story of the Mississippi Saints*, (Beagle Creek Press: Boise, Idaho, 1995), 48

arch was true. Upon confirming this shocking news, Brown no longer wanted to preach "to the world," so he returned home to recover.[2]

After resting, Brown traveled to Itawamba, Mississippi, with Elder William Matthews. They left on 2 September 1844 and fell in company with Elder James Cummings. After baptizing three persons, he and Elder Mathews returned to Monroe County on the 17th of September. Mid-October found John Brown leaving Monroe County to attend a "quarterly conference" in Noxubee County, where he was called to preside. While at the conference, Brown baptized two men and conferred the priesthood on two others. Brown returned home 29 October, where he "preached occasionally in the regions 'round about as opportunity could afford."[3] While at home in Monroe County, Brother Benjamin Clapp returned from Nauvoo and told Brown he had been called as a member of the 8th Quorum of the Seventy. Brother Clapp, one of the presidents of the 8th Quorum, ordained him to that office 12 November 1844.[4] John Brown and Benjamin Clapp then traveled to the Little Bear Creek Branch in Franklin County, Alabama. They had organized this branch earlier on 20 November. After spending a short time at the branch, they returned to Monroe County before leaving again to visit branches in Noxubee and Kemper Counties in Mississippi. After spending time in those counties, Brown traveled with Brother Preston Thomas to Oktibbeha, Chickasaw, and Pontotoc counties. Brown continually preached and strengthened local members while serving in these areas. In February 1845, Brother Brown met Abraham O. Smoot and his family. Smoot had been called to preside over missionary work in Alabama and surrounding areas.[5]

---

2. John Brown reminiscences and journals, 1843-1896; Volume 1, 1843 May-1860 April; Church History Library,
   https://catalog.churchofjesuschrist.org/assets/d8284095-dc09-4b4d-a9b4-92e62c18bf30/0/26, <accessed: September 23, 2021>
3. Ibid.
4. John Zimmerman Brown, Autobiography of Pioneer John Brown, 1820-1896, (Stevens & Wallis, Inc. Salt Lake City, Utah 1941) 47
5. Ibid, 49

Early Church Branches in the South

Many missionaries impacted the growth of the church in north-eastern Mississippi and northwestern Alabama during the mid-1840s. John Brown and Benjamin Clapp are just two of many who brought their message to Southern settlers. Amazingly, from August 1843 to June 1844, Clapp baptized 118 converts, and John Brown baptized sixty individuals.[6] Even though many of these ministers came from the North, many individuals and families living in the area accepted their message and became united with The Church of Jesus Christ of Latter-day Saints. The need to organize small groups of believers, or branches, became apparent, and several local units were created to provide a place for residents to worship together and gain strength from each other. The opportunity to meet in a beautiful church was usually not an option, so the members would usually meet in the homes of members. Missionaries would visit the small branches to baptize, provide support, call individuals to various positions, and preach. Abraham O. Smoot, whom John Brown met in February 1845, was called by church leaders to preside over the branches in Alabama and surrounding areas. Smoot left Nauvoo, Illinois, 4 November 1844 after receiving a "parting blessing" under the hands of John Taylor. He spent three months preparing himself and his family to leave Nauvoo.[7]

Abraham O. Smoot

Elder Smoot arrived in Lauderdale County, Alabama, 22 December 1844 after traveling through several other states, including Kentucky and Tennessee. The long, arduous journey took weeks to complete. As

---

6. LaMar C.Berrett, "History of the Southern States Mission, 1831-1861" (1960). Thesis and Dissertations. 4525. 253. https://scholarsarchive.byu.edu/cgi/viewcontent.cgi?article=5524&context=etd, <accessed 25 September 2021>
7. Abraham Owen Smoot, 1815-1895. Typescript journal, 1844 May-1845 April. 27/54 https://catalog.churchofjesuschrist.org/assets/9d9be8eb-14f7-4214-b708-1076b5d81a6a/2/28, <accessed: 26 September 2021>

Elder Smoot traveled, he visited family, made new contacts, and preached when the opportunity arose. Like earlier missionaries serving in the South, Smoot spent many nights with members of the church. Smoot's first visit to the small branch in Lauderdale County was spent with a Brother Mare, who was an elder in the branch.[8] He visited many small branches during the ensuing months. On the first of January 1845, Elder Smoot visited members in the Russellville branch of the church in northeastern Alabama. While there, he preached at the house of Brother Griffin on the "dispensation of the fullness of times to a small but attentive congregation, which seemed to be much interested in the subject of the restoration."[9] On 3 January, Smoot traveled sixteen miles to the Bar Creek (Little Bear Creek) branch. While there, he shared with the Saints the reason he was in Alabama and then taught "on the authenticity of the *Book of Mormon.*" Next, he accompanied Brother Griffin to visit two sick ladies who had requested an appointment.[10] Smoot's heavy travel schedule then took him to the Sipsey branch in Tuscaloosa County, Alabama. Benjamin Clapp met Abraham Smoot 29 January 1845. Clapp was seeking subscriptions for the Nauvoo temple. Not knowing that Benjamin Clapp had received the authority to collect money for the temple, Smoot interviewed Clapp. During the interview, Benjamin presented a letter signed by four of the twelve apostles and members of the temple committee.[11]

On 1 February, Elder Smoot traveled on Centerville Road to a meeting house in Tuscaloosa, Alabama, where he hoped to attend a Baptist gathering. Smoot requested an appointment to preach, which was denied. Other arrangements were made, and Abraham addressed "an attentive audience" by candlelight.[12] Elder Smoot left on 4

---

8. Abraham A, O. Smoot, "Smoot Diary, Vol. 1, 1836-1846," L. Tom Perry Special Collections, Harold B. Lee Library, Brigham Young University,220, https://contentdm. lib.byu.edu/digital/collection/MMD/id/27235, <accessed 6 October 2021>

9. Ibid, 222

10. Ibid.

11. Ibid, 223-226

12. Abraham Owen Smoot, 1815-1895. Typescript journal, 1844 May-1845 April,

February to visit the Bogue Chetto Branch to inspire and uplift those members. Next, a visit to a branch came on 6 February 1845 when he left the Bogue Chetto Branch for the Five Mile Branch in Perry (now Hale), Alabama. Smoot described the evening with the Saints, writing, "We preached by candlelight to the Saints with the same good spirit that characterised [*sic*] the previous evening meeting. It gave the Saints much comfort." Regarding his travels later that night, Smoot wrote, "Passed through Marion County [Alabama], and traveled during the day thirty miles." Amazingly, the very next day, Smoot left Five Mile Branch and traveled twenty-five miles to Tuscaloosa County, where he spent the night with Hardy Clemons.[13] Abraham Smoot celebrated his thirtieth birthday 17 February 1845 by getting his boots mended and spending the night with a Brother Skinner. This followed a two-day conference at the Sipsey branch in Alabama.[14]

Evidence indicates that Smoot met several people who would later become part of the Mississippi Pioneer group in 1846 during his travels. Among others, he mentioned meeting Brother John Holladay, John Brown, and Benjamin Mathews.[15] Abraham continued traversing the area of northeastern Mississippi and northwestern Alabama. Over the next three months, he logged hundreds of miles visiting the small fledgling branches in the area. His last known entry as the leader of the Southern Mission came 20 April 1845. He taught a group in Tuscaloosa County, Alabama, on the authenticity of the *Book of Mormon*. He concluded the day by debating with an "Esquire Blocker" concerning a negative book written by John C. Bennett. He wrote about the experience:

41/54, https://catalog.churchofjesuschrist.org/assets/9d9be8eb-14f7-4214-b708-1076b5d81a6a/2/40, <accessed 5 October 2021>

13. Abraham A, O. Smoot, "Smoot Diary, Vol. 1, 1836-1846," 228, https://contentdm.lib.byu.edu/digital/collection/MMD/id/27243, <accessed 5 October 2021>

14. Ibid, 229

15. Ibid, 231-232

> At the close of my discourse, Esquire Blocker, being employed by a Hireling Priest by the name of Thompson, presented to the people Dr. John C. Bennet's book on the Exposure of Mormonism, but the congregation, becoming disgusted, left the speaker to his own shame, and gave their attention to my remarks on J. C. Bennet's character.[16]

Through Abraham Smoot's account of his missionary travels, we discover several early branches of the church in Mississippi and Alabama. Additional research has added to our understanding of these early branches. The Big Sandy, Five Mile, Sipsey, Russellville, Little Bear Creek, Hamilton, and Moscow/Marion comprised the branches in northeastern Alabama. These young branches declared membership of seven to fifteen members. The main branch in northeastern Mississippi was the Buttahatchie Branch in Monroe County. The 1846 Mississippi Pioneer Company departed from there.[17]

John Brown's Travels Between Mississippi and Nauvoo, Illinois

The challenges in Nauvoo became so intense in early 1845 that the Quorum of the Twelve Apostles sent out a letter requesting all "young, middled [sic] aged and able-bodied men to Nauvoo to defend the place and help build the temple; to carry with them their arms and ammunition."[18] John Brown, along with six other men from the surrounding area, answered the call and prepared to leave their homes and families to travel to Nauvoo. They began their journey north on 14 March 1845 by walking from Monroe County, Mississippi, to Memphis, Tennessee, approximately 165 miles over rough roads. Fortunately, they used a light wagon to carry their luggage and other necessities. From Memphis, the travelers chartered a steamboat to St. Louis, Missouri, where they purchased ammuni-

---

16. Ibid, 239
17. Mormon Places, "Mormon Branches in the South," http://mormonplaces.byu.edu/map.html?, <accessed 12 October 2021>
18. John Zimmerman Brown, Autobiography of Pioneer John Brown, 1820-1896, 56

tion. Brown and the others kept the guns stored in a long box covered with blankets. The travelers continued from St. Louis, where they boarded the steamer *War Eagle* 24 March. After twenty-six hours on the *War Eagle*, Brown and his companions arrived in Nauvoo, Illinois, where they rented a small room to sleep in.[19]

Brown's arrival in Nauvoo in late March allowed him to attend the church's conference from 6 April to 8 April, which he thoroughly enjoyed. On 17 April 1845, John penned a letter to his wife in Mississippi in which he told Elizabeth that he and his friends worked on the temple. According to Brown's letter, the temple should be covered by the summer, and some of the rooms would be finished. Following these needed steps, the "twelve will commence giving the Saints their endowments, washings, and anointings." John deeply missed his wife and told her in his letter that he wanted to travel to get her and bring her back to Nauvoo in July. He believed he would be sent out on a mission in the fall but hoped he could spend the fall and winter with her. John begged Elizabeth to write immediately upon receipt of his letter. "Don't wait a single day," he pleaded. Interestingly, her mailing address read simply: Elizabeth Brown, Athens, Monroe County, Mississippi.[20] Precisely one month later, on 17 May 1845, John penned another letter to Elizabeth. His first sentence reveals a profound desire to see his wife face-to-face instead of "writing with ink and paper six hundred miles off."[21] Brown describes in detail his surroundings as he wrote the letter.

> I am now sitting upon a stool in front of a window and have the whole room to myself. On my right is a beer barrel, the upper disk is furnished with a painted bucket and a tin cup; Brother Mathews's pantaloons and a bowie knife; on my left are saddle bags, bed clothes and a trunk; in my rear stands four rifles, hang three pistols, stand two flour barrels, nearly empty, set four stools, one trunk and a small box.

19. Ibid.
20. Ibid, 57-58
21. Ibid, 59

Also, a long box which is used for a table. It is now covered (not with a cloth, four such a thing was never on it) with delft plates, knives, and forks, iron spoons, and tin cups.[22]

Brown's detailed description of the room he was writing provides a glimpse at the trappings of life in the mid-1840s.

John Brown left Nauvoo 3 June 1845 with his friends William Crosby, John H. Bankhead, and William Mathews. His destination was Monroe County, Mississippi, where he sought to be united with his wife. The journey began on the steamer *Mermaid*, which took them to St. Louis after twenty-four hours on the Mississippi River. From St. Louis, the party boarded the *New Missouri* on its first voyage. John reached Memphis 6 June and traveled the final distance to Aberdeen, Mississippi, in a carriage. The entire journey from Nauvoo to Aberdeen covered 800 miles and took eleven days to complete. John was pleased to find the family healthy, and he determined to take his wife back to Nauvoo. John stayed home for only a few days before he left Monroe County with his wife and traveled back by way of his mother's home in Perry County, Illinois. John and his wife obtained a two-horse wagon to complete the arduous overland trip. The couple left Monroe County on 27 June and arrived in Perry County on 9 July. Cross-country journeys in the mid-1840s were dangerous and tedious. The mileage from Monroe County to Perry County was less than half the distance from Monroe County to Nauvoo, yet the journey took four days longer to complete. John had not seen his mother in two years and was taken aback by how frail she appeared. Yet, his mother entertained the couple for several days while John preached and became reacquainted with old friends. John and Elizabeth arrived back in Nauvoo 29 July 1845, where he rented a room, bought a city lot from William Hyde for twenty-five dollars, and commenced building a home for his family. The transaction was recorded on December 20, 1845, by W. W. Phelps.[23]

---

22. Ibid, 60-61
23. Ibid, 63-64

With great anticipation, John looked forward to welcoming a new baby and enjoying the companionship of his wife. Tragically, shortly after arriving back in Nauvoo, his wife gave birth to a son who lived for only about one hour. Brown named his son Samuel and buried his remains "on the northeast corner of my lot and raised a small heap of bricks on his grave." September 1845 witnessed a significant increase in mob activity around Nauvoo, which brought business to a grinding halt. Despite the struggles with the mob, Brown finished building his home in Kimball's addition in the city of Nauvoo. During the month of September, church leaders made the determination to abandon Nauvoo and head west the following spring. During this time, William Crosby and his family arrived in Nauvoo and lived with John and Elizabeth in their partially-completed home. With the directive to leave Nauvoo and head into the unknown, Brown knew he needed to return home to Mississippi to settle business and personal affairs. Before doing so, John and Elizabeth received their endowments in the temple. He rented his home to an unnamed individual and left the structure in the care of William Hyde, with the instructions to sell the home and use the proceeds to help Hyde's family in the wilderness. John Brown, along with William Crosby, William Mathews, and George P. Dykes, left the city of Nauvoo 14 January 1846, bound for Monroe County, arriving on 22 February 1846. Before leaving Nauvoo, Brigham Young told John to leave families behind, organize a group of Saints from the South, travel west, and meet up with the Saints from Nauvoo "in the Indian Country." In less than two months, Brown and several others would leave their homes in the South and head into the vast uncharted territory of the West, seeking a place where he and other members of the church could live their religion without outside interference.[24]

NAUVOO TEMPLE

The construction of the Nauvoo Temple may be rated as one of the

---

24. Ibid, 64-66

most monumental structural accomplishments on the Western frontier in the mid-1840s. After being forced out of both Kirtland and Missouri, most of the Saints were extremely poor. Many members of the church lost tremendous amounts of money after being forcibly removed from Missouri in the winter of 1838-1839. Yet, amid extreme scarcity, Joseph Smith declared in July 1840 that a temple must be built in Nauvoo, and he requested individuals "to bring everything you can bring and build a Temble [Temple] unto the Lord a house unto the mighty God of Jacob."[25] In a revelation dated January 1841, the Saints were commanded to build a temple and hotel. The cornerstone was laid 6 April 1841, and church members volunteered labor, money, and tithing to complete the temple. John Brown participated in the construction of the temple during his time in Nauvoo. About his experience, he wrote, "We worked on the temple during the day and whittled and whistled through the streets at night, keeping everything in order and guarding the city against mobs. There was no need of a curfew bell in those times; none were seen upon the streets except those on duty."[26] Men, such as John Brown, took the place of a police force for Nauvoo following the repeal of the Nauvoo Charter by the Illinois legislature.

Building construction came under the direction of a committee composed of Reynolds Cahoon, Alpheus Cutler, Elias Higbee, and Hyrum Smith. A wooden baptismal font was completed in the fall of 1841, and proxy baptisms for the deceased were moved from the Mississippi River to the basement of the temple. The first baptisms in the temple began November 1841. The temple stood approximately 158 feet tall and measured 128 by eighty-eight feet at the base. The first two floors contained offices and assembly halls, while the third-floor attic held offices, dressing rooms, and endowment rooms. The temple also served for a time as a meeting place for Sunday services.

---

25. "Discourse, circa 19 July 1840, as Reported by Martha Jane Knowlton Coray–B," p. [9], The Joseph Smith Papers, https://www.josephsmithpapers.org/paper-summary/dis course-circa-19-july-1840-as-reported-by-martha-jane-knowlton-coray-b/1 <accessed 13 November 2021>
26. Leonard J. Arrington, "Mississippi Mormons," *The Ensign* (June 1977), 45-51

The temple was dedicated 20 April and 1 May 1846, following the Saints forced expulsion from Nauvoo.[27]

EXPULSION OF THE SAINTS FROM NAUVOO

Members of The Church of Jesus Christ of Latter-day Saints were forced from their homes in Nauvoo by local citizens who despised the tenets of the church, hated Joseph and Hyrum Smith, and viewed the members living in Nauvoo and surrounding areas as a threat. Following rejections from the states of Ohio, Missouri, and now Illinois, the only choice seemed to be leaving the United States and fleeing west. The determination to vacate Nauvoo by the spring of 1846 was a monumental task. Thousands of people needed to be organized, with needed food, necessary leadership for the wagon trains, and the construction of hundreds of wagons. The departure was first set for the spring of 1846.[28] However, due to increased pressure from local settlers, the first group to leave Nauvoo departed 4 February 1846. They crossed the Mississippi River to Iowa to set up temporary camps during the bitterly cold winter of that year. Several hundred others followed the first group and set up camp in Iowa.[29] One noted historian, William Hartley, determined three distinct phases took place during the flight from Nauvoo. Brigham Young's Camp of Israel began 1 March 1846 and did not conclude until this company finished crossing Iowa to the eastern bank of the Missouri River. The next departure included an estimated 12,000 members and ended with thousands spread out across Iowa. In September 1846, the

27. "Temple, Nauvoo Illinois" The Joseph Smith Papers, A Summary of the Nauvoo Temple construction, https://www.josephsmithpapers.org/place/temple-nauvoo-illi nois?highlight=Temple,%20Nauvoo,%20Illinois, <accessed 13 November 2021>
28. William G. Hartley, Glenn Rawson, Dennis Lyman, Bryant Bush, editors, *History of the Saints*, William Hartley, "Exodus from Nauvoo," (American Fork: Covenant Communications, Inc., 2012), 18-19
29. Leonard J. Arrington, *Brigham Young: American Moses*, (Chicago: University of Illinois Press, 1985), 127

last group left Nauvoo at gunpoint following a surrender to an armed militia.[30]

PARTICIPANTS FROM MISSISSIPPI AND ALABAMA IN 1846

After arriving back home, John Brown and those who would participate in the trek into the unknown had a limited amount of time to prepare a group to travel west, as requested by Brigham Young. Arriving in Monroe County in the latter part of February and making the needed arrangements to leave for an unknown destination in the West within forty-five days must have seemed almost unattainable. Who would be willing to leave family, land, homes, friends, and their way of life in the South for an unknown destination outside of the United States? For those who were leaving wives and children at home, who would take care of their needs? How should the land be disposed of, and what legal issues should be addressed before departing? With these and other questions needing resolutions, John Brown and his friends assembled a resolute group of men, women, and children willing to leave every earthly possession to travel toward an undetermined location and start from nothing to rebuild their lives and homes. Brown noted the group, now known as the Mississippi Company, consisted of approximately fourteen families and six individuals as they began the journey from northeastern Mississippi.[31] Most of those who comprised the Mississippi Company came from Monroe County, Mississippi, and Marian County, Alabama. Some of the participants owned large plantations and slaves, and others worked smaller plots of land. Some were single, while others were traveling with their families, including children. Evidence indicates there were forty-three adults—nineteen women and twenty-four men—and many children when they departed Mississippi on Thursday, 8

---

30. Hartley, *History of the Saints,* William Hartley, "Exodus from Nauvoo," 19
31. Autobiography of Pioneer John Brown, 1820-1896, 66-67

April 1846.[32] The following individuals are known to have agreed to leave their homes and go west. Here is a brief introduction of the documented participants.

As noted earlier, **John Brown (1820-1896)** married **Elizabeth Crosby (1822-1906)** 21 May 1844 in Monroe County, Mississippi. Because of his missionary work in the South, his marriage into the Crosby family, and the direct request from Brigham Young to go west with a group of Saints from the South, John Brown is one of the central participants in this remarkable story. Brown departed alone with the Mississippi Company in April 1846 and left Pueblo in September 1846 to return home.[33] **Absalom Porter Dowdle (1819-1897)** and his wife, **Sarah Ann Holladay (1828-1915)**, daughter of plantation owner John Holladay, left with the original Mississippi Saints. According to Dowdle's personal account, a daughter, **Sarah Catherine Dowdle (1846-1936)**, was born "on the banks of the Arkansas River"[34] after arriving at Pueblo. **George Washington Gibson (1800-1871)**, his wife, **Mary Ann Sparks (1802-1871)**, and his family joined the movement west after being a member for only one year. The Gibson family consisted of George, Mary Ann, and nine children ranging from two to twenty-one years of age.[35] Shortly after arriving in Pueblo, George was stricken with mountain fever.[36] **James Harmon (1801-1851)**, with his wife, **Mary Ann Blanks (1808-1897)**, left for the West with their four children after selling their land holdings and other assets. According to a letter written by their daughter Josephine in 1926, a son, **John Taylor Harmon (1847-1926)**, was born

---

32. Norma Bates, "The Forgotten Pioneers, Part II, Crossroads Newsletter of the Utah Crossroads Chapter Oregon -California Trails Association, (Fall 1997, Vol. 8, No. 4), https://user.xmission.com/~octa/newsv8n4.htm#Forgotten%20Pioneers, <accessed 21 November 2021>

33. Autobiography of Pioneer John Brown, 1820-1896, 70

34. Absalom Porter Dowdle, 1819-1897. Absalom P. Dowdle autobiography , https://catalog.churchofjesuschrist.org/assets/4bd7e829-80dd-4098-b5d9-d2443e7b4cdb/0/0 <accessed: November 22, 2021>

35. Kate B. Carter, Compiler, "Mississippi Saints," *Our Pioneer Heritage*, 20 volumes, Daughters of Utah Pioneers, Salt Lake City, Utah, 1959, 2: 436-437

36. Ibid.

at Pueblo 6 April 1847, just prior to leaving for the Salt Lake Valley.[37] [38]

John Holladay (1798-1862) and his wife, **Catherine Beesley Higgins (1797-1877)**, settled in Marion County, Alabama. Like many others in the Mississippi Company, they sold their land holdings (a large plantation) and started west with their six children. Shortly after arriving in the Salt Lake Valley, they settled in the Big Cottonwood Canyon area, which was later named Holladay in honor of John, who served as the first bishop of the community.[39] **Allen Freeman Smithson (1816-1877)**, along with **Letitia Holladay (1824-1849)**, another daughter of John Holladay, departed with their four children for the hoped-for reunion with other members of the church who were forced out of Nauvoo. Sadly, Letitia died shortly after arriving in the Salt Lake Valley. Allen's brother **William Cox Smithson (1804-1889)** and wife **Lucinda Wilson (1813-1899)** obtained the faith necessary to leave their home and embark into the unknown. They traveled with six children from one to twelve years of age. Another brother, **James Albert Smithson**, returned to the South with John Brown in September 1846.[40] **George Washington Sparks (1819-1906)** and **Lusianna "Luanna" Roberds (1818-1895)** loaded up their wagon with a few supplies and their two-year-old son, as well as a four-month-old baby girl named Mary Ann "Polly" Sparks. Sadly, she died 8 January 1858 near San Bernardino, California, and is buried in the Pioneer Memorial Cemetery.[41]

Benjamin Franklin Mathews (1819-1888) embarked on the journey west with his wife, **Temperance Weeks (1817-1879)**, and

---

37. Ibid, 449-451

38. James Harmon, *Family Search*, <KWVQ-NCM>, https://www.familysearch.org/tree/person/details/KWVQ-NCM, <accessed 19 June 2024>

39. Ibid, 447

40. Autobiography of Pioneer John Brown, 1820-1896, 70

41. Ibid, 455-456, Information on the birth and death of Mary Ann "Polly" Sparks located online at "Find a Grave," Ancestry https://www.ancestry.com/discoveryui-content/view/83132826:60525?tid=&pid=&queryId=04c6b71908e29912bc5906c48164797b&_phsrc=huy24&_phstart=successSource, <accessed 23 November 2021>

their three young children, including an infant. Benjamin purchased "two heavy wagons, which he loaded with provisions, bedding and a few implements, and a third lighter wagon which was made as comfortable as possible for riding and sleeping purposes."[42] Following a brief courtship, **William (Billy) Harvey Lay (1817-1886)** married **Sytha Solena Crosby (1817-1881)** 18 December 1841 at Aberdeen, Monroe County, Mississippi.[43] Billy left his wife and children in Monroe County when he first traveled with the Mississippi Company. He returned to his family from Pueblo in the fall of 1846, only to find his wife had suffered a terrible tragedy during his absence. During Billy's absence of seven months, Sytha traveled to the town of Aberdeen, near their plantation, for some shopping. She noticed three men leaning against a saloon wall, leering at her, but she paid them little notice. The term "Mormon Crosby witches" was an expression that followed the Crosby women who had joined The Church of Jesus Christ of Latter-day Saints while living in Monroe County. On the same day, Sytha was violated by the men she had seen earlier. For some time following the assault, she remained sequestered in her home, kept company with other women she trusted, and did not allow the children to be alone. The men who assaulted her were never brought to justice.[44]

Daniel Monroe Thomas (1809-1894) married **Ann Crosby (1812-1878)** on 17 March 1845 in Monroe, Mississippi. He left Monroe County with the Mississippi group without his family and returned in the fall of 1846. Thomas made it to the Salt Lake Valley with the Edward Hunter/Jacob Foutz wagon train of 1847. The Hunter/Foutz wagon train left eastern Nebraska Territory 19 June 1847 and arrived in the Salt Lake Valley 1 October 1847. He traveled with his wife, child, and extended family during this second trip west.[45] **George Washington Bankhead (1819-1898)** left with the Mississippi

---

42. Ibid, 456
43. Charmaine Lay Kohler, *Southern Grace: A Story of the Mississippi Saints,* (The Beagle Press, Boise, Idaho, 1995) 44
44. Ibid, 56-57
45. Mormon Pioneer Overland Travel "Edward Hunter/Jacob Foutz Company (1847),

Company for the West. After remaining in Pueblo for a short period, he returned to the South with John Brown and others on 1 September 1846.[46] **William Crosby (1808-1880)** married **Sarah Jane Harmon (1808-1888)** 4 March 1832 in Monroe, Mississippi. William left his family in the South while he journeyed west. He also left Pueblo in September 1846 to return home. William was the father-in-law of Daniel Monroe Thomas, William Harvey Lay, and John Brown.[47] William Crosby received his elder's license 22 April 1844[48] and presided over the branch in Monroe County, Mississippi, before leaving with the Mississippi group.[49] **William Christopher Ritter (1824-1875)** married **Sarah Ann Lowry (1825-1876)** in Monroe County 17 March 1845.[50] Tragically, Ritter's life was cut short after he, along with six other men, were buried in an avalanche in Big Cottonwood Canyon in 1875. William worked as a "snaker" at the Richmond mine when the accident occurred. Snakers were men who took the ore from the mine and traveled down the mountain on rawhides.[51] **John Roberds (1800-1880)** married **Martha Tucker Walpole (1817-1897)** 2 September 1834 in Monroe County. They and their five young children departed with the Mississippi Saints in 1846. Evidence indicates he arrived with his family in the Salt Lake Valley 29 July 1847 after spending the winter at Pueblo.[52]

---

https://history.churchofjesuschrist.org/overlandtravel/companies/342/edward-hunter-jacob-foutz-company, <accessed 25 November 2021>

46. , "Mississippi Saints," *Our Pioneer Heritage*, Vol. 2, 467

47. *Southern Grace: A Story of the Mississippi Saints*, 11

48. "License Record Book," p. 123, The Joseph Smith Papers, <accessed November 26, 2021> https://www.josephsmithpapers.org/paper-summary/license-record-book/145

49. Autobiography of Pioneer John Brown, 1820-1896, 44

50. William Christopher Ritter Sr., *Family Search*, The Church of Jesus Christ of Latter-Day Saints, https://www.familysearch.org/tree/person/details/LH2W-5PY, <accessed 27 November 2021>

51. William Christopher Ritter Sr., *Family Search Memories*, The Church of Jesus Christ of Latter-Day Saints, https://www.familysearch.org/tree/person/memories/LH2W-5PY, <accessed 27 November 2021>

52. Historical Department journal history of the Church, 1830-2008; 1840-1849; 1847 July-December; Church History Library, https://catalog.churchofjesuschrist.org/assets/a84034e2-b2c3-43fd-9821-261211f6fda7/0/111, <accessed: November 27, 2021> In this compiled list his name is listed as Roberts, not Roberds.

As noted earlier, the Mississippi Company left Monroe County, Mississippi, on 8 April 1846, with high hopes of meeting other Saints on the trail west. Brown wrote that he formed a team with William Crosby, Daniel Monroe Thomas, William (Billy) Lay, James Harmon, and George W. Bankhead for the trek west. This band remained close throughout the trek to Pueblo. When John Brown traveled back home from Pueblo 1 September 1846, he took all but James Harmon with him. In addition, James Smithson and John Holladay traveled with him. Providentially, on the return trip, these men encountered the Mormon Battalion 11 September 1846 as they traveled on the Santa Fe Trail. This unplanned meeting allowed three separate detachments from the Battalion to winter in Pueblo.[53] This is their incredible story of tenacity and devotion.

---

53. Michael N. Landon, Brandon J. Metcalf, *The Remarkable Journey of the Mormon Battalion,* (American Fork, Utah: Covenant Communications, 2012), 40-41

4

SANTA FE TRAIL

The Santa Fe Trail played an important role in the story of the company from Mississippi and the three Mormon Battalion detachments that wintered in Pueblo. During the mid-1800s, the trail was an invaluable east-to-west trade route. Goods were taken from Missouri to New Mexico and sold for enormous profit. Those living in New Mexico used the trail to take their goods to the United States. The trail began in Independence, Missouri, and extended to Santa Fe, New Mexico. The profits earned by those traveling the trail contributed to the Mexican American War of 1846. Following the American victory, the use of the trail expanded, particularly after mail service was introduced in 1849. The trail lost its importance in 1880 following the completion of the Santa Fe railroad.[1] Spain ruled Mexico until a revolution in 1821 forced Spain to grant Mexico its independence. Mexico could then trade with the United States. At the same time, a financial panic in Missouri became so severe that farmers could not sell their products locally and needed to ship their products to faraway New Orleans. A Missouri salt maker, William

---

1. Britannica, The Editors of Encyclopedia. "Santa Fe Trail". *Encyclopedia Britannica*, 3 Jun. 2021, https://www.britannica.com/topic/Santa-Fe-Trail. <accessed 12 April 2023>

Becknell, found himself broke and on the verge of going to jail. What caused Becknell to journey to Santa Fe is not known, but he started a journey from Franklin, Missouri, with five other men in September 1821. His trek took nearly two and a half months to complete. Becknell is credited with establishing the Santa Fe Trail.[2]

The overall length of the Santa Fe Trail extended approximately 800 miles. Initially, the trail commenced in Franklin, Missouri, but by 1827, the starting point moved to Independence, Missouri. From Independence, the trail passed through Kansas, Oklahoma, Colorado, and New Mexico. A route named the "Cimarron Cutoff" served as the original trace. The "Mountain Branch" was longer but contained better watering locations. This longer path was used primarily after 1845. During the early years, pack mules were used to take products to New Mexico, but oxen and mules were later used to pull wagons loaded with products from around the world.[3] Cotton cloth, silk goods, and even playing cards were in demand during the early years of the trail's existence. In return, traders received "silver pesos, mules, and beaver pelts."[4]

EARLY FREIGHTING OVER THE SANTA FE TRAIL

The estimated amount of freight carried over the trail from 1822 to 1843 is staggering. During the first four years, from 1822 to 1825, approximately $127,000 of sellable merchandise traveled the trail, primarily hauled by mules. The men needed for the trips totaled 350, with sixty-three wagons. The next four years witnessed $385,000 of merchandise, 440 men, and 190 wagons seeking their fortunes in

2. Harry C. Meyers, "A History of the Santa Fe Trail," Santa Fe Trail Association, https://www.santafetrail.org/the-trail/history/history-of-the-sft/, <accessed 12 April 2023>

3. "Trail Beginnings & Geographic Setting," National Park Service, https://www.nps.gov/articles/santa-fe-trail-beginnings.htm, <accessed 12 April 2023>

4. "More Trails Facts & the Decline of the Santa Fe Trail," National Park Service, https://www.nps.gov/articles/santa-fe-trail-decline.htm?utm_source=article&utm_medium=website&utm_campaign=experience_more&utm_content=small, <accessed 12 April 2023>

New Mexico. Fast-forwarding to the years 1840 to 1843, the results are even more astounding. A total of $1,000,000 of product, 630 men, and 410 wagons traveled the Santa Fe Trail seeking a place to sell their merchandise.[5] Trips further south than Santa Fe were undertaken, with some trains going as far south as Chihuahua, Mexico. The average gross profit returns for these adventurous traders equaled about 50 percent, which, after expenses, provided a return of between 20 and 40 percent. However, the travel time of over two months, deaths on the trail from accidents, overwhelming thirst, attacks by the Indigenous tribes who lived on or near the trail, and natural disasters created an environment where all profit could evaporate like a mirage of water in the desert.[6]

Sensing an opportunity to benefit from the increased goods coming into the area, Mexican officials levied duties and other taxes that were, at times, arbitrary. As the number of products flowing into the area increased, "customs-collecting became a lucrative source of income for Mexican officials." In 1839, Mexican citizens were excused from real estate taxes due to the high volume of products arriving from the freight wagons on the Santa Fe Trail. For a period, a flat rate of $500 per wagon was levied. This taxation led to larger wagons being used, with more mules or oxen pulling them. Shippers would hide items within the wagons or use false axle trees to conceal products. At times, the traders would remove products from one wagon and transfer the items to a different one. Bribery became a common and expected practice. The year 1839 witnessed 139 wagons arriving in Santa Fe. Thus, local officials could tap into a tremendous source of revenue—a source that would return year after year.[7]

---

5. Josiah Gregg, *Commerce of the Prairies, Volume II*, http://www.kancoll.org/books/gregg/index.html#contents, <accessed 12 April 2023> originally published in 1844 and 1845, Transcribed by Dick Taylor and John Maier; produced by John Maier, Dick Taylor, Lynn Nelson, and Susan Stafford.

6. Ibid.

7. Walker Demarquis Wyman, "Freighting on the Santa Fe Tail, 1843-1866," Iowa Research Online, Master's Thesis, 5-6, https://na-st01.ext.exlibrisgroup.com/01IOWA_INST/upload/1681332500926/Freighting%20on%20the%20Santa%20Fe%3F%20Trail%201843-1866.pdf?Expires=1681332634&Signature=rZHBNn2HLU

A Successful Journey on the Santa Fe Trail in 1829

One successful trip on the Santa Fe Trail began in April or early May 1829. By this time, the small village of Independence had begun asserting itself as an important component of Western trade. Concerning Independence, historian David Lavender wrote, "The town, a collection of log stores and taverns only two years old, was already achieving dominance as the starting place of the prairie trade."[8] Traveling on the trail to Santa Fe required that all participating in the caravan work together. This particular caravan consisted of thirty-eight wagons and seventy-nine men. Included in the group were survivors of a failed 1828 mission. During their previous year's excursion, several bags of silver were buried on an island on the trail. Charles and William Bent, who later would establish Bent's Fort, were also a part of this group. Charles was elected captain of this wagon train. The captain's job was to determine messes for cooking, arrange the wagon train, locate campgrounds, and determine who would work the hated night watches during the trek.[9]

Second Lieutenant Philip St. George Cooke, freshly graduated from West Point, served in a military group that traveled with the caravan as protection. (Cooke would later lead the Mormon Battalion from Santa Fe to the California coast.) The soldiers, with their ox-drawn wagons, would lead out ahead of the merchants, followed by the rest of the participants. The scouts traveled ahead of everyone.

---

glelqmpH4Jyn3jED3FZ9aUSphUm-l732G5uebGWuje54isFk2fHDjhgCTi~RT-UO7u
Q917nEwyXPzE8EHrp4aSoZXECoop4~-
92Vw3IMYYxT0XTMUZtojYhLXFJehORebYxmhH~3vCh1tZIbKh
Nkgx9e4Bm~5BAC-1Rngekac9BFVyiJqWts9XlgMh-ribtMGCgvTbO6j189NFObk
XGG-sqbuNnD-
djChxqFB3iYhG~gpQS2T6tPpS6ILzT4c11tKK9x0UbrWb3LdCfZcFfwo6MAdzTw
JFc6ltzR08nM3jdRrZxrDUo3DkjEgVnVfBaB2r7ZaCpjgkTQ__&Key-Pair-Id=APKA
J72OZCZ36VGVASIA, <accessed 12 April 2023>
8. David Lavender, *Bent's Fort*, (Garden City, New York, Doubleday & Company, 1954), 88
9. Ibid, 91

Hunters would spread out searching for game, and loose livestock followed from the rear. Wagons would often travel in two-wide or even four-wide lines for protection against the Indigenous population. In 1829, huge herds of buffalo still roamed the prairie, and the hunters took advantage of the situation. As the wagon train continued down the trail, they located a small cannon buried in the ground, which Charles had pulled out and put in working order.[10] The caravan continued slowly toward its objective of Santa Fe.

The military escort was only allowed to travel with the traders to a certain point along the trail. Their orders were to wait along the Arkansas River until the fall when the caravan would return. On 10 July 1829, preparations were made to cross the Arkansas River. Although shallow, the slow-moving river contained shifting channels and quicksand. To keep the wagons from sinking, teams were doubled or even tripled. After several hours, the crossing was completed. Shortly after the river crossing, the wagon train extended out over one-half mile, which placed the company in a vulnerable situation. Traveling ahead of the company, William Bent sighted a band of Indigenous warriors. He forced his mule to turn around and rushed back to the unsuspecting men in the caravan. After arriving back with the traders, defensive positions were taken up, and a short skirmish ensued. During the conflict, the small cannon found earlier was utilized. The noise and explosion of sand sent the warriors scrambling for cover. In the meantime, a small contingent was sent to locate the soldiers, and when the military arrived, the warriors left. During the skirmish, one man was killed, and some of the livestock died, but the product was unscathed. Fortunately for the traders, when word reached Taos about the approaching wagons, ninety-five trappers were sent to escort them to Taos and, eventually, to Santa Fe.[11] This particular caravan reached its destination safely.

---

10. Ibid, 93
11. Ibid, 97-99

CHARLES BENT, WILLIAM BENT, AND CERAN ST. VRAIN

Charles Bent, William Bent, and Ceran St. Vrain all came from respected families in St. Louis, Missouri. Little is known about how the two Bent brothers met St. Vrain. All three men participated in trapping during the mid-1820s, so if they did not know each other from their time in St. Louis, it is likely their paths crossed during a beaver trapping excursion. As the profitability of the beaver trade faltered, these three men began looking at another area where they could make their fortunes—Santa Fe and the Southwest. Evidence indicates that no one else had more impact on trade in the Southwest than these three men during the early days of the Santa Fe Trail. Charles Bent was older than William, and he worked as a partner in the Missouri Fur Company from 1824 to 1828. Following the demise of that company, Charles purchased equipment and departed for New Mexico in 1829. William was smaller, and his complexion was darker than Charles's. Both brothers were energetic and shrewd in business, but considerate to friends and "loyal to their country." St. Vrain began trading American products in 1825, and he called Taos home. He was a skillful negotiator, yet he used gentleness and compassion in his interactions with others. In 1832, a partnership was formed between the three men when they entered the Indian trade on the Arkansas. In the year 1835, the company finished the construction of Bent's Fort on the north side of the Arkansas River.[12]

BENT'S FORT

Bent's Fort on the Santa Fe Trail played an important role for those who stayed in Pueblo during the winter of 1846-1847. As noted earlier, William Kartchner and James Harmon worked as blacksmiths at the fort. The Bent brothers and St. Vrain constructed the non-mili-

---

12. Janet Lecompte, *Pueblo, Hardscrabble, Greenhorn, The Upper Arkansas, 1832-1856,* (University of Oklahoma Press, Norman, 1978), 13-14

tary fort on the Cimarron route of the old Santa Fe Trail. One of St. Vrain's assets was that he knew the Mexican culture well, which aided the three partners greatly since the fort stood on Mexican soil. In writing about the fort, historian David Lavender noted the construction of the "mud castle" brought about the "American expansion into the Southwest."[13] The rectangular fort faced east and measured 137 feet by 178 feet in size. The walls of the fort stood fourteen feet in height and measured three feet thick. The fort was constructed almost entirely of adobe, and on two opposite corners of the fort, round towers rose eighteen feet into the air for protection. Although not yet completed, by the fall of 1833, the mud castle was far enough along to open for business.[14] The fort contained clerks' offices, servants' quarters, sleeping rooms, and a dining hall. A barber shop and a tailor shop were added to the accoutrements within the fort. The second story sported a billiard table and a bar.[15] Thus, they had made the fort an inviting location for those who traveled the dust-choked Santa Fe Trail.

Due to the business connections of the Bent brothers and St. Vrain, the fort offered products from around the world. Merchandise such as glass beads from Italy and the Czech Republic, sugar from Cuba, coffee from Central and South America, Hudson Bay blankets from England, cloth from France and England, and guns from Belgium, England, and the Eastern United States comprised the incredible variety of products offered by this obscure fort in the middle of the "American Desert." Mountain men, trappers, Mexicans, and Native Americans constituted the majority of customers at the fort. To trade for the goods at the fort, Native American women would prepare a buffalo hide. A buffalo brain was used to tan the inside of the hide, which took about ten days to prepare. In exchange for their efforts, the finished robes were worth about three dollars in

---

13. David Lavender, *Bent's Fort*, 15
14. Ibid, 136-139
15. Janet Lecompte, *Pueblo, Hardscrabble, Greenhorn*, 13

trade amount, or roughly $110 in 2020 dollars.[16] Bent's Fort survived during the years before the Mexican American War began by trading with those living in and around the fort. During the war, the fort was a major supply depot for the tons of freight needed to support the war effort, as well as a resting place for the hundreds of soldiers marching their way west. The end of Bent's Fort came quickly. The purpose of the fort was to trade with the Indigenous people living in upper Arkansas. Following the end of the Mexican American War, the military sent troops that camped near the fort. These new troops were to "control the Indians and protect travelers and settlers."[17]

Three events took place that brought an end to Bent's Fort. The first was Charles's death in 1847. Next came the horrific cholera epidemic that swept across the area in 1848. Finally, Vincent St. Vrain failed in his attempt to sell the fort to the US Army. William knew the end was near.[18] As noted earlier, the fort was not built to fight the Indigenous people—it brought products to those living on the plains. Something had to give. According to one account, William ordered the employees to take everything of value out of the fort and place the items in wagons. The fixtures filled twenty wagons, which in turn were pulled by six yoke of oxen. He then loaded his children and wife (who was named Yellow Woman) onto the caravan, and the entire group traveled to a creek five miles down the Arkansas River. William then rode back to the fort, rolled kegs of powder into the main parts of the fort, set fire to the wooden roofs, and rode back to the camp.[19] He built trading houses near the new camp and later, in 1853, built another fort.[20] The empire built by Charles and William Bent and Vincent St. Vrain now stood in the twilight of its existence.

---

16. Interview with Park Ranger Alicia LaFever, Bent's Old Fort National Historic Site, La Junta, Colorado, 29 April 2022.

17. Janet Lecompte, *Pueblo, Hardscrabble, Greenhorn,* 204

18. Bent's Old Fort, National Historic Site by the National Park Service History Library, http://npshistory.com/publications/beol/index.htm#:~:text=It%20is% 20thought%20that%20William,and%20a%20catalyst%20for%20change. <accessed 15 April 2023>

19. David Lavender, *Bent's Fort,* 315-316

20. Bent's Old Fort, National Historic Site

THE OREGON TRAIL

The most famous of the routes used during America's Manifest Destiny of Western expansion was the Oregon Trail. This remarkable track from western Missouri to Oregon, Washington, California, and Utah allowed hundreds of thousands of individuals to leave their homes in the East for their dreams in the West. The first pioneers to reach the Oregon Territory, apart from explorers and mountain men, were two Protestant missionaries from Canada. Their main purpose was to convert the Native people to Christianity. Although these valiant early missionaries failed in that undertaking, they did establish a foundation for settlement in Oregon and paved the way for future expansion. Shortly thereafter, Dr. Marcus Whitman and his small entourage of missionaries first traveled west in 1836 with fur caravans.[21] The 2,000-mile trail to Oregon originated in Independence, Missouri. However, a few years later, a crowded steamboat landing and the cholera epidemic in Independence caused a move to Westport and other locations further up the Missouri River. Another town, St. Joseph, provided stiff competition as a relevant starting point for pioneers heading west. Although it was better known as the birthplace of the Pony Express, St. Joseph attracted many pioneers to begin their four-to-six-month journey there.[22]

MANIFEST DESTINY

Although discussion of western expansion in the United States began in the 1830s, the idea of Manifest Destiny provided additional justification for settling the West. John L. O'Sullivan, an influential journalist during the mid-1800s, promoted the ethical, political, and financial justifications for populating the country from the Atlantic to

---

21. Dr. Jim Tompkins, "The Road to Oregon," Oregon California Trails Association, unpaginated, https://octa-trails.org/school-resources/, <accessed 1 May 2023>
22. Dr. Jim Tompkins, "Many Roads Leading Pioneers & Emigrants Westward," Oregon California Trails Association, unpaginated, https://octa-trails.org/articles/origins-of-the-oregon-trail/, <accessed 1 May 2023>

the Pacific. In 1839, O'Sullivan expressed his views concerning the future of America, writing, "This is our high destiny, and in nature's eternal, inevitable decree of cause and effect, we must accomplish it. All this will be our future history, to establish on earth the moral and dignity and salvation of man."[23] A few years later, in 1845, he authored an article supporting the annexation of Texas and formalized the term Manifest Destiny. He pled for Americans to rally to them, as he put it, "manifest destiny to overspread the continent allotted by Providence for the free development of our yearly multiplying millions." [24] O'Sullivan was not a proponent of military force, but his two-word phrase influenced Western expansion and territorial conquest.

Concerning the future state of California, which was then governed by Mexico, O'Sullivan wrote, "Imbecile and distracted, Mexico never can exert any real governmental authority over such a country."[25] Not everyone could be included in Manifest Destiny. Millions were still shackled by the bonds of slavery. Native Americans were forcibly removed from their ancestral homes and relocated. The conquest of Mexico and other takeovers can be traced to the concept of Manifest Destiny. Even though it could not be enjoyed by all, the rallying cry to move west rang true to many Americans who sought a better life. Western expansion sent Americans west on various trails— the most important of which was the Oregon Trail. Americans chased their dreams of rich farmland in the Northwest, religious freedom in the Utah Territory, or gold in California. Within a few decades, the United States of America extended from the East Coast to the Pacific Coast.

---

23. John L. O'Sullivan, "An American Journalist Explains "Manifest Destiny"," *SHEC: Resources for Teachers*, <accessed April 26, 2023>, https://shec.ashp.cuny.edu/items/show/1939.
24. John O'Sullivan, "Annexation," 1845, Bill of Rights Institute, p. 2 https://pdcrodas.webs.ull.es/anglo/OSullivanAnnexation.pdf, <accessed April 27, 2023>
25. Ibid. p. 5

INDEPENDENCE, MISSOURI

The town of Independence lies in western Missouri, on the south side of the Missouri River. The area became a part of the United States due to the Louisiana Purchase of 1803. In the 1830s and 1840s, Independence was on the western edge of the frontier. Lewis and Clark stopped at the future site of the town during their epic journey to the Pacific Ocean in 1804. Missouri entered the Union as a slave state in 1821 due to the Missouri Compromise. In 1827, a plat was created for the town of Independence, and slaves constructed a log courthouse for the new town. Unfortunately, the courthouse functioned as a pigpen in the evenings, which brought an onslaught of fleas. To eliminate the fleas, the judge ordered sheep to be brought in to clear out the fleas before holding court.

Eugene T. Wells provides an early account of the importance of Independence to the western migration. He wrote:

> Independence was the rendezvous point for the emigration of 1838 and, in the succeeding years, was the major outfitting point for that area.... In 1844, an estimated $50,000 was spent in Independence by the Oregon emigrants. The succeeding year (1845), the local merchants stocked outfits and goods for 8,000 emigrants to the Northwest.[26]

Wells also described how the area around Independence looked in May 1846, which was the same month and year the Mississippi Company had arrived. Wells wrote, "The roads into Independence are lined with wagons, but weather conditions are unfavorable." [27] Apparently, the road out of town fared no better. "The first five miles of the roads leading from Independence to the Trace, we found in a

---

26. "Early Santa Fe, and Oregon and California Trails in Jackson County Missouri, Based on first hand documentation," p. 1, Downloaded from Oregon California Trails Association Website.
27. Ibid.

vary [*sic*] bad condition for wagons."[28] After a few years, pioneer companies moved upriver to Weston and St. Joseph. The year 1850 witnessed nearly double the number of emigrants traveling west; however, the number of those using Independence fell.[29]

SOUTH PASS

During the years the Great Platte River Road system was used, roughly 500,000 pioneers traveled to the West.[30] The Oregon Trail, the Mormon Trail, the Pony Express Trail, and the numerous other routes that led west would not exist without what is now called the "South Pass." Concerning this incredible opening, eminent historian Will Bagley wrote, "South Pass will forever be noted for its critical role in the lives of the half-million Americans who crossed it between 1840 and 1869 on their way to new homes in the West."[31] Travel over the South Pass began slowly in the early 1840s, but following the discovery of gold in California, "a mighty river of families, wagons, and cattle" utilized the South Pass to reach Oregon, Washington, Utah, and California.[32] As Charles T. Stanton crossed South Pass on 18 July 1846, he wrote with exuberance, "Thus the great daydream of my youth and of my riper years is accomplished. I have seen the Rocky Mountain[s]—have crossed the Rubicon and am now on the waters that flow to the Pacific!"[33] The South Pass, which stands at an altitude of 7,412 feet, opened the West to hundreds of thousands of individuals.[34]

---

28. Ibid.

29. Merrill J. Mattes, *The Great Platte River Road: The Covered Wagon Mainline Via Fort Kearny to Fort Laramie,* (Lincoln, University of Nebraska Press, 1969), 108

30. Merrill J. Mattes, *Platte River Road Narratives,* (Urbana and Chicago, University of Illinois Press, 1988), 5

31. Will Bagley, *South Pass Gateway to a Continent,* (Norman, University of Oklahoma Press, 2014), 21

32. Ibid, 114

33. Ibid, 134

34. Ibid, 24

STORIES OF THE OREGON TRAIL FROM 1846

In addition to the Mississippi Company traveling west on the Oregon Trail in 1846, others started west that year. According to noted trail historian Merrill J. Mattes, the number of emigrants who went west in 1846 totaled about 3,000.[35] The former governor of Missouri, Lilburn W. Boggs, traveled the trail that year with his son William Montgomery Boggs. They were with the Donner party near Devil's Gate when members of the ill-fated Donner wagon train were convinced to take a "shorter" route to California called the Hastings Cutoff. Their tragic story may be one of the most heartbreaking accounts of the entire pioneer western migration. The two Boggs men elected to go to Fort Hall. William H. Russell led the largest wagon train traveling west that year. Most of his group was traveling to California. The train of 100 wagons he began the journey with at one point swelled in size to 150. While on the trail, the company broke up into smaller groups for efficiency. Russell warned those in Independence that "2,000 Mormons had crossed the Missouri River 'with artillery' but appeared friendly."[36] As noted in chapter four, John Brown wrote about the hysteria that existed in Independence concerning members of The Church of Jesus Christ of Latter-day Saints.

J. Quinton Thornton and his wife departed Quincy, Illinois, 16 April 1846—just eight days after the Mississippi group left Monroe County. Near Independence, they joined a large group under the direction of W. H. Russell. The new group contained seventy-two wagons, which afforded greater protection on the trail. After traveling for about two months, Thornton describes meeting a company on the trail traveling east for the United States. Their description of the West was not impressive. On 27 June 1846, Thornton wrote:

---

35. Ibid, 2
36. Ibid, 74-87

A company of travelers, consisting of persons of both sexes, some of whom were from Oregon and some from California, returning to the states, were camped upon a plain about a mile distant. They presented a very woebegone appearance and brought us, moreover, an evil report of those lands. The Californians affirmed that the country was wholly destitute of timber and that wheat could not be raised in sufficient quantities for bread; that they had spent all their substance and were now returning to commence the world anew, somewhere in the vicinity of their former homes.[37]

One can only imagine how this news about the West impacted the trail weary travelers. Mr. Thornton ceased writing in his journal shortly after arriving at Fort Laramie.

James Miller Harrison left Iowa for Oregon on 1 April 1846. He traveled in a wagon train named the Iowa Company, which consisted of forty-one wagons and 500 head of cattle. During the early portion of the trek, he described the beauty of the plains and recalled the breathtaking sight of "the long string of white covered wagons moving slowly and majestically over the high rolling prairies, covered [the venue with] the deepest blue." He also witnessed little girls gathering flowers and seeing an occasional deer or antelope. Their troubles began upon arriving at the Little Blue River. The waterway was swollen from recent rains, and crossing was extremely difficult. One wagon crossing the Blue turned over with a woman and two children inside. Several men jumped in and saved the occupants. After crossing the Little Blue, the pioneers rested for a day.[38] Another incident took place shortly after the river crossing. Some men from the wagon train went duck hunting on a pond of water near their camp. One of the

---

37. Transcribed by Louise Ridge, "Oregon and California in 1848," p. 1, 10, Oregon California Trails Association, Diary-of-J.-Quinn-Thornton-1846.pdf, <accessed 1 May 2023>

38. James Miller Harrison, *Across the Plains to Oregon,* Typed copy of an article written by James Harrison about his journey over the Oregon Trail. Located at Internet Archive, p. 2-3, https://archive.org/details/james.-miller.-harrison.-or.-trail-0001/page/n1/mode/2up, <accessed 2 May 2023>

men shot a duck, but unfortunately, the ball traveled across the pond and hit B. Stark, the captain of the wagon train, in the shoulder.

As the wagon train reached buffalo country near the Platte River, Harrison noted it was hard to keep men attending their duties within the wagon train—so great was their desire to kill a buffalo. He also indicated something near the river caused men to fall asleep during the day. Teamsters would doze off as they walked beside the wagons, and men on horseback would "find themselves bobbing." Although most in this pioneer company got along well, several in the wagon train became frustrated with the many complications that arose on the trail. Apparently, nothing could be done to satisfy this group of individuals. The grumbling continued to the point that consideration was given to splitting the company.[39]

One man was killed by Native Americans on the company's trek west. During a nighttime thunderstorm, the cattle stampeded and strayed miles from the encampment. The next morning, a group of men went searching for them. Harrison and one Mr. Trimble went looking for the stray livestock together. They took no firearms with them. Around sundown, the two men located the cattle and began rounding them up. The two were ambushed. About six warriors surrounded Harrison. During the scuffle, his clothing was torn off his body. As he tried to escape, Mr. Trimble was shot in the back and killed. For some reason, those who had surrounded Harrison rode off to join with those around Trimble. As Harrison gathered his wits, he located his spare clothing and began walking back to camp. In time, he met other men from the wagon train. Due to the circumstances, the men traveled back to camp rather than trying to locate Mr. Trimble's body. Trimble's body was never recovered, and he became one of the many who died on the Oregon Trail.[40] Although the number of pioneers who used the Oregon Trail in 1846 was limited, their successes and failures provide stories of great value.

---

39. Ibid, 3
40. Ibid, 4-5

5

FROM MONROE COUNTY, MISSISSIPPI, TO PUEBLO

Those traveling in the Mississippi Company came from diverse backgrounds. Some owned plantations and were considered the elite of that time. Others farmed smaller plots of land and were not prosperous by any worldly standard. Some were married with families. A few single men traveled in the group. In the 1840s, homes were heated by wood, and indoor plumbing with hot and cold running water was nonexistent. Life was tough, and many diseases that are now virtually eradicated ran rampant. Yellow fever, typhoid, malaria, measles, and numerous other sicknesses brought death to many. The oldest of the company to leave Monroe County was John Holladay at forty-nine years of age, which was considered old at the time. The average life span during the 1840s in the Antebellum South was thirty-seven years.[1] Two infants traveled in the group. The youngest was Mary Emma Smithson, born on 1 March 1846, just over a month before the wagon train headed west. Mary Ann Sparks came into the world on 18 January 1846, making her just three months old.

---

1. "Life and Death in the Antebellum Era 1800-1850, http://www.legacy.com/life-and-death/the-antebellum-era.html, <accessed 30 November 2021>

One can only imagine the difficulty of journeying with a newborn baby during the months of arduous travel.[2]

The same day the Mississippi Company left Monroe County, the group of Saints that fled Nauvoo, Illinois, under the direction of Brigham Young were bogged down in Iowa with continuous rain. Brigham Young rode out to examine the road west and returned to declare the road was not fit for travel. Men were then engaged to make the trail passable."[3] Two days after the Mississippi Company began their trek west, the ship *Brooklyn* rounded the southern tip of South America. Mercifully, this passage was uneventful, with children playing on the deck of the ship. After traveling up the coast of Chile, their supply of water became green and filled with algae. The passengers had been at sea for nearly three months and desperately desired to stand on land again.[4]

The Trek Begins

Absalom Porter Dowdle described how the Mississippi Saints began their trek west. Concerning the beginning of their journey, he wrote,

> Time went one [*sic,*] and we were on our way, but we did not know where we were going, only to meet the train from Missouri. We traveled all day, and at night, we camped. We had to hunt a trail all the way. We never saw a house on the way, but we had an old Indian with us for a guide, and he knew the country very well. We had to guard our mules and watch for Indians. It was hard, and as for me, I had

---

2. Mormon Pioneer Overland Travel, "Mississippi Company," https://history.churchof jesuschrist.org/overlandtravel/companies/392/mississippi-company, <accessed 30 November 2021>

3. Historical Department journal history of the church, 1830-2008; 1840-1849; 1846 January-July, Church History Library, https://catalog.churchofjesuschrist.org/assets/ dd163195-554a-403e-bc9f-7299b106c7d2/0/163, <accessed 8 December 2021>

4. Richard O. Cowen and William E. Homer, *California Saints: A 150 Year Legacy in the Golden State*, BYU Religious Studies Center, https://rsc.byu.edu/book/california-saints, <accessed 17 December 2021> unpaginated

never driven two spans of mules in my life, and Sarah had never ridden in a covered wagon in her life.[5]

Their destination was unknown. Their only directive was to meet other Saints near Grand Island on the vast plains of what is now Nebraska.[6] Armed with faith in God, they moved out from their homes with the hope of meeting another group of Saints traveling west. Because they were planning to return in the fall, John Brown's team of six traveled with one wagon. Brown's description regarding the beginning of the journey only states the group crossed the Mississippi River at Iron Banks and then traveled through the state of Missouri to Independence.[7] In what appears to be a description of the river ferry crossing at Iron Banks, Absalom wrote the following:

They had built a big thing like a boat to take us across the river. It would hold two or three wagons at a time. The river was about two miles across. That wasn't so bad, and I was happy to be on our way, but we did not know where we were going. I used to say just God knows, but what was the difference? There was no peace anywhere. We landed on the other side with our old faithful guide, and he was acquainted with all the country. Four days on the way it started to rain and thunder and lightning until we had to stop for two days.[8]

Iron Banks was located on the eastern side of the Mississippi River in southwestern Kentucky, near present-day Columbus, Kentucky. After crossing the river at Iron Banks, the team of travelers reached what is now the state of Missouri.

---

5. Absalom Porter Dowdle, 1819-1897. Absalom P. Dowdle autobiography, https://cat alog.churchofjesuschrist.org/assets/4bd7e829-80dd-4098-b5d9-d2443e7b4cdb/0/0, 38-39 <accessed: November 27, 2021>
6. Richard E. Bennett, *We'll Find a Place: The Mormon Exodus 1846-1848,* (Salt Lake City, Utah, Deseret Book, 1997) image 158 of 1475, online Book available through Deseret Bookshelf, https://read.deseretbook.com/login?next=%2F, <accessed 6 July 2024>
7. John Zimmerman Brown, Autobiography of Pioneer John Brown, 1820-1896, (Stevens & Wallis, Inc. Salt Lake City, Utah 1941) 66
8. Absalom P. Dowdle autobiography, 41-42

Iron Banks, Kentucky

The crossing at Iron Banks was a crucial point for those needing to traverse the Mississippi. Having a bridge spanning the mighty river was only a dream in the 1840s. Whether taking product east from the Missouri side of the river or leaving to settle somewhere in the West, Iron Banks offered a needed location to negotiate the treacherous river. Several years before the Mississippi Saints arrived at Iron Banks, Native Americans who had been forcibly removed from their ancestral homes crossed the Mississippi at Iron Banks. Andrew Jackson ignored a Supreme Court ruling in favor of the Cherokee tribe, who had battled for three years to remain on their own land, with the declaration, "That's John Marshall's decision; now let's see him enforce it." A detachment of approximately 1,200 Cherokee left Fort Payne in northeastern Alabama on 1 October 1838, bound for the new Indian Territory in what is now Oklahoma. They traveled on what is now known as the Benge Route, which took them to the Iron Banks crossing in western Kentucky. Evidence indicates that their crossing took place at the same location as the Mississippi Company.[9] Concerning the existence of an actual ferry at Iron Banks in the 1840s, John Kelly Ross, a local historian from Columbus, Kentucky, wrote:

> The ferry at Iron Banks, i.e., Columbus, was operating at least as early as 1829. The June 25, 1869, "The Charleston Courier" of Charleston, MO, ran this ad, "FERRY NOTICE / The Steam Ferryboat, YOUNG EAGLE, makes regular trips from Columbus, Kentucky, to the Missouri shore.... This ferry has been established about forty years and is the natural crossing point for travelers and movers going to and coming from the West." The City of Columbus, founded in 1821,

---

9. "The Exodus of the Cherokee to the West," Kentucky Great River Road, https://kygrro.org/jupiter/history/trail-of-tears/, <accessed 8 December 2021>

owned the ferry franchise and every few years would put it up at auction for lease to the highest bidder.[10]

After crossing the river at Iron Banks, the small group landed in the southeastern portion of what is now Missouri. Their next stop—Independence, Missouri—where members of the church were forcibly removed in the winter of 1838 to 1839. After traveling in a north-westerly direction, the company arrived at Independence on 26 May 1846, following a journey of 640 miles.[11]

ADDITIONAL TRAVELERS

Independence in 1846 was the westernmost settlement in the United States. Trappers, Mexican traders, Indians, and enthusiastic pioneers found this entrance to the frontier exhilarating. Following their arrival at Independence, John Brown's team gained friends and family from Perry County, Illinois. **Robert Crow (1794-1876)**, his wife **Elizabeth Brown (1795-1870)**, and their nine children ages eight to twenty-six then joined the Mississippi Company. Elizabeth was a cousin of John Brown, the key figure in organizing this pioneer group. They were together as a family on the edge of the frontier. Another family that joined the Mississippi Saints at Independence was **George Washington Threlkel (1820-1900)** and his wife **Matilda Jane Crow (1824-1906)**. Matilda was the daughter of Robert Crow. Tragedy struck the Threlkel family shortly after arriving in the Salt Lake Valley in 1847. Their three-year-old son Milton drowned in City Creek 11 August 1847, thus becoming the first death of the arriving Saints. Concerning the anguish experienced by the mother, Howard Egan wrote, "The grief of both of the parents was great, but that of the agonized mother baffles all description. She laughed, wept, walked to and fro, alternately, refusing all attempts at consolation from her

---

10. John Kelly Ross, local historian in Columbus, Kentucky, direct communication with Mr. Ross. Information in possession of Erick Wadsworth.
11. Autobiography of Pioneer John Brown, 1820-1896, 66

friends, being, apparently unable to become resigned to her domestic melancholy bereavement."[12] Incredibly, just four days following the death of her son, a daughter, Harriet Ann Threlkel, was born.[13] **William Kartchner (1820-1892)** and his wife **(Margaret Jane Casteel (1825-1881)** also met John Brown and company in Independence. **James Albert Chesney (1824-1869)**, who was born at Cooper County, Missouri, also joined the pioneer company at Independence.[14] [15] This intrepid team of emigrants from various parts of the South, Missouri, and Illinois was now ready to begin their trek west on the Oregon Trail.

John Brown describes the hysteria that existed during this time concerning members of The Church of Jesus Christ of Latter-day Saints from those outside of the church. He wrote:

> There was great excitement here. Rumor said Ex-Governor Boggs had started to California and the Mormons had intercepted him on the way and killed and robbed several companies, etc. They tried to persuade us not to go on the plains on account of these Mormons, but we told them that we were not afraid.[16]

Brown also noted that while at Independence, there were now twenty-five wagons. William Crosby was selected as captain of the wagon train, with Robert Crow and John D. Holladay as counselors for the company.

---

12. Howard Egan, *Pioneering the West, 1846 to 1878: Major Howard Egan's diary*, (Richmond, Utah: Howard Egan Estate, 1917) 120-121 https://archive.org/details/pioneer ingwest1800began/page/120/mode/2up, <accessed 15 December 2021>

13. Harriett Ann Threlkel, "Family Search," Church of Jesus Christ of Latter-day Saints," https://www.familysearch.org/tree/person/details/KL87-ZD6, <accessed 15 December 2021>

14. James Albert Chesney, "Family Search," <K2WC-PY4> Church of Jesus Christ of Latter-day Saints," https://www.familysearch.org/tree/find/name?self=James%20al bert%20%7CChesney%7C0%7C0&gender=male&birth=%7C1824-1824%7C0%7C0& death=%7C1869-1869%7C0%7C0, <accessed 16 December 2021>

15. Margaret Jane Casteel, *Family Search*, <KWJ6-WGG>, https://www.familysearch. org/tree/person/details/KWJ6-WGG, <accessed 3 June 2024>

16. Autobiography of Pioneer John Brown, 1820-1896, 66-67

Mississippi Saints Traveled the Oregon Trail

The most important element for a successful trip on the trail was the type of wagon, and the animals used to roll the wagon west. The composition of the wagon train itself was important, but frequently, wagon trains were split up on the trail due to disagreements among the emigrants. Oxen accounted for about 60 percent of the livestock used, while horses and mules made up the other 40 percent. Oxen were slower than both mules and horses, but Indians had no use for that animal and would rarely steal them. Oxen could also forage on the available grasses on the trail. Typically, four oxen were needed to pull the lumbering wagons. The oxen could also pull plows and perform other labor after arriving at the emigrant's new home. The pioneer wagons could haul a load between 1,600 and 2,500 pounds, and the box was generally two feet high and eleven feet long. Using the best material, such as oak, hickory, or other hardwoods, produced a wagon that could last through the long journey west. The canvas covering was often bent at a height of five feet above the wagon bed and was usually double-covered with a rain-proof canvas. Wagon tongues, axles, and spokes often wore out on the trail, so spare parts were typically carried under the wagon bed. Water barrels, grease buckets, whips, goads, and 100 feet of heavy rope completed the needed running gear. The heaviest and most important feature for the pioneers was their food supply. One early guidebook recommended 200 pounds of flour, 150 pounds of bacon, ten pounds of coffee, twenty pounds of sugar, and ten pounds of salt.[17] This is not an appealing diet, but met the basic needs.

Travelers faced many stream crossings and a lack of trees for firewood. Trail expert Merrill Mattes noted that often stream crossings needed to have their steep banks "cut down with spades." Furthermore, he wrote, "Wagons were frequently lowered and hoisted

---

17. Merrill J. Mattes, *The Great Platte River Road: The Covered Wagon Mainline Via Fort Kearny to Fort Laramie,* (Lincoln: University of Nebraska Press, 1969), 37 - 40

with ropes and chains, and double-teaming—all stout shoulders to the wheel—often a necessity." This thoroughfare, unlike our current superhighways, was constantly twisting around the prairie contours in search of higher ground or a smoother route.[18] One important stopping place just over the Missouri border in Kansas was named Alcove Springs, "which typically took pioneers about two weeks to reach." Often, trekkers stopped there to rest. The Donner party of 1846 stopped at the springs, where, sadly, one of their group, Sarah Keyes, died.[19] After several weeks on the trail, emigrants reached Nebraska. After experiencing mud, dust, thunderstorms, daily diarrhea, homesickness, mosquitoes, breakdowns, accidents, and Indian attacks, the emigrants had become trail-hardened.[20]

A definitive departure date for the Mississippi Saints, who did not arrive at Independence until Tuesday, 26 May 1846, and undoubtedly needed to update their supplies for the trip west, is not provided. However, they arrived "among the buffalo" on 25 June 1846.[21] Evidence indicates that the buffalo roamed areas near the Platte River valley during the mid-1840s. Estimating 320 miles from Independence to the current site of Fort Kearny State Park and assuming a travel distance of fifteen miles per day, the Mississippi Company possibly departed from Independence during the second week of June 1846. When the wagon train, now led by Captain William Crosby, left for the West, Brown noted they began with twenty-five wagons. An additional group that was traveling to Oregon joined the Southern company during the first part of the journey. The following account by John Brown details an interesting experience they had after traveling for a few days:

When we got out into the Indian Country, our Oregon friends found out that they were in company with a lot of Mormons. They were a

---

18. Ibid, 142-143

19. Paul and Hellen Henderson, *Maps of Manifest Destiny*, (Gering, Nebraska, Legacy of the Plains Museum, 2004),4

20. Ibid, 8

21. Autobiography of Pioneer John Brown, 1820-1896, 67

little uneasy and somewhat frightened and began to think that we did not travel fast enough for them. They left us and the next day we passed them and left them in the rear. They were a little afraid to go on not being strong enough. This repeated again. At length, they traveled with us til [sic] we got to the Platte River where we met a company of six men from Oregon, and when they saw six men who had traveled the road alone, they took courage, having 13 or 14 men in company. So, they left us again and we rested a day for repairs, so we saw them no more.[22]

Following this incident, the company was now down to fifteen wagons and twenty-four men. In addition, members of the Fox Tribe took one yoke of oxen belonging to George Threlkel. Brown described a time when, on 27 June, "a buffalo calf came running into the train of wagons. The dogs, teamsters, and everyone else took after it, running through the train several times, and it finally got into the loose herd, and the dogs driven out, it became contented."[23]

Shortly after arriving in buffalo country, the company met a man who had tried to float the Platte River with trappers. The gentleman's name was Hosea, and rather than trying to continue down the Platte River, he remained with the Mississippi Saints for several days before heading back to the mountains.[24] The Platte River was exceedingly difficult to float because of the shallowness of the river, numerous sandbars, and the absence of a main river channel. Francis Parkman, who departed Independence in the spring of 1846 (just before the Mississippi group), met a fleet of eleven boats stocked with buffalo robes and beaver pelts roughly 300 miles below Fort Laramie. Because of the shallowness of the river, the journey from Fort Laramie took a full month to complete. According to the record, "Fifty times a day the boats had been aground: indeed, those who navigate the Platte invariably spend half their time upon sand-bars."[25]

---

22. Ibid.
23. Ibid.
24. Ibid.
25. Ottis B. Sperlin, Ph,M. editor, *Francis Parkman's The Oregon Trail*, (New York: Long-

Hosea taught the group about proper camp life and the intricacies of approaching buffalo.

CROSSING THE PLATTE RIVER AND ARRIVING AT ASH HOLLOW

The exact location where the Mississippi pioneers crossed the Platte River is unknown. However, the date of the crossing was 30 June, and they arrived at a location called Ash Hollow 1 July.[26] Once pioneers passed the convergence of the North and South Platte rivers, they needed to find a place to ford the South Platte. Several crossings were available, but most emigrants chose a location called the California Crossing. Francis Parkman crossed the Platte (likely at the same crossing) about three weeks before William Crosby's company. He described the crossing in impressive detail:

> First, the heavy ox-wagons plunged down the bank and dragged slowly over the sand-beds; sometimes the hoofs of the oxen were scarcely wetted by the thin sheet of water, and the next moment, the river would be boiling against their sides and eddying fiercely around the wheels. Inch by inch, they receded from the shore, dwindling every moment until at length, they seemed to be floating far out in the very middle of the river. A more critical experiment awaited us; for our little mule-cart was but ill-fitted for the passage of so swift a stream.[27]

Parkman watched their mule-cart become a "motionless white spec" in the middle of the river. The mules began losing their footing, the wheels on the mule-cart began sinking into the river, and their supplies were drenched by the river water that rose over the sides of the cart. Parkman and his fellow travelers jumped into the water and

---

mans, Green, and Co., 1910) 68-69 https://archive.org/details/francisparkmanso01park/page/n5/mode/2up?ref=ol&view=theater, <accessed 24 December 2021>

26. Autobiography of Pioneer John Brown, 1820-1896, 67

27. *Francis Parkman's The Oregon Trail*, 79

pushed the mules to the other bank. Finally, the exhausted group of men and animals reached the other side of the Platte.[28] Perhaps the Mississippi group faced similar challenges during their crossing.

Following their crossing of the Platte River, the Mississippi Company continued moving west. Brown shared how challenging it was to travel on the Oregon Trail without knowing where they were to meet other "Saints en route from Nauvoo." His haunting words portray the silence and loneliness associated with traveling the vast stretches of open territory.

> Nothing to be seen or heard but the movements and noise of vast herds of wild animals on the naked plains, buffaloes, antelope, wolves, prairie dogs, and rattlesnakes, not even a tree or bush on part of [the] route to vary the monotony. As far as man was concerned, all was dismal and silent as the grave... a spirit of uneasiness began to manifest itself on the company. It was quite evident that the little party was alone in the wild waste. We were now a long way beyond the point where we were to meet our brethren, after we passed that point, we were virtually out at sea without chart or compass. No instructions as to where we should land.[29]

These Southern Saints, who were by now feeling the disappointment of not meeting any who had fled Nauvoo, began to realize the seriousness of their situation. They were now hundreds of miles from civilization, encircled by wild animals, and surrounded by those whose land they were trespassing on. They began to lose any hope of connecting with others of their faith on the lonely trail west. Their next stop of any consequence was Ash Hollow.

------

28. Ibid, 79-80

29. Brown, John, 1820-1896. Autobiographical sketch, undated., 26-27 https://catalog.churchofjesuschrist.org/assets/6c67a206-04f7-410a-be89-1396dc4a3c26/0/26, <accessed 30 December 2021>

ASH HOLLOW

One of the more well-known stopping points along the Oregon Trail was Ash Hollow. Emigrants who rested there discovered fresh water, grass, firewood, and welcome shade. This hollow gained its name from the numerous ash trees that grow in the area. To enter Ash Hollow, many traveled down the steep slope of Windlass Hill, which lies to the south. Due to the extreme incline, wagons were assisted down the hill using ropes. An abandoned cabin operated as a temporary post office for those traveling west.[30] The size of Ash Hollow is underwhelming. The length is about four miles and runs about 2,000 feet wide, rim to rim. The depth of the landmark stands at roughly 250 feet.[31] The Mississippi group entered Ash Hollow on 1 July 1846, one day after the river crossing. On 29 June 1846, just before crossing the south fork of the Platte River, the company encountered a violent storm during the night that caused tents to collapse and forced many to sleep inside wagons. Once morning came, the troupe found themselves "almost frozen."[32] During their stay at the hollow, Brown and a companion crossed the North Platte River in search of the "trail of the emigrating Saints." Brown was hopeful that perhaps other companies of those heading west had used the north side of the Platte River in their journey. They discovered no evidence of anyone traveling on the opposite side of the North Platte River, so he and his companion returned to camp to report their findings. After hearing the pair's report, the apprehension of those in the company increased dramatically, and several in the company desperately wanted to turn back.[33] However, they had traveled too far to stop now.

---

30. "Ash Hollow." *Explore Nebraska History,* https://mynehistory.com/items/show/232, <accessed 31 December 2021>
31. Mattes, *The Great Platte River Road,* 281
32. Autobiography of Pioneer John Brown, 1820-1896, 67
33. Brown, John, 1820-1896. Autobiographical sketch, undated., 28

FORT LARAMIE

One can only wonder what went through the minds of these secluded pioneers isolated on the plains of Nebraska. After traveling for almost three months on their trek west, the anticipation of linking with other members of the church now faded away like morning dew under a hot sun. Nevertheless, the company moved forward toward its still-unknown destination. Fortunately, Fort Laramie, Wyoming, stood about 120 miles northwest of Ash Hollow, where these devoted emigrants would find new hope and a place to stay during the upcoming winter. The group moved west from Ash Hollow, passing Chimney Rock on 6 July 1846. [34] They continued traveling west, arriving near Fort Laramie in early July.[35] In 1846, Fort Laramie was not a military base but was occupied by mostly French men who had married Sioux wives and felt safe from Indian interference.[36] Francis Parkman described the fort as follows:

> Fort Laramie is one of the posts established by the "American Fur Company," who well-nigh monopolize[d] the Indian trade in this whole region.… The little fort is built of bricks dried in the sun, and externally is of an oblong form, with bastions of clay, in the form of ordinary blockhouses, at two of the corners. The walls are about fifteen feet high and surrounded by a slender palisade… the main entrance has two gates, with an arched passage intervening. A little square window, quite high above the ground, opens laterally from an adjoining chamber into this passage; so that when the inner gate is closed and barred, a person without may still have communication with those within, through this narrow aperture.[37]

Unfortunately, any hope of meeting another group of Saints trav-

---

34. Ibid, 68

35. Ibid, this estimate is based on the company traveling 15 - 20 miles per day from the day they passed Chimney Rock.

36. Mattes, *The Great Platte River Road*, 484

37. Ottis B. Sperlin, Ph, M. editor, *Francis Parkman's The Oregon Trail*, 94

eling west was crushed completely when they met a returning group of California travelers who told them no members of their church were on the trail ahead of them.

Now, the need to find a suitable place for winter was crucial. This small company of pioneers desperately needed assistance, or their dream of settling in the valleys on the western side of the Rockies with other Saints was doomed. A remarkable occurrence took place upon the arrival of the Mississippi Saints at Fort Laramie. Near the fort, the travelers met a French trapper named John Richard (anglicized version pronounced Reshaw).[38] Richard was camped near the fort at a place called Goshen Hole, where he traded robes with the Mississippi Company. He then invited them to winter in Pueblo with him, even volunteering to lead them there. Pueblo was 250 miles south, supplies could be readily acquired there, and the small village was positioned on the headwaters of the Arkansas River. A council meeting was held, and after much discussion, the unanimous conclusion was to travel south to Pueblo. John Richard gathered his two wagons loaded with furs and began the journey south with the beleaguered Mississippi Company on 10 July 1846. Richard knew the route to Pueblo and understood where camping places existed. Perhaps his most important asset was that he understood the Native American culture and could speak their language. The need for Richard's expertise quickly became evident. After traveling south for several days, the company came close to the South Platte River in present-day Colorado. Concerning the incident, John Brown wrote:

Before reaching the South Platte, the Cheyanne Indians came upon us. There appeared to be thousands of them, men, women, and children.

---

38. Leonard J. Arrington, "Mississippi Mormons," *Ensign,* The Church of Jesus Christ of Latter-day Saints, https://abn.churchofjesuschrist.org/study/ensign/1977/06/missis sippi-mormons?lang=eng&adobe_mc_ref=https%3A%2F%2Fwww.churchofjesuschrist. org%2Fstudy%2Fensign%2F1977%2F06%2Fmississippi-mormons%3Flang%3Deng& adobe_mc_sdid=SDID%3D299785A6F971257F-005EC177F1DFE1EC%7CM CORGID%3D66C5485451E56AAE0A490D45%2540AdobeOrg%7CTS% 3D1641071928, <accessed 1 January 2022>

They demanded tribute for passing through their country. They wanted us to make them a feast. What to do, we did not know, all the provisions we had would not make them one square meal. Mr. Reshaw [Richard] told us to make some mush and bake some bread and go through the performance of a feast and ask them to excuse the scanty meal, as there was so few of us, and this was the best we could do.[39]

During this encounter, a young member of the Cheyanne Tribe wanted to buy the wife of a Mississippi Company member. The young brave was smitten by the woman's long black hair. So, he went to John Richard, along with the woman's husband, and told him he wanted the man's wife. The husband responded that this lady was the only wife he had, and he "did not want to sell her." The young Cheyanne insisted on a trade and offered five horses for the exchange. The husband's reply was still no. The answer insulted the young brave. The suitor said he was wealthy and would treat the man's wife well. The situation quickly deteriorated, so Richard took matters into his own hands. He knew the Cheyanne's culture and customs, so he began talking with them directly. He explained that the Americans differed from the Cheyanne because they did not like selling their wives to strangers. Richard explained that he had lived among the Native Americans for five years before they would sell him a wife. Fortunately, after passing a few gifts among the group, the problem was resolved, and the company was permitted to pass on. The Cheyanne were not seen again for the rest of the journey to Pueblo. After crossing the south fork of the Platte River, the troupe traveled upriver to the current location of Denver.[40] The company continued traveling south until it reached the village of Pueblo on 7 August 1846. Their journey from Monroe County, Mississippi, to Pueblo,

---

39. John Brown, 1820-1896. Autobiographical sketch, undated, 30
40. Ibid, 31-32

Colorado, covered over 1,400 miles and took four months to complete.[41]

---

41. Autobiography of Pioneer John Brown, 1820-1896, 69-79

6

WINTER IN PUEBLO

The current town of Pueblo, Colorado, is situated on the Arkansas River, 112 miles south of Denver. Precipitation amounts to roughly twelve inches annually. Pueblo sits in what is called the "banana belt" and receives less snow than other major cities in the state. The population in Pueblo stood at 106,595 in the 2010 Federal census.[1] By the 2020 census, the town reached a population of 111,876 residents.[2] In the early 1840s, Pueblo offered an excellent location for frontiersmen and trappers. Bent's Fort was nearby, the Arkansas River provided needed water, trees were available, and the climate was conducive for growing food. Wild game provided the necessary meat and skins for hides. In addition, direct routes to eastern markets supplied an opportunity to turn furs into cash. Longtime Pueblo resident Mary M. Lindenmuth wrote that over the years, Pueblo was known by various labels. Fort Pueblo, Hardscrabble, Upper Pueblo, Greenhorn, and Fort El Pueblo were a

---

1. Familypedia, "Pueblo, Colorado," https://familypedia.fandom.com/wiki/Pueblo,_Colorado#Fort_Pueblo, <accessed 26 January 2022>
2. United States Census Bureau, https://www.census.gov/quickfacts/pueblocitycolorado, <accessed 19 April 2022>

few of the names used by those who gave accounts of the area.[3] A fort, or trading post, was built in 1842 by several traders living in the area. Names associated with the founding of Fort Pueblo are George Simpson, J. B. Doyle, and Alexander Barclay. Barclay had worked at Bent's Fort during the previous four years.[4] The post stood on the Cherokee Trail and Trappers Trail, and it was near the Santa Fe Trail, which seemed a perfect location. Evidence indicates the trading post was enclosed with rooms arranged in a square facing a center courtyard. The structure was large enough to hold as many as 100 people.[5]

DIFFERENT VIEWS OF FORT PUEBLO FROM THE PAST

Kit Carson, Richens Lacy Woolton, and James Beckwourth were a few of the more noteworthy mountain men to spend time at Fort Pueblo. Interestingly, in June 1844, John C. Freemont traveled by the post and wrote the settlement "appeared in a thriving condition."[6] Others held different opinions about Pueblo. In 1845, a gentleman named Andrew Drips, an Indian agent familiar with Pueblo, wrote a scathing letter to the Superintendent of Indian Affairs in St. Louis, Missouri. In part, his letter read:

> I would particularly call the attention of the department to a description of traders who reside in the vicinity of the Mexican country on the waters of the Arkansas. They cultivate corn, etc., which they trade to the Indians for robes and skins, with which they proceed to Santa Fe and Taos to barter for whiskey, flour, etc. They defy a United States agent, and want of a proper force at the latter's command permits them to act with impunity. They reside in two villages, one on the

---

3. Mary Lindenmuth Scarcello, *Mormon Pioneers in Pueblo, Colorado 1846-1900,* (Mary Lindenmuth Scarcello, 1993), 32-33. Copy of the book in possession of the author.
4. David Lavender, *Bent's Fort,* (Garden City, NY, Doubleday & Company, 1954) 212
5. Legends of America, "Fort Pueblo, Colorado," https://www.legendsofamerica.com/fort-pueblo/, <accessed 2 February 2022>
6. Legends of America, "Fort Pueblo, Colorado,"

American side and the other within the Mexican line. They are a mongrel crew of Americans, French, Mexicans, and half-breeds and, generally speaking, are unable to procure employment on account of past misconduct. In fact, they are no better than outlaws.[7]

Steven Watts Kearny realized the smuggling of liquor created problems in and around Fort Pueblo and recommended the stationing of a sub-agent at nearby Bent's Fort, which lay about seventy miles southwest. The Mexican American War and Kearny's involvement in that conflict blocked any effort to stop the unlawful trade of alcohol, and no sub-agent was stationed at Bent's Fort.[8]

The Mississippi Company entered this world of contraband runners, trappers, and fur traders and called the area home from early August 1846 until the spring of 1847. Although minuscule when compared to Winter Quarters, on the western banks of the Missouri River, Pueblo became the Winter Quarters for the Mississippi Company and the three detachments of the Mormon Battalion that wintered there. Similarities are worth noting. First, both locations were meant to be transitory resting spots. Second, both sites were outside the United States. Third, both were organized on land occupied by others. Native Americans called the area around Winter Quarters home, while Mexico claimed the land around Pueblo. Fourth, births, marriages, and deaths occurred at both settlements. Last, both settlements were occupied predominantly by members of The Church of Jesus Christ of Latter-day Saints as they sought a place to live in peace. After years of forced removal from one location to another, the desire to live in a setting free from outside harassment was of utmost importance.

---

7. Ibid.
8. Ibid.

JOHN BAPTISTE RICHARD: PILOT OF THE MISSISSIPPI COMPANY

John Baptiste Richard (Reshaw) met the bone-weary pioneers while he was at Goshen Hole (near Fort Laramie) and guided them to Pueblo. Did this unscheduled meeting on the high plains of what is now Wyoming happen accidentally, or was the encounter a divinely-directed rescue for the Mississippi Company, who wandered for months in the harsh environment known as the Oregon Trail? Whether meeting Richard near Fort Laramie was accidental or divinely orchestrated, Mr. Richard's role in piloting the Mississippi Company to Pueblo likely saved their lives. John Baptiste Richard became famous for his entrepreneurial abilities, fur trading, and as a notorious whiskey smuggler. He could barely read or write, but he possessed an uncanny intellect that more than made up for his lack of formal education. One noted author wrote that Richard "is reputed to have been the first trader to smuggle in contraband whiskey and trade it to the Indians of the northern plains."[9]

> His dress was rather singular; his black curling hair was parted in the middle of his head and fell below his shoulders; he wore a tight frock of smoked deerskin, very gayly [sic] ornamented with figures worked in with dyed porcupine quills. His moccasins and leggings were also gaudily adorned in the same manner, and the latter had, in addition, a line of long fringes reaching down the seams.[10]

John Richard dressed like a mountain man and lived a mountain man's life, and he seemed to relish his lifestyle.

Mr. Richard was born on 14 December 1810 in St. Charles, Missouri. John's father worked in the mountains of the West with

---

9. Jefferson Glass, *Reshaw: The Life and Times of John Baptiste Richard*, (High Plains Press, Glendo, Wyoming, 2014) xi

10. Leroy R. Hafen and Frank M. Young, "The Mormon Settlement in Pueblo, Colorado, During the Mexican War," (The Colorado Magazine, Vol. IX, No. 4, July 1932), 124 fn5

such trappers as William Sublette and William Ashley. John Richard formed many partnerships with other mountain men, but he also worked closely in business with his siblings. One brother, Joseph Richard, lived at Fort Pueblo at the time John piloted the Mississippi Company there. One reason Richard likely headed to Fort Pueblo centered on the fact that Taos, now in the state of New Mexico, was an important location to pick up whiskey and other contraband. Taos was well known for distilling alcohol as early as 1825, and John used their services for his illicit whiskey runs. Unfortunately, when John reached Fort Pueblo, he learned that proceeding to Taos was impossible due to the Mexican American War. He reluctantly stayed in Pueblo until 6 November 1846, which hurt John financially. After arriving in Pueblo, the Mississippi Company received definitive news concerning Brigham Young and the Saints from Nauvoo.[11] In the spring of 1846, the main body of church members expelled from Nauvoo traveled no further west than the western bank of the Missouri River in Nebraska Territory.

Evidence indicates that ten years after guiding the Mississippi group to Pueblo, Richard assisted members of a rescue team of the Martin and Willie handcart companies. As news reached Brigham Young about handcart travelers snowed in between John Richard's bridge, near present-day Casper, Wyoming, and South Pass, he immediately organized rescue parties. Dan Webster Jones assisted in the deliverance of the stranded pioneers. Following the rescue, Jones and a few helpers remained at Devil's Gate Fort for several grueling winter months to protect the possessions of the beleaguered handcart company. Daniel Jones described their near-starvation situation:

Things looked dark, for nothing remained but the poor raw hides taken from starved cattle. We asked the Lord to direct us what to do. The brethren did not murmur but felt to trust God. We had cooked

---

11. Ibid, 18, 63-67

the hide after soaking and scraping the hair off until it was soft and then ate it, glue and all.[12]

Men became sick just thinking about eating something so disgusting. By mid-February, the men subsisted on cattle hides, wrappings from the wagon tongues, old moccasin soles, and "a piece of buffalo hide that had been used for a foot mat for two months."[13] On the brink of starvation, Jones described meeting a group of men from the Platte River Bridge.[14] This party brought several butchered cattle from John Richard's own stock.[15] In the span of ten years, John Baptiste Richard (Reshaw) saved two distinct pioneer groups of The Church of Jesus Christ of Latter-day Saints.

EXPERIENCES IN PUEBLO

John Brown noted that when the Mississippi group arrived in Pueblo, six to eight mountaineers were living in the vicinity with their families. Their wives were Native American and Spanish. The residents of Pueblo "received us very kindly, and they seemed pleased to see us."[16] Tragically, one day before arriving at Fort Pueblo, George Therlkill, a son-in-law of Robert Crow, encountered a grizzly bear while he and William Lay pursued a wounded deer. After startling the grizzly, the bear battered both men to the ground and mauled George Therlkill's head. Fortunately, other members of the Mississippi Company came to the rescue of Therlkill and Lay and destroyed the bear. Francis Parkman described George Therlkill as "a tall, shambling fellow, who... wore brown homespun trousers, much too short for his legs, and a pistol and bowie knife stuck in his belt. His head and one eye

---

12. Daniel Webster Jones, *Forty Years Among the Indians*, (Juvenile Instructor Office, Salt Lake City, Utah, 1890) 81
13. Ibid, 82
14. Ibid.
15. *The Life and Times of John Baptiste Richard*, 111
16. John Zimmerman Brown, Autobiography of Pioneer John Brown, 1820-1896, (Stevens & Wallis, Inc. Salt Lake City, Utah 1941) 70

were enveloped in a huge bandage of linen."[17] After arriving at Fort Pueblo, the Mississippi group traveled downriver from the fort to create their new Winter Quarters. This offered privacy and created a short distance from their neighbors living at the fort.[18]

After receiving commitments from the mountaineers to provide them with supplies and corn in exchange for labor, the Southern trekkers harvested cottonwood trees and tirelessly began erecting cabins. Janet Lecompte described the results of their efforts: "Their town was in a broad and well-timbered bottom of the Arkansas [River]. A single long street was lined with houses, each about fourteen feet square, built of cottonwood logs laid horizontally and chinked with mud."[19] In addition, a small building was erected to serve as a church, schoolhouse, and social hall.[20] John Brown, the organizer of the Mississippi travelers, departed Pueblo to walk back to his home in the South. He organized a small church group before leaving and instructed the group to remain in Pueblo until word came from the main body of the church about future travels. John Brown left the village of Pueblo on 1 September 1846. Accompanying Brown on the journey home were William Crosby, D. M. Thomas, John Holladay, William Lay, James Smithson, and George W. Bankhead. These men left families behind in Alabama and Mississippi. Also traveling with this group was a man by the name of Wales Bonny, who stayed with Brown's group until Independence, Missouri.[21] After a three-day march, the travelers reached Bent's Fort, where they learned about a group of forty-five men working as teamsters for the

---

17. William E. Parrish, "The Mississippi Saints," The *Historian* 50, no.4 (August 1988): 496

18. The Mississippi Saints: A Unique Odyssey of Southern Pioneers, "The Mississippi Saints: A Unique Odyssey of Southern Pioneers," in *Far Away in the West: Reflections on the Mormon Pioneer Trail,* edited by Scott C. Esplin, Richard E. Bennett, Susan Eason Black, and Craig K. Manscill (Provo, UT: Religious Studies Center; Salt Lake City: Deseret Book, 2015), 161-86

19. Janet Lecompte, *Pueblo, Hardscrabble, Greenhorn: Society on the High Plains, 1832-1856,* (Norman: University of Oklahoma Press, 1990), 180

20. The Mississippi Saints: A Unique Odyssey of Southern Pioneers, 172

21. Ibid, fn29, 182

United States government who had left the fort two days earlier, bound for the east. Four days later, Brown and company caught up with the teamsters and traveled with them for protection. John Brown and his associates met the Mormon Battalion on the Santa Fe Trail on 12 September 1846.[22] The story of this unexpected meeting and the remarkable results for both the emigrants in Pueblo and members of the Mormon Battalion is an important facet of this book.

BIRTH OF THE FIRST BABY

William Decatur Kartchner described his first few days in Pueblo, in which a disagreement between Kartchner and Robert Crow resulted in hard feelings. William Kartchner felt Crow broke an obligation to provide provisions for him and his family, causing the Kartchner family to make camp under a cottonwood tree. Fortunately, John Brown contributed flour and bacon to the Kartchner family with a promise of future security. William wrote about the birth of his baby:

> When we arrived at the Pueblo on [the] Arkansas River, we found farms of corn cultivated by Indians mostly and traders who had Indian squaws for [the] wife of whom we bought corn and prepared for Winter Quarters, building a row of log houses on the opposite bank of the river from Fort Pueblo. **On the 17ᵗʰ of August 1846, our first little angel daughter was born,** [bold font added], under the tree under these destitute circumstances. Not knowing where succor was to come from to make Bro. Brown's promises [were] fulfilled, but when our baby was a week old, a messenger was sent from Bents Fort eighty miles below for a blacksmith, and the man bought a horse for me to ride, and I recommended James Harmon as gunsmith who accompanied us.[23]

---

22. John Zimmerman Brown, Autobiography of Pioneer John Brown, 70
23. Connie Mikesell Hale, 1946 –. William D. Kartchner memoirs, undated, 13 https:// catalog.churchofjesuschrist.org/assets/3d2b6c1f-2a28-42c3-a9a8-93c04ba38108/0/13, <accessed 16 February 2022>

William and James Harmen, who was also a blacksmith, left the next day for Bent's Fort. Kartchner left his wife and newborn baby "to the kindness of Catherine Holladay." Following two days of hard riding, the pair arrived at the fort. Fortunately, both Kartchner and Harmon found work. William worked as a blacksmith, welding and setting wagon tires, mostly for the US Army. He earned two dollars a day and stayed at the fort until late in the fall. During his time at the fort, he and his companion "lay hard and slept cold." This sleeping arrangement caused William to develop an attack of rheumatism, which caused him to return to Pueblo sick. Despite his ill health, Kartchner had earned enough money at Bent's Fort to purchase "corn and an old wagon."[24]

Kartchner noted, "During my absence, the part of the Mormon Battalion who was sick under [the] command of Capt. S. Brown and Higgins had come to our camp and built a row opposite our row of log cabins for Winter Quarters and place[d] over the doors signs for sport." William also wrote, "The soldiers annoyed Capt. Brown by writing and dropping near his quarters poetry, calling him the Old Linn Mall." One night during the winter, an alarm sounded concerning 500 Spaniards who were allegedly planning to attack the village. Drums called men into line to command them to fight the anticipated onslaught. The feared invasion turned out to be a band of elk, not the dreaded enemy. Still unable to walk, Kartchner relied on his wife to gather firewood, requiring her to walk "in snow knee deep many times to the grove 100 yards and carried a limb from the cottonwoods for fuel during my confinement with rheumatism." Shortly, word was received that the main body of church pioneers would leave Winter Quarters on the Missouri River to head west in the spring of 1847. This main group would meet a portion of the Mississippi Company at Fort Laramie. During his sickness, Kartchner worked to repair his wagon "sitting on the bed" while his wife and friends carried needed parts of the wagon to him. He also helped

------

24. Ibid.

other members of Pueblo repair their wagons for the anticipated spring departure.[25]

UNIQUE MEMBER OF THE FORT PUEBLO AREA

The people living in the Fort Pueblo area before the arrival of the Mississippi Company held their own set of mores and values. They lived hundreds of miles from civilization and developed their standards suitable to the harshness of their environment. As noted earlier, for the most part, the Southern Saints were welcomed to the locale. One individual in particular, Valentine J. "Rube" Herring, stands out among his peers for not only welcoming the newcomers to the area but declaring to all who would listen that he believed their religion was true. Rube was free-spirited, having been trapped with Nathaniel Wyeth in 1835 before becoming an independent trapper. He is described as eccentric, good-looking, sulky, unsmiling, and silent. He stood tall, with long arms and straight black hair that hung down to his shoulders. His clothing included buckskin breeches that shrunk up to his calves. Rube located a *Book of Mormon,* which he would read aloud in his booming voice day and night. Such a reading of the book brought much badgering from the other mountain men and their families. Undeterred by the taunting, he continued to assert his belief in the new religion and the *Book of Mormon.* One factor that might have created the bond between Rube and the Southern Saints was the belief that he would lead the group to their next destination. When Rube learned the company no longer needed his expertise to guide them, his conviction concerning the beliefs of his new friends from the South quickly changed. Tradition holds that without flinching, he grabbed his *Book of Mormon,* flung it into the Arkansas River, and then turned around and "spat out a quid of tobacco and his Mormonism altogether."[26]

----

25. Ibid.

26. Janet Lecompte, *Pueblo, Hardscrabble, Greenhorn:* The Upper Arkansas, 1832-1856, (Norman, University of Oklahoma Press, 1978), 183-184

Manomas Gibson Andrus's Recollections of Pueblo

George Washington Gibson and his family arrived at Pueblo with his wife, Mary Ann Sparks, and their nine children, ranging in age from two to twenty-three years old. One daughter, Manomas Lavinia Gibson Andrus, related a unique memory from her time in Pueblo during an interview in 1936. Although only five years of age during her winter in Pueblo, Manomas recounted an evening of revelry that turned deadly. She told the story in the following words:

> There were assembled at Pueblo along with the few Mormon pioneers, quite a number of traders and trappers who did a good bit of drinking and gambling. One night, some of these men were gambling in a building next to the cabin occupied by the Gibsons. An argument arose over the card game, and the Gibson children were terrified of the thought of what was going on so near them, as they could hear every word of the snarling, swearing men. Suddenly, there were shots. One man was killed.

The killer fled into the wilderness, hoping to evade capture. Next, Manomas related how gunfire boomed through the night while a group of men pursued the killer, eventually finding him. He was killed that night. The unofficial posse brought the man back to Pueblo for burial. Her father built a coffin from rough logs, and the man was buried.[27] No one else recorded this event taking place, so the account may be hyperbole.

In addition to the terrible evening when gunshots and mayhem ruled, Manomas Gibson also remembered the kindness of several of the people who lived in Pueblo. Her father fell ill on the journey west,

---

27. Utah Historic Records Survey, "Pioneer Personal History Interview with Manomas Lavinia Gibson Andrus, St. George, Utah," https://collections.lib.utah.edu/details?id= 700171, <accessed 5 April 2022>

and for a time, it was felt he might die. In her own words, Manomas depicted how some of the residents of Pueblo assisted her family:

> I do remember well, though, the kindness of the Spanish women living in Pueblo and their immaculate cleanliness. Though their homes were of logs, as I remember them, the floors were scrubbed snowy white, and everything seemed spotless to me.
>
> Father being too sick to work, we were dependent upon the kindness of the people for our food, and well, I remember having these kind women take me and my baby brother to their homes and give us our dinner. And such good dinners they were, too. Most of the homes had their flowers and gardens, so the people seemed very well fixed to our childish eyes.[28]

As Manomas continued remembering her childhood in Pueblo, she also recollected her mother dealing with a few of the Native Americans living in and around Pueblo. Her mother was preparing green beans for dinner as several Native Americans sat on the floor, watching her mother work. When a green bean accidentally hit the floor, they were quickly grabbed by their unsolicited guests. Once the bean was scooped off the floor, one of the men quickly placed the bean in his mouth, then promptly spat the bean at her mother, who paid no attention to the interruption. She simply "went on with her work."[29]

THREE MORMON BATTALION DETACHMENTS WINTER IN PUEBLO

John Brown and his companions were traveling back to Mississippi from Pueblo when they found the Battalion on 12 September 1846 as

---

28. Kate B. Carter, compiler, *Our Pioneer Heritage,* 20 Vol. (Salt Lake City, Utah: Daughters of Utah Pioneers, 1966) 2:437
29. Ibid, 437-438

they were camped on the Arkansas River.[30] This meeting, which many consider divinely orchestrated, likely saved the lives of countless men, women, and children who were connected to the Battalion. Shortly after this encounter, Battalion commander Lieutenant Smith ordered Captain Nelson Higgins to take a guard of ten men, along with some of their wives and children, to the village of Pueblo to winter. Many men were not happy with this decision, as Brigham Young had counseled the Battalion to stay together under any circumstances.[31] Even so, Captain Higgins left for Pueblo with his detachment on 16 September 1846. Two other detachments followed later.

Brown also encountered John D. Lee and his traveling companions two days after encountering the Mormon Battalion. Lee recorded the event in his diary:

Soon after, we discovered several men on horseback with three or four wagons in co—coming towards us, which, when they came up, proved to be Br Wm Crosby, John Brown, John D. Holloday [Holladay], Geo W Bankhead and Daniel Thomas from Miss. Co. Bro Crowsby [Crosby] said that he led a co forty-three persons and nineteen wagons—when at Independence Mo they made enquiery [*sic*] for the Mormon camp, was told that a co had crossed the South Fork of the Platt River took the Origon Trace and had bent their course westward; hearing nothing more definite about the camp, rolled on, took up the North Fork to the Fort Laramey, passed near the foot of Grand Island and located at Fort Perbelow [Pueblo] on the Arkansas River, as distance of 250 ms from Ft Laramy and 25 ms from the foot of the mountains.[32]

---

30. John Zimmerman Brown, Autobiography of Pioneer John Brown, 1820-1896, (Stevens & Wallis, Inc. Salt Lake City, Utah 1941), 70

31. Historical Department journal history of the Church, 1830-2008; 1840-1849; 1846 August-December; Church History Library, image 391-392/1154, https://catalog.chur chofjesuschrist.org/assets/c8703fa3-c68c-495e-aadc-63c50f024f41/0/394, <accessed: 23 June 2022>

32. Lee, John D. and Juanita Brooks, "Diary of the Mormon Battalion Mission." *New Mexico Historical Review* 42, 3 (1967), 188, https://digitalrepository.unm.edu/cgi/view content.cgi?article=2036&context=nmhr, <accessed 25 June 2022>

Further discussion dealt with improvements made at Pueblo. The company had planted pumpkins, melons, and turnips. In addition, the group prepared to plant wheat and other spring crops—unless directed otherwise. Brown informed Lee that those living in Pueblo utilized Bent's Fort for certain supplies. The Mississippi Saints desperately wanted to leave Pueblo in the spring to connect with the main body of the Saints. However, the available wagons and teams were not sufficient to carry twelve months' provisions. Brown and his companions sought direction from John D. Lee concerning the future migrations of their families, who were still in Mississippi and Alabama. Lee told them to continue home, and he would bring their plight before the "council." Following the council's decision, a letter would be sent that would provide the desired direction.[33]

The second detachment to leave the Mormon Battalion was led by Captain James Brown. His group departed Santa Fe at 10:00 a.m., 18 October 1846. Before leaving, an incident took place that allowed roughly twenty able-bodied men to travel with their wives to Pueblo. Colonel St. George Cooke had ordered that only those who were sick would join the Brown detachment, while the wives of healthy men would travel alone. After unsuccessfully trying to obtain help from officers in the Battalion, John Hess and John Steele approached Colonel Cooke with a request to allow the healthy married men to accompany their wives to Pueblo. Cooke quickly rebuffed their request. Hess then insisted that Alexander Doniphan, commander of all forces in Santa Fe, make the final decision. Cooke reluctantly agreed to ask, and Doniphan altered Cooke's decision. The healthy husbands accompanied their wives to Pueblo.[34]

Lieutenant William Willis led the last group to winter in Pueblo. At the time, this detachment was jettisoned from the main Battalion, and Cooke noted that twenty-two men were too sick to march and

---

33. Ibid.

34. John William Hess, 1824-1903. Autobiography and journal of John W. Hess , https://catalog.churchofjesuschrist.org/assets/719b5bb9-ea56-4bba-815f-49aa5b1d944f/0/7, <accessed 10 December 2022>

"encumbered the wagons."[35] Concerning this group of soldiers being removed from the main body of the Battalion, Levi Hancock wrote:

> I found that all our sick had to go to Puebelo [*sic*] Accordingly, Lieu Willis was called upon to go with them about two o'clock they started from our camp, and such a sight I never saw they was stowed away in the wagon like so many dead hogs no better way could be done it was said I went to the Lieu and asked him if he would see that they was well taken care of when he had it in his power to do it and gave him my hand he griped it, and I could say no more neather could he many gave me there hand and wept.[36]

The company, led by Lieutenant William W. Willis, departed for Santa Fe on November 10, 1846. They began their march with sick soldiers and little food.[37] According to Joseph Skeen, the Willis detachment traveled three miles on the first day. He recalled the entire group received only four yokes of "worn out" oxen for the long journey to Santa Fe.[38] Colonel Cooke added three more men to the Willis group on 11 November 1846. Cooke noted that "evident improvement" was now taking place as the main Battalion continued its march to the ocean.[39] One can picture the interaction Battalion members experienced with the Mississippi Saints, the mountain men, and others living in Pueblo that winter of 1846-1847.

---

35. Ibid.

36. Levi W. Hancock papers, 1832-1878; Journal, 1846 October-November; Church History Library, 27/63 https://catalog.churchofjesuschrist.org/assets/a083026f-8e0b-455c-b011-75a0135281da/0/26?lang=eng, <accessed 22 January 2023>

37. Kevin Henson, *Map N Tour*, Mormon Battalion Association, Copyright 2018-Kevin Henson & Map-N-Tour, Inc., http://www.mapntour.com/viewer/?c=487, <accessed 25 January 2023>

38. Joseph Skeen, 1816-1882. Joseph Skeen reminiscences and diary, 1846 July-1847 May   , https://catalog.churchofjesuschrist.org/assets/b800a06b-bbcf-4d49-bca7-b384e4edcc2e/0/33?lang=eng, <accessed 23 February 2023>

39. Philip St Cooke, Report from the Secretary of War, 15

POPULATION OF PUEBLO

Because there is no original list of who left northeast Mississippi in April 1846, an exact count of Mississippi Saints who wintered in Pueblo is difficult to construct. However, evidence indicates that the population of Pueblo swelled to between 290 and 300 men, women, and children during the winter of 1846 to 1847.[40] Integrated in this count is roughly eighty from the Mississippi Company, including men, women, and infants who were born in Pueblo after their arrival. Due to extensive research by individuals within the Mormon Battalion Association, we know the precise number of men, women, and children from the Battalion who wintered there. A total of 139 soldiers, twenty-nine women, thirty-six children, six officer servants, and three other adults called Pueblo home during that winter.[41] The total number of Battalion members who arrived in Pueblo was 150; however, due to seven deaths and four men who left for Iowa, the adjusted number is 139 men. Also, as noted in an earlier chapter, Lydia Gibson, daughter of Mississippian George Washington Gibson, married Gilbert Hunt, son of Captain Jefferson Hunt.[42]

THE BATTALION'S TIME IN PUEBLO

The time the Mormon Battalion spent in Pueblo presented several challenges that created discord among the rank-and-file soldiers and their leaders. One issue that caused misunderstanding between the soldiers and their supervisors was the difficult circumstances surrounding the marches of two detachments. One was Captain Brown's group, and the other was under the leadership of Lieutenant Willis. Both marches were extremely difficult and resulted in several

---

40. "The Forgotten Pioneers, (CTN 2: Folder 5), Norma B. Ricketts Papers, Banc Mss 2007/199, The Bancroft Library, University of California Berkley,
41. Mary Ann Kirk, "The Mormon Battalion Pueblo Detachments," Power point presentation, 13 December 2021, Mormon History Association, https://www.youtube.com/watch?v=STdzDvVws3o, <accessed 30 January 2023>
42. Ibid.

deaths. Brown's detachment reached Pueblo about 2 p.m. the afternoon of the 17th of November, and the Higgins detachment and the Mississippi Saints welcomed the newly arrived soldiers and their families.[43] Daniel Tylor described the extraordinary reception:

> The greeting which occurred between comrades and old friends, husbands, and wives, parents and children, when the two detachments met, was quite touching. A thrill of joy ran through the camp, which none but those living martyrs can fully comprehend.[44]

When the men and their families arrived at Pueblo, the first order of business was to build eighteen log houses in addition to those already built by the Mississippi Company and the Higgins detachment. Only two days after arriving, the group went to work felling trees for the homes.[45] The small dwellings stood fourteen feet square and were constructed mainly out of cottonwood trees that grew in the area. Amazingly, the cabins were occupied by early December. Soon after, those now living in Pueblo constructed a thirty-by-twenty-foot meeting house opposite the rows of cabins within a grove of cottonwood trees.[46] George Ruxton described the setting:

> In the wide and well-timbered bottom of the Arkansas, the Mormons had erected a street of log shanties, in which to pass the inclement winter. These were built of rough logs of cottonwood, laid one above the other, the interstices filled with mud, and rendered impervious to wind or wet. At one end of the row of shanties was built the "church"

---

43. Norma Baldwin Ricketts, *The Mormon Battalion,* (Logan, Utah, Utah State University Press, 1996), 236

44. Daniel Tyler, *A concise History of the Mormon Battalion in the Mexican War: 1846-1847,* (Forgotten books 2022, originally published 1881), 171

45. John Steele reminiscences and journals, 1846-1898; Journal, 1846 July-1877 May; Church History Library, https://catalog.churchofjesuschrist.org/assets/fc3ad50a-97ba-4f1e-9049-2b273f380c77/0/44, <Accessed 20 November 2022>

46. Norma Baldwin Ricketts, *The Mormon Battalion,* 237

or temple—along building of huge logs, in which prayer-meetings and holdings-forth took place.[47]

The happy greetings among family and friends soon subsided as the realities of life and their situation in Pueblo—on a frontier far from home and temporary at best—became apparent. On 24 November, two men were reported as deserters. A search party was sent out to locate them and bring them back for trial and punishment. They were located and brought back to the village. The alleged deserters, William Castro and Jackson Shoup, simply went hunting.[48] Jealousies and arguments began breaking out among the men and the officers. John Steele felt the "petty officers" were overly strict with the rank-and-file Battalion members. The entire detachment was paraded three times a day, and all privileges were taken away from the men. Referring to Battalion officers—Captain James Brown in particular— Steele wrote, "We all feel the hands of tyrants. There is not a privilege that is not taken from us."[49] In early January 1847, Battalion officers in Pueblo called the men together and declared there would be no card playing, dancing, or ill-speaking against officers. All soldiers should be out of another soldier's barracks by 8:00 p.m., under penalty of being sent to the guard house and court-martialed the next day. If a woman broke one of the requirements, she could be discharged. John Steele felt the entire village was under martial law.[50]

Leading men and women can be a thankless undertaking, and many who were under the command of Captain James Brown felt he was unfair, picked favorites, and drove them to exhaustion. Members of the Mormon Battalion fell under two lines of authority, which were diametrically opposed to one another. One was the military, which is

---

47. Leroy R. Hafen, editor, George Frederick Ruxton, *Life in the Far West*, (Norman, University of Oklahoma Press, 1951) 204

48. John F. A. Yurtinus, *A Ram in the Thicket: The Mormon Battalion in the Mexican War*, Ph.D. Dissertation, B.Y.U., 1975, 314

49. John Steele reminiscences and journals, 1846-1898; Journal typescript, 1959 July; Church History Library, https://catalog.churchofjesuschrist.org/assets/2097df47-8eb2-4def-8289-4103fe6d9616/0/22, <Accessed 21 November 2022>

50. Ibid.

authoritarian in nature and demands complete obedience to orders. When a direct order is given, those receiving the directive must comply with the demand or face the consequences of disobedience. The second line of authority involved church leaders, particularly Brigham Young. For members of The Church of Jesus Christ of Latter-day Saints, his word was law. Those who disobeyed his direction felt not only his ire but, in their minds, possibly risked their salvation due to their disobedience. For example, Brigham Young told Battalion members to keep together and not split into different groups during their time in military service. However, the organization of the Battalion itself led to complications during the long, grueling marches. Having wives and children travel with the Battalion created the crucial need to split Battalion members on three occasions. When the splits happened, Battalion members looked on those placed over them from within their ranks as members of the church—not as a military leader capable of giving orders. With so many young men between the ages of eighteen and twenty-one belonging to the Battalion, one can understand how difficult living in the wilderness under strict military rules would be. Those who wintered in Pueblo did the best they could in the setting they found themselves in.

A Perilous Journey From Pueblo to Winter Quarters

Battalion members William Tippetts and Thomas Woolsey left the relative comfort of Pueblo to undertake a perilous journey across the plains to a place called Sarpee's Point on the Missouri River. This small village was just below Winter Quarters and was a site where provisions were available. The men began their journey two days before Christmas 1846. On their first travel day, they lost their way, and it took an entire day to locate the trail again. By the seventh day out, they camped on Cherry Creek, near present-day Denver, Colorado. Upon reaching the south fork of the Platte River, Tippetts and Woolsey headed east and followed the Platte. The cold became so extreme that the "extremities of the tails of our mules were frozen."

Wood was scarce, and the men only knew the general direction of where they were traveling. The wind and cold were so brutal that Tippetts noted the ice on the river was ten inches thick. After traveling about 200 miles on the open plains, the men located wood for a fire, so they stopped for three days.[51]

Their provisions ran out, which forced them to live on what they could kill. During this point of extreme malnourishment, a small herd of buffalo came into view. They killed one, which provided the needed nourishment. Shortly thereafter, they were taken captive by a group of Pawnee warriors and held for a day and a night. Fortunately, the two men escaped from their imprisonment, and they "rode until dark and camped in the brush." Shortly after escaping the first captivity, the two men were forced to stop by seven Pawnee warriors who searched the two men "and took what they wanted." They left this situation and rode again until dark before hiding in some timber. The next day, they crossed the ice of the frozen Platte River. After a few more days of travel, they came to the Elk Horn River, which they crossed by throwing sand on the ice to keep their mules from slipping. After crossing the Elk Horn, they were stopped by a group of people, one of whom spoke English. Tippetts asked the man who spoke English where they were located. They were told that Winter Quarters stood only sixteen miles away. Thus, after a trip of fifty-two days, the men arrived at Brigham Young's house on 15 February 1847.[52] The two bedraggled men were invited to enjoy a dinner with those at Brigham Young's house. Shortly after dinner, Tippetts left Young's home and located his family. Tippetts wrote, "Throughout all our experiences, I acknowledged the hand of the Lord in our preservation and our arrival in safety among our friends and families on the

---

51. Historical Department journal history of the Church, 1830-2008; 1840-1849; 1847 January-June; Church History Library, image 328/1138, https://catalog.churchofje suschrist.org/assets/75cc4e9f-bfcb-4ac2-8309-19d1a3e82e8e/0/327, <accessed 17 July 2023>

52. Ibid, 330/1138

Missouri River."[53] Their cross-country journey was an incredible act of courage for both William Tippetts and Thomas Woolsey.

An Uprising

Toward the latter part of January 1847, news arrived that an uprising had taken place in Taos, New Mexico, and all the "White people" living there were killed. The governor of New Mexico, Charles Bent, was among those who lost their lives. Bent had traveled to Taos to show his support for the government and law. He left Santa Fe without any escort and took his wife and children with him. After a ride of four days, Governor Bent and his traveling companions arrived on the outskirts of Taos. They rode into town and arrived at his home before settling in. Later that evening, the streets in Taos filled with a frenzied mob. Bent was warned to flee, but he chose to remain. Tragically, early in the morning following his arrival, the antagonists broke into the home, shot the governor in the stomach, and filled his body with arrows. Charles Bent died in his residence and was buried by friends in a grave the Native Americans could not locate. The governor's wife and children survived the horrific reign of terror.

Simeon Turley owned a ranch outside of Taos. He had lived among the people since 1830 and employed many Mexicans and Native Americans living in the area. Turley was certain he was safe, but that conviction was shattered by an onslaught of 500 rebels attacking the ranch with arrows and musket balls. The eight or ten defenders fought valiantly but were overwhelmed by the sheer number of attackers. Three men survived, including John Albert, who escaped the slaughter. John eventually arrived at Pueblo, where he warned the settlement of the uprising.[54]

The frightening news about the uprising came to the attention of

---

53. Ibid.
54. David Lavender, *Bent's Fort*, (Garden City, New York: Doubleday & Company, 1954), 277-285

those in Pueblo on 25 January 1847 as the residents were preparing for dinner. John Steele noted the man who brought the news spent two days on the trail reaching Pueblo, and his hat had several musket-ball holes. The man also mentioned he had "killed eight Spaniards himself."[55] Although Steele does not mention the man's name, evidence strongly indicates the person was John Albert. The residents of Pueblo quickly sprang into action. The cattle were rounded up and taken to a safe location, with twelve men to guard them. In addition, all livestock was gathered to a spot where they could be relatively safe. Families were assembled for some measure of protection.[56] In addition, messengers were immediately dispatched to Bent's Fort and the surrounding area to warn them of the insurrection. The small cabins were linked together to form a stockade, and pickets kept guard around the clock. Soldiers and families were prepared to fight to the death or breakout.[57] Those living in Pueblo stayed on high alert until 25 February 1847, when word arrived that the rebels had been destroyed and travel was again open between Pueblo and Santa Fe. The settlers in Pueblo celebrated at the meeting house until midnight.[58]

WOMEN OF THE MISSISSIPPI SAINTS

George Ruxton, in his book *Life in the Far West*, stated the Mississippi Saints living in Pueblo during the winter of 1846 to 1847 were "a far better class than the generality of Mormons and comprised many wealthy respectable farmers." He continued that the group contained "good hunters" and that "they were able to support their families upon the produce of their rifles." Ruxton also noted the ladies of the group wintering in Pueblo "sported their tall, graceful figures at the frequent fandangos [dances]."[59] The women who were counted among the

55. John Steele reminiscences and journals, 1846-1898; Journal typescript
56. Ibid.
57. John F. A. Yurtinus, *A Ram in the Thicket*, 300
58. Norma Baldwin Ricketts, *The Mormon Battalion*, 247
59. George F. Ruxton, *Life in the Far West*, (William Blackwood and Sons, Edinburgh,

Mississippi Company that called Pueblo home during the months from August to May were, for the most part, "cultured and refined southern belles, and they brought a more permanent style of homelife that had not been seen in the area."[60] The company included several wives and their daughters. Sarah Ann Dowdle, the wife of Absalom Porter Dowdle (the presiding elder over the small branch in Pueblo), came from a wealthy plantation family in the South and enjoyed the privileges associated with such a life. One can only imagine how difficult it was for her to live in an alien environment, leaving her home and family in the South and living with the constant fear of attacks from Native Americans or the army.

Other women in the village included Mary Ann Sparks Gibson and her daughters Mary, Lydia, Francis, Laura, and Manomas, all of whom resided on the banks of the Arkansas River during the winter of 1846 to 1847. Lydia married a Mormon Battalion member, Gilbert Hunt, who wintered in Pueblo after arriving in a detachment under the direction of Captain James Brown. Gilbert and Lydia married on 23 April 1847—just before the camp left for the Salt Lake Valley.[61] Romance blossomed for another daughter of Mary Ann Sparks Gibson. Mountain man Bill New met the Gibsons' oldest daughter, Mary, during their stay in Pueblo. Following the departure of the Gibsons to Utah, Bill followed the family there and brought his twenty-three-year-old bride back to Pueblo in 1847. Mary was now the mother to Bill's two children, Nancy and Jane. The couple lived in Greenhorn, where Mary gave birth to a child named Gethro. Tragically, a group of Native Americans killed Bill in 1850.[62]

Mary Ann Blanks Smithson Harmon, wife of James Harmon, who accompanied William Kartchner to Bent's Fort, resided in Pueblo

---

and London, 1868) 189 https://archive.org/details/lifeinfarwest00ruxtuoft/page/188/mode/2up?view=theater, <accessed 11 April 2022>

60. Mary Lindenmuth Scarcello, *Mormon Pioneers in Pueblo, Colorado 1846-1900*, (Mary Lindenmuth Scarcello, Pueblo, CO. 1993) 49

61. Widow's Pension Brief, "Mexican War Pension," Family Search, https://www.family search.org/tree/person/memories/KWVS-NSJ, <accessed 14 May 2022> page 79

62. Lecompte, *Pueblo, Hardscrabble, Greenhorn, The Upper Arkansas*, 183

with her three young daughters: Paralee, age twelve; Sarah, age six; and Josephine, age two. Sarah Ann Lowry Ritter called Pueblo home for the winter. No daughters lived in her simple log home during the winter of 1846-1847. The daughters of Martha Roberds included Lodesky, Mary Beth, Harriet, and Francis—ages ten, six, five, and one, respectively.[63] The Roberds did not leave for Utah with the Mississippi Company in the spring of 1847. They remained in southeastern Colorado until the spring of 1848. At that time, the family traveled with a group of mountaineers who were headed to California. During the year in the Pueblo area, the Roberds first moved ten miles outside of town with the intent of raising crops. However, after a short time, the family moved back to Pueblo for safety. The family then moved to Hardscrabble. A short time later, they moved to another fort, which John managed during the winter. After four moves in less than a year, they finally left southeastern Colorado. Their journey took them to Salt Lake City, where they resided until 1850. From Salt Lake City, the family trekked to Northern California, where they arrived in late July 1850.[64]

Letitia Holladay Smithson and Lucinda Wilson Smithson, wives of brothers Allen and William Smithson, called Pueblo home for this winter season. Letitia's daughters, Sarah Catherine and Mary Emma, were both young. Sarah was only four years old, while Mary began the journey from Mississippi as a one-month-old baby.[65] Sadly, Letitia died in August 1849, leaving Allen a widower with five children. Allen married Jennett Burton Taylor on 16 December 1849 in the Endowment House.[66] Five daughters of Lucinda lived in the Pueblo area during the winter of 1846 to 1847: Sarah Elizabeth, age

---

63. Church History Biographical Database, "Mississippi Company," (Church History Library, Salt Lake City, Utah) https://history.churchofjesuschrist.org/chd/organiza tion/pioneer-company/mississippi-company-1846?lang=eng&timelineTabs=allTabs, <accessed 15 May 2022>

64. "R. T. Roberds," in An Illustrated History of Southern California (Chicago: The Lewis Publishing Company, 1890), 554-555, https://archive.org/details/illustrated histofsc00lewi/page/n5/mode/2up?view=theater, <accessed 15 May 2022>

65. Carter, compiler, *Our Pioneer Heritage*, Vol. 2, 452

66. Ibid, 453

thirteen; Susan Eliza, age nine; Martha Serilda, age seven; Almira Lucinda, age four; and Ferebea, age three.[67] Tragically, several years following their stay in Pueblo, Sarah Elizabeth met an untimely death while living with her husband and children in San Bernardino, California. Sarah married Rollins Don Carlos Shepard on 1 January 1852. Sarah, Don, and their three children were living in San Bernardino in 1862. Don worked for the church hauling freight, and during one of his freight trips in 1862, Sarah and her three daughters, Sarah Jane, Helen Lucinda, and Harriet Elvira, drowned during a terrible flood.[68] This flood became known as California's Great Flood of 1862.

Lusianna Roberds Sparks and her small infant daughter, Mary Ann "Polly," resided in Pueblo during that winter. Sadly, Polly died in San Bernardino, California, on 8 January 1858.[69] Temperance Weeks Mathews, wife of Benjamin Matthews, survived the winter in Pueblo with her three young daughters: Sarah Jane, age seven; Mary Elizabeth, age five; and Sallie E., an infant, who constituted Temperance's children. Evidence is inconclusive about whether Elizabeth Adeline Henderson, wife of William Mathews, brought fourteen-year-old Elizabeth Jane, eight-year-old Marie Celeste, one-year-old Elvira Narcissa, and a newborn infant daughter named Martha Rosanna with the Mississippi Company. However, due to the efforts of noted historian Norma Ricketts concerning those who stayed in Pueblo, the names of the mother and her children are included here.[70] Harriet Wheeler Young, Clara Decker Young, and Ellen Sanders Kimball are well known for entering the Salt Lake Valley with Brigham Young's vanguard wagon train in 1847. Not as

---

67. Church History Biographical Database, "Mississippi Company,"
68. Sarah Elizabeth Smithson, "Family Search," <L21V-GRR> Church of Jesus Christ of Latter-day Saints, https://ancestors.familysearch.org/en/L21V-GRR/sarah-elizabeth-smithson-1833-1862, <accessed 20 May 2022>
69. Mary Ann "Polly" Sparks, "Family Search <LD5DH-3LQ>, Church of Jesus Christ of Latter-day Saints, https://ancestors.familysearch.org/en/LD5H-3LQ/mary-ann-%22polly%22-sparks-1846-1858, <accessed 20 May 2022>
70. Norma Ricketts, "The Forgotten Pioneers, Part II," Crossroads Chapter, Oregon California Trail Association, (Fall 81997, Vol. 4, No. 4), 12

well known is the fact that Elizabeth Crow, Harriet Crow, Elizabeth J. Crow, Isa Vinda Exene Crow, Ira Miranda Crow, and Matilda Jane Therlkill also entered the Salt Lake Valley with Brigham Young on 24 July 1847.[71]

---

71. John Zimmerman Brown, Autobiography of Pioneer John Brown, 74

7

TRAVEL FROM PUEBLO TO THE GREAT SALT LAKE VALLEY IN 1847

ROBERT CROW PARTY LEAVES PUEBLO

Robert Crow led a company of seventeen eager emigrants who had wintered in Pueblo, but he decided to leave the village early to meet the vanguard wagon train led by Brigham Young at Fort Laramie. This group left Saturday, 17 April 1847, with "five wagons, one cart, eleven horses, twenty-four oxen, twenty-two cows, three bulls, and seven calves."[1] This small contingent traveled in a north-westerly direction until reaching Fort Laramie. Thomas Bullock noted meeting Robert Crow and George Threlkel on 1 June 1847. Crow's company arrived at the fort sixteen days earlier while they waited for the vanguard wagon train to arrive. Crow and Threlkel told Thomas Bullock that the remainder of the people living in Pueblo would begin coming north around the first part of June, as the Battalion was now furnished with three months of provisions.[2]

---

1. Mary Lindenmuth Scarcello, *Mormon Pioneers in Pueblo, Colorado 1846-1900*, (Mary Lindenmuth Scarcello, 1993), 108. Copy of the book in possession of the author.
2. Thomas Bullock journals, 1843-1849; Journal, 1847 April-June; Church History Library, image 80/126, https://catalog.churchofjesuschrist.org/assets/d6c2dec4-173b-4653-a8e1-1cf7e4d6a8ce/0/79?lang=eng, <Accessed 5 June 2023>

According to Horace K. Whitney, the names of those traveling with the Crow group included members of the Crow family: Robert Crow, his wife Elizabeth, and their children Benjamin, Harriet, Elizabeth Jane, John McHenry, Walter H., William P., and twins Ira and Isa. In addition, George W. Therlkill, his wife Matilda, James Therlkill, and their children Milton and James traveled with Crow. (Though this is how Whitney recorded their names, the correct spelling of the surname is Threlkel). Matilda Threlkel was the daughter of Robert and Elizabeth Crow. Non-family members included Archibald Little, James Chesney, and Lewis B. Myers. Amazingly, this contingent from Pueblo still possessed five wagons, one cart, eleven horses, twenty-four oxen, twenty-two cows, seven calves, and three bulls. Lewis Meyers had two wives and several children still at Pueblo, and he was torn between going back to Pueblo or continuing west with the vanguard. One day, he even started toward Pueblo but then returned and continued west with the Crow group. This entire group stayed together and traveled west within the second division of the vanguard wagon train.[3]

MEETING BRIGHAM YOUNG'S VANGUARD WAGON TRAIN AT FORT LARAMIE

Both the vanguard group and Robert Crow's band were now within 350 miles of Fort Bridger. During that time, Bullock entered in his journal the price of provisions at Fort Laramie. Calico, cotton, and yarn were one dollar per yard, a butcher knife ran one dollar each, buffalo robes ran from three to five dollars per robe, and buckskins were from two to three dollars each. The prices for livestock ran forty dollars each for a horse, fifteen dollars for a pony, and twenty-five dollars for a cow.[4] Of meeting the wagon train from Pueblo, William Clayton noted the main pioneer company was camped about two

---

3. Horace K. Whitney journals, 1843; 1846-1847; Journal, 1847 March-July; Church History Library, image 77/124, https://catalog.churchofjesuschrist.org/assets/d6546b00-e1a7-47c1-8554-bbe481467f5a/0/76?lang=eng, <accessed 13 June 2023>
4. Ibid, 83/126

miles from the fort and experienced "much joy to meet with brethren in this wild region of the country, and also because we should have some news from the brethren in the army."[5] The seventeen members of the Robert Crow contingent brought the total of the pioneer camp to 161 souls. Due to his knowledge of the mountains, Lewis B. Myers traveled with the Crow family to function as a hunter and guide.[6]

Now that the Crow party was blended into the main pioneer wagon train, other essential business needed addressing. Church leaders desired additional communication with those still in Pueblo. Brigham Young sent Amasa Lyman, a member of the Quorum of the Twelve Apostles, Mormon Battalion members Thomas Woolsey and John H. Tippetts, and Roswell Stevens south to meet those who wintered in Pueblo. These men left on 3 June 1847 at 11:15 a.m., traveling with horses and mules. Brigham Young, Heber C. Kimball, Willard Richards, and Orson Pratt accompanied the four men to the Laramie Ford, where a short council was held, and the group was dedicated to God and blessed.[7]

Brigham Young wrote letters to Captain James Brown and Absolom Dowdle, which he sent via Amasa Lyman. Thomas Woolsey was handed 349 letters for Battalion members and was appointed Deputy Postmaster. Brigham Young instructed Woolsey to bring back any undeliverable letters.[8] Before leaving Laramie Ford, President Young gave further instructions that he wanted to be given to Battalion members. First, the Battalion had accomplished the designs of getting the Battalion to Mexico. Second, those living in Pueblo must not follow James Brown to Mexico but instead "go to California." For those who were disobedient, Amasa was given the authority to call new officers "who would do right." Third, if any of

---

5. William Clayton, "William Clayton's Journal; a daily record of the journey of the original company of "Mormon" pioneers from Nauvoo, Illinois, to the valley of the Great Salt Lake," (Salt Lake City, The Deseret News, 1921), 206-207, Internet Archive, https://archive.org/details/williamclaytonsj00clay/page/206/mode/2up, <accessed 6 June 2023>
6. Ibid, 215
7. Ibid, 212-213
8. Thomas Bullock journals, 1843-1849; Journal, 1847 April-June; 84/126

the Battalion was in Santa Fe, they were to come back and join the trek west. Finally, President Young voiced his anger with President Buchanan because his orders were to enlist no more than "1//3 Mormons in his army." The council, as noted earlier, began at 11:15 a.m. and concluded at 11:27 a.m. The four men crossed the river and went on their way toward Pueblo.[9]

The blended wagon train was now prepared to travel together. On 4 June, the wagon train began moving west again. During that day's travel, Robert Crow's cart turned over, but no damage was done. The next day was Sunday, so following a worship service, the wagons only traveled four miles before stopping for the night. Howard Egan noted that William Clayton "put up a guide board every ten miles." As the vanguard wagon train continued west, several Oregon-bound wagons camped nearby.[10] In addition to acting as a guide for the Crow group, Lewis B. Myers hunted game for the family to eat. A few days after leaving Fort Laramie, he killed a deer. William Clayton noted that Robert Crow's group was not willing to share this deer meat with others, which created conflict among the group. The mandate to share harvested meat was an important rule within the camp. Robert Crow indicated that if more meat was located, he would be willing to share. Later, Clayton learned that the Crow family relied completely on Myers for their food. They only ate what Myers killed.[11] During the same period, Robert Crow came near death as he tried "to yoke a pair of wild steers." Several men were assisting Robert when his legs became entangled with lariats and the steers as they tumbled to the ground. Fortunately, the rope was cut, and Crow escaped injury.

Another challenge faced the Crow family. On 8 June 1847, Harriet Crow, Robert's sixteen-year-old daughter, stopped for a drink of water. She stepped on the wagon tongue to get her drink. The startled

---

9. Ibid, 84/126

10. Howard Egan, *Pioneering the West, 1846 to 1878:* (Richmond, Utah, 1917), 66, https://archive.org/details/pioneeringwest1800began/page/66/mode/2up, <accessed 8 June 2023>

11. William Clayton, "William Clayton's Journal; a daily record of the journey of the original company of "Mormon" pioneers, 223

oxen bolted forward, and the wagon ran over her leg just below the knee and her foot just over her toes. She screamed out in agony, and most thought she had broken her leg. Fortunately, her leg was only badly bruised but not broken. One of the women on the train washed her foot with camphor, and Harriet was placed in a wagon before the group continued.[12] After several days of travel on the Oregon Trail, the wagon train met Jim Bridger and two companions on Monday, 28 June 1847, as he was traveling east to Fort John (Laramie). Bridger consented to spend the night with the vanguard wagon train, and he informed church leadership of his opinion of the geography toward which they were traveling. Following a meal, Bridger met one-on-one with President Brigham Young.[13] Samuel Brannon and two companions arrived in camp on the thirtieth, and Brannon provided the group with a glowing review of California.[14]

SELECTED INDIVIDUALS SENT AHEAD TO PREPARE THE ROAD INTO THE VALLEY

On 13 July 1847, some of the members of the vanguard wagon were sent ahead to carve out a road to the Salt Lake Valley. Apostle Orson Pratt took leadership of this company. Among the party of forty-two men selected to proceed ahead of the main wagon train was John Brown (the same John Brown who originally put the 1846 Mississippi Company together). Additionally, Robert Crow and three of his sons —Benjamin, John, and Walter—moved ahead. Others from the Crow group selected for the advanced company included George Threlkel, James Chesney, and Lewis B. Meyers. Green Flake, Oscar (Crosby) Smith, and Hark (Lay) Wales also contributed to this special advanced team.[15] These three men were enslaved, owned by several Mississippi

---

12. Ibid.
13. Ibid, 277-278
14. Howard Egan, *Pioneering the West, 1846 to 1878:*, 90
15. Horace K. Whitney journals, 1843; 1846-1847; Journal, 1847 March-July; Church History Library, image 116/124, https://catalog.churchofjesuschrist.org/assets/d6546b00-e1a7-47c1-8554-bbe481467f5a/0/76?lang=eng, <accessed 13 June 2023>

converts who traveled with the vanguard train from Winter Quarters. They were among the first from the vanguard wagon train to enter the Salt Lake Valley on 22 July 1847.[16]

On 21 July 1847, Orson Pratt and Erastus Snow experienced their first view of the Salt Lake Valley. At last, following months of perilous cross-plains travel, numerous river crossings, severe thunder and lightning storms, and sickness, these two men were the first to view the valley. During the ensuing years, thousands of members of The Church of Jesus Christ of Latter-day Saints would call this valley and other locations in the West their home.

> Mr. Snow and myself ascended this hill from the top of which a broad open valley about twenty miles wide and 30 long lay streatched [*sic*] out before us and at the N. end of which the broad waters of the great Salt Lake glistened in the sunbeams.... After issuing from the mountains, among which we had been shut up for many days and beholding in a moment such an extensive scenery open before us we could not refrain from a shout of joy which almost involuntarily escaped from our lips the moment this grand and lovely scenery was within our view.[17]

Pratt and Snow immediately descended from their hilltop view and entered the valley. Pratt noted they "traveled a circuit of about twelve miles before we left the valley."[18] The advanced party reentered the valley on 22 July 1847, while Brigham Young and the balance of the vanguard company arrived on 24 July 1847.[19]

---

16. Benjamin Kiser, "Biography of Green Flake," 100 Century of Black Mormons, J. Willard Marriott Library, The University of Utah, https://exhibits.lib.utah.edu/s/century-of-black-mormons/page/flake-green#?c=&m=&s=&cv=&xywh=-1117%2C-62%2C3255%2C1246, <accessed 12 June 2023>

17. Orson Pratt autobiography and journals, 1833-1847; Journal, 1846 February-July, 1847 May-July; Church History Library, image 101/168, https://catalog.churchofjesuschrist.org/assets/45de59d3-2bec-47fd-a2f8-86021538309a/0/100?lang=eng, <accessed 10 June 2023>

18. Ibid.

19. Ron Rood, Linda Thatcher, "Mormon Settlement," History to Go, Utah Department

Three women traveled in the 1847 vanguard wagon train from the starting point in Winter Quarters. Clara Decker Young, wife of Brigham Young; Ellen Sanders Kimball, wife of Heber C. Kimball; and Harriet Wheeler Young, wife of Lorenzo D. Young, are credited with being the first women to enter the valley in July 1847. Their stories of entering the valley are generally understood. However, an often-overlooked fact is that seven other women entered the valley at the same time. Robert Crow's wife, Elizabeth, and her daughters Harriet, Elizabeth J., Ira, and Isa, as well as Matilda Jane Threlkel, all entered the valley in July 1847 after wintering in Pueblo.[20] Unfortunately, the stories of these women are less well known.

THE SECOND PARTY LEAVES PUEBLO

Fourteen days after the Crow group left Pueblo, John G. Smith, a private in Company D, left the village on Sunday, 2 May 1847. Daniel Tylor wrote that he departed with one wagon, three yoke of oxen, "and others" and began their trek to Fort Laramie. After a march of two days, the travelers reached a spring then known as "Soda Fountain." Tylor described the area, with its many naturally carbonated springs and rock formations, as an excellent location for scientific research.[21] The probable location where Smith and his group stopped is now known as Manitou Springs, Colorado. The distance from Pueblo to Manitou Springs is forty-nine miles, which would fit into the two days it took for Smith and company to reach the unique springs.[22] According to Thomas Bullock's list, John G. Smith (and likely those who traveled with him) entered the Salt Lake Valley on 29

of Cultural and Community Engagement, https://historytogo.utah.gov/mormon-settle ment/, <accessed 12 June 2023>

20. Joseph Fielding Smith, *Essentials in Church History*, (Utah, Deseret Book Company, 1979) fn a 374, Joseph Fielding Smith did not include Isa Crow in the names of the Crow family women to enter the valley. Her name is included as one who entered the valley July 1847.

21. Daniel Tyler, *A Concise History of The Mormon Battalion in the Mexican War, 1846-1847*, (Salt Lake City: Historian's office, 1881), 197

22. Trippy, www.trippy.com, <accessed 20 June 2023>

July 1847.[23] Even though Smith and his group left Pueblo on the second of May and the balance of the Battalion and Mississippi families left later that month, they entered the Salt Lake Valley together.

MISSISSIPPI FAMILIES AND CAPTAIN JAMES BROWN HEAD TO FORT LARAMIE

Before the largest group left Pueblo, some important issues needed to be addressed. Battalion members desired to know who could discharge them from service and where they should go from Pueblo. Soldiers wanted money owed to them for their service to the United States. Finally, the need for adequate provisions for a march from Pueblo needed to be addressed. To resolve the first issue, John Brown and other officers traveled to Santa Fe to determine when the Battalion could be released and what their next orders were. Upon their return on 9 April 1847, the word came that no one in Santa Fe had authority for the Battalion's discharge, and additional orders could not be issued.[24] Captain Brown and Captain Higgins appointed themselves to travel to Santa Fe for the soldiers' money. Brown charged the men two-and-a-half percent each for any money they collected. Brown also demanded that the men give him power of attorney before he would provide any of their earned pay. Upon returning from this second trip to Santa Fe, Brown reported they now had orders to "go to California and start on the 25th of May with two-and-a-half months of provisions."[25]

Most of the Mississippi Company and the Battalion members, along with their families, left Pueblo for Fort Laramie on 24 May

---

23. Names of Pueblo soldiers and Mississippi brethren , https://catalog.churchofje suschrist.org/assets/ab774142-989d-4df6-a024-1f3a90e5bbd3/0/0, <accessed 20 June 2023> John G. Smith's name appears on the second row, forth name from the bottom of Bullock's list.

24. John Steele reminiscences and journals, 1846-1898; Journal, 1846 July-1877 May; Church History Library, images 59-60/226, https://catalog.churchofjesuschrist.org/assets/fc3ad50a-97ba-4f1e-9049-2b273f380c77/0/59?lang=eng, <accessed 21 June 2023>

25. Ibid, 61/226

1847.[26] One Battalion member noted the distance from Pueblo to Fort Laramie totaled 315 miles.[27] Evidence indicates this group may have taken a route known as the Trappers Trail, which connected Fort Laramie with Taos, New Mexico, and the Santa Fe Trail.[28] This is likely the same trail John Richard used to guide the Mississippi Company from the Fort Laramie area to Pueblo. Portions of the old trail are parts of today's Interstate 25 and US Highway 85 in southern Colorado. Several trading posts were established along the trail, and several military units used all or portions of the trail. John C. Freemont traveled on the trail during his 1842 expedition. Stephen W. Kearney's journey of 1845 also utilized the Trappers Trail.[29] Philip St. George Cook, who later led the Mormon Battalion from Santa Fe to the Pacific Ocean, also participated in this expedition. He described his feelings as he passed Pike's Peak immediately after a thunderstorm.

> But suddenly, with a direful crash amid the Titanic rocks, there came a wondrous glare that revealed through a vista of the black array of clouds, Mount Pike, splendid, sublime, serene, amid the chaotic war! —like a *Fata Morgana*, turned to stone. I was speechless.[30]

The El Pueblo Museum, located in downtown Pueblo, is an excellent location to learn about trapping and trade during the 1840s. Lee Whiteley authored an excellent article about the Trappers Trail, where

---

26. John F. Yurtinus, *A Ram in the Thicket: the Mormon Battalion in the Mexican War*, Master's Thesis, August 1975, 318

27. Thomas Hayward, 1814-1893. Hayward Thomas reminiscences and journal , image 16/45,   https://catalog.churchofjesuschrist.org/assets/f848fe68-f60e-4559-a138-fbb8ae3646a9/0/15?lang=eng, <accessed 29 June 2023>

28. Lee Whiteley, *"The Road to Fort Laramie's Back Door," Overland Journal*, (Volume 16, Number 4, Winter 1998-1999): 2

29. Ibid, 7-8

30. Philip St. George Cooke, *Scenes and Adventures in the Army*, (Philadelphia: Lindsay & Blakiston, 1859), 411,
   https://quod.lib.umich.edu/m/moa/aja3344.0001.001/413?page=root;rgn=full+text;size=100;view=image, <accessed 30 June 2023>

he noted several additional locations one can enjoy traveling north on Interstate 25, Colorado Highway 105, and State Highway 392.[31]

BATTALION MEMBERS' ACCOUNTS OF THE TRAIL FROM PUEBLO TO FORT LARAMIE

Fortunately, several members of the Mormon Battalion recorded, or later recalled, their travel from Pueblo to Fort Laramie. Members of the group from Mississippi and Alabama were not as consistent in recording details of the experience. During the first part of their journey, the travelers followed Fountain Creek, where they encamped for a short period while waiting for provisions from Bent's Fort. During their encampment, Captain Higgins returned to Pueblo to locate missing cattle. During their short encampment on Fountain Creek, guards were placed around their campsite to protect their livestock.[32] The party then continued its journey toward Fort Laramie. The caravan traveled eighteen miles on 29 May 1847 and camped at what Joseph Skeen and John Steele called James Camp.[33] During the night, a terrible wind, rain, and hail storm swept through the site before their tents could be set up, which, in the words of Joel J. Terrell, produced a "very disagreeable" night.[34] Jimmy's Camp is just east of Colorado Springs, Colorado.

Weather consistently created havoc for the Mississippi Company, Battalion members, and their families. After traveling eighteen miles on May 31st, another violent thunderstorm struck the camp.

---

31. *Lee Whiteley, "The Road to Fort Laramie's Back Door,"* 15

32. Joseph Skeen, 1816-1882. Joseph Skeen reminiscences and diary, 1846 July-1847 May , image 46/60 /https://catalog.churchofjesuschrist.org/assets/b800a06b-bbcf-4d49-bca7-b384e4edcc2e/0/45?lang=eng, <accessed 30 June 2023>; Daniel Tyler, *A Concise History of The Mormon Battalion,* 198; Steele reminiscences and journals, image 62/226

33. Joseph Skeen, 1816-1882. Image 46/60; Steele reminiscences and journals, image 62/226

34. Joel Judkins Terrell, 1801-1883. Joel J. Terrell diary ,image 73/101 https://catalog.churchofjesuschrist.org/assets/e36554e1-15f7-43dc-a399-d83878be3a35/0/72?lang=eng, <accessed 4 July 2023>

Concerning the storm, Terrell wrote, "Before we got here, it hailed and rained very hard, which was very bad on us and our animals." Terrell noted he stood as "officer of the guard" that evening, and he became so wet that he received little rest during the night.[35] One can only begin to imagine how uncomfortable that night was for all involved. As the company continued moving north on the Old Trappers Trail, they reached Cherry Creek on 1 June 1847, where they located good grass for their livestock. The voyagers reached the south fork of the Platte River on 3 June 1847. They were now 145 miles from their Winter Quarters of Pueblo and faced the daunting task of crossing the Platte River.[36] The Platte River was running high that year, which made the crossing challenging. The fording began Saturday, 5 June, at noon. To cross, wagon boxes were raised, and blocks of wood were placed on the underside to keep the loads within the wagons dry.[37] After the crossing was completed, the company traveled a short distance, camped, and rested for the next two days.[38]

Meeting Amasa Lyman on the Trail

The trek north continued again on 7 June 1847. The next important stop as they continued their march to Fort Laramie came when they reached and crossed Crow Creek. Unfortunately, there was little wood or water at this camping spot. John Steele's entry in his diary wryly noted there was an "abundance of prickly pairs."[39] The troupe was continuing their march northward when, to the delight of the entire camp, they met Amasa Lyman and the small contingent he traveled with on Friday, 11 June 1847. John Steele described the event, writing, "Came twenty miles and camped on Poll Creek. There is a good spring here. After we got our tents pitched, there was a cry made

---

35. Ibid, 73-74
36. Steele reminiscences and journals, image 63/226
37. Daniel Tyler, *A Concise History of the Mormon Battalion in the Mexican War, 1846-1847,* (Originally published in 1881; Republished by Forgotten Books 2012), 198
38. Steele reminiscences and journals, image 63/226
39. Ibid, image 64/226

that Wolsey and Tippets was to come with Amas A Lyman. I went with all speed and found it so."[40] As noted earlier, Brigham Young had appointed Thomas Woolsey Deputy Postmaster, and Woolsey brought letters from friends and family in Winter Quarters and other locations on the Missouri River. Joel J. Terrell was also thrilled with seeing his fellow church members, but he was disappointed with having to pay for the mail, as he expressed by writing, "[Woolsey] came to our camp which gave some of us much satisfaction, others distress of mind. At any rate, it gave us another chance to part with one dollar more of our hard earnings, it was joy and grief for me."[41] Sadly, Andrew J. Shupe received a letter from his wife announcing the death of his father, mother, and his brother John. He noted the news was "mortifying" to him.[42]

Remarkably, the same day Amasa Lyman and his small band left Fort Laramie, the Mississippi Company, and Battalion members reached the south fork of the Platte River.[43] A unique event took place during Lyman's travel south. On 9 June 1847, after traveling "a short distance," one of the travelers killed a pelican, which they ate for breakfast. Lyman wrote in his journal that the pelican's wingspan from the tip of each wing was seven feet, and the bird was "fat."[44] Brigham Young sent Apostle Amasa Lyman with specific instructions to give to those who wintered in Pueblo. From a campsite on Horse Creek, on Sunday, 13 June 1847, Amasa Lyman set about quelling the negative feelings Battalion members felt for each other—particularly to their leaders—and to help Battalion members remember their covenants. Lyman felt his remarks met with "apparent satisfaction,"

---

40. Ibid.

41. Terrell, Joel Judkins, 1801-1883, image 75/101

42. Andrew Jackson Shupe, 1815-1877. Andrew J. Shupe diary , image 127/32, https://catalog.churchofjesuschrist.org/assets/2e32a4b2-18e8-49bc-a86b-83dab3a13f69/0/26?lang=eng, <accessed 6 July 2023>

43. Steele reminiscences and journals, image 63/226

44. Amasa M. Lyman collection, 1832-1877; Journals, 1832-1877; Journal, 1847 April 8-September 10; Church History Library, images 13-14/68, https://catalog.churchofje suschrist.org/assets/48a3e398-d725-435c-93f4-d89eb0e7747b/0/0?lang=eng, <accessed 6 July 2023>

and the group expressed a willingness to improve their behavior.[45] One week later, he followed up with additional counsel concerning the need to be "men of God."[46] John Steele wrote that Lyman counseled the listeners to stop playing cards, discontinue swearing, and return to God. Steele also noted that the apostle stated the things within the Battalion were "not as bad as he expected to find."[47] Other Battalion members also felt Lyman's remarks were well-received.

Captain James Brown was so moved by Lyman's remarks that he publicly acknowledged some of his imperfections. However, John Steele noted that after Brown conceded his faults, he went on "to run down his boys" and declared that he "was not going to be counseled by any private soldier."[48] The Mississippi Company and Mormon Battalion members continued heading north to Fort Laramie. On 16 June 1847, as they neared the fort, a Sioux war party appeared on the horizon. The sudden appearance of a well-armed war party of Native Americans created alarm among the travelers. Joel Terrell recorded that once the Sioux realized these pioneers were not a war party of Crow, "with whom they were at war, but finding the mistake they all commenced shaking hands with us and you may depend they went the whole hog at that they gladly escorted us to Laramy."[49] The company was now within one mile of the fort. Once at Fort Laramie, they learned the vanguard was traveling twelve days ahead.[50] After learning they were within striking distance of Brigham Young's wagon train, the group left early on the morning of 17 June 1847. During this time, near Fort Laramie, the company located some of the livestock that was stolen earlier.[51] From Fort Laramie, the company traveled the Oregon Trail, utilizing signs put up at camping locations

---

45. Ibid, image 15/68
46. Steele reminiscences and journals, image 65/226
47. Ibid, image 64/226
48. Ibid, image 65/226
49. Terrell, Joel Judkins, 1801-1883, image 77/101
50. Norma Baldwin Ricketts, *The Mormon Battalion, U. S. Army of the West, 1846-1848,* (Logan, Utah, Utah State University Press, 1996), 251
51. Shupe, Andrew Jackson, 1815-1877, image 128/186

by the vanguard group.[52] By the time they reached the ferry on the Platte River, the band was only one day behind Young's wagon train.

The company continued their march to the Salt Lake Valley, and they reached the Platte River on Sunday, 27 June 1847, where they found a group left behind by Brigham Young to ferry pioneers across the water. The greeting was a joyous occasion for all involved. On the 28th, Captain Brown ordered thirteen men to locate more stolen live-stock and the "Frenchman" who had taken the animals and sold them to other emigrants. Brown also directed this advance party to over-take Brigham Young's wagon train.[53] This advanced group traveled to the Green River before catching up to where the vanguard was camped, about two miles below the river ferry. They were ferried across the river and escorted to Brigham Young's camp. The men were met with "cheers and a Hosanna to God and the Lamb." This long-awaited reunion took place on 4 July 1847.[54]

FOURTH OF JULY 1847: IN CALIFORNIA AND ON THE TRAIL

Three noteworthy proceedings took place on the date acclaiming our country's independence and at the same time as the above-mentioned event. One wedding, a salutation in Los Angeles, and a non-celebration each took place on 4 July 1847. Battalion member Private Norman Sharp left a widow, Martha Jane Sargent Sharp. Martha faced the strain of raising a new baby alone in the temporary location of Pueblo following the loss of her husband. Fortunately for Martha, Harley Mowrey arrived in Pueblo as a member of the Higgins detach-ment. During the winter, she and Harley developed a relationship that later resulted in a marriage on the Oregon Trail. Battalion member

---

52. Daniel Tyler, *A Concise History of the Mormon Battalion in the Mexican War, 1846-1847,* (Forgotten Books, 2012), 201, www.forgottenbooks.org.
53. Shupe, Andrew Jackson, 1815-1877, image 129/186
54. Andrew Jensen, "Day By Day with the Utah Pioneers 1847," Copyright by *The Salt Lake Tribune,* (Provo, Utah, Community Press, 1997) 93

Abner Blackburn wrote an interesting account of their courtship and marriage:

> There was a couple of young folks in the company spooning and licking each other ever since we started on the road. The whole company was tired of it, and they were persuaded to marry now and have done with it and not wait until their journey's end. The next evening, we had a wedding and a regular minister to unite them, and after come the supper with the best the plains could furnish. Then came the dance or hoe down. The banjo and violin made us forget the hardships of the plains.

Love blossomed, and a marriage took place along the Sweetwater River. As noted by Blackburn, those traveling with the couple enjoyed the diversion from the hardships of the trail.[55]

Most of the Mormon Battalion soldiers who reached the Pacific coast were released from service after their year in the military. The majority either went to Northern California or traveled to Utah Territory. Before the Battalion members departed the area, they helped build a fort "capable of holding two hundred soldiers and of withstanding a siege until aid could come from San Diego, San Francisco, or Monterey."[56] For Battalion members who remained in the Los Angeles area, a unique celebration took place on 4 July 1847. Several Battalion members, along with a group of "natives," were sent to San Bernardino to cut down the largest trees they could find to construct a flagpole for the unfinished fort's dedication. After a lengthy and worrisome wait, the caravan was seen returning to Los

---

55. Abner Blackburn, and Will Bagley. 1992. *Frontiersman : Abner Blackburn's Narrative*. [Publications in the American West Series, V. 30]. Salt Lake City: University of Utah Press., 60-61

56. Laurance Landreth Hill, *La Reina, Los Angeles in three centuries, 1781-1929: A volume commemorating the fortieth anniversary of the founding of the Security Trust and Savings Bank of Los Angeles, February 11, 1889,* (Family Search, Salt Lake City), image 43/210, https://www.familysearch.org/library/books/records/default?search=La%20Reina:%20Los%20Angeles%20in%20Three%20Centuries&sort=_score&perpage=10&page=1&fulltext=1&, <accessed 15 July 2023>

Angeles hauling two tree trunks. One measured ninety feet tall, while the other tree reached roughly seventy-five feet in height. Each tree was hauled by twenty yoke of oxen "with an Indian driver on each one." The two trees were spliced together, which created "a flagpole for the city 150 feet high that could be seen by all men."[57] During their time in the mountains, this small group fought with Native Americans, killing three and bringing back the ears of their victims "strung upon a string." The writer of the article wrote, "[Battalion members] were singing one of their interminable songs of Zion—a paean of delivery from the hands of the Philistines."[58]

The vanguard wagon train, led by Brigham Young, continued their trek to the Salt Lake Valley. The pioneer camp was next to the Green River in what is now the state of Wyoming. Their destination of the Salt Lake Valley would not be reached for another twenty days. It was a day filled with Sunday preaching and some rest. However, due to the number of times church members were driven from location to location, many chose not to celebrate the country's independence that Sunday. Memories of the deaths of their first prophet-leader and his brother, the difficulties endured at Winter Quarters, and being forced out of Ohio, Missouri, and Illinois were engraved into their hearts and minds. They were fleeing the United States for a setting in which they could live their religion (which seemed so puzzling to other citizens) in peace. Wagon train member John Smith wrote, "We do not feel to celebrate the birthday of the Independence of the United States, as we have been driven from its borders because we worshipped God according to his laws. A public meeting was held at 2 p.m., at which Elders Pratt and Taylor made some particularly good remarks."[59] The Fourth of July 1847 brought together a happy couple for a wedding, provided a distinctive celebration in Los Angeles and

---

57. Ibid.
58. Ibid.
59. Historical Department journal history of the Church, 1830-2008; 1840-1849; 1847 July-December; Church History Library, image 27/1034, https://catalog.churchofje suschrist.org/assets/a84034e2-b2c3-43fd-9821-261211f6fda7/0/26, <accessed 15 July 2023>

created painful emotions for a homeless contingent on the Oregon Trail.

ENTERING THE SALT LAKE VALLEY

From this point on, Battalion members traveled with the vanguard wagon train to Fort Bridger, where they located and arrested the person who stole the animals. Some of the men returned to the contingent led by Captain Brown, while six men, including Andrew Shupe, remained with the vanguard.[60] During their travel to Fort Bridger, they passed through South Pass and the Continental Divide on 13 July and then camped on the western side of Pacific Springs.[61] They were continuing their forward progress when, on Friday, 16 July, several Battalion members fired their guns in celebration of the first anniversary of their enrollment with "Uncle Sam." They were now at the Green River, which they crossed after raising their wagon boxes.[62] Since no one held the military authority to discharge the men, they were now in the awkward position of being under the direction of both Captain James Allen and their spiritual leader, Brigham Young. When they were camped near Fort Bridger, another complaint was lodged against Captain Brown by Battalion member Ebeneezer Hanks, who alleged that Brown took provisions belonging to other soldiers.[63]

By 25 July, the weary Mississippi Company, Battalion members, and their families were now nearing the end of their long, exhausting journey, which for the Mississippi Company encompassed almost the entire width of the country. It was at this point that Amasa Lyman offered additional counsel. He stated that now that the gentile persecutions had been left behind, the biggest threat to the future would

---

60. Shupe, Andrew Jackson, 1815-1877, image 130/186
61. Franklin Allen, 1890d. Franklin Allen diary, image 28/123, https://catalog.churchof jesuschrist.org/assets/1d58315c-8252-40e1-b43e-2bb7e8c97ca3/0/27?lang=eng, ,accessed 16 July 2023>
62. Ibid, image 29/123
63. Steele reminiscences and journals, image 70/226

come from "devils in our own mist."[64] By Wednesday, 28 July 1847, after working their way through much undergrowth and a rough trail, the travelers caught their first views of the valley below, including earlier arrivals to the valley as they planted crops. Some men met them and said the trip to the valley was another twelve miles. The next day, 29 July 1847, the Mississippi Company, Battalion members, and their families finally entered the Salt Lake Valley.[65] The members who left Mississippi in April 1846 and Battalion personnel who left families and friends in and around Winter Quarters were now at their hoped-for Zion. But many challenges still lay ahead.

GEORGE WASHINGTON GIBSON FAMILY REMAIN IN PUEBLO

As noted earlier, George Washington Gibson fell ill during his travels across the plains before arriving at Pueblo. His recovery during the winter of 1846 to 1847 took longer than they had hoped. There is supporting information showing that the Gibson family likely remained in Pueblo until George fully recovered. Alexander Barkley noted he purchased corn from the family in February 1848.[66] Andrew Jensen recorded the Gibson family entering the Salt Lake Valley on 29 July 1847, along with the other Mississippi Company and Mormon Battalion members. However, the names contained on this list were written much later from memory by Marion J. Shelton, the son of Mormon Battalion member Sebert Crutcher Shelton, who was thirteen years old when they arrived in the valley.[67] Thomas Bullock prepared a detailed list of those who arrived on 29 July 1847 in August 1847. Apart from Lydia Hunt, who had married Battalion

---

64. Ibid.

65. Ibid, image 71/226

66. Janet Lecompte, *Pueblo, Hardscrabble, Greenhorn; The Upper Arkansas, 1832-1856,* (University of Oklahoma Press; Norman, 1978), 186

67. Historical Department journal history of the Church, 1830-2008; 1840-1849; 1847 July-December; Church History Library, image 223/1034, https://catalog.churchofje suschrist.org/assets/a84034e2-b2c3-43fd-9821-261211f6fda7/0/222, <accessed 1 August 2023>

member Gilbert Hunt while living in Pueblo, no other members of the Gibson family are listed on his report.[68]

During the winter of 1846-1847, Mary Gibson met mountain man and trapper William New. The exact date of their marriage is not known, but the 1850 federal census indicates they were living in Taos Territory, New Mexico. William (Bill) was forty-eight years old, and Mary Gibson New indicated her age as twenty-five. Bill's three children by another mother were Jethro, Nancy (age twelve), and ten-year-old Jone. The children were born at Greenhorn, the Platte River, and the Arkansas River, respectively.[69] William and Mary were living at Greenhorn in 1848 when Mary gave birth to a child they named Gethro. Tragically, Indians killed William in 1850. Mary Gibson New may have been the first white woman to live in such a "primitive place."[70] In his autobiography, Kit Carson described the death of William New following a pursuit of Native American warriors:

> Two of the men with me on this enterprise have since been slain by the same tribe of Indians; Sergent Holbrook, a brave and gallant soldier, was killed in the battle of Ceneguilla in 1854, and William New, a brave and experienced trapper, was killed at Rayado a few months after our pursuit of the Indians that had stolen our horses.[71]

Lydia Gibson Hunt wrote her sister Mary and William New were married during their stay in Pueblo. New apparently promised the Gibson family he would bring Mary to Utah as soon as he could

---

68. Names of Pueblo soldiers and Mississippi brethren 1847, images 2/4, https://catalog.churchofjesuschrist.org/assets/ab774142-989d-4df6-a024-1f3a90e5bbd3/0/2, <accessed 1 August 2023>

69. William New household, 1850 U. S. census, Taos, Territory,, New Mexico image 191/227; Ancestry.com, https://www.ancestry.com/discoveryui-content/view/11150807:8054, <accessed 1 August 2023>

70. Janet Lecompte, *Pueblo, Hardscrabble, Greenhorn*, 183

71. Milo Milton Quaife, *Kit Carson's Autobiography*, (Family Search, Salt Lake City, Utah), image image 186/252, https://www.familysearch.org/library/books/viewer/760471/?offset=&return=1#page=186&viewer=picture&o=search&n=0&q=William%20New%20, <accessed 1 August 2023>

"arrange his business affairs." Tragically, Mary died "one or two years later" before she could reunite with her Gibson family. Mary and William's child was sent "to relatives in the East to be educated."[72] Pueblo's connection to the Mississippi Company was now over.

72. Lydia Hunt, "The Gibsons by Lydia Hunt," (Family Search: Salt Lake City, Utah), <KVP1-25T> https://www.familysearch.org/photos/artifacts/37086492?p= 49234562&returnLabel=George%20Washington%20Gibson%20(KWJ1-3B)&return Url=https%3A%2F%2Fwww.familysearch.org%2Ftree%2Fperson%2Fmemories%2FK WJ1-43B, <accessed 1 August 2023>

8

EARLY SETTLEMENTS IN UTAH TERRITORY AND THE MISSISSIPPI SAINTS OF 1848

IMMEDIATELY FOLLOWING ARRIVAL IN JULY 1847

Among the issues facing the newly arriving settlers in the Salt Lake Valley, three crucial matters stood out. First, it was now August, so winter would soon arrive, and crops needed to be planted. Second, permanent dwellings must be constructed, both for protection from the elements and for defense against the Indigenous people on whose land they were now settling. It was a paradoxical situation —members of The Church of Jesus Christ of Latter-day Saints, who were themselves forced from various settlements in the United States, were now inhabiting ground from which another culture would eventually be forcibly removed. Third, members of the vanguard wagon train and Battalion members desperately wanted to reunite with their families and bring them west. Concerning the need for sustenance, preparation for planting began at noon, Friday, 23 July 1847, near the current intersection of East Temple and First South in Salt Lake City. Several plows were broken on the first day due, in part, to the dry soil, but three plows and one harrow (a tool used after plowing to even out the dirt for planting) continued throughout the day. At 2:00 p.m., several men built a dam across City Creek to provide water to the parched ground. Soaking the ground made the plowing much easier.[1]

Prior to the previously-mentioned ground preparation, a committee of five was organized to search out the best location for planting potatoes, corn, beans, and other crops. Those appointed were Shadrack Roundy, Seth Taft, Stephen Markham, Robert Crow, and Albert Carrington. These men immediately left the meeting to go to work. Three men, Charles A. Harper, Charles Shumway, and Elijah Newman, were assigned to round up plows and locate other men to assist them. In addition, Hensen Walker, William Wadsworth, and John Brown were called to "supervise the moving and rigging up of scythes." Stephen Markham was also appointed to make sure the needed livestock was available to change out every four hours. Each man in the company was allowed to "plant his own potatoes and seeds as he pleased."[2] William Clayton reported that by 10 August 1847, approximately eighty acres had been plowed or planted. At this point, the need to work on housing took priority.[3]

Howard Egan noted that during a meeting on 1 August 1847, the determination was made to "employ the Spanish mode of building houses with adobes, clay or dirt moulded [*sic*] and dried in the sun."[4] Under the direction of Heber C. Kimball, members of the Mormon Battalion formed three companies to build a livestock corral. The decision was also made to place houses inside a fort or stockade for

---

1. Historical Department journal history of the Church, 1830-2008; 1840-1849; 1847 July-December; Church History Library, image 173/1034, https://catalog.churchofje suschrist.org/assets/a84034e2-b2c3-43fd-9821-261211f6fda7/0/172, <accessed 19 August 2023>

2. Thomas Bullock journals, 1843-1849; Journal, 1847 June-September; Church History Library, image 46/126, https://catalog.churchofjesuschrist.org/assets/ 4db0776e-281f-4989-aacc-aa20fe1c9cac/0/45?lang=eng, <accessed 19 August 2023>

3. William Clayton, "William Clayton's Journal; a daily record of the journey of the original company of "Mormon" pioneers, 342-343, https://archive.org/details/william claytonsj00clayy/page/340/mode/2up, <accessed 17 August 2023>

4. Howard Eagan, *Pioneering the West, 1846 to 1878: Major Howard Eagan's diary, also thrilling experiences of pre-frontier life among Indian, their traits, civil and savage, and part of autobiography inter-related to his father's*, (Richmond, Utah; Howard Eagan Estate, 1917), image 114/302, https://archive.org/details/pioneeringwest1800began/page/114/ mode/2up, <accessed 24 August 2023>

protection. Due to the shortage of timber in the area, those assembled voted to build the fort and houses from adobe. At this point, roughly 450 settlers were living in the Salt Lake Valley. Work on the fort began immediately, with some of the men making molds for the adobe bricks.[5] Two men, in particular, supported the propriety of using adobe to construct the homes. A.P. Rockwood stated that building a log home with dimensions of sixteen by eighteen feet would cost forty dollars to build, while one built of adobe would cost half as much. Both Samuel Brannan and Lieutenant Willis supported the erection of adobe homes. Brannan noted he had a worker in California who, with three additional men, could build a thirty-square-foot house and put a family in the home in one week.[6]

The adobe fort, with the crudely constructed homes inside, provided a better location to live than covered wagons. The wall stood nine feet high and twenty-seven inches thick on ten acres between present-day "Third and Fourth West and Third and Fourth South." Twenty-seven homes were built to house 160 families during the winter of 1847-1848.[7] As early as the spring of 1849, residents began moving away from the fort, and most people had left their homes in the fort by 1851. The number of people arriving in the valley and the opportunity to live on land provided by their leaders created a short life for the fort. For those who lived within the walls of the stockade, the duration of shelter there was brief. The current location of the ten-acre Pioneer Park in Salt Lake City is the only tribute to those early pioneers.[8]

Shortly after arriving in the Salt Lake Valley, some Battalion members became dissatisfied with the amount of time they had been away from their families, and their dissatisfaction led to action. On 11

---

5. William Clayton, "William Clayton's Journal;

6. Historical Department journal history of the Church, 1830-2008; 1840-1849; 1847 July-December, image 251/1034, <accessed 24 August 2023>

7. Ronald O. Barney, editor, *The Mormon Vanguard Brigade of 1847, Norton Jacob's Record,* (Logan, Utah, Utah State University Press, 2005) 242

8. Brad Westwood, "The Legacy of Salt Lake City's Pioneer Fort," Utah Department of Cultural & Community engagement, https://community.utah.gov/the-legacy-of-salt-lake-citys-pioneer-fort/, <accessed 24 August 2023>

August, about a dozen Battalion men secretly left the valley to travel back to reunite with their families. This group was followed by others.[9] Four different groups were organized by Brigham Young to retrace their steps back over the same trail to Winter Quarters. The first party of four men left the valley on 2 August 1847. The next band, consisting of eleven men, principally a detail of hunters, departed on 11 August. A set of seventy men left on 16 August, while the final group, under the direction of Brigham Young, began the long trek back to Winter Quarters on the 25th of August.[10] Although the trip over the trail east did not run as smoothly for the teams not led by Young as the travel west had, each of the groups eventually arrived back at Winter Quarters. Brigham Young's group arrived about an hour before sunset on 31 October 1847. Young remarked, "We have accomplished more than we expected. The one hundred and forty-three men who started, some of them sick, are all well. Not a man has died, and we have not lost a horse, mule, or ox except through carelessness."[11] Those living in the valley would now fend for themselves without Brigham Young and with new arrivals coming before winter.

EARLY YEARS OF SETTLEMENT

The Salt Lake Valley and surrounding areas were quickly populated by immigrating Saints. In 1847 alone, thirteen additional companies settled in the Utah Territory. The year 1848 saw six pioneer companies enter the Great Basin area. By 1850, an additional twenty-eight pioneer trains had entered the greater Salt Lake City area. Thus, between 1847 and 1850, forty-eight companies of pioneers had left the Midwest for the Salt Lake Valley.[12] The Utah Territory was orga-

---

9. William Clayton, "William Clayton's Journal, 345
10. Ronald O. Barney, editor, *The Mormon Vanguard Brigade of 1847,* 234
11. Historical Deptartment journal history of the Church, 1830-2008; 1840-1849; 1847 July-December; Church History Library, image 793/1034, https://catalog.churchofje suschrist.org/assets/a84034e2-b2c3-43fd-9821-261211f6fda7/0/792, <accessed 14 September 2023>
12. Mormon Pioneer Overland Travel, "The Church of Jesus Christ of Latter-Day

nized in 1850, and peace between church leadership and the government was tenuous from the beginning. As early as 1846, Brigham Young had written President James K. Polk, stressing that members of the church were loyal Americans who desired to establish a US territorial government once they arrived in the Great Basin, which was then held by the government of Mexico.[13] Several times in the intervening years, Young petitioned the federal government to establish a territory, with church members filling political appointments. When these tactics failed, Young threatened to create an independent state.[14]

Five years of sending petitions resulted in a new territorial government. Brigham Young was appointed governor, and several church leaders held key positions in the new administration. However, in 1851, Washington sent several non-Mormons to the new territory. One filled the position of Territorial Secretary, a second served as an Indian subagent, and the third functioned as a federal judge.[15] Officials in Washington did not trust the leaders of The Church of Jesus Christ of Latter-day Saints, and the settlers in the Great Basin felt betrayed by those serving in the federal government. LDS leaders wanted their territorial government to "exercise political, legal, and cultural power for the fullest measure of self-rule in the place they chose to settle."[16] The federal government detested these efforts at theological rule. Shortly after the political appointees arrived in Salt Lake City, an event took place that fanned the flames of resentment on both sides. On 24 July 1851, Daniel Wells, a general in the Utah militia, spoke at a celebration of the arrival of the first band of Mormon pioneers four years earlier. During his remarks, Wells stated the United States was under a curse because of the persecution of the Saints several years earlier. He predicted America would seek

---

Saints," http://history.lds.org/overlandtravels/searchPage?lang=eng#, <accessed 12 March 2023>

13. Ronald W. Walker, "The Runaway Federal Officers," *Journal of Mormon History*, Vol. 39, No. 4, (Fall, 2013), 54

14. Ibid, 3

15. Ibid, 12

16. Brent M. Rogers, *Unpopular Sovereignty, Mormons and the Federal Management of Early Utah Territory*, (Lincoln and London, University of Nebraska Press, 2017), 40-41

help from the Mormons, and they would step forward to the rescue.[17] Shortly after the inflammatory speech, several of the newly arrived appointees fled the state, and the stage was set for increased animosity between church members in Utah Territory and citizens living in the East.

During the first years in the Salt Lake Valley, many residents lived in wagons and tents. Those who lived in cabins found their existence very primitive. Mary Isabelle Horne described the log houses as small and further explained the circumstances in the home, writing, "The ground was full of snakes which used to crawl around our houses, but these were soon killed or frightened away." She further noted, "The timber was so full of bugs that it was years before they were entirely subdued. The mice also were very numerous, running over us by day and by night and destroying considerable clothing."[18] Proper clothing was also in short supply during the early years. Talking about his footwear, Parley P. Pratt noted, "Myself and some of them were compelled to go with bear [sic] feet for several months." Another resident of the valley stated, "I have all the clothes I have on my back."[19] As noted earlier, six pioneer companies settled in the Salt Lake Valley in 1848. The wagon trains led by three men—Brigham Young, Heber C. Kimball, and Willard Richards—brought 2,417 souls to the basin.[20] This brought the total number of residents living in the valley to about 4,800 people at the end of 1848.[21] By the end of 1852, the majority of Saints who had been driven from Nauvoo had migrated to the valley. Then, gatherings began from Great Britain and Scandinavia, which added an average of 3,000 new arrivals each year. Thus, by 1857, about 35,000 Latter-day Saints had gathered in the

---

17. Ibid, 24

18. Glenn Rawson, Dennis Lyman, and Bryant Bush, edited by William G. Harley, *History of the Saints: the Great Mormon Exodus and the Establishment of Zion,* (American Fork: Covenant Communications, 2012), 137

19. Ibid, 138

20. Ronald O. Barney, editor, *The Mormon Vanguard Brigade of 1847, Norton Jacob's Record,* (Logan: Utah State University Press, 2005), 285fn55

21. Leonard J. Arrington, *Brigham Young: American Moses,* (Chicago: University of Illinois Press, 1985), 172

Great Basin. In 1869, three years after the 1866 European migration, about 75,000 Saints were living in the valley and surrounding areas.[22]

During the second year of settlement, hunger continued to plague the Saints living in the Great Basin area. The arrival of 2,000-plus people taxed food supplies to the limit. While the winter of 1847-1848 had been mild, the winter of 1848-1849 was severe. One report indicated that one to three feet of snow covered the ground for several weeks, and the temperature fell to "33 degrees below freezing point."[23] Cattle starved, and people reverted to eating rawhides, sego lilies, and thistles. By February 1849, a committee appointed to investigate the food supply determined there was enough flour on hand to provide about three-quarters of a pound of breadstuffs a day until the next harvest. A voluntary rationing was implemented, and those who had excess food were asked to turn over their surplus to the bishop for distribution to the poor. James Flake wrote in a letter to Amasa Lyman that the price of cattle was extremely high, and the crops on Cottonwood Creek were not "very good." He noted he needed to purchase a large quantity of "provisions for the family."[24] Flake had the means to purchase food for his family. The majority of those living in the valley did not.

The cold winter, nagging hunger, and poor harvest of the preceding fall caused some of the settlers to question whether the Great Basin was the right "gathering place of the Saints." A few began openly declaring that California was superior "in every way" and that the Saints should relocate. Many valley residents moved to California to settle. Evidence indicates that a great majority of those living in Winter Quarters were also skeptical of the future of the Great Basin Colony. However, Brigham Young would not be influenced by the

---

22. Ibid

23. Leonard J. Arrington, *Great Basin Kingdom: an Economic History of the Latter-day Saints, 1830-1900,* (Cambridge: Harvard University Press, 1958), 58

24. Amasa M. Lyman collection, 1832-1877; Correspondence, 1841-1877; Incoming letters, 1849; James M. Flake letter to Amasa M. Lyman; Church History Library, https://catalog.churchofjesuschrist.org/assets/e7634519-c929-4272-bd07-cb54f3099c67/0/0?lang=eng, <accessed 2 May 2024>

views of those who desired to relocate to California. In his typical direct style, he stated, "We have the finest climate, the best water, and the purest air that can be found on the earth; there is no healthier climate anywhere."[25] Brigham Young was unwavering in his determination that the Salt Lake Valley was to be the gathering place for the Saints.

In September 1848, arrangements were made to distribute land to those living in the Salt Lake Valley. Brigham Young and Heber C. Kimball apportioned city lots to applicants, and permission was granted to begin building on the lots. Unmarried men did not qualify for lots, but polygamists were entitled to a lot for each separate family. The initial lots were taken quickly, so a new plat was surveyed, and additional lots were provided for those who were late submitting applications. Plats were divided into nineteen ecclesiastical wards, each under the supervision of a bishop who supervised ditch building, tree planting, bridge construction, and fence assembly.[26] The desire to secure an inheritance of land was paramount for those who settled in the valley. Following an afternoon meeting, men crowded into the office "to secure their inheritances and also to register their names for lots in the big field." On the first day alone, 776 applications were filed, which represented 9,630 acres or fifteen square miles. Of those applying, 240 sought five acres, 335 wanted ten acres, and 153 desired twenty acres. The remaining applications were for fifteen, forty, and eighty acres.[27] People continued to swarm the application office, and by 9 October, 863 people had taken up 11,005 acres of land. The original plan was to lay the city out for ten miles to the north and ten miles to the south.[28] Church leaders distributed relatively small parcels for equality and productive use. This system of land allocation provided the best means to distribute the scarce water supply for the

---

25. Ibid, 60-62
26. Ibid, 51
27. Journal History of the Church, 1896-2001: 1840-1849; 1848 July-December, Church History Library, The Church of Jesus Christ of Latter-day Saints, Salt Lake City Utah (2 October 1848, Book 71)
28. Ibid, 9 October, Book 71

largest number of lots. Fencing could be completed cooperatively, and the city was of sufficient size for appropriate social contact among the residents and to assist in defending against the Native American population.[29]

The continual influx of emigrants created a need to find suitable locations outside of the Salt Lake Valley. Parley P. Pratt guided a large exploring party to southern Utah, which led to the expansion from the Salt Lake base. Soon, settlements were organized in the northern and southern portions of the Salt Lake Valley. Following the founding of these towns in 1847 and 1848, other areas were settled, such as Provo, in the Utah Valley; Nephi, in the Salt River Valley; Manti, in the Sanpete Valley; and Richfield, Cedar City, Las Vegas, and San Bernardino. Eventually, settlements were pushed into southern Colorado, New Mexico, eastern Utah, Idaho, and Arizona.[30] During the first decade following the arrival of the vanguard group to the Salt Lake Valley, nearly 100 communities had been organized and settled. Most of the settlements were made under the direction of Brigham Young, but there were also many self-directed migrations to different locations in the Great Basin.[31] These self-directed settlements were often spin-offs from established towns. Families sought to improve their situation by finding better locations on the fringes of an existing village. The primary justifications for seeking a better setting were housing and food for the family.[32] Thus, a site would need good soil, sufficient water for crops and livestock, grass for grazing, and ample building materials to construct a dwelling.[33] Whether the settlements were by decree from Brigham Young or individuals relocating inde-pendently, there was always a form of religious purification enveloping the settlement process. As one respected historian noted, "Making the waste places blossom as the rose, and the earth to yield

---

29. Arrington, *Great Basin Kingdom*, 52

30. Arrington, *Brigham Young: American Moses*, 171

31. Glen M. Leonard, "Seeking an Inheritance: Mormon Mobility, Urbanity, and Community," *The Journal of Mormon History*, Vol. 40, No. 2, (Spring 2014), 21

32. Ibid, 27

33. Ibid, 30

abundantly of its diverse fruits, therefore, was more than an economic necessity; it was a form of religious worship."[34]

THE MISSISSIPPI COMPANY OF 1848

A second group from Mississippi emigrated west in 1848. Included in this company were four of the original men who left Mississippi in 1846. John Brown, William Crosby, William Lay, and George Bankhead were each part of the first group of Mississippians to travel west. These men also left Pueblo for home in September 1846.[35] The men, women, and children in this company, including the enslaved, left Mississippi for Winter Quarters, Nebraska Territory, 10 March 1848. They walked 800 miles over land and traveled roughly 200 miles on water. The latest arrival to Winter Quarters was John Bankhead and those traveling with him. Included in this party were George Bankhead, John D. Holladay, Francis McKowin, William Lay, Elizabeth Crosby, John Brown, William Crosby, and Eccles Truly. John and Moses Powell entered Winter Quarters 3 May 1848, while Robert Smith and John Lockhart settled at the departure point 17 May 1848.[36] These Mississippi Saints traveled in two companies from Winter Quarters. A smaller group united with Heber C. Kimball, while the large one traveled with the William Richards wagon train.

The Heber C. Kimball wagon train, which included 663 individuals, left Winter Quarters 7 June 1848 and arrived at Salt Lake City 24 September 1848. John and George Bankhead, John Lockhart, and Francis McKowin were anxious to reach the Salt Lake Valley, so they

---

34. Leonard J. Arrington, "Religion and Economics in Mormon History," BYU Studies Quarterly, Vol. 3: No. 3-4 (1961), 7 https://byustudies.byu.edu/PDFViewer.aspx?title=4583&linkURL=3.3-4ArringtonReligion-50d6000c-39cd-45f8-9f93-48ccc8137eda.pdf, <accessed 18 April 2015>

35. John Zimmerman Brown, Autobiography of Pioneer John Brown, 1820-1896, (Stevens & Wallis, Inc. Salt Lake City, Utah 1941), 70

36. Camp of Israel schedules and reports, 1845-1849; Mississippi company, report, 1848 May; Church History Library, image 1/2, https://catalog.churchofjesuschrist.org/assets/b2446f27-3ec6-4bdb-a85e-55298202eaac/0/0, <accessed 17 September 2023>

chose to travel ahead of their Mississippi counterparts.[37] **John Bankhead (1814-1884)**, his wife **Nancy Crosby (1825-1915)**, and John's younger brother, **George Bankhead (1819-1898)**, united themselves with Kimball's company. John and Nancy's three young children accompanied their parents. **Francis McKown (1791-1869)** and his wife, **Margaret Lockhart (1794-1848)**, traveled west with the Kimball company. They were accompanied by their seven children from four to twenty-one years of age. **John Lockhart (1802-1849)**, and his wife, **Margaret Towery (1806-1864)**, headed west for the Salt Lake Valley with their five children, who ranged in age from six years to twelve years old. This group from Mississippi expanded slavery into the Salt Lake Valley. John and Nancy Bankhead brought six unnamed enslaved people with them, and George Bankhead came with five unnamed enslaved people. Francis McKown and his wife Margaret brought two enslaved people.[38] This emigration of enslaved persons and the expansion of slavery into the valley would create challenges for individuals and the church for the next 130 years—until 1978.

The Willard Richards Company departed Winter Quarters on 3 July 1848 and arrived in the Salt Lake Valley between 10-19 October 1848. This group contained a combined total of 526 people when it left Winter Quarters. The wagon train was divided into two companies, one under the direction of Richards and the other led by Amasa Lyman, whose group started west on 1 July 1848. **John Brown (1820-1896)** and his wife, **Elizabeth Crosby (1822-1906)**, along with an eleven-year-old enslaved girl named Betsy, traveled in the Amasa Lyman group. Others in this group included **William Crosby (1808-1890)**, his wife, **Sarah Jane Harmon (1808-1888)**, two children, and five enslaved people. The enslaved were named Violet, age fifty; Rose, age fifteen; Grief, age thirty-two; Nelson, age thirteen; and Henderson, age eleven. The Crosby family matriarch, **Elizabeth**

---

37. Brown, Autobiography of Pioneer John Brown, 1820-1896,, 98

38. Nauvoo (Illinois); City Court. Nauvoo City Court docket book, 1844 February-1845 May , https://catalog.churchofjesuschrist.org/assets/faa87b6f-3343-4486-927a-a5347ebae3c5/0/64?lang=eng, <accessed 23 January 2024>

Crosby (1785-1849), traveled with the group, along with three enslaved: Tobe, age forty-eight; Edy, age twenty-one; and Mary, age eighteen. **William Harvey Lay (1817-1886)** and his wife, **Sytha Crosby (1817-1881)**, traveled with their five children, ranging in age from a newborn to six years old. In addition, they were accompanied by two enslaved girls, Harriet, age twenty-one, and Lucy, age twelve. The last of the Mississippi group transporting the enslaved were **Robert Smith (1804-1891)**, his wife, **Rebecca Smith (1810-1899)**, and their five children, ranging in age from one year to fourteen. Smith took nine enslaved persons with him. Their names were Rande, age twenty-six; Biddy, age twenty-eight; Ellen, age ten; Hannah, age twenty-six; Harriet, under one year old; Ann, age eleven; Lawrence, age five; Nat, age three; and Jane, six months old.[39]

John Eccles Truly (1813-1863) traveled with the Willard Richards Company; he appears to have traveled alone. **Margaret Richey (1804-1852)** traveled with her three children, John, Eliza, and William. Her oldest son, John, was fifteen, Eliza was ten, and William was eight when they began their long journey west. **John Powell (1812 - 1877)**, along with his wife, **Sarah Powell (1813 - 1883)**, traveled to Utah Territory with four children: Lucinda, Robert, William, and Moses. Lucinda was born in 1835, Robert in 1838, William in 1841, and Moses in 1845. **Willis Boss (1827-1887)** traveled alone with the company. **Daniel Tyler (1816-1906)**, a member of the Mormon Battalion, traveled with his wife, **Ruth Tyler (1820-1897)**, and their children Perintha, age nine and Emily, age one.[40] **George Wardle (1820-1901)** and his wife, **Fanny Wardle (1821-1881)**, traveled with the John Brown group in the Willard Richards company. George also participated in the vanguard wagon train in 1847. He returned to

---

39. Camp of Israel schedules and reports, 1845-1849; John Brown's company of 10, report, 1848 June; Church History Library, image 1,2/2, https://catalog.churchofje suschrist.org/assets/82b3a69e-d5ec-4752-a52f-e9816e27c554/0/1,   <accessed   20 September 2023>
40. Ibid.

Winter Quarters before going back to Utah Territory in 1848.[41] **Andrew Lytle (1812-1870)** and his wife, **Hannah Lytle (1816-1893)**, began their travels west with three children: Olive, age eleven; Cyrena, age nine; and Heber, age two.[42] Most of those traveling in this company eventually settled in other areas after arriving in Utah Territory.

Eliza P. Lyman traveled with the Willard Richards company and arrived in the Salt Lake Valley on 19 October 1848. She was the daughter of Edward Partridge and one of the plural wives of Amasa Lyman. She described the experience of childbirth on the plains during her migration from Winter Quarters while also noting why she and other members of the church were fleeing from the United States:

> Platte Dealton Lyman born, at about 6 o'clock on Sunday morning. This is the second son that I have born in a wagon, and I still think it is a most uncomfortable place to be sick in. He was born on the east bank of the Platte River opposite Fort John or Laramie. This journey thus far has not been very pleasant for me, as I have been very nearly helpless all the way, but it is all right, as we are going from the land of our oppressors where we can raise our children in the fear of the Lord and where they will never suffer by the hands of our enemies as we have done.[43]

After arriving in the valley, Eliza described the area, writing, "We are now at our journey's end for the present. The weather is beautiful. The country barren and desolate. I do not think our enemies need

---

41. George Wardle and Family, *Family Search*, Salt Lake City, Utah, https://www.family search.org/tree/person/details/KWJC-HRX, <accessed 20 September 2023>

42. Camp of Israel schedules and reports, 1845-1849; John Brown's company of 10, report, 1848 June

43. Eliza P. Lyman journal, 1846 February-1885 December, 1927; Journal, 1846 February-1885 December; Church History Library, image 41/142, https://catalog.chur chofjesuschrist.org/assets/07e3a758-6ad9-4bf2-8afd-284a31fa49ce/0/41, <accessed 26 September 2023>

envy us, this locality, or ever come here to disturb us."[44] Eliza lived in a room at the fort until they could move to a lot in town.[45]

FOUNDING OF HOLLADAY, UTAH

As of July 2022, the population of Holladay, Utah, stood at almost 31,000 people. The beginnings of this now thriving community took place in the spring of 1848. Many of the Mississippi pioneers of 1847 and 1848 settled in the Cottonwood area, known today as Holladay, in honor of John D. Holladay, which became the first settlement in Utah outside of the fort in Salt Lake City.[46] Many of the pioneers in the early days of Utah drew lots to obtain land. This process was utilized for the settlement of Holladay. John Holladay, Sr. was the captain of ten, so the drawing of lots for property fell to him. William D. Kartchner, a member of the original Mississippi Company, provides his account of the founding of Holladay, Utah:

> Our ten draw was on a high bench six miles S. E. of the city, and our captain, John Holladay Sen., asked permission of his capt[ain] for us to locate three miles further South at a larger spring. It was granted and soon we moved out there and built a row of small houses and fenced a field.[47]

Like for other settlers in the Salt Lake Valley, personal circumstances in the new settlement were often challenging. Regarding his situation, Kartchner wrote, "My rheumatism had now settled in my

---

44. Ibid, 42/142
45. Ibid.
46. Robert Wagstaff Contributor, *Founding of Holladay Utah,*(Pioneer Magazine, 1986, Vol. 33, No. 6, December-January), page 8, https://ia600703.us.archive.org/31/items/SUPPM19866NovDec/SUPPM-1986-6-NovDec_text.pdf, taken from a manuscript written by Emily McDonald in 1915.
47. William D. Kartchner, *Journal of William D. Kartchner,* image 38/102, file:///C:/Users/Owner/OneDrive/Documents/Mississippi%20Company/Mississippi%20Saints%20Company%20Participants/William%20Kartchner%20KWNV-G3N/William%20D.%20Kartchner%20MS%203267.pdf

ankles and feet, and I stood on my knees to do the ditching my portion of that fence."[48]

During this trying time through the early years of the new settlements, food and suitable shelter were extremely difficult to obtain. The Kartchner family ran out of flour, which forced the family to kill their last ox. Kartchner noted he could not slaughter the animal himself, as it was like "killing one of my family." Fortunately, his neighbor George Sparks killed the animal for him. The creature was so malnourished that the meat provided by the ox was "very poor beef but was very good boiled with thistle roots." Eventually, Kartchner located and purchased a bushel of wheat from Parley P. Pratt. Kartchner offered a ten-dollar gold piece to Pratt for payment, but Pratt refused. The conditions in the valley were such that Pratt bartered for one ton of hay for payment—rather than gold.[49] It is possible this is an indication that even church leadership suffered from a lack of basic food items during the years 1848 to 1849.

John Holladay approached William Kartchner in the latter part of June 1848 while eating a small portion of bread. Holladay asked Kartchner, "What under heaven's are we to do for bread?" This was not a rhetorical question but a concern coming from a community leader who was worried about those living in the area. In response, Kartchner told him to cheer up and pointed to a green field of grain growing nearby. Wheat would eventually be available. Kartchner wrote that at the time this interaction happened, he had not tasted "bread or any substance of grain for more than two months." Holladay offered Kartchner a piece of bread, which he eagerly devoured. Corn represented another important source of food. Unfortunately, a member of the community named William Matthews planted his corn too early, and hard frosts hit the area, killing the crops that were already planted. Unlike Kartchner, Matthews had other seeds to plant. Kartchner waited until 10 May 1848 to plant his corn. His corn grew well and produced six to eight ears to the hill, and the harvest was

---

48. Ibid.
49. Ibid.

sufficient for three families in the fall of 1848. Such were the conditions at Holladay, Utah Territory, in the year 1848.[50]

That same year, those living in Holladay also endured an invasion of pests that swept over the Salt Lake Valley. These insects consumed crops desperately needed by the settlers. To save their harvests, many Holladay families turned water on the land to wash the crickets off. In all likelihood, their crops would have been destroyed without the appearance of thousands of seagulls from the shores of the Great Salt Lake to devour the vermin. Once the gulls were full, they winged to the lake, regurgitated their food, and flew back to wolf down more "Mormon crickets," as they came to be known. Many who lived through this experience were convinced their crops would have been lost without the "miracle" of the seagulls.[51] John R. Young, a pioneer of 1847 who lived in the Salt Lake Valley, gave this account:

As the summer crept on and the scant harvest drew nigh, the flight with the crickets commenced. Oh-how we fought and prayed, and prayed and fought the myriads of black, loathsome insects that flowed down like a flood of filthy water from the mountains above. And we should surely have been inundated and swept into oblivion, save for the merciful Father's sending of the blessed seagulls to our deliverance.[52]

Those who settled in the Holladay area—and throughout Utah—faced daily challenges as they eked out a living from the land on the high deserts of the Salt Lake Valley.

---

50. Ibid, 39/102

51. Robert Wagstaff contributor. *Founding of Holladay*, Utah Pioneer Magazine, 1986, Vol. 33, No.6, December - January, https://archive.org/details/SUPPM19866NovDec/page/n7/mode/2up, p. 8, <accessed 1 January 2024> The original article was written by Emily McDonald, and was enclosed in the cornerstone of the old Holladay chapel, which was dedicated 13 June 1915.

52. Historical Department journal history of the Church, 1830-2008; 1840-1849; 1848 January-June; Church History Library, image 757/856, https://catalog.churchofje suschrist.org/assets/23fbe214-4d8a-499c-a07f-93dcef404b38/0/756?lang=eng, <accessed 2 January 2024>

MEMBERS OF THE MISSISSIPPI COMPANY WHO SETTLED HOLLADAY

Many members of the Mississippi Company settled in Holladay during the years 1848-1849. Although several of the original settlers relocated to other localities, the thought of living on land outside of the old fort in Salt Lake City must have been inviting. As mentioned earlier, the male members of the Mississippi Company who are known to have settled in Holladay are the following: George Bankhead, Absolom Porter Dowdle, John Bankhead, John D. Holladay Sr., George Washington Gibson, John D. Holladay Jr., Benjamin F. Matthews, and Allen Freeman Smithson.[53] Two other former members of the Mississippi Company who settled in the Holladay area were William D. Kartchner and George Washington Sparks.[54] The settlers quickly formed a church branch, and John D. Holladay Sr. was selected as the presiding elder. A small meetinghouse served as the venue for the weekly services. However, some members elected to travel to Salt Lake City for Sunday services.[55]

Further growth of Holladay took place in the fall of 1848 with the arrival of another group from the South. Shortly after arriving in the Salt Lake Valley, this group, which included enslaved people, quickly traveled to the Holladay area. John D. Holladay was able to greet his son, John D. Holladay Jr., whom he had not seen for two years. William Crosby connected with his enslaved man, Oscar Crosby, and Green Flake reunited with his enslaver during the fall of 1848. Upon arriving in the Cottonwood area, the Southern pioneers found both Oscar and Green held to their commitment to build log cabins for their enslavers.[56] Many of these Southern settlers were related to each

---

53. John Holladay life story, regarding the settlement of Holladay comes from the book *Holladay-Cottonwood, Places and Faces (Utah)*, by Stephen L. Carr, 1987. PDF account held by Erick Wadsworth.

54. William D. Kartchner, *Journal of William D. Kartchner*, image 38/102

55. John Holladay life story, regarding the settlement of Holladay, p. 3

56. Jay M. Todd, *The Founders of Holladay: A Historical Context*, unpaginated, pdf copy in possession of Erick Wadsworth.

other, and all came from a common Southern culture. In addition, this area south of Salt Lake City itself, near Holladay and Big Cottonwood Creek, presented an excellent location for the enslavers to settle with those who were enslaved. As noted earlier, in the year 1851, a large group of settlers left their homes to settle in San Bernardino, California. Many residents from Holladay, along with the people they enslaved, answered the call to leave their homes for an unknown area in Southern California with Amasa Lyman and Charles C. Rich.[57]

A System of Slavery Permitted in Utah Territory

Sectarian issues between the North and South over the issue of slavery strained the very fabric of the country and threatened to destroy the balance of power within the Union. The Missouri Compromise of 1820 was threatened due to the land acquired during the Mexican American War. Henry Clay of Kentucky proposed resolutions that he hoped would create a path to the resolution of the impasse. His proposals were debated for seven months, but his solutions were voted down. Steven A. Douglas presented alternative legislation, which passed both houses. This legislation became known as the Compromise of 1850, which permitted the formation of the Utah and New Mexico Territories and accepted California as a state. The law was approved 9 September 1850. Utah was officially a territory of the United States, with the necessary territorial leadership. In addition, the right to vote was mandated for every "free white male inhabitant above the age of twenty-one years" who resided in the territory.[58] According to federal law, those who were citizens but did not have white skin were denied the right to vote on a federal level. The need for those who were white-skinned to elevate themselves over those with Black skin continued with the passage of this law.

---

57. Ibid.

58. Milestone Documents, *Compromise of 1850 (1850),* Washington National Archives, unpaginated, https://www.archives.gov/milestone-documents/compromise-of-1850#page-header, <accessed 5 October 2023>

Church members had fled the United States in hopes of settling in a location where they could live their religion without facing the wrath of other citizens. The place where the Saints settled became a part of the United States following the American victory over Mexico. Once again, church members were a part of the country they had been forced to leave. Compounding the challenges faced by church members was the public announcement in 1852 concerning polygamy. The practice of marrying more than one wife has been secretly observed since its inception. Once announced, the public outcry against polygamy compared this practice to "white slavery." The white public viewed women who married a man with other wives as being caught in a web of humiliation and exploitation—even lower than those who enslaved Black people in the South. Debates even took place regarding which was worse—slavery or polygamy. Polygamy was often determined to be worse than Southern slavery.[59]

Historian William Parrish noted that the enslaved people who traveled with their enslavers from Mississippi and other southern states realized *no change* in their status upon arrival in Utah Territory. Furthermore, the forty-plus enslaved people who traveled with the Mississippi company constituted roughly half of the enslaved population that emigrated during the years 1847 to 1848. Parrish also wrote that free Black people lived in the Utah Territory from these early migrations as well. Although many early church leaders expressed displeasure with the institution of chattel enslavement, the legislature of Utah Territory, which was composed of local and general church leaders, enacted a law permitting the enslavement of Black people in the territory during the first legislative session. At the same time, some began to move "within the church to deny Black members full priesthood rights."[60]

Governor Brigham Young officially supported the law permitting Black servitude in Utah Territory. He also declared his belief that

---

59. W. Paul Reeve, *Religion of a Different Color, Race and the Mormon Struggle for Whiteness*, (New York: Oxford University Press, 2015), 140-142
60. William E. Parrish, "The Mississippi Saints," *The Historian, A Journal History*, Vol. L, No. 4 (August 1988), 504

Black people would remain in servitude due to their lineage—as descendants of Cain.[61] The Utah Territory Legislature passed "An Act in Relation to Service" 4 February 1852. The law included provisions for educating enslaved people and punishment for sexual relations between the enslaver and the enslaved. Furthermore, the law addressed the need for "comfortable habitations, clothing, bedding, sufficient food and recreation" for the enslaved people who were brought into Utah Territory. The legislation required that people who were enslaved should receive schooling for "not less than eighteen months between the ages of six and twenty years." Also, any punishment directed at an enslaved person should be "guided by prudence and humanity."[62] Under the direction of Governor Young, the first legislature in Utah Territory passed the enslavement law. Although the wording of the bill appears to seek certain rights for the enslaved, those who lived under the rule of their enslavers in Utah Territory now witnessed the enactment of a law permitting their continued enslavement. Although the law was not as strongly worded as Southern chattel slavery, the results were fundamentally the same. The enslaved noticed little or no improvement from their time in the South.

Although the legislature approved the Act in Relation to Service, one person, Orson Pratt, delivered a strong denunciation of allowing slavery in the Utah Territory. He moved for the bill to be rejected "in toto." During his remarks, Pratt declared:

Shall we then assume the same position in this our young and flourishing territory that those pirates that trafficked in human blood and pulled the slave from his native land, tore him from his wife children

---

61. Church History Department Pitman Shorthand transcriptions, 2013-2023; "The Lost Sermons" publishing project files, 1852-1867; Brigham Young, 1852 February 5; Church History Library, https://catalog.churchofjesuschrist.org/assets/e6a939a0-3402-4771-814d-4eaf2547e613/0/0?lang=eng, <accessed 12 October 2023>
62. Amy Tanner Thiriot, *Slavery In Zion: A Documentary and Genealogical History of Black Lives and Black Servitude in Utah Territory, 1847-1862,* (Salt Lake City, University of Utah Press, 2022), Appendix A, 431-432

and bound him out in foreign country to serve there all the days of his life shall we introduce this evil in our midst no I hope wisdom light and intelligence enough within the bosoms of this honorable council to spurn the idea [with] indignation.[63]

Pratt concluded his speech by stating it was preposterous to him that they should enslave people in the new territory after having church members "damned to slavery" in several states. Binding "the African because he is different from us in color [is] enough to cause the angels in heaven to blush."[64] Pratt's speech had no impact on the outcome of the legislation. The majority of enslaved people who were brought to Utah remained in their trapped condition until their enslavers took them to California, which was a free state. Most of the enslaved taken to California still did not receive their freedom from their enslavers until years after arriving. For those in Utah Territory, it was not until 1862 that slavery was outlawed in all US territories by the federal government.[65]

---

63. Church History Department Pitman Shorthand transcriptions, 2013-2023; Addresses and sermons, 1851-1874; Orson Pratt, 1851-1875; Orson Pratt on slavery, 1852 January 27; Church History Library, https://catalog.churchofjesuschrist.org/assets/b15e28f1-0725-40d8-8607-7554ca44b6e9/0/0?lang=eng, <accessed 5 October 2023>

64. Ibid. This is a transcription by LaJean Purcell Carruth from the papers of George D. Watt. Although words are missing, the feelings of Orson Pratt come across powerfully.

65. Ronald G. Coleman, *Blacks in Utah History: An Unknown Legacy,* (Utah State Historical Society, First Addition, 1976), 117

9

THE SETTLEMENT OF SAN BERNARDINO, CALIFORNIA

SAN BERNARDINO BEFORE 1851

San Bernardino was established in 1851 and is considered one of the oldest towns in the state of California. The first significant group to settle in San Bernardino came from Utah Territory, and most were members of The Church of Jesus Christ of Latter-day Saints. This group stayed until 1857. The population in 1860, just three years after the town's residents departed for their return to Utah Territory, was only 940 inhabitants. By 2023, the population of San Bernardino, California, stands at 223,044 residents.[1] The first non-Indigenous persons to enter the area came in 1769. Gaspar de Portolá traveled from San Diego with a military detachment and marched just west of what is now San Bernardino County. A pack train of 100 mules and supporting livestock accompanied Portolá's band. They found nomadic Native tribes living in a "barren" empire. The land provided needed clothing, shelter, weapons, and medicine.[2]

---

1. San Bernardino, California Population 2023, World Population Review, unpaginated, https://worldpopulationreview.com/us-cities/san-bernardino-ca-population, <accessed 7 October 2023>
2. William Cox Robinson, "The story of San Bernardino County," Family Search

In 1839, a large land grant known as Rancho San Bernardino was issued to Don Antonio Maria Lugo on behalf of his son José del Carmon Lugo. This grant permitted the settlement of San Bernardino and Yucaipa valleys. This first settlement failed.[3] In 1842, Lugo and his wife, Dolores, received a land grant totaling about 35,000 acres. Lugo paid $800 in "hides and tallow" for the land. Several families tried living on the land grant area, but the lure of residing in Los Angeles, where the family had homes, coupled with the harshness of farming and ranch life, led to another failure to settle the land in San Bernardino. In addition, the constant harassment by horse thieves provided another justification to remain in Los Angeles. Therefore, the Lugos family allowed their "trusted ranch foremen" to take care of their land.[4] The 35,000 acres owned by the Lugo family would later play a prominent role in the settlement of San Bernardino.

A number of members of the Mormon Battalion, who received their discharge in Southern California, passed through the San Bernardino area on their return to Utah Territory. These Battalion members were impressed by the warm climate and land, which they believed provided an excellent place for settlement. Several of these men expressed their desire to establish a settlement in the area to Brigham Young, who at first opposed the idea.[5] The most prominent of the Battalion members who looked upon the San Bernardino area as an excellent place to settle was Captain Jefferson Hunt. He and his two sons were among the early enlistees into the Battalion in 1846. While stationed at Los Angeles, Hunt undertook several trips within

---

International, p. 3-4, https://www.familysearch.org/library/books/records/item/810435-the-story-of-san-bernardino-county?offset=, <accessed 7 October 2023>

3. Ibid, 18

4. Nick Cataldo, "How the Lugo family, owners of Rancho San Bernardino, rose to prominence," *The Sun,* unpaginated, https://www.sbsun.com/2023/06/26/how-the-lugo-family-owners-of-rancho-san-bernardino-rose-to-prominence/, <Accessed 17 October 2023>

5. Manuscript histories of the Church in the United States, circa 1910-1971; Manuscript history of Church activities in San Bernadino, California, 1850-1860; Church History Library, image 5/239, https://catalog.churchofjesuschrist.org/assets/2eeb16d3-7205-4aad-add3-2d4d123db880/0/4?lang=eng, <Accessed 17 October 2023>

the Southern California area and from Utah Territory to San Bernardino between the years 1847 and 1851. Hunt was so impressed with the Rancho del Chino, near San Bernardino in Southern California, that he negotiated with the owner, Colonel Isaac Williams, to purchase the property. However, the owner decided to hold on to his land to see if a better offer might materialize.[6] Two apostles of the church were sent to California in 1849. Amasa Lyman and Charles C. Rich were sent to ascertain "the expediency or not of holding an influence in the country."[7] Within twenty months, Rich and Lyman would lead a group from Utah Territory to California to establish a new settlement.

THE FOUNDING OF SAN BERNARDINO, CALIFORNIA

Brigham Young reluctantly gave his approval for a settlement in California at his office on 23 February 1851. One reason to establish a settlement in the San Bernardino area was its relative closeness to San Diego, which offered the opportunity to establish a trail for emigrating Saints and freight to Salt Lake City. In addition to a settlement in Iron County, Utah Territory, San Bernardino would be one of the resting places on the trail from San Diego to the Salt Lake Valley.[8] The First Presidency addressed the justification for the proposed settlement in Southern California in their fifth general epistle to the church on 7 April 1851. The letter covered many key issues for church members, including the need to shun every evil, the ongoing worldwide missionary efforts, and laying the temple cornerstone. The

---

6. A. Harvey Collins, "At the End of the Trail: The Mormon Outpost of San Bernardino Valley," *Annual Publication of the Historical Society of Southern California*, Vol. 11, No. 2 (1919): 70, https://www.jstor.org/stable/41168773?seq=6, <accessed 22 November 2023>

7. Edward Leo Lyman, *The Rise and Decline of Mormon San Bernardino*, (BYU Studies, 29:4) 43, https://byustudies.byu.edu/wp-content/uploads/2020/02/29.4LymanRise-6b2ff325-f11a-4581-ac60-ca88036f01e1.pdf, <accessed 19 October 2023>

8. Manuscript histories of the Church in the United States, circa 1910-1971; image 6/239

motive behind founding a settlement outside of Utah Territory was expounded:

> Elders Amasa Lyman and Charles C. Rich left this place early in March with others, the camp amounting to about one hundred and fifty wagons (some of which were to stop and locate themselves in Iron County) for the purpose of establishing a settlement in the southern part of California, at no great distance from San Diego, and near Williams's ranch and the Cajone pass, between which and Iron Count we desire to establish settlements as speedily as possible, which Elder Lyman will commence on his route, if practicable, so as to have a continue line of stations and places of refreshment between this point and the Pacific, which route is passible [sic] during the winter months.[9]

In the same communication, church leadership requested that the "English Saints" stop emigrating "by the route through the states and up the Missouri River" and wait for further direction from church leadership. This could save "some three thousand miles of inland navigation through a most-sickly climate and country." The First Presidency wanted the new emigration pattern to begin in the fall of 1852. Their desire was to have the emigrating Saints sail from England to Panama, cross over the Isthmus of Panama to the Pacific Ocean, and then sail to San Diego. From there, the emigrants would travel north through San Bernardino and other stopping points to the Salt Lake Valley.[10] However, the hoped-for new emigration pattern did not materialize, and the migration routes remained virtually unchanged for the balance of the worldwide church's emigration years.

President Young and his counselors wrote a letter to Elders Lyman

----

9. Fifth general epistle of the Presidency, 1851 April 7, Church History Library, (Salt Lake City, Utah) CR 1234 1, https://catalog.churchofjesuschrist.org/search/_simple/ Fifth+General+Epistle+of+the+Presidency%2C+1851+April+7/_fdigital@inc:true? lang=eng+%3Flang%3Deng, <accessed 24 October 2023>
10. Ibid.

and Rich on 17 March 1851 detailing what their roles were to be on this mission. They were instructed to "gather the Saints in California around you and build up a stronghold."[11] The two leaders were charged with finding a location that would create rest stops connecting San Diego with the Salt Lake Valley. President Young instructed both men to diligently collect tithing, both in-kind (volunteer labor or goods) and cash. The desired tithing was cash, and the funds were to be forwarded to the "First Presidency, or the Trustee in Trust for the establishment of Zion in this place (Salt Lake Valley)." Finding the best locations to produce cotton, wine, olive oil, and sugar cane constituted another important aspect of their mission to California. The letter closed with a directive to focus on assisting Parley P. Pratt as he undertook his mission to the islands of the Pacific Ocean and "as opportunity presents, plant the Standard of Salvation in every country and kingdom, city and village on the Pacific, and the world over as fast as God shall give you the ability."[12]

MISSISSIPPI SAINTS, AND THE TREK TO SOUTHERN CALIFORNIA

Many people from the South, including those known as Mississippi Saints, accepted the call to settle in Southern California. Among those was William D. Kartchner. During the winter of 1850, Amasa Lyman and Charles C. Rich issued calls for families to leave their homes in the Utah Territory and settle in California. One can imagine the feelings held by many when asked to relocate so soon after arriving in the Salt Lake area. Kartchner noted that when he received the call to leave home, he declined. Upon hearing about Kartchner's refusal to relocate, Amasa Lyman told Kartchner that if he refused to go, Lyman would make sure he would be called on "a worse mission." Kartchner

---

11. Amasa M. Lyman collection, 1832-1877; Correspondence, 1841-1877; Incoming letters, 1850-1852; First Presidency letter to Amasa M. Lyman and Charles C. Rich; Church History Library, image 1/ 4, https://catalog.churchofjesuschrist.org/assets/1aaf2de8-6281-4a11-838b-b786f4b479a6/0/0, <accessed 25 October 2023>
12. Ibid, image 3/ 4

wisely changed his mind and traveled with the original group of settlers. The families prepared for the trip to California during the winter of 1850, and Kartchner was able to meet others who were embarking on the same journey.[13]

According to noted historian Leonard J. Arrington, Southerners comprised only 3 percent of church pioneers who came west, but their accomplishments are remarkable. First, as detailed in this book, they headed west in 1846, which was a full year before Brigham Young's vanguard wagon train. Second, they established the first settlement outside of Salt Lake City, which at the time was called Cottonwood.[14] This early village is now the city of Holladay, Utah. The founding of another settlement outside of Utah was their next commission. The Southern members, along with the enslaved people who traveled with them, began this journey into the unknown. Traveling with William D. Kartchner were Allen Freeman Smithson and John D. Holladay.[15]

An understanding of who took enslaved persons to San Bernardino comes from in-depth research found in the book *Slavery in Zion*, by Amy Tanner Thiriot. Her investigation revealed the widow Agnes Flake owned two individuals: Green and Elisabeth. Green Flake did not travel to California but remained behind with Brigham Young. William and Sarah Crosby took Toby, Grief, Oscar, Nelson, Mary, and Henderson to San Bernardino. Daniel and Ann Thomas removed Philemon and Tennessee to California. Robert and Rebecca Smith (who were not part of the original Mississippi Company of

---

13. Connie Mikesell Hale, 1946-. William D. Kartchner memoirs, undated. , image 55/74, https://catalog.churchofjesuschrist.org/assets/3d2b6c1f-2a28-42c3-a9a8-93c04ba38108/0/54?lang=eng, <accessed 26 October 2023>

14. Leonard J. Arrington, "Mississippi Mormons," *Ensign Magazine*, (June 1977), https://www.churchofjesuschrist.org/study/ensign/1977/06/mississippi-mormons?lang=eng#title1, <accessed 31 October 2023>

15. Amasa M. Lyman collection, 1832-1877; Papers; California papers, 1849-1855; Church History Library, image 21/38,https://catalog.churchofjesuschrist.org/assets/efe74d0e-f6ec-4a48-9e47-bc3b0f728dc5/0/20, <accessed 4 December 2023> Names not appearing on Amasa Lyman's list: Allen Freeman Smithson, Agnes Flake. George and John Bankhead appeared on the list for California, but did not go.

1846) compelled Hannah, Biddy, Ellen, Ann, Harriett, Ann, Lawrence, Nelson, Jane, and Charley to journey with them to San Bernardino. William and Sytha Lay took Hark and Harriet. This forced Hark to leave his wife and one son in Utah Territory. In addition, an unnamed man traveled to California with William and Sarah Crosby. Hark and the unknown man were owned by John Bankhead, who remained in Utah Territory with his brother, George.[16] In total, Southerners took about two dozen enslaved persons with them to San Bernardino.

Brigham Young's strategy for settlements in areas outside of Utah included the calling of a presiding authority, or bishop, to supervise the settlement along with approximately twenty families. To Young's surprise, even though the place to settle was not yet finalized, 437 individuals were waiting at Payson to travel to California. This massive company contained 150 wagons, 588 oxen, 336 cows, twenty-one young stock, 107 horses, fifty-two mules, and 437 men, women, and children. Having so many wanting to leave the Utah Territory angered Brigham Young. He was so upset he did not speak to those who wanted to leave. He later wrote, "I was sick at the sight of so many of the Saints running to California, chiefly after the God of this world." Heber C. Kimball strongly scolded those who were not asked to go and urged them to stay. In addition to the company heading to California, several families were called to settle an "Iron Mission" in present-day Cedar City, Utah. Notwithstanding the irritation felt by President Young and other church leaders, this large company of emigrating Saints, missionaries, and Iron County settlers departed Payson for their various destinations on 24 March 1851.[17]

The entire journey from Payson, Utah, to the San Bernardino, California, area took about eight weeks. The company arrived during the latter part of June and early July. While a few disobeyed counsel to remain in the area, most of the group camped at a site called

---

16. Amy Tanner Thiriot, *Slavery in Zion*, (Salt Lake City, University of Utah Press, 2022), 98-100

17. Joseph Snow Wood, "The Mormon Settlement in San Bernardino, 1851-1857" (Ph. D dissertation, University of Utah, 1968), 71, https://collections.lib.utah.edu/details?id=1461923, <accessed 27 October 2023>

Sycamore Grove to await further instructions. This location, just north of Cajon Pass, provided a well-earned stopping point near their journey's end.[18] One of the first items of business for the newly arrived church members was to select the necessary church leaders. The first conference held in California took place Saturday and Sunday, 5 and 6 July 1851. During the two-day meeting, church members sustained Brigham Young as president of the church and Heber C. Kimball and Willard Richards as his counselors. Charles C. Rich nominated David Seely as president of the organization in San Bernardino. Seely then nominated Samuel Rolfe and Simeon Andrews as his counselors. Rich then nominated twelve men to serve in a group called the high council. These men served under the direction of the newly-called stake presidency in administering to the spiritual and physical needs of those living in the area. William Crosby was called as "acting bishop" for the location. He nominated Robert M. Smith and Albert Collins as his counselors. The voting was unanimous for those nominated.[19]

During this special conference, Amasa Lyman accepted the responsibility as overall leader of the settlement, with Richard R. Hopkins as clerk. Apostle Charles C. Rich was second in command. Both Lyman and Rich addressed the gathering of church members at this special conference. Apostle Rich set forth the reasons for coming to California, which included the need to live righteously and the necessity of "planting a standard of righteousness on the Pacific coast for the gathering of the Saints who had already, and might hereafter come to California." Amasa Lyman's short remarks cautioned the Saints to settle differences within the church and not seek solutions from the laws of the United States. He presented a resolution requiring, "this people as a body to covenant that they will not fellowship

---

18. Connie Mikesell Hale, 1946-. William D. Kartchner memoirs, undated, image 56/74
19. Manuscript histories of the Church in the United States, circa 1910-1971; Manuscript history of Church activities in San Bernadino, California, 1850-1860; Church History Library, image 15/239, https://catalog.churchofjesuschrist.org/assets/ 2eeb16d3-7205-4aad-add3-2d4d123db880/0/14?lang=eng, <Accessed 21 November 2023>

any the belong to the Church who will go to law, brother with brother, seeking redress of the laws of the land." Lyman's resolution carried unanimously.[20] Due to past experiences, which included being forced out of their homes on several occasions, church members held little faith in the laws of the land.

SNAPSHOT OF LIFE IN SAN BERNARDINO, CALIFORNIA 18511857

During the early years, the Saints living in San Bernardino t bonded with each other and with their church leaders. They worked tirelessly to help each other with their daily labors. By working together, the dwellings were quickly constructed, the fort was erected promptly, and plowing and planting the huge fields proceeded with resolve. Togetherness empowered these settlers every day during their first years together, separated by hundreds of miles from their former homes in Utah Territory. Unfortunately, enterprises that begin with great anticipation are often overcome with frustration. For those living in San Bernardino, as the days turned into months and the months turned into years, unanticipated setbacks interrupted the early feelings of camaraderie. Yet, these faithful men, women, and children, including the enslaved individuals they brought with them, worked hard during their years in the area to create a successful settlement.

1851

Due to the failure to acquire Rancho del Chino, church members desperately needed a place to settle. Unexpectedly, the owners of Rancho de San Bernardino, which allegedly contained 80,000 to 100,000 acres of beautiful, rich farmland, now appealed to the settlement leaders. This beautiful land was owned by José Maria Lugo, José Del Carmen Lugo, Vicente Lugo, and their brother-in-law, Diego

---

20. Ibid.

Sepulveda. The three brothers and Sepulveda's wife were children of Don Antonio Maria Lugo, a prominent landowner in Southern California. Amasa Lyman, Charles C. Rich, and other leading men in the colony approached the ranch owners with an offer to purchase. The men agreed to purchase the land for $77,000. Financing was needed to complete the purchase, so a team traveled to San Francisco to secure money. Lyman finalized the obtaining of money for the ranch, while Rich located $8,000 of much-needed provisions for the new colony. Charles Rich returned to the camp first, while Amasa secured $7,000 to bind the sale of the land. The transfer of title for Rancho de San Bernardino began on 22 September 1851 with the transfer of the binder to the landowners.[21]

The new settlers immediately moved out of Sycamore Grove and worked their way down the steep Cajon Pass to the newly acquired land. Dwellings were an urgent need for these new colonizers, and the work progressed rapidly. According to Richard R. Hopkins, the branch clerk, most homes were finished by the 22nd of November.[22] Native tribes living at the Colorado River formed an alliance with Indigenous people throughout the Southern California area, and several settlers in outlying areas were killed. All livestock around San Bernardino were gathered into a central area and watched over by guards. Jefferson Hunt was appointed "commander-in-chief" over all the forces in the area. On Tuesday 25 November 1851, the entire community met and determined to build a fort immediately. The settlement also needed arms and ammunition to fortify itself against a possible attack. The needed guns and ammunition arrived quickly from a garrison stationed at Chino. Both Amasa Lyman and Charles

---

21. Charles C. Rich collection, 1832-1908; Diaries, 1833-1862; Volume 8, 1849 October 8-1851 September 22; Church History Library, images 100-103/110, https:// catalog.churchofjesuschrist.org/assets/29f0479b-c38f-4df9-a095-c94caa189eda/0/99? lang=eng, <accessed 22 November 2023>

22. San Bernardino Branch (California, 1851-1857). 1851 Nov.-1853 Dec. and 1855 July-1856 May. Image 63/149, https://catalog.churchofjesuschrist.org/assets/ 12c1b4e9-61db-407b-8694-e612e9304bb2/0/62?lang=eng, <accessed 22 November 2023>

C. Rich believed that all the current residents of San Bernardino could live within the fort.[23]

The fort stood on eight acres, and the fort's dimensions measured 300 feet wide and 760 feet long. Split cottonwood and willow tree trunks were sunk three feet into the ground, and the edges were tightly joined together. The logs rose a full twelve feet in height. This construction was utilized on the north and south ends, as well as along the east side of the fort. Houses were relocated from various locations in the town and placed with the outer walls of the cabins joined together, creating a tight barrier. Eighty-eight dwellings provided homes for the settlers inside the compound, with additional sleeping quarters made from covered wagon beds. A free-flowing stream ran through the fort to provide water. Captain Jefferson Hunt made certain men stand guard day and night. Although issues continued for several months with the Native Americans in the area, no attack was ever made on the fort. Once the danger ended, people began moving from the fort back to "their own land."[24] The fort's main entrance was on the east side, with the gates opening outward. Gates also stood on the west and north sides. More than 100 families and a significant number of single men lived in the fort during the time of the crisis.[25] The settlers finished the fort fully on 15 December 1851.[26]

In addition to church leadership, San Bernardino needed judges and constables. The local authorities granted permission to elect three justices of the peace and two constables. Accordingly, on 20 November 1851, Jesse D. Hunter of San Bernardino was elected as one of the judges, and Abner Blackburn, formerly of the Mormon Battalion, was elected as one of the township's constables.[27] The new settlers needed food to survive, so raising crops to both consume and sell was a priority of the highest order. By mid-December, a survey of

---

23. Ibid, 65
24. Ibid, 74
25. Manuscript histories of the Church in the United States, image 25/239
26. San Bernardino Branch (California, 1851-1857).image 72/149
27. Ibid, 63

the first wheat field, which contained about 1,300 acres, began. Plowing commenced 18 December 1851. Preparing and planting crops took precedence over almost every other activity and became "the all-absorbing object" of these hearty pioneers. The plows moved "through the ground in all directions." Christmas that year passed by the settlers with little notice due to their focus on basic human needs, such as constructing basic dwellings, building a fort, and preparing the ground for planting.[28] Thus ended the year 1851.

1852

By the end of January 1852, grass in the area still provided little nutrients for the oxen, so the planting lagged behind the desired schedule. The weakened oxen could only plow for half a day. However, it was felt that a few warm days would quickly resolve the issue. By early March 1852, the settlers began replacing their oxen with horses, which improved their ability to prepare and plow the fields.[29] The colonists purchased the horses from cattle drovers who passed through the area and wanted the oxen to add to their herds. The horse trade worked out so favorably the Saints began purchasing wild horses at a low price and training them. In addition, by bartering the oxen for horses, an additional $6,000 was raised to help complete the down payment for the ranch. With this and other funds, Amasa Lyman, Charles C. Rich, and others traveled to Los Angeles to secure the deed for Rancho de San Bernardino on Saturday, 21 February 1852. Lyman and Rich returned on 29 February with the news the warranty deed for the ranch was now secured. The men paid another $18,000 toward the ranch purchase and financed a note of 52,500 dollars for two years.[30]

During the first six months of 1852, those living in San Bernardino were still bonding together to help each other and their

28. Ibid, 73-74
29. Manuscript histories of the Church in the United States, image 38/239
30. San Bernardino Branch (California, 1851-1857).images 80-83/149

leaders. On Monday 23 February 1852, while Amasa Lyman and Charles C. Rich were obtaining the warranty deed for the ranch, the stake president (the church leader for San Bernardino) invited residents to plow and sow their fields in their absence. A "large number" turned out the next day to work on the two men's fields.[31] On 9 March 1852, the survey for the city of San Bernardino began. About the same time, numerous grape vines arrived. During the year 1852, many church members were rebaptized to show their commitment to their earlier baptisms. A council house was erected, and the first conference was held there in April 1852. The town residents completed a road to their source of timber about nine miles away. Construction took 1,000 man-hours to complete. At the same time, school began for 125 children, and a sawmill and a grist mill began operating. Of that time, Richard Hopkins wrote, "Such unanimity of feelings as that which existed among us had scarcely been witnessed in such a degree before."[32]

On 3 June 1852, a ranch owner filed a lawsuit against one of his neighbors. Both parties appeared before the justice of the peace and requested a jury trial. Referring to the event, Richard Hopkins noted, "It is to be hoped that this is the last time our gentile [a term given to those not belonging to the church] neighbors will bring their difficulties to us to settle," showing how church members felt about outsiders.[33] The year's harvest was so bounteous that the citizens built a storehouse to hold the grain. The residents celebrated the Fourth of July on the fifth. The entire town "came together at the big field" for the celebration. The festival developed slowly "until the entire crop of Gen. Rich's wheat was cut, bound, and put up." By mid-July, the colony had surveyed and planted 20,000 vines on forty acres.[34] The rich soil of Southern California brought about an abundant harvest in

---

31. Manuscript histories of the Church in the United States, image 37/239
32. Ibid, images 39-42/239
33. San Bernardino Branch (California, 1851-1857).image 97/149
34. "Latest From San Bernardino," *Deseret News*, Salt Lake City, Utah, 4 September 1852, page 2, https://newspapers.lib.utah.edu/details?id=2578807, <accessed 25 November 2023>

1852, which resulted in a great festival held at the bowery. Leaders offered speeches extolling what the future held for the citizens of San Bernardino.[35] December 1852 brought torrential rains, causing roofs of several adobe homes to collapse. The rains continued for several days, but that did not stop a Christmas celebration with 125 children to take place on Friday 24 December 1852.[36] It was only a year earlier that the settlers "took little notice" of the Christmas season.

1853

The fledgling community continued to prosper, and with that prosperity came a desire for more independence from outside influences. San Bernardino residents wanted their own county. In April 1853, Jefferson Hunt introduced a bill to the state legislature to form San Bernardino County from the eastern part of Los Angeles County. The bill passed, and two members of the church were elected county commissioners. Church members David Seely and Henry G. Sherwood served with John Brown and Isaac Williams. In June 1853, Jefferson Hunt was again elected to the state legislature. Other church members elected include:

- Daniel M. Thomas, County Judge
- Robert Clift, Sheriff
- Richard R. Hopkins, Clerk
- T. S. Sparks, District Attorney
- William Stout, Assessor and Superintendent of Schools
- H. B. Sherwood, Surveyor
- W. J. Cox, Coroner

The new county judge quickly convened a session with two

---

35. Eliza Persis Russell Robbins Crafts, *Pioneer Days in the San Bernardino Valley*, (Redlands, California, 1906), 27-28, https://archive.org/details/pioneerdaysinsan00craf/page/28/mode/2up <accessed 25 November 2023>
36. San Bernardino Branch, California, 1851-1857, 126/149

recently-appointed associate judges. This first session resulted in levying taxes for both schools and county needs, dividing the county into three townships, and designating appropriate voting locations. Shortly thereafter, San Bernardino city was incorporated, Amasa Lyman was elected mayor, and the formation of the city council took place. The leadership of both the county and city was under the control of church members.[37] The demographics of the area began changing. By 1853, several residents of San Bernardino were not members of the church, and like in other areas where church members previously settled, philosophical battle lines were drawn. Another group that met with discrimination from others was Jews. Three Jewish settlers called San Bernardino home during the 1850s. Marcus Katz, Lewis Jacobs, and Isaac R. Brunn all established stores in the town.[38] As the notoriety of San Bernardino's rich land spread to other areas across the county, more newcomers sought it out as an appealing location to settle.

A serious issue facing church members living in San Bernardino in 1853 centered on the amount of land Amasa Lyman and Charles C. Rich thought they had originally purchased. The legal document used by the sellers of the ranch was written in Spanish. Even with an interpreter present during the negotiations, the two buyers overlooked something. The original land grant the pair had purchased actually contained significantly less land than they thought. Instead of 80,000 to 100,000 acres, the total was only 35,000 acres—less than half of what they thought was purchased. The buyers were allowed to select any ground they wished from the land that they had believed they purchased, but the effects were devastating. In addition to the loss of land, this new development would allow large amounts of government land to come to market at a much-reduced price. The entice-

---

37. Joseph Snow Wood, "The Mormon Settlement in San Bernardino, 1851-1857", 120-121

38. Marilyn W. Mills collection, circa 1847-1998; "Building a Community: San Bernardino 1847-1857"; Church History Library, image 208/285, https://catalog.chur chofjesuschrist.org/assets/52c70461-e8a5-44a2-acf4-31992ce9de35/0/207?lang=eng, <accessed 26 November 2023>

ment for church members and "gentiles" to purchase the cheaper government land now became an issue.[39]

In 1853, the wheat crop was hit by rust, which lowered expectations for the year's harvest. Residents still held out hope for a decent harvest to supply bread and a little surplus. The anticipation of a bounteous fruit harvest still ran strong. Three sawmills now operated, and lumber was selling for fifty dollars per thousand board feet. Two runs of burrs to grind the wheat into flour were purchased, and the flour mill anticipated production in short order. At the time, flour sold for six-and-a-half cents per pound.[40] Sadly, in August 1853, Marshall Hunt slipped into a threshing machine, tearing his leg off almost at the knee. The doctor amputated his leg just below the knee with the hope that another surgery would not be necessary. Also in August, Francis Lyman opened a store in San Bernardino.[41]

1854

The *Deseret News* published a glowing report concerning the advantages of San Bernardino. The paper reported the population of the town stood at more than 1,000 inhabitants, with the prospect of continuing growth. The article stated that San Bernardino would become "the most beautiful city of California." The newspaper noted with the formation of the county, the "Mormons have a little government of their own." The size of the new county ran thirty miles east to west and sixteen miles north to south. The article further reported that church members are looked upon as "good neighbors," and "little is said of the polygamic doctrine; and for the sake of peace they will probably not introduce the practice into the state."[42] It may be of

---

39. Edward Leo Lyman, *The Rise and Decline of Mormon San Bernardino*, 47
40. "Extracts," *Deseret News*," Salt Lake City, Utah 29 October 1853, page 2, https://news papers.lib.utah.edu/details?id=2579659, <accessed 27 November 2023>
41. Manuscript histories of the Church in the United States, image 70/239
42. "The Mormons in San Bernardino," *Deseret News*, Salt Lake City, Utah, 16 February 1854, ;page 2, https://newspapers.lib.utah.edu/details?id=2582156, <accessed 27 November 2023>

interest to note that several men living in San Bernardino were living in polygamy. The year 1854 began with Amasa Lyman and Charles C. Rich writing a letter to Brigham Young. Both men suffered from illnesses which they were just not recovering from. A self-inflicted death in the community was brought to light in the letter, which had occurred 28 December 1853. Around 5:00 p.m. in the afternoon, a man walked to a field near his home and swiped his throat with a knife. His son discovered him just before he died. The father "bid him farewell and asked him to take care of his mother." Also in the letter, both men expressed confidence in being able to meet the March payment for the ranch. One of the tasks delegated to Lyman and Rich was the collection of tithing and forwarding it to Utah, particularly tithing received in cash. In the letter, both men noted funds were available for church leadership in Salt Lake City—to use as they see fit.[43]

Concerning the changing population in San Bernardino, a missionary passing through from Cedar City, Utah, expressed a rather scathing view of the dynamics the city now faced, both from church members and others. He wrote:

The city of San Bernardino is situated on a beautiful rolling prairie, with streams flowing through it, fringed with sycamore, black walnut, cottonwood, and many other kinds of trees…. The city is inhabited by Jews, Gentiles, Latter-day Saints and Mormons, making rather a mixed set of inhabitants. I found a good many people here who came from different parts of the Bee Hive State and had become dissatisfied with the affairs in that place and were going to seek happiness in the gold mines of California, where they can be free from the laws of God, and be solely amenable, in time, to the laws of men, which no doubt will be more congenial to their feelings.[44]

---

43. "Letter," *Deseret News*, Salt Lake City, Utah, 16 February 1854, page 3, https://news papers.lib.utah.edu/details?id=2582168&q=San+Bernardino&sort=rel&year_start=1854&year_end=1854, <accessed 28 November 2023>

44. "Extracts," Deseret News, Salt Lake City, Utah, 24 August 1854, page 3, https://

The harvest of 1854 was good, but the settlers were impacted by heavy rain during the month of August. Adobe houses were ruined, grain was destroyed, and the downpour saturated the soil eighteen inches deep.[45] Even with the changes from earlier years, 1854 ended with a bright hope for the future of the settlement.

1855

Challenges continued escalating in Southern California in 1855. Daniel M. Thomas wrote a letter to James Lewis in Parowan describing the economic situation in San Bernardino at the time. He wrote, "One-half of those who have left Utah for this place and upper California would be glad to be back in the valleys of the mountains, trying to get employment but can find none. As regards to money it has left this place entirely." Thomas described the fiscal climate as "very dull."[46] Amasa Lyman wrote about heavy rains that fell in January of that year, yet the plan in 1855 was to plant 4,000 to 5,000 acres of wheat and barley. Referring to those who were settling in the area, he wrote, "few of them have as yet manifested a disposition to renew their identity with the church by rebaptism." However, Lyman also mentioned, "There are some here who love the cause of truth."[47] Both men held a pessimistic view of the economy and of those coming to the area from Utah.

At a special conference held 23 June 1855, David Seeley, the stake president, was tried for striking Lewis Jacobs on the head with a stick

newspapers.lib.utah.edu/details?id=2580768&q=San+Bernardino&sort=rel&year_start=1854&year_end=1854, <accessed 28 November 2023>

45. "From San Bernardino," *Deseret News,* Salt Lake City, Utah, 21 September 1854, page 3, https://newspapers.lib.utah.edu/details?id=2580903&q=San+Bernardino&sort=rel&year_start=1854&year_end=1854, <accessed 28 November 2023>

46. "San Bernardino California, *Deseret News* Salt Lake City, Utah, 11 January 1855, page, 2, https://newspapers.lib.utah.edu/details?id=2581721&q=San+Bernardino&sort=rel&year_start=1855&year_end=1855, <accessed 28 November 2023>

47. "Miscellaneous Correspondence," *Deseret News,* Salt Lake City, Utha, 11 January 1855, page 11, https://newspapers.lib.utah.edu/details?id=2570571&q=San+Bernardino&sort=rel&year_start=1855&year_end=1855, <accessed 28 November 2023>

"that endangered his life." Seeley took responsibility for his actions and pleaded for forgiveness. A motion was passed, and the conference dropped David Seeley as stake president while allowing him to retain his membership. During the proceedings, Charles C. Rich requested that missionaries be sent to various locations in California to "preach the gospel, and endeavor to raise $35,000, the amount yet due on the mortgage." Amasa Lyman would preside over the northern portion of the state, while Rich would supervise the southern part. The next day, attendees voted to "make a last strong effort to meet the debt on the ranch." A total of eighty men volunteered to help raise the money, and they were called to their special mission two days later. On 27 June, Amasa Lyman wrote a letter seeking help to pay off the ranch debt. On a tragic personal note for Charles C. Rich, he buried his son, Morris Macron Rich, Saturday 20 June 1855. Morris suffered for seven weeks before succumbing to his illness.[48] The missions met with limited success in resolving the debt on the ranch. Thus, the settlers decided to send roughly 100 men to the gold mines in California to earn money to eliminate the ranch debt.[49]

The work in the gold mines was to take place until harvest time. Amasa Lyman wrote, "We are expecting to start in the beginning of the ensuing week a party to work in the mines to raise some money between this time and harvest to be applied in payment of the ranch." He continued with further details:

These parties we propose to furnish with supplies from our place and thus turn a portion of our produce into cash and thus make the results of their labor and gold available at the point the means thus procured be applied to the credit of the men furnishing the same, less the amount of whatever we may expend for them in supplies.[50]

---

48. Charles C. Rich collection, 1832-1908; Diaries, 1833-1862; Volume 9, 1855 May 10-July 1; Church History Library, image 29-31,https://catalog.churchofjesuschrist.org/assets/a803d91f-d00b-4e88-ab81-1680be2cb6ac/0/28?lang=eng, <accessed 30 November 2023>
49. Manuscript histories of the Church in the United States, image 100/239
50. Amasa M. Lyman collection, 1832-1877; Correspondence, 1841-1877; Outgoing

The ranch debt hung over Lyman, Rich, and those who lived in the San Bernardino area like a bad dream. Amasa Lyman finished his letter with remarks about the upcoming harvest. He noted the harvest appeared satisfactory and covered "some six thousand acres."[51] Considering the handiwork involved with such a large acreage, the resilience and tenacity of these pioneers and the enslaved people who lived with them remains an extraordinary accomplishment.

1856

The Pacific Circus came to San Bernardino in early February 1856, bringing a nice diversion from the daily struggles. Large crowds attended the performances. Later in the month, Charles C. Rich again stated the need to remove the debt against the ranch. Rich told those gathered that he would take livestock as partial payment for the land, and where a deed could not be presented, he would provide a bond for the deed. A special conference was held in mid-March in which ten individuals were cut off from the church. During the conference, Charles C. Rich warned those attending of the need to "live up to their covenants," or they could be removed from church membership as well. As the conference continued, several men were called on missions to various parts of the world, as well as to California. The need to pay down the debt was again presented. During one of Rich's talks, he told the congregation he would shortly be leaving San Bernardino for a mission to Europe. He did not leave the area for several more months. An opposition political party began declaring their desire to break San Bernardino "of the Mormon rule." Not surprisingly, an election was held 5 May 1856, and members of the church were elected to the various city posts—by an almost unanimous vote. The opposing party only received twenty-six votes in the

---

letters, 1845, 1850-1875; Amasa M. Lyman letter to Brigham Young; Church History Library, images 5/8, https://catalog.churchofjesuschrist.org/assets/46062ad9-074b-4d73-a618-24fc272180eb/0/4, <accessed 30 November 2023>
51. Ibid.

election, which fanned the ever-increasing negative feelings toward church members.[52]

California experienced a drought in 1856. The weather throughout the state was excessively hot, which dried out the grass cattle normally used for grazing. Large herds of cattle were driven into the mountains to keep the livestock from starvation. Harvest throughout the state was expected to be light, except for barley and corn. The same drought conditions were experienced in San Bernardino as well.[53] The first horse race in San Bernardino took place Saturday, 23 August 1856, which was well-attended. According to the local scribe, "thousands of dollars changed hands" during the races. A stabbing took place in San Bernardino on the night of 27 August at a local restaurant. The person responsible for the stabbing worked on a surveying crew in the area.[54] On 22 October 1856, a group of citizens living in San Bernardino formed a library association. A.P. De Lind served as librarian, and Daniel M. Thomas as assistant librarian.[55] An interesting side note concerning a particular resident of San Bernardino comes from Brigham Young. During a discourse delivered on 28 September 1856, he talked about Sister Turley and her husband, who worked all week only to walk weekly to church and back home—a distance of twenty or thirty miles—to attend their meetings.[56]

With all the challenges facing members of the church who settled in San Bernardino, a newspaper editorial presents a view of how

---

52. Manuscript histories of the Church in the United States, images, 100-117/239
53. "San Bernardino, CA," *Deseret News*, Salt Lake City, Utah, 2 July 1856, page 5, https://newspapers.lib.utah.edu/details?id=2573162&q=San+Bernardino&sort=rel&year_start=1856&year_end=1856, <accessed 1 December 2023>
54. San Bernardino Branch (California, 1851-1857). 1856 July-1857 Dec. , image 12/96 https://catalog.churchofjesuschrist.org/assets/12c1b4e9-61db-407b-8694-e612e9304bb2/1/13?lang=eng, <accessed 1 December 2023>
55. "Correspondence," *Deseret News*, Salt Lake City, Utah 2 January 2815, page 8, https://newspapers.lib.utah.edu/details?id=2571854&q=San+Bernardino&sort=rel&year_start=1856&year_end=1856, <accessed 1 December 2023>
56. "Remarks," *Deseret News*, Salt Lake City, Utah, 8 October 1856, page 2, https://news papers.lib.utah.edu/details?id=2574081&page=2&q=San+Bernardino&sort=rel&year_s tart=1856&year_end=1856, <accessed 1 December 2023>

those with this strange religion were viewed by others. An article published 20 December 1856 in the *Los Angeles Star* offered a pleasant view of the city. Following a trip to the city, the following thoughts appeared in this Los Angeles paper: "We were glad to find that considerable progress has been made in city improvements since the period of our former visit. Several new stores have been erected; the old one have been improved, and the number of persons engaged in trade considerably increased." The paper noted the current population of the city stood at "about 3,000." The weekly also reported the mortgage against the ranch property was now "released from all liabilities." The harvest of 1856 produced 30,000 bushels of wheat, 15,000 bushels of barley, 7,000 bushels of corn, and 200 bushels of oats. Due to the drought, the potato harvest failed. The same period witnessed the production of 1,700 pounds of butter, 5,000 pounds of cheese, and 13,000 dozen eggs. San Bernardino County now contained seven sawmills, one grist mill, and two shingle mills that cut 500,000 wood shingles.[57] Against overwhelming odds, remarkable progress had been made during these first years in Southern California.

1857

A "most violent earthquake" struck Southern California on Friday, 9 January 1857. One individual described how walls in most of the houses in the San Bernardino area cracked, and water in streams flew several feet in the air during the event. Trees in the area swayed back and forth "as if in a strong gale." The earthquake struck with two major shocks. One lasted two minutes, and the second persisted for about one minute.[58] The local recorder in San Bernardino reported a

---

57. "San Bernardino," *Los Angeles Star,* Los Angeles, California, 20 December 1856, Volume VI, Number 32, https://cdnc.ucr.edu/?a=d&d=LASTAR18561220.2.11&e=-------en--20-LASTAR-1--txt-txIN-San+Bernardino------, <accessed 2 December 2023>

58. "Correspondence," *Deseret News,"* Salt Lake City, Utah, 11 February 1857, page 5, https://newspapers.lib.utah.edu/details?id=2575174&q=San+Bernardino&year_start=1857&year_end=1857&facet_paper=%22Deseret+News%22, <accessed 2 December 2023>

partial eclipse of the sun on 25 March 1856. That same day, those opposing the church increased their agitation of members. One group of apostates (former church members) allegedly induced a group of Indigenous people living in the area to share leftover spoils with them once the Mormons were driven from the state. Louis Rubidoux, a wealthy landowner who lived about ten miles from San Bernardino, also began accepting some of the arguments of the apostates, which hardened his feelings against former friends.[59]

Several situations arose that created divisions between church members and their neighbors. One event happened when a former member of the church homesteaded on property he believed was not owned by Amasa Lyman and Charles C. Rich. Jerome Benson arrived at San Bernardino in 1854 and settled on property roughly three miles southeast of the city, which he believed was on government land. However, he had settled on privately owned property, so he was ordered to leave by the owners. He refused, so the sheriff was called to evict him. Benson called on his friends, whom church members called apostates, to help him. Earthworks were pitched around his house, and the group armed themselves for resistance. A cannon that had been used at the previous year's Fourth of July celebration was also brought to Benson's home. Although no fight is known to have taken place at Benson's home, the rift between those of the Independent Party (the apostate group) and church members continued to widen. Benson's home became known as Fort Benson. In the end, Benson gained possession of the land and received a clear title.[60]

The first stage of failure for the church settlement in San Bernardino commenced in 1857. The most serious blow to the settlement came with the departure of Amasa Lyman and Charles C. Rich. The burden these two men felt during their efforts to create a successful settlement in Southern California seems almost immeasur-

---

59. San Bernardino Branch, 43/96

60. John Brown, James Boyd, *History of San Bernardino and Riverside Counties;* v. 1, Digitized by Family Search International, page 47, https://www.familysearch.org/library/books/viewer/791081/?page=79&viewer=picture&o=info&n=0&q=#page=78&viewer=picture&o=info&n=0&q=, <accessed 3 December 2023>

able, but a summons from Brigham Young (the man sustained by Lyman and Rich as a prophet) to leave San Bernardino for Europe left little choice. They would leave San Bernardino as instructed. Their departure virtually sealed the fate of the fledgling community. As the hostility between members of the church and other settlers increased, the end of this settlement seemed inevitable. Amasa Lyman and Charles C. Rich began the long, wearisome journey from San Bernardino on Saturday, 18 April 1857 at 3:00 p.m.[61] The hole Lyman and Rich left behind is felt from the following note, written just two days following their departure: "Our city looks lonesome and deserted in consequence of the absence of Br. Lyman and Rich and those who accompanied them."[62]

The final blow to the settlement came when federal troops were ordered to Utah to put down what was considered open rebellion. With the dispatch of federal troops, Brigham Young issued a call for all settlements outside of Utah to return. Many members obeyed the recall directive and sold the property they worked so hard to improve —in most cases, at a considerable loss. In one instance, "a good four-room house well located and furnished, was sold for $40.00—with a buggy, a cloak, and a sack of sugar thrown in for good measure."[63] The pioneers who arrived in 1851, filled with confidence and faith that their settlement would succeed were now buried under an avalanche of negative news from Utah, the departure of their two beloved leaders, and the increasing animosity from their neighbors. Among those faithful pioneers stood the Mississippi Company and the enslaved who left their homes as early as April 1846.

MISSISSIPPI SAINTS

In April 1851, Charles C. Rich, who owned slaves, listed the names of

---

61. San Bernardino Branch, 48/96

62. Ibid, 49/96

63. L. A. Ingersoll, *Ingersoll's Century Annals of San Bernardino County 1869-1904* Los Angeles, L. A. Ingersoll, 1904, page 147-148, https://archive.org/details/ingersollscentur00ininge/page/n7/mode/2up?ref=ol&view=theater, <accessed 4 December 2023>

those who would "be subject to the council of Elders Lyman and Rich" during their time in Southern California. In addition to the Mississippi group and those not members of the church, Rich listed the names of five enslaved people. Oscar, Grief, Toby, Nash, and Phil Crosby each had their names listed on the document. This is one of the few known times that the names of enslaved individuals were acknowledged in a positive light.[64] As noted earlier, a fort was built soon after the arrival of the settlers in San Bernardino. Several of the Mississippi Company lived inside the fort, including John D. Holladay, William D. Kartchner, William Crosby, Daniel M. Thomas, Agnes Flake (widow), and "Lizzie Flake," an enslaved woman. Thomas's records indicate Crosby lived in four cabins; it is likely slaves lived in the one not occupied by Crosby, his wife, and his family. Thomas's father-in-law, Jacob Casteel, also lived inside the fort. Most of the people listed above had families. Several individuals and families elected to live outside the fort. Joshua Casteel, Margaret Casteel Thomas's brother, made camp outside the fort.[65]

Several of the Mississippi Company served in leadership positions within the local government or the church. William Crosby served as a bishop from the first conference held at Sycamore Grove in 1851 until he left for Utah with others who responded to Brigham Young's directive to return. Crosby often spoke at the weekly Sunday meetings. His wife, Sarah Jane Harmon, possessed a remarkable singing voice and often shared her talent with others. Crosby was elected as a member of the three-man board of county supervisors, and he was part owner in a sawmill. In 1853, the citizens of San Bernardino County elected Daniel M. Thomas as the county judge.[66] At a conference held in October 1855, Thomas was serving as a counselor to San

---

64. Charles C. Rich collection, 1832-1908; Papers, 1832-1908; California papers, 1851-1856; Church History Library, images 1-3/18, https://catalog.churchofjesuschrist.org/assets/ce36fd4c-5107-468d-8ed6-48d773b49223/0/0?lang=eng,   <accessed 5 December 2023>

65. John Brown, James Boyd, *History of San Bernardino and Riverside Counties;* v. 1, image 73/639

66. L. A. Ingersoll, *Ingersoll's Century Annals of San Bernardino County 1869 – 1904,* page 141

Bernardino stake president William J. Cox. William Crosby was sustained as "the Presiding Bishop of the Stake," and members upheld John D. Holladay as a member of the high council.[67] Although not among those who settled in San Bernardino, Absolom Porter Dowdle spoke at a special meeting, which was packed with congregants, on Tuesday, 7 December 1852. He was traveling through the area on his return from a mission to Australia.[68] Dowdle crossed the plains in 1846 with the original Mississippi Company.

Other less well-known members of the Mississippi Company who lived in San Bernardino were likely rebaptized as a symbol of their continued commitment to the church. Attending Sunday services, fasting, and praying daily were likely an integral part of their worship. Their daily life focused on survival. They would have prepared, plowed, planted, and harvested crops from the large fields for the entire settlement and grown their food for their families. At harvest time, all colonists were assigned to labor in the communal fields.[69] They would have been among those who guarded the fort during times of trouble. These settlers would have volunteered for military duty, helped build the road to the timber, and assisted in building the sawmills, grist mills, and other needed structures for the community. The labors of these devoted colonists were a crucial component of the success of San Bernardino during the early years.

Of equal importance to the success of San Bernardino were the enslaved people who were taken from Utah, in most cases without their consent, to settle in Southern California. Concerning the impact of Black pioneers on western migration and growth, African American Studies professor Ronald G. Colman wrote the following:

---

67. "Minutes," *Deseret News,* Salt Lake City, Utah 31 December 1856, page 5, https:// newspapers.lib.utah.edu/details?id=2574816&page=2&q=San+Bernardino&year_s tart=1856&year_end=1856&facet_paper=%22Deseret+News%22,,   <accessed   5 December 2023>

68. Ibid, image 60/239

69. *The San Bernardino County Sun,* September 30, 1951, Page 36. via Newspapers.com (https://www.newspapers.com/article/the-san-bernardino-county-sun-mormon-col/ 136388864/, <accessed 7 December 2023> clip page for Mormon Colony in Sharp Contrast to the Mother Lode by user erickwadsworth

"Black pioneers were both slave and free, Mormon, and non-Mormon. They shared the experience of journeying to a new land and participating in its settlement and subsequent development."[70] One enslaved member who lived in San Bernardino by the name of Grief Embers held a position of trust in the colony. "Uncle" Grief Embers, who was enslaved by William Crosby, had the responsibility to blow a large horn to either warn the colony of an impending crisis or to call the entire community to gather at a specific location. Grief "used his horn to summon men from the grain fields, to call meetings and seems to have enjoyed his unique role."[71] A written description of Grief's personality is as follows:

> Grief was certainly not somber or withdrawn, by all accounts, he was one of the most liked members of the community. In fact, the pioneers called him "Uncle Grief," a term of affection reserved for elderly or respected persons.... After the Mormons left, he and his family used the name Embers.[72]

Independence Day 1852 was "ushered in by the sounding of the Bishop's horn (Uncle Grief's six-foot instrument), at which signal the entire strength of the camp came together to celebrate the patriotic day."[73] In September 1871, Grief sought the office of Coroner of San Bernardino. He ran against two other men and came in second.[74]

While living in Mississippi, Elizabeth "Lizzy" Flake was taken

---

70. Ronald G. Colman, "Blacks in Utah History: An Unknown Legacy," Utah Department of Cultural & Community Engagement, (1976) page 116, https://collections.lib.utah.edu/ark:/87278/s6wd3zxj/420661, <accessed 7 December 2023>

71. *The San Bernardino County Sun*, September 30, 1951, Page 36. via Newspapers.com (https://www.newspapers.com/article/the-san-bernardino-county-sun-mormon-col/136388864/, <accessed 7 December 2023>, clip page for Mormon Colony in Sharp Contrast to the Mother Lode by user erickwadsworth

72. Marilyn W. Mills collection, circa 1847-1998; "Building a Community: San Bernardino 1847-1857"; Church History Library, image 218/285, https://catalog.churchofjesuschrist.org/assets/52c70461-e8a5-44a2-acf4-31992ce9de35/0/217?lang=eng, <accessed 7 December 2023>

73. Ibid, 219/285

74. Ibid, 227/285

from her family at the age of four and enslaved. Lizzy lived with her enslaver, Agnes Flake until Agnes passed away in 1855. One account of Agnes's death details that Elizabeth "slept by the side of her bed and kept watch over her, waking up with a word when anything was wanted."[75] Thus, if the account is accurate, Elizabeth watched over her enslaver through the end of the woman's life. Due to Agnes's illness, Elizabeth cared for her three sons during her time in San Bernardino. Elizabeth also made adobe bricks used for housing in the fort. She alerted other enslaved people that they were being held illegally in San Bernardino. Elizabeth married Charles H. Rowen, and the marriage was formalized in 1867. Together, they brought three children into the world. Their daughter, Alice Rowen Johnson, became one of the first Black people to receive her college degree, and she taught in nearby Riverside, California. Elizabeth selflessly cared for her enslaver's children, raised three of her own, and never stopped helping other enslaved persons find their freedom. Lizzy and Charles "became leaders in the community and fought slavery."[76] Lizzy passed away at the age of ninety-seven at her home on I Street. She was "highly esteemed" by the community.[77] Her journey from enslavement at the age of four to freedom, marriage, children, and property ownership stands as a witness to her indomitable spirit. She and other enslaved people somehow found freedom in the face of overwhelming odds.

When the pioneers crossed the state line into California, the enslaved individuals who traveled with the company were now free. However, enslavers were not anxious to lose their free labor. Thus,

---

75. Flake family history book, page 288, Family Search, https://www.familysearch.org/photos/artifacts/131588284?p=56238632&returnLabel=James%20Madison%20Flake%20(KWJ5-CQP)&returnUrl=https%3A%2F%2Fwww.familysearch.org%2Ftree%2Fperson%2Fmemories%2FKWJ5-CQP, <accessed 9 December 2023>

76. T. Michelle Tucker, "Lizzy Flake Rowen," *Hutchens Museum/Institute*, https://johnhutchingsmuseum.org/lizzy-flake-rowan/, <accessed 9 December 2023>

77. *The San Bernardino County Sun*, March 31, 1908, Page 4. via Newspapers.com (https://www.newspapers.com/article/the-san-bernardino-county-sun-obituary-o/136538187/, <accessed 9 December 2023> clip page for Obituary of Elizabeth Flake Rowen, by user erickwadsworth

several slave owners used fear of freedom to keep enslaved people. Despite this, over time, the people who had been enslaved found freedom and left those who had owned them. With freedom, husbands and wives would no longer be forcibly separated. As noted earlier, Hark Lay was torn from his wife and son because his enslaver lived in Utah and chose not to settle in San Bernardino. In 1851, Robert Smith brought twelve enslaved individuals from Utah to San Bernardino. Five years later, in 1856, a disaffected Smith decided he would move to Texas with the enslaved individuals. During legal proceedings, Smith told the court he had supported his enslaved individuals and had exerted "no greater control than his own children."[78] Smith was not allowed to take them out of the state. One quote from the judge sums up how the law viewed the issue: "If a woman might deliberately surrender herself to slavery, she could not carry her offspring to that fate. It is the first grand thought of the Constitution —LIBERTY IS INALIENABLE."[79] At last, an isolated group of enslaved people, after decades of confinement, could now experience the sweet taste of freedom. The departure of the white settlers in 1857 allowed the formerly-enslaved to experience life as never before. They became involved in the communities where they lived, purchased homes and property, and relished the joy of freedom—something they had never experienced.

---

78. "Suit For Freedom," *Los Angeles Star*, Volume 5, Number 38, 2 February 1856, https://cdnc.ucr.edu/?a=d&d=LASTAR18560202.2.11&e=-------en--20-LASTAR-1--txt-txIN-Suit+For+Freedom-------, <accessed 9 December 2023>
79. Marilyn W. Mills collection, circa 1847-1998; "Building a Community: San Bernardino 1847-1857," image 239/285

1 0

THE MISSISSIPPI COMPANY
AND THE COTTON MISSION

Eight members of the original Mississippi Company participated in the Cotton Mission in the southern Utah Territory. The families of William Harvey Lay, William Crosby, Daniel Monroe Thomas, Allen Freeman Smithson, his brother William, William Matthews, William D. Kartchner, and George Washington Gibson each lived in the Cotton Mission area during a portion of its existence. The first seven men and their families were involved with the San Bernardino colony, and when Brigham Young ordered families to return, they chose to live in the southern Utah Territory. William Lay and William Crosby selected Santa Clara as the place to settle. Daniel Monroe Thomas, William D. Kartchner, and William Matthews each elected to live in Beaver City. Allen and William Smithson resided in Washington Village, near the current city of St. George, Utah. Evidence indicates George Washington Gibson and his family moved to Duncan's Retreat, near the Virgin River, about 1862.[1] These

---

1. Locations of the Mississippi Company who settled in southern Utah Territory located 1860 federal census records through "Family Search" using ID number as follows: William Harvey Lay (LLQF-Y3B), William Crosby (KWV7-BJY), Daniel Monroe Thomas (KWVP-8S3), Willam Mathews (KWVW-8SX), William D. Kartchner (KWNV-G3N), Allen Freeman Smithson (L5R3-PBF), William Cox Freeman (K2HF-

devoted Saints from Alabama and Mississippi left their homes in the South eleven years earlier to find their Zion in the West. Since arriving in Utah in 1847 and 1848, the members of this group answered Brigham Young's directive to establish settlements throughout the western United States. More details about the lives of the members of the Mississippi Company and their time in the Cotton Mission will be shared in a later chapter.

WHY A COTTON MISSION?

Following their eviction from Nauvoo, Illinois, the distrust toward those who were not members of the church ran deep within the circles of church leadership, as well as the overall church membership. Just days after the arrival in the Salt Lake Valley of Brigham Young's vanguard wagon train, he stated the following to a crowd of church members:

> We do not intend to have any trade or commerce with the Gentile world, for so long as we buy of them we are, in degree, dependent upon them. the Kingdom of God [cannot] rise independent of the Gentile nations until we produce, Manufacture, and make every article of use, convenience, or necessity among our own people.... So we shall need no commerce with the nations. I [am] determined to cut every thread of this kind and live free and independent, untrammeled by any other of their detestable customs and practices.[2]

The person who was revered as a prophet by his followers thundered after only a few days in the valley that church members should never support those who were not members of the church. The church was now in a geographic location that would allow its members to become an independent society, which, up to this point,

---

WCJ), George Washington Gibson (KWJ1-43B), https://www.familysearch.org/en/, <accessed 26 January 2024>
2. Ronald O. Barney, editor, *The Mormon Vanguard Brigade of 1847, Norton Jacob's Record,* (Logan, Utah, Utah State University Press, 2005) 229

had been impossible. Business interaction with "Gentiles" was unacceptable. Indeed, every article of food, clothing, or shelter should be grown, crafted, or constructed in Utah Territory. The desired self-sufficiency now seemed attainable.

According to noted historian Leonard J. Arrington, during the first six years of the 1850s, the establishment of a self-sufficient society seemed practicable. Settlements were expanding, and the Saints were obtaining a level of independence from Gentiles. The future appeared bright. Then, several setbacks blocked the Saints' path to total independence. First, the undertaking of iron and sugar production during the early 1850s failed. Next, the invasion of grasshoppers and the drought of 1855 and 1856 significantly reduced the anticipated harvest, and the brutal winter that year destroyed large amounts of livestock. The strong language of the Reformation movement by church leaders may have influenced some church members to participate in the ill-fated Mountain Meadows Massacre. The final blow came with the arrival of federal troops in Utah Territory and the removal of Brigham Young as governor.[3] Even though the total independence from the world they had hoped for fell short of expectations, the necessity of self-sufficiency continued to hold center stage. Planting, growing, and producing cotton remained a top priority for church leaders. Thus, the movement to the southern portions of Utah continued.

Exploring Southern Utah

Far fewer Mississippi Saints served in the southern Utah Territory's cotton mission than San Bernardino. However, recognizing the service of those who scratched out a living in the deserts of southern Utah is crucial to understanding those faithful men and women who left their homes in 1846. The unplanned beginning of the Cotton Mission in southern Utah Territory commenced shortly after the

---

3. Arrington, Leonard J. *Brigham Young: American Moses*, (Chicago, University of Illinois Press, 1985), 300

arrival of Brigham Young's vanguard wagon train in July 1847. Days after arriving in the Salt Lake Valley, Young determinedly asserted that he wanted "every hole and corner from the Bay of San Francisco to the Hudson Bay known to us." Young's desire to establish settlements for the thousands of Latter-day Saints who would emigrate to their hoped-for Zion took top priority. He knew preparing the area for those who would follow during the next two decades demanded swift action.[4] Months later, Young offered a more subdued but no less focused view of the next steps needed for the western settlement of church members by writing, "We soon hope to explore the valleys three hundred miles south and also the country as far as the Gulf of California with a view to settlement and to acquiring a seaport." One key component of Brigham Young's actions to locate areas for future settlement was the formation of a southern exploration group under the direction of Apostle Parley P. Pratt in November 1849.[5]

John Brown, the driving force of the original 1846 Mississippi Company, served under Parley P. Pratt on his exploration of southern Utah. Parley P. Pratt organized the group at Brown's home on Thursday, 23 November 1849. John Brown was called to captain fifty for the organization. The group obtained sufficient livestock and wagons for their supplies, as well as riding and pack animals to explore areas where wagons could not travel. The company was well-armed and carried enough items to trade with the Indigenous people they would encounter. Pratt and his band left Brown's house for the unknown lands of southern Utah on 24 November 1849. On the first night out, snow covered the ground to a depth of over eight inches. With much difficulty, they reached the Utah Valley the next day. Following several days of snowstorms, Pratt's party reached Juab Valley, near present-day Nephi.[6] The journey of discovery by this fifty-man company likely influenced the settlement of many locations

---

4. William B. and Donna T. Smart, *The 1849 Southern Exploring Expedition of Parley P. Pratt,* p. 125, file:///C:/Users/Owner/Downloads/pratt-exploration1.pdf, ,accessed 8 January 2024>

5. Ibid, 126.

6. John Brown, 1820-1896. John Brown journal extract , image 1/56, https://catalog.

found along their path.[7] In addition to John Brown, several members of the 1846 Mississippi Company participated in this exploration, including William Matthews, John D. Holladay, and John Bankhead.[8] On 26 December 1849, a contingent of twenty men departed from the larger group to explore the Rio Virgin and the St. George areas before reuniting with their companions on 8 January 1850.[9] In just a few short years, hundreds of missionaries would be called to settle in the far south of Utah Territory.

Settlement of Parowan, Utah

The settlement of a location further south in Utah Territory came as a direct result of Pratt's exploration of southern Utah in the winter of 1849 to 1850. Less than one year following Pratt's journey of discovery, an article appeared in the *Deseret News* on 16 November 1850, listing the names of 100 men needed to settle an area approximately seventy miles north of the current city of St. George, Utah. George Albert Smith and Ezra T. Benson served as the leaders of this mission south. Those participating in the journey were to be ready to begin their trek south by 1 December 1850. Carpenters, mill wrights, shoemakers, joiners, blacksmiths, sawyers, and one surveyor were needed to participate in the new settlement. Seeds for planting, plows, spades, shovels, and hoes constituted the basic items needed for survival during the winter months. Large quantities of wheat, beef cattle, potatoes, radishes, beets, and squash provided food until crops could be planted and harvested.[10] Many of these courageous pioneers left their homes after less than two years in the Salt Lake Valley and traveled

---

churchofjesuschrist.org/assets/baaaf846-47f1-4a83-b11b-b54d712f6bb5/0/2?lang=eng, <accessed 8 January 2024>

7. Rick J. Fish, *The Southern Utah Expedition of Parley P. Pratt 1849-1850,* unpublished Master's Thesis, image 144/224, file:///C:/Users/Owner/Downloads/The%20Southern%20Utah%20Expedition%20of%20Parley%20P.%20Pratt_%201849-1850.pdf

8. Ibid, 124/224

9. Ibid, 126/224

10. "Untitled," *Deseret News*, Salt Lake City, Utah, 16 November 1850, page 2, https://newspapers.lib.utah.edu/details?id=2569019, <accessed 10 January 2024>

over 230 miles south to establish the town of Parowan, Utah Territory.

Details of those who traveled south indicate the diversity of the group and the sheer size of the organization. Two carriages and 101 wagons transported the group to the settlement. A total of 169 individuals, including 120 men, thirty-one women over the age of fourteen, and eighteen children under fourteen, worked their way to southern Utah Territory. Livestock consisted of 368 oxen, 100 horses, twelve mules, 146 cows, and twenty beef cattle. Interestingly, fourteen dogs, eighteen cats, and 121 chickens accompanied the pioneers. A six-pound brass cannon, 129 guns, fifty-two pistols, nine swords, 1,001 rounds of ammunition, and forty-four saddles provided ammunition and comfort for those who rode during the trip. One Black church member, likely enslaved, traveled to the new settlement. His name was John Burton. His name appears with the designation "colored."[11] John Burton originally traveled to the Salt Lake Valley with Daniel M. Thomas and Ann Crosby Thomas. He died in Parowan in 1865 and is buried in the Parowan City Cemetery.[12] During his life in Parowan, Burton developed a personal relationship with the leader of the church unit there. This respected leader, John Calvin Smith, died on the evening of 30 December 1855. John Burton, likely the lone Black resident of Parowan, was among those by his leader's side when he died. His name was listed as "Black John."[13] John Burton began his life under the yoke of slavery and experienced the horrors of total captivity by another human. His life concluded with the respect of those with whom he lived—evidenced by his burial in the city cemetery.

---

11. Annals of the Southern Utah Mission, circa 1903-1906; 1847-1869 (Book A); Church History Library, images 3-5/162m https://catalog.churchofjesuschrist.org/assets/3faee6c9-545e-42fd-9c67-41745a5e3622/0/4?lang=eng, <accessed 14 January 2024>

12. Amy Tanner Thiriot, *Slavery in Zion*, (Salt Lake City, University of Utah Press, 2022), 187-188

13. Parowan Stake historical record, 1855-1860; Typescript, 1981; Church History Library, image 85/90, https://catalog.churchofjesuschrist.org/assets/1871c41a-3166-4a4e-9dbc-2d241d8dfcf8/0/0?lang=eng, <accessed 15 January 2024>

The devotion of many who settled in Parowan is evident from the following words, which were offered shortly after the pioneers arrived. These thoughts come from an individual who just left his home to answer a call from their prophet. One can feel the strength of his conviction:

> For what cause have we come to this place, what has induced us to come but to keep the commandments of God? We left the US to roll forth the Kingdom of God, so have come to this place to lay the foundation for future settlements in these valleys, not to do our own will but the will of those who sent us…. We should concentrate our faith and prayers to sustain him, who is our leader, who is at our head, set over us to lead and guide, in doing this, we shall be blessed and accomplish the mission whereunto we have been sent or called.[14]

Unfortunately, the Iron Mission never achieved the desired result of an efficient iron manufacturing plant. Unforeseen issues plagued the mission. The furnace and linked structures were built too close to the banks of Coal Creek. The ground was spongy, and the creek constantly flooded. The lack of a circulating currency within the Utah Territory added to the challenges of keeping the workforce compensated. Employees were credited on company books, but the company store inventory could not keep up with the credit held by the workers. Difficulties with the Indigenous people in the area and undertrained management were factors in Brigham Young's decision to close down the plant.[15]

---

14. Iron County Mission historical record, 1850-1859; Volume 1, 1850-1859; Church History Library, image 4/52, https://catalog.churchofjesuschrist.org/assets/8b1abad0-973c-4865-9112-20326fbfe071/0/0?lang=eng, <accessed 13 January 2023>

15. Morris A. Shirts, *The Iron Mission*, Utah History Encyclopedia, unpaginated, https://www.uen.org/utah_history_encyclopedia/i/IRON_MISSION.shtml, <accessed 13 January 2024>

FIRST COTTON GROWN IN DAVIS COUNTY, UTAH TERRITORY

Let us pause and reflect on why the southern Utah climate and land were necessary to grow cotton and other semi-tropical crops. Remarkably, the first known cotton grown and harvested in Utah Territory came from Reddin A. Allred, who lived in Davis County in northern Utah. Allred detailed his experience to the *Deseret News*. "Last season, I came to the valley and brought with me two or three dozen cotton seeds, which I planted on the 15th of May, and to my satisfaction, it grew and matured before the frost interfered." Allred was convinced that 1,000 acres of land existed for planting and harvesting cotton every year. Briefly, excitement ran high for growing cotton in northern Utah. Editors for the *Deseret News* asked residents to write their friends in cotton growing areas to ask for a pound of cotton seeds. The seed could be mailed in tin boxes for one dollar per pound. Their plea ended with this request, "Who will begin it? Now is this time. Don't let another mail pass without sending your orders." With all the initial enthusiasm, raising cotton in northern Utah never gained traction. Allred himself pointed out that "all the farms in the valley will not mature this crop, from the fact that the frost makes its appearance very early in the lowlands."[16] The elevation of the Salt Lake Valley made it almost impossible to determine precisely when a frost would hit—even on land against the mountains. The Saints also needed to determine whether cotton should be raised in the Salt Lake Valley at the expense of needed other crops.

SETTLEMENTS EXPANDING IN SOUTHERN UTAH TERRITORY

During the early 1850s, church leaders continued to search for settlements where self-sufficiency could flourish and a climate where warm weather crops might thrive. As noted earlier, the experiment in

---

16. "Local Correspondence," *Deseret News*, 6 November 1852, page 2.

Southern California launched with high hopes. Unfortunately, hopes for a shorter route for emigration and a location to grow cotton, grapes, tobacco, figs, hemp, rice, and other crops suitable for the climate were dashed when the federal troops invaded Utah Territory and Brigham Young directed those in San Bernardino to return to Utah. The push to southern Utah, where semitropical products might thrive, intensified following the founding of Parowan. George A. Smith offered a glimpse into the settlements in southern Utah in a December 1852 letter to the *Deseret News*. Smith's letter noted that sixty families were now settled in Cedar City, and "the crops there have exceeded any that I know of in the territory."[17] Smith further noted:

> Six miles south of Cedar is a Fort called Walker, containing three families with nine men capable of bearing arms. Mr. Shirts is making salt there. About nineteen miles South of this—on the first water South of the rim of the basin, in Washington County, attached to Iron County, John D. Lee, and Elisha H. Groves and company are building a Fort on Ash Creek called "Harmony," 15 men are capable of bearing arms; 51 loads of lumber had been taken there from Parowan, about 50 miles, and six teams are constantly employed hauling more.[18]

By the end of 1852, settlements in southern Utah began in earnest, and the Cotton Mission soon officially began.

A mission to the Indigenous people of southern Utah Territory moved forward under the direction of Brigham Young. During the October Conference of 1853, fifty families were directed to strengthen the southern settlements and "labor among the Indians." George A. Smith and Erastus Snow were authorized by the First Presidency to call these resolute pioneers. Rufus C. Allen led the group, and he left on April 8, 1854. Rufus had just returned from a

---

17. "Local Correspondence," *Deseret News*, 11 December 1852, page 2, https://newspa pers.lib.utah.edu/details?id=2579613&month_t=%22december%22&year_start=1852& year_end=1852&facet_paper=%22Deseret+News%22, <accessed 18 January 2024>
18. Ibid.

mission to South America with Parley P. Pratt. In addition to serving as missionaries to the Native population in the area, these individuals were to strengthen Iron County settlers and begin settling further south in Washington County. Interestingly, Parowan's population at the time stood at 392 people, and Cedar City's residents equaled 455 inhabitants. The travelers arrived at the camp of John D. Lee in Harmony, Utah Territory, on 16 May 1854 and waited for Brigham Young to arrive for further instructions.[19] Church leadership wanted to carve out a road from Harmony, across the Black Ridge, and down to the Virgin River, and Brigham Young and other leaders expressed that desire to the group. Many at the time felt that building a road over the treacherous terrain to the Virgin River was not possible, and they voiced their opinions. Despite this, Heber C. Kimball predicted a road would be carved out and that a temple would be built in the vicinity of the Virgin River.[20]

Rufus Allen and his group of missionaries continued south, arriving in Santa Clara in June 1854. They located a group of Native Americans, numbering 200 souls living in the area. This group of Indigenous people welcomed the newcomers with open arms. In return, the missionaries shared techniques for sowing and planting crops that could improve how they were currently laboring. By December 1854, Jacob Hamlin, Thales H. Haskell, Ira Hatch, Samuel Knight, and Augustus P. Hardy were directed by Rufus Allen to settle permanently in Santa Clara. Soon, log dwellings were constructed, and a dam was placed to assist with irrigation in the summer months. The local inhabitants were reluctant to build a dam because they felt the creek would dry up in the summer and no one would have access to water. Hamlin promised the entire group that both Indigenous people and the missionaries now living in the area would have enough water for the irrigation of crops.[21]

Jacob Hamlin became extremely sick—so much so that Augustus

---

19. Annals of the Southern Utah Mission, circa 1903-1906; 1847-1869 (Book A), images 20-22/162
20. Ibid, 23/162
21. Nellie M. Gubler, "History of Santa Clara, Utah, *Washington County Historical Society,*

P. Hardy quickly departed to Fort Harmony, seeking medicine and better food than what was available at Santa Clara. Hardy continued heading north until he reached Parowan, where he received additional medicine for Hamlin. On the same trip, one Sister Hardy, who was from one of the southern states, gave Hardy a quart jar filled with cotton seeds. These seeds would become the first to travel south of Parowan. The dam was now completed and reached 100 feet in length and fourteen feet in height, which allowed water to reach the town and the surrounding area. The water also allowed the missionary settlers and the Indigenous people to cultivate and farm together. The two parties farmed 100 acres together. The year 1855 produced good crops, which provided the settlers much-needed nourishment. The partnership of Native Americans and missionaries worked very well that first summer.[22]

Amazingly, the quart of cotton seed was planted, cultivated, and harvested that same year. This first crop of cotton grown in southern Utah Territory yielded enough cotton to produce thirty yards of cloth. Not only was the harvesting process important, but the seed needed to be separated from the lint by hand since there was no cotton gin available. Three ladies receive credit for creating the cloth. Caroline Beck Knight, Maria Woodbury Haskell, and Syman Curtis separated the cotton lint from the seed, then used a hand-spinning wheel and treadle looms of "the most primitive make" to fashion the cotton into cloth. A sample of the cloth was sent to Brigham Young's office, where it was placed on display. A Virginian who saw the cloth declared "it was as good as any he had ever seen. It was beautifully white, fine, and silky."[23]

Robert D. Covington, a native of North Carolina, was called to southern Utah Territory in April 1857. Covington and twenty-eight other families were directed to establish a permanent settlement,

---

(Washington County, Utah, 1915) unpaginated, https://wchsutah.org/towns/santa-clara4.pdf, <accessed 20 January 2024>
22. Annals of the Southern Utah Mission, circa 1903-1906; 1847-1869 (Book A), images 30-31/162
23. Ibid, 32/162

grow cotton, and establish a settlement in the area where St. George now stands. The site selected was named Washington City.[24] Although Covington and those who traveled with him hailed from the South and were familiar with growing cotton, those who actually planted, cultivated, and harvested cotton in the South were generally enslaved people—not plantation owners. According to a report given by George Albert Smith in 1861, those who settled in this dry, hot area were "terribly homesick and discontented to the present time."[25] Although the town site was fifty to ninety miles from a wheat grinder or blacksmith, about thirty of the original settlers remained in the harsh conditions and faced the daily hardships head-on. Cotton failed miserably in the first year because the settlers did not know how to irrigate the crop. However, their ability to grow and harvest cotton improved each year to 1860, when Smith issued his report on settlements in the southern Utah Territory.[26]

Developments between the years 1857 and 1864 added to the population called to grow cotton in southern Utah Territory. The closing of San Bernardino due to the Utah War in 1857 brought fifty families. Thirty families of Swiss emigrants were summoned to settle in Santa Clara. A call was issued at the 1861 October General Conference for 309 families to serve a mission to grow cotton. An additional appeal was issued in 1862 for 200 more families. In 1864, fifty or sixty families were requested to settle south of St. George on a river named Muddy. An additional 1,000 persons were summoned to serve in the 1860s and 1870s. The harshness of the environment, soil saturated with alkali, blistering hot weather, constant flooding of the Virgin River, grasshoppers, and worms understandably caused many to leave the mission. Only twenty families remained in Washington,

---

24. Dennis R. Lancaster, "Dixie Wine," (Master's thesis. Brigham Young University, 1972, image 20-21/174, https://scholarsarchive.byu.edu/cgi/viewcontent.cgi?article=5861&context=etd, <accessed 22 January 2024>

25. Historical Department journal history of the Church, 1830-2008; 1860-1869; 1861 July-December; Church History Library, image 413-415/696, https://catalog.churchof jesuschrist.org/assets/631a8c58-f671-4540-b46b-5bb265d97e8e/0/412?lang=eng, <accessed 22 January 2024>

26. Ibid, 415/696

Utah Territory, by June 1861. Fortunately, the arrival of new missionaries in the 1860s brought a much-needed uplift for those already living in the southern Utah Territory.[27]

The war between the states produced an even stronger push toward self-sufficiency among church leaders. The isolated members of the church in the mountains of the West were now faced with the absolute necessity to live in almost total self-reliance. Of the 309 families called in October 1861, fewer than 200 traveled south and completed their mission. The company called to this mission was told this responsibility was as important as being called to preach the gospel to the nations of the earth. In addition to growing cotton and other crops that could thrive in warm soil, another objective for this company was to establish the city of St. George.[28] Roads to connect the various communities took on a crucial importance as more people were sent to the area. The Washington County Court set up local precincts to support a road connecting Harmony to Washington, and the Utah Territorial Legislature approved funding for road projects in the area.[29]

The increased pressure on the leadership in Salt Lake City to bring church members to total self-reliance did not always flow into the hearts of church members who were comfortably settled in their homes in the northern Utah Territory. The request for 200 additional volunteers to move south in 1862 was met with a lukewarm response. Concerning those who were asked to volunteer, George Albert Smith observed, "There were a few who came up and gave their names, but the great mass of brethren did not feel to do so." He continued by recalling how those who first settled in the San Pete Valley were also discouraged in the beginning. He compared the feelings of early San

<hr>

27. Georgene Cahoon Evans, "The Cotton Mission," *Utah History Encyclopedia,* unpaginated, https://www.uen.org/utah_history_encyclopedia/c/COTTON_MISSION.shtml <accessed 23 January 2024>

28. Ivan J. Barrett, "History of the Cotton Mission," (Master's thesis, Brigham Young University, 1947, image 119-122/348, https://scholarsarchive.byu.edu/cgi/viewcontent.cgi?article=5505&context=etd, <accessed 25 January 2024>

29. Annals of the Southern Utah Mission, circa 1903-1906; 1847-1869 (Book A), images 84-85/162

Pete settlers to those in southern Utah Territory and commented, "Now there has recently been just such a feeling regarding Washington County, but the past years' experience has demonstrated more fully that most excellent cotton, sugar cane, grapes, peaches, and many other commodities of life can be successfully raised there, in that desert looking country."[30]

The first two men to reach the St. George Valley were Robert Thompson and William Fawcett. They entered the site where the new town was to be built on 25 November 1861. The location of St. George lay five miles from the village of Washington. The arrival of the primary group of missionaries in the St. George area happened on 1 December 1861. Other missionaries continued entering the valley daily, rapidly increasing the number of settlers. Erastus Snow oversaw the first meeting, which took place on 4 December 1861. This essential gathering took place approximately one-half mile "due east of where the temple now stands."[31] The skills of those who left their homes to settle in southern Utah Territory were varied. Of those who signed up for the mission, twenty-nine men listed their occupation as farmers, fourteen men worked as blacksmiths, eight were coopers, and five worked as masons. Musicians, schoolteachers, carpenters, tanners, dam builders, and other crucial workers brought needed skills to the settlement. Interestingly, one person who specialized in making castor oil, a drum major, and a sailor accompanied the group.[32] Church leadership selected individuals with different vocations to create an opportunity for successful settlements in the southern Utah Territory.

Many early settlements along the Virgin River no longer exist. These settlements began with hope, but the river destroyed the dreams of the families who were striving to obey their leaders and carve out life in a hostile environment. Virgin City held a total popu-

---

30. "Remarks," *Deseret News*, 25 March 1863, page 1, https://newspapers.lib.utah.edu/details?id=2593834, <accessed 24 January 2024>

31. Annals of the Southern Utah Mission, circa 1903-1906; 1847-1869 (Book A), image 104/162

32. Ibid, images 90-100/162

lation of sixteen families in 1860, and by 1880, thirty-six families resided there. The village of Grafton had seven families in 1870, but by 1880 only five families remained. Eleven families resided in Duncan's Retreat in 1879 and grew to thirteen families ten years later. Settlements such as Rockville, Shunesburg, and Springdale each began with a few families. However, eventually, these settlements vanished into the hot desert air of southern Utah Territory.[33] Sadly, each of these communities bordered the Virgin River, which provided needed water but was also a key reason for the demise of these towns. Continual floods wiped out entire fields. Grafton was even relocated following a flood. Like so many other locations in southern Utah Territory, nature forced both settlements and individuals into submission and broke their determination.

One crop was grown that provided better bartering power than cotton. Grapes for wine became an important crop for many in the mission. A speech by George A. Smith appeared in the *Deseret News* in 1868, praising the population of St. George that had grown from its incorporation in 1862 to 1,500 inhabitants by 1868. Concerning the growing of grapes, Smith stated the "inhabitants enjoy the satisfaction of being able to produce what fruit they need for home use, and quantities of wine which they expect to export." [34] By 1875, there were 544 acres of grapes planted, which produced a staggering total of 3,409,200 pounds and yielded 6,260 bushels per acre.[35] By 1870, wine-making outfits were prevalent, with operators in St. George producing from twenty-five to 2,500 gallons annually. Santa Clara, Washington, Leeds, and Tocqueville, as well as other areas in southern

---

33. W. Paul Reeve, "A Little Oasis in the Desert: Community Building in Hurricane, Utah, 1860-1930, (Master's Thesis, Brigham Young University, 1994, image 37/199, https://scholarsarchive.byu.edu/cgi/viewcontent.cgi?article=6064&context=etd, <accessed 31 January 2024>
34. "News From the South," *Deseret News*, 19 February 1868, page 1, https://newspa pers.lib.utah.edu/details?id=2601344&page=7&month_t=%22february%22&year_s tart=1868&year_end=1868, <accessed 31 January 2024>
35. Dennis R. Lancaster, "Dixie Wine," (Master's thesis. Brigham Young University, 1972, image 53/174

Utah Territory, were actively producing wine.[36] The tithing office in St. George produced 600 gallons of wine in 1889, which was the result of one-tenth of the grapes harvested during the year.[37] The weaker cotton market provided a growth opportunity for grapes and wine.

ACCOUNTS FROM THE COTTON AND MUDDY MISSION

One of the more unique individuals to serve in the Cotton Mission was George A. Hicks. He and his family answered the call to serve in 1861. Like others who went south, he sold his property at a loss. He began his journey to the southern Utah Territory in late November with a "heavy heart." He commented that he often wanted to run away from the mission, but he never did. He strongly believed the majority of those who settled in Washington were Southern sympathizers. He noted that he and one other man were the only "Union men in Washington." Following his arrival, he was only able to construct a brush wickiup for his family to live in due to a lack of time and money. George Hicks, along with several others in the settlement, started a "dramatic company" to provide entertainment for the other town residents. Hicks raised cotton as directed, but he looked at others who raised grain, which could be sold to freighters from California, as being wiser than himself.[38] What set George apart from others was his ability to tell stories and write songs. Hicks despised polygamy and felt the Mormon Reformation produced little good. He publicly criticized John D. Lee during the time he and the family lived in Harmony, and he was not hesitant to complain about church leaders.

In 1864, Hicks wrote a song about the Cotton Mission that caused

---

36. Ibid, image 75/174

37. Ibid, image 76/174

38. George A. Hicks autobiography, 1878; Autobiography, 1835-1926; Church History Library, image 99-101/118, https://catalog.churchofjesuschrist.org/assets/9ba5befb-eabd-4b5a-8ec6-b1653f08b318/0/0?lang=eng, <accessed 30 January 2024>

leaders to criticize him and other settlers to celebrate his words. He entitled his poem "Once I Lived in Cottonwood." Here are two stanzas from his twelve-verse song, which show his wit and struggles with the mission:

"I feel so weak and hungry now; I think I'm nearly
　　dead;
'Tis seven weeks next Sunday since I tasted bread.
Of carrot tops and lucerne greens, we have
　　enough to eat,
But I'd like to change my diet off for buckwheat
　　cakes and meat.

I brought this old coat with me, about two
　　years ago,
And how I'll get another one, I'm sure I do not
　　know.
May providence protect me against the wind
　　and wet,
I think myself and Betsy, these times will ne'er
　　forget.

Hicks performed this song as often as he could, and this resulted in the leadership becoming very frustrated with him. However, it is possible these few lines of witty verse provided a needed reprieve for others who experienced similar feelings about their situation. To his credit, Hicks completed his mission before returning to northern Utah. Following his mission, Hicks expressed his feelings about the mission, saying, "At one time England sent her convicts to Bondsman's Land, Russia sends hers to Siberia, but in Utah the Church sends hers to the Cotton Farm of Southern Utah."[39]

---

39. Fred Esplin, "Siberia or Southern Utah? A mission of mercy 'to the cotton farm,' *St. George News,* 26 November 2023, https://www.stgeorgeutah.com/news/archive/2023/11/26/fce-siberia-or-southern-utah-a-mission-of-mercy-to-the-cotton-farm-of-southern-utah/. <accessed 30 January 2024>

William Henry Thompson was born in England in 1828 and first emigrated to the United States in 1855 as a young man of eighteen years. He joined the church in Providence, Rhode Island, in 1859 and traveled to Utah Territory in 1861 in the Ira Eldridge wagon train. Before leaving Providence, William married Matilda Young on 12 June 1859. William worked as a silversmith and could not find work after arriving in Utah Territory, so he volunteered to serve in the Cotton Mission in 1861. He was a skilled teamster, so he drove Orson Pratt's teams to southern Utah, arriving at Adventure (Rockville) at the mouth of Zion's Canyon on 3 December 1861. The couple lived in a wagon box during their first few months. Residents along the Virgin River suffered forty days of continuous rainfall during the winter of 1861-1862, which caused terrible floods on the Virgin River. William, Matilda, and their new daughter left Adventure for St. George with Orson Pratt, arriving on 1 March 1862. William worked as a teamster and carpenter during much of his time in St. George and Washington.[40]

William spent the remainder of his life in southern Utah. He worked as a teamster, carpenter, militiaman, and Wilford Woodruff's bodyguard during the time federal marshals were cracking down on polygamy. Tragically, William's entire family became sick with chills and fever during the winter of 1866. Matilda died on 23 February 1866. Before her death, she asked William to take their two girls to the Thomas Cottom family so the children would be cared for. Thomas was an old childhood friend of William's, and Matilda was confident her children would be well cared for. William and Matilda also had a three-week-old son. William walked door to door, seeking a woman who could nurse the little boy. Formula and cow's milk were not utilized at that time. William and Matilda's two daughters were placed in a home at Pine Valley. Pine Valley stood thirty-five miles from William's home, but he would walk the thirty-five miles as often

---

40. Several editors, *Autobiography, William Henry Thompson*, p. 1,4, Document provided by Melvin Thompson, a direct descendent of William. Article in possession of Erick Wadsworth

as possible to see his daughters. During the construction of the St. George Temple, William was named lead carpenter, making him responsible for placing the heavy timbers, setting up and running the woodworking machinery, and placing the boiler in the temple. William wrote that Brigham Young himself asked him to "go in there [pointing to the temple] and work for nothing and board yourself and stay until you have further orders. Will you do it?" William said yes, which led to thirty-seven years of continuous service in the St. George Temple.[41]

In an effort to strengthen the cotton-growing efforts in southern Utah Territory, 158 men received a call to serve in an area on the Muddy River, near the confluence of the Muddy and Virgin Rivers, during the October general conference of the church in 1867. Of those called, about eighty eventually traveled south to serve in this new mission.[42] One of the families called to serve in the Muddy Mission was that of John and Margaret Esplin. The sacrifices they made to serve are representative of the experiences of so many other individuals and families. John and Margaret lived in relative comfort on a productive farm in the first adobe house built in Nephi, Utah Territory. They devised a plan in which John would travel to the mission immediately with one of his sons while the other children would remain in Nephi to help Margaret and the farm. The father left for the Muddy River at the end of October 1867—after only a few weeks to prepare. John, who joined the church in Scotland, must have been shocked at the site of the vast desert upon arrival at the Muddy River. John and his son settled in St. Joseph, which was named after Joseph W. Young, an early pioneer and nephew of the prophet. Like so many other pioneers, the two men lived in wagon boxes set on the ground. The two men struggled to build a one-room adobe home out of mud bricks they made themselves. The rest of the family arrived in

---

41. Ibid, 7
42. Ivan J. Barrett, "History of the Cotton Mission," (Master's thesis, Brigham Young University, image 195/348

the fall of that year.[43] Those who served in the Muddy Mission met with similar challenges as those who settled along the Virgin River, including grasshoppers, lack of water, the distance from needed supplies, and irritated Indigenous people already living in the area.

William Wood, another person called to the Muddy Mission, left Salt Lake City with his family on 20 November 1867. During the previous three weeks, he sold his property, wound up his business affairs, and began his journey to the mission. He began with two spans of good horses and felt well-equipped for the trek. Concerning his trip to the mission, he wrote, "But the unseen tests ahead which was our lot to meet were the greatest hardships it had been my lot to endure."[44] Upon arrival, William received two parcels of land. A two-and-a-half-acre piece to raise hay on and five acres to farm. William described the ground for hay as "swampy and wet," and the farmland was covered with mesquite brush with thorns as long as a "darning needle." He described the challenges of clearing desert land:

> The thorns were strong enough to pierce a hole through a leather strap. You could do nothing with it unless you used a pitchfork to bend the brush over and then chop it off. When the top was cleared, you had to work and dig out the roots, which was oftimes very large. I have taken them out four or five feet inside the ground. I hired an Indian and, in a few weeks, had all the brush cleared, which gave us quite a pile of firewood.[45]

He planted two-and-a-half acres of cotton and harvested "a few bales of cotton." William harvested his hay from the swampy ground by cutting a small quantity at a time, raking it up, and carrying it out

---

43. Fred Esplin, *Sagebrush Saints,* (Provo, Utah, Brigham Young University Press, 2021),, 161-163

44. William Wood, 1837-1916. William Wood autobiography , image 39/71, https://cat alog.churchofjesuschrist.org/assets/a1c08d7a-6f76-46e4-8d27-a2185b930249/0/38? lang=eng, <accessed 29 January 2024>

45. Ibid, 49/71

on his back to dry ground.[46] The Muddy Mission ended in 1872 when the area became part of Nevada, and officials from that state introduced higher taxes and demanded back taxes. Most residents moved back to the Utah Territory.[47]

Church leaders continually tried to create a successful environment for those serving in the Cotton and Muddy Missions. A large cotton factory was built at St. George. Brigham Young directed the establishment of the United Order (for certain locations), which provided an opportunity for the settlers to have all things in common; each person could work with others for the betterment of the entire community. In addition, tithing storehouses were utilized to provide food for the missionaries. Yet, the inability to trade goods and services with those who were not members of the church, plummeting cotton prices after the Civil War, little to no cash, and the unforgivingly harsh environment doomed the overall financial success of the mission. The completion of the continental railroad in 1869 might have signaled the final chapter of the Cotton Mission—even though many continued to grow cotton.

The Cotton Mission did not realize the total self-reliance desired by church leaders during the turbulent mid-nineteenth century. Nevertheless, the gifts these valiant growers provide us today are almost immeasurable. The city of St. George, Utah, stands as a testament to the tenacity of the early settlers. The area is filled with beautiful homes, delightful lawns, and gardens filled with fruit. Southern Utah is lined with beautiful farms, orchards, and vineyards. Two temples built by The Church of Jesus Christ of Latter-day Saints now stand in southern Utah. The St. George Temple and the Red Cliffs Temple (Washington, Utah) are testaments to the resilience of the early settlers. Each drop of sweat and every tear that fell stands as a tribute to their effort. These ordinary people—men, women, and children filled with weaknesses similar to our own—provide an example to remember.

---

46. Ibid.
47. Ibid, 55/71

11

REMEMBERING BLACK MEN AND WOMEN EXPLORERS AND PIONEERS

As noted earlier, the Mississippi Saints brought several enslaved men and women to Utah Territory. This chapter is devoted to Black men and women—both enslaved and free—who contributed to the settlement of Utah Territory and other locations in the West. For decades, the stories of Black men and women who helped settle the West were suppressed under the shroud of slavery. Enslavers viewed the enslaved as property, and they received little to no credit for the amazing work they accomplished during the early discovery and settlement of the western United States. Their efforts should be remembered with equal significance to the more well-known explorers and settlers. The memories presented in this chapter provide a glimpse into the past, portray inspiring accomplishments and commonplace incidents, and offer a glimpse into the impact of Black men and women on Western settlement and adventure. These accounts are the result of extensive research conducted by resolute historians and scholars to uncover narratives of those who otherwise might be forgotten.

York: Enslaved Member of the Corps of Discovery

One remarkable story from the early 1800s comes from the journey across the country now known as the Lewis and Clark Expedition. York's birth date is unknown, but he likely entered life a few years after William Clark, who was born on 1 August 1770, and they may have grown up together.[1] Clark enslaved York as his body servant, which saved York from the horrific life in the fields. His assignment likely meant he received better food, lived in the same house as William, and wore clothes similar to his enslaver. York fed his enslaver during meals, shaved him, assisted him in dressing, and attended to all the needs of William Clark. York's other roles included traveling with William on business trips and being responsible for his safety, which meant York always remained close to Clark—both day and night. The years of service with Clark allowed York to develop "highly polished manners" and social skills.[2] Through the years Clark and York spent together, one should remember York was always a slave and subject to the desires of William Clark. However, Clark's selecting of York for the Lewis and Clark Expedition provided an opportunity to experience a degree of freedom.

The name of the woman York married, the date of the wedding, and whether York and his wife had children together remains a mystery. Due to the Lewis and Clark journey west, York and his bride were separated for almost three years. Before heading west, the Corps stopped near the mouth of the Missouri River to construct a fort for the winter. Here, likely for the first time, York worked alongside white men in an almost equal capacity while clearing land, setting up tents, cutting trees, and constructing rudimentary huts. After five months at their Winter Quarters, York and the other men loaded 23,000 pounds of supplies on the boats to begin their journey west.

---

1. Robert B. Betts, *In Search of York, The Slave Who Went to the Pacific With Lewis and Clark*, (Boulder, Colorado, Colorado Associated University Press, 1985), 84
2. Ibid, 95-96

The provisions included gifts for the Indigenous people they would meet, food, instruments, and books.[3] York was about thirty-four years old at the time the Lewis and Clark Expedition departed for the Pacific Ocean. He stood large in stature, was exceptionally strong, and might have been a little overweight. York's responsibilities increased during the Corps' lengthy time on the trail. During an early portion of the journey, Clark noted how York tended to Sgt. Charles Floyd as he lay near death. He also served as a caregiver to Sacagawea and others who became sick during the expedition.[4]

According to Meriwether Lewis, the amount of meat needed to support the Corps of Discovery for twenty-four hours was a staggering four deer, an elk, or one buffalo. Wild berries, greens, and fish supplemented the diet when the wild game available changed. York carried a gun during the journey west, which allowed him to hunt and harvest big game. York's Black skin, which kept him and other Black men, women, and children enslaved, brought him newfound fame when interacting with Indigenous groups. To several western tribes, black was a sacred color. Shoshoni warriors painted their faces black to indicate they fought bravely during a battle. York's Black skin created a "powerless slave" in the American culture, but his skin meant "powerful warrior" to the Shoshonis.[5] A singular event for York took place upon arrival at the Pacific Ocean. He was allowed to vote, along with other Corps members, concerning the location of Fort Clatsop during the winter of 1804 to 1805. This brought him the honor of being the first Black man to have any type of recorded vote in North America.[6]

York's interactions with the Nez Percé caused them to continue an oral history of his impact on their tribe. One legend noted the Nez

---

3. Rhoda Blumberg, *York's Adventures with Lewis and Clark, An African American's Part in the Great Expedition,* (New York, New York, HarperCollins, 2004), 12-18
4. Michael Haynes, "York," *National Park Service,* https://www.nps.gov/jeff/learn/histo ryculture/york.htm, <accessed 16 August 2024>
5. Rhoda Blumberg, *York's Adventures with Lewis and Clark, An African American's Part in the Great Expedition,* 47
6. Ibid, 58

Percé wanted to slaughter the members of the Corps of Discovery after emerging from the Bitterroot Mountains on their return home. However, they feared "Raven's Son" might retaliate, and the group was allowed to pass through.[7] For unknown reasons, William Clark refused to release York from his enslavement following their triumphant return home. Once again, York became Clark's personal body servant and was still enslaved. In the fall of 1809, "misconduct" by York caused a falling out with Clark. One possible reason for the acrimonious split was after spending time with his wife in Kentucky, York told Clark he would rather live with another enslaver to be close to his wife than continue his enslavement with Clark.[8] Infuriated, Clark sold York to another enslaver named Young, who had a reputation for physically abusing enslaved people. In 1832, Clark told Washington Irving he freed several slaves, including York. Evidence indicates York received his manumission between 1811 and 1815.[9]

The Corps of Discovery entered St. Louis on 23 September 1806 after an absence of almost two-and-a-half years. York, along with the other members of the team, received an exuberant welcome home. However, York's moment of basking in public adulation quickly ended. Once again, his skin color immediately categorized him as inferior to all other white men and women. York's name never officially made the list of members of the Corps of Discovery. Sacagawea and her baby were also not listed. Every other enlistee received double pay for their time and 320 acres of land. Both York and Sacagawea received nothing.[10] Although York never received the honors of the other members of the Corp of Discovery, his successful

---

7. Shoshi Parks, "York Explored the West with Lewis and Clark, but His Freedom Wouldn't Come until Decades Later," unpaginated, *Smithsonian Magazine*, https://www.smithsonianmag.com/history/york-explored-west-lewis-and-clark-his-freedom-wouldnt-come-until-decades-later-180968427/, <accessed 20 August 2024>

8. Rhoda Blumberg, *York's Adventures with Lewis and Clark, An African American's Part in the Great Expedition*, 78

9. Shoshi Parks, "York Explored the West with Lewis and Clark, but His Freedom Wouldn't Come until Decades Later,"

10. Rhoda Blumberg, *York's Adventures with Lewis and Clark, An African American's Part in the Great Expedition*, 76

two-and-a-half-year mission across the country stands as a witness to the human capacity to accomplish the seemingly impossible. York experienced success unheard of as an enslaved individual—particularly among the Native inhabitants. He guided, hunted, trapped, nursed, and worked as almost an equal among the men of the Corps. It's possible the journey of Lewis and Clark across the country might have failed without the efforts of an obscure enslaved Black man who carried the name of York.

Mountain Man: James Beckwourth

James Beckwourth (Beckwith) was born a slave. His father was a white enslaver; his mother was an unnamed enslaved African woman. Evidence indicates James was born on 26 April 1798 in Frederick County, Virginia. His father, Jennings Beckwith, moved the family to the Louisiana Territory around 1809 and purchased land near Portage des Sioux, located within forty-five miles of present-day St. Louis, Missouri.[11] Jim's father allowed him to enroll in two years of school, where he learned to read and write. Shortly thereafter, Jim apprenticed with two blacksmiths but left their employ following an argument. In 1822, he mined at Galena, Illinois. He soon tired of mining and left for New Orleans on a steamboat. He returned home after coming down with yellow fever while in New Orleans. Jim's wanderlust grew to the point where, in 1824, he signed up for an overland trapping expedition with William Henry Ashley. Before he left for the West, his father appeared in a St. Louis Court and executed a deed of manumission freeing Jim.[12]

As a free man, Jim Beckwourth could now pursue his dream of exploring the American West. As a member of the Ashley supply expedition, he served as a groom, blacksmith, and bodyguard for William Ashley. He participated in the first Rocky Mountain

---

11. William E. Foley, James Pierson Beckwourth (Beckwith) 1798-1866, *Missouri Encyclopedia*, The State Historical Society of Missouri, unpaginated, https://missouriencyclopedia.org/people/beckwourth-beckwith-james-pierson, <accessed 6 March 2024>
12. Ibid.

Rendezvous in the summer of 1825. During his time in the West, Beckwourth was trapped alongside such well-known mountain men as Jim Bridger, Hugh Glass, Thomas Fitzpatrick, and Jedediah Smith. At different times, he served as a guide for military operations and operated trading posts.[13] Beckwourth arrived in the Salt Lake Valley more than twenty years before Brigham Young's vanguard wagon train. For a short period, he and other mountain men lived in the Cache Valley, located in the northern portion of the current state of Utah. The first annual rendezvous happened in the summer of 1825, near the current town of McKinnon, Wyoming. Jim describes this incredible gathering in his own words:

> When all had come in, he [William Ashley] opened his goods, and there was a general jubilee among all at the rendezvous. We constituted quite a little town, numbering at least eight hundred souls, of whom one-half were women and children. There were some among us who had not seen groceries, such as coffee, sugar, etc., for several months. The whisk[e]y went off as freely as water, even at the exorbitant price he sold it for. All kinds of sports were indulged in with a heartiness that would astonish more civilized societies.[14]

Like other mountain men of his era, James Beckwourth often embellished his own accomplishments. However, his achievements are of great value. Beckwourth spent years living with the Crow Tribe after warriors allegedly captured him while trapping Jim Bridger. Upon his capture, he was led to a Crow village, and after much discussion, it was decided Jim was a brave warrior who had been lost for twenty years. Chief Big Bowl became Beckwourth's father, and

---

13. American History Central Staff, edited by Randal Rust, *James Beckwourth*, American History Central Website, unpaginated, https://www.americanhistorycentral.com/entries/james-beckwourth/, <accessed 7 April 2024>

14. T. D. Bonner, *The Life and Adventures of James P. Beckwourth, Mountaineer, Scout, Pioneer, and Chief of the Crow Nation of Indians,* (London, T. Fisher Unwin. 1892), 79, https://archive.org/details/adventuresoflife00beckrich/page/78/mode/2up?q=Rendezvous+, <accessed 7 April 2024>

almost immediately, he received the choice of "three very pretty daughters to marry." The name of Beckwourth's new wife was Stillwater, and following the wedding ceremony, he was troubled by the memory of his wife back in St. Louis. Nevertheless, Beckwourth's new life afforded him the ability to "trap in their streams unmolested and derive more profit under their protection than if among my own men." James resolved to guard his secret and do his best to help the Crows "subdue their enemies.[15] Following his capture, Beckwourth went three years without seeing a white man.[16]

Mountain man James Beckwourth traded and trapped with the Crow people for almost twenty years, but in the fall of 1842, he married a woman in Taos, New Mexico, named Louise Sandoval. James and his new wife moved to a place on the Arkansas River that became Fort Pueblo. Beckwourth claimed he helped found Fort Pueblo in 1842, but further research indicates this did not happen. However, he did move to the adobe trading post in October 1842, when it had existed for just a few months.[17] Thus, he had some justification for his claim of being one of the founders. This location later became a sanctuary for the Mississippi Saints, who went west in 1846, and for three detachments of the Mormon Battalion.

Beckwourth continued to impact western development. He operated a hotel in Santa Fe, worked as a guide for the United States Military, and helped suppress the Taos Revolt of 1847.[18] Perhaps one of Samuel Beckwourth's most significant achievements regarding western settlement was the discovery of what is now known as Beckwourth Pass in 1850. The discovery of the pass led to the creation of a road from near Reno, Nevada, to Marysville, California. Beckwourth's pass provided a much easier crossing of the Sierra Nevada than the Donner Pass. In the spring of 1851, he led a wagon

---

15. Ibid, 132-134
16. Ibid, 129
17. Janet Lecompte, *Pueblo, Hardscrabble, Greenhorn: the Upper Arkansas, 1832-1856,* (Normon: University of Oklahoma Press, 1978) 42
18. William E. Foley, James Pierson Beckwourth (Beckwith) 1798-1866, *Missouri Encyclopedia*

train of settlers over the newly constructed trail. Pioneers and gold seekers used the trail heavily until about 1855. Beckwourth constructed a ranch and trading post just west of the actual pass.[19] Emigrants utilized the Beckwourth Ranch as a resting place after crossing the pass. He described the travelers as "weary, way-worn travelers," and he indicated that their wagons were "holding together by a miracle."[20] James Beckwourth probably died in late October 1866 while living again with the Crow Tribe.[21] His impact on western expansion in the early- to mid-nineteenth century stands unparalleled among the mountain men of his time.

Explorer: Jacob Dodson

Jacob Dodson, a freeborn Black man, traveled thousands of miles with John C. Fremont as they explored the uncharted vistas of the American West and Southwest between 1843 and 1847. Jacob was only eighteen years old when he first traveled with Fremont.[22] Dodson originally began his service with Fremont as his personal servant; however, he eventually earned his position as a full-fledged member of the group. Thirty-nine members began the 1843 to 1844 journey, but eleven of the original members left the exploration party, providing Dodson an opportunity to become one of the most valuable members of Fremont's second exploration of Utah, California, and other locations in the West.[23] One account indicated Jacob Dodson felt a strong attachment to Thomas Hart Benson, a powerful senator from Missouri. This narrative indicated Dodson served as Fremont's

---

19. "The Beckwourth Trail, *James Pierson Beckwourth, 1798-1866,* https://beckwourth. org/Biography/index.html, unpaginated, <accessed 6 March 2024>
20. T. D. Bonner, *The Life and Adventures of James P. Beckwourth, Mountaineer, Scout,* 427
21. William E. Foley, James Pierson Beckwourth (Beckwith) 1798-1866, unpaginated
22. Ronald G. Coleman, *Blacks in Utah History: an Unknown Legacy,* (Digitized by J. Willard Mariott Library, University of Utah, 1976), 115, https://collections.lib.utah. edu/ark:/87278/s6wd3zxj/420661, <accessed 9 March 2024>
23. John Rae, *The Prairie Dance: From Fact to Fiction,* online publishing 2022, file:///C:/ Users/Owner/Downloads/The%20Prairie%20Dance_%20From%20Fact%20to%20Fic tion%20-%20John%20Rae.pdf, image 16/107, <accessed 9 March 2024>

"personal servant" on both the second and third expeditions.[24] Fremont viewed Dodson's participation in his exploration as so significant he wrote the following description: "Jacob Dodson a free young colored man of Washington City, who volunteered to accompany the expedition, and performed his duty manfully throughout the voyage."[25]

During Fremont's return journey to the United States from the West, he left Jacob with J. B. Bernier to "take charge of the party which was to remain at the Dalles [Oregon, on the Columbia River]."[26] Dodson's tireless effort during Fremont's western exploration earned him a distinctive degree of respect from the United States government. Dodson volunteered to serve in the military as a private during the Mexican American War, beginning 7 July 1846. He served in Captain Richard Owen's company of the California Battalion until 14 April 1847. He was mustered into the military at a time when most Black men served either as servants or were enslaved by military leaders. The compensation for his service in the military did not happen until 21 February 1856 and included the following justification for his payment: "All that we propose in this bill is to give him what he would have received if he had been of a different color—in other words, if he had been a white man."[27] Dodson received the full pay of a private, minus the $281 Freemont paid him during the time he served in the military.[28]

Jacob Dodson played a key role, along with John C. Fremont, in securing victory for the United States against Mexico in 1846. On one

---

24. John Charles Fremont, *The expeditions of John Charles Fremont*, (University of Illinois Urbana-Champaign, 1970), 428fn, https://archive.org/details/expeditionsofjoh01fr/page/428/mode/2up?q=Benton, <accessed 10 March 2024>
25. Ibid, 427-428
26. Ibid, 561
27. United States. Congress. The Congressional Globe: Containing the Debates, Proceedings, Laws, Etc., of the First and Second Sessions, Thirty-Fourth Congress, book, 1856; Washington D.C.. page, 482, https://digital.library.unt.edu/ark:/67531/metadc30791/m1/484/?q=Jacob%20Dodson, <accessed 11 March 2024>, University of North Texas Libraries, UNT Digital Library, https://digital.library.unt.edu; crediting UNT Libraries Government Documents Department.
28. Ibid.

occasion, they completed an 800-mile horseback journey in just eight days to warn another group of soldiers about an imminent attack on their forces. He also helped secure victory in the town of Los Angeles by carrying a gun and fighting alongside his military companions.[29] By 1848, Dodson returned to his home in Washington, DC, where he worked as a Senate messenger for a period. The outbreak of the Civil War in 1861 caused him to offer his services in raising a unit of 300 African Americans to fight for the Union. The reply stated that the Union had no intention of using "colored soldiers."[30] Jacob Dodson traveled thousands of miles exploring the West, served in the military during the Mexican American War, and tried to raise troops to fight for the Union during the Civil War. His accomplishments stand as a testament to his tenacity in the face of overwhelming odds.

Long-Awaited Monument Dedication

On 22 July 2022, M. Russell Ballard, Acting President of the Quorum of the Twelve Apostles of The Church of Jesus Christ of Latter-day Saints, dedicated a long-overdue monument comprising three bronze statues honoring Green Flake, Oscar (Crosby) Smith, Hark (Lay) Wales, Jane Elizabeth Manning James, and her two sons, Silas and Sylvester. The dedication took place 175 years after Green Flake drove a wagon into the Salt Lake Valley. The memorial honors free and enslaved Black men and women who participated in the western migration and recognizes their sacrifices. The project to memorialize those whose efforts have been unnoticed for decades took four years of planning and development to complete. Mauli Junior Bonner, who spearheaded the undertaking, stated, "At the end of it all, we're talking about difficult things—enslavement with other pioneers. That's hard, and it's heavy. But at the end of the day, we're all family... we're still

---

29. Author unknown, "The Ride of Jacob Dodson," *African American Veterans Monument*, video, https://heroes.aavmwny.org/mexican-war, <accessed 9 March 2024>

30. John Rae, *The Prairie Dance: From Fact to Fiction*, online publishing 2022, image 16/107

family and children of God." The statues are located at the Place Heritage Park in east Salt Lake City, Utah.[31]

GREEN FLAKE

Green Flake, perhaps the most well known of the three enslaved men to enter the Salt Lake Valley in July 1847, was born on the William Jordan Flake plantation in Anson County, North Carolina. Evidence indicates he was born on 8 January 1828 and was taken to Mississippi sometime in the 1840s.[32] John Brown baptized Green on 7 April 1844 during his mission to the South. About the occasion, Brown wrote, "I also baptized two Black men, Allen and Green, belonging to brother Flake."[33] In early 1847, John Brown left Monroe County, bound for Winter Quarters. Brown and his group arrived just a few days before the vanguard wagon train began the westward march. He took with him four enslaved men. Brown described the mud and cold on the journey as "very severe." He noted the "negroes suffered most." Brown further wrote, "My boy, whose name was Henry, took cold and finally the winter fever set in which caused his death on the road." Another unnamed enslaved man died at Winter Quarters.[34] With only a short time to prepare, Green Flake, Oscar (Crosby) Wales, and Hark (Lay) Smith, along with John Brown, joined Brigham Young's vanguard wagon train west.

Green Flake and the other enslaved people chosen to participate in this journey west were crucial components of this journey. Green is

---

31. Scott Taylor, *Church News: A living Record of the Restoration,* unpaginated, https://www.thechurchnews.com/2022/7/22/23278589/the-story-behind-the-new-pioneers-of-1847-monument-honoring-black-pioneers/, <accessed 11 March 2024>

32. Benjamin Kiser, "Biography of Green Flake, *Century of Black Mormons,* J. Willard Marriott Library Digital Exhibitions, https://exhibits.lib.utah.edu/s/century-of-black-mormons/page/flake-green#?c=&m=&s=&cv=&xywh=-1118%2C-63%2C3258%2C1247, <accessed 13 March 2024>

33. John Zimmerman Brown, Autobiography of Pioneer John Brown, 1820-1896, p. 46, https://archive.org/details/autobiographyofp00brow/page/46/mode/2up,   <accessed 13 March 2024>

34. Ibid, 73

credited with driving the first wagon into the valley. By the time Brigham Young arrived, crops were already being cultivated. When his enslavers arrived in 1848, a cabin built by Green was ready for them. Flake married Martha Crosby, half sister to Hark (Lay) Wales and Oscar (Crosby) Smith, while she was still enslaved. Together, Green and Martha had two children, Lucinda and Abraham. The family lived in Union, Utah Territory, for most of their lives. Green remained an active member of the Union Ward throughout his life.[35] Brigham Young provided land for the family in Union, and Green held a deep admiration for the prophet throughout his life. Concerning that affection, one of Flake's descendants later recalled, "Green shed many tears at the death of Brigham Young, helped dig his grave, and was at the funeral of the beloved President."[36]

Green Flake farmed and mined during the years he lived in Union. The town was near the mouth of Big Cottonwood Canyon, so when a mining boom began in the early 1870s, Green elected to try his hand at that risky venture. Flake, with other Black and white men and women, formed a mining company.[37] The name of one of Green's mines was Evergreen Consolidated Mining and Tunnel Company. The *Salt Lake Tribune* offered a glimpse of how perilous mining could be with a delinquency notice in November 1875, which listed Green Flake, Hark Wales, and others for non-payment of the mortgage.[38] Miners worked all year long—even during the long Utah winters. Tragically, in the winter of 1882, a massive avalanche swept down the Cottonwood Canyon and engulfed the cabin of a young family. When Green and Martha's daughter, Lucinda Stevens, and her husband,

---

35. Jonathan A. Stapley and Amy Thiriot, "In My Father's House are many mansions," *The Church of Jesus Christ of* Latter-Day Saints, unpaginated, https://history.churchofje suschrist.org/content/pioneers-in-every-land/in-my-fathers-house-are-many-man sions?lang=eng <accessed 13 March 2024>

36. Amy Thiriot Tanner, *Slavery in Zion,* (Salt Lake City, Utah: University of Utah Press, 2022) 222

37. Ibid, 143

38. "Delinquent Sale," *Salt Lake Tribune,* November 17, 1875, page 3, https://newspa pers.lib.utah.edu/details?id=12974803&page=11&q=Delinquent+Sale&year_start= 1875&year_end=1875, <accessed 15 March 2024>

George, heard about the tragedy, they traveled up the canyon and dug through the tons of snow covering the cabin. At the peril of their own lives, they recovered the bodies of Charles and Elizabeth Tackett and their four little children.[39] The *Salt Lake Herald-Republican* carried a report of the bodies being recovered but made no mention of the names of those involved with the recovery.[40]

Green's notoriety for having entered the valley with Brigham Young's vanguard allowed him to share this experience at the 24th of July celebrations throughout his lifetime. Martha died in 1885, and the town of Union began losing its charm. In 1896, Green moved to Grays Lake, Idaho, to live with his son until he died in 1903. The family returned his body to the Union to be buried.[41] Green Flake entered life enslaved, traveled to Utah Territory as an enslaved man, married, raised children, and died in the home of his son, Abraham, on 20 October 1903. One measure of his legacy comes from an article published in the *Deseret News*: "The deceased was a faithful Latter-day Saint and to his dying day bore testimony to the divine mission of the Prophet Joseph Smith."[42]

HARK (LAY) WALES

Hark Lay Wales came into this world around 1825 as an enslaved member of the John Crosby family in Monroe County. His enslaver died in 1841, and the probate record valued Wales at $550. Crosby's daughter and her husband, Sytha and William Lay inherited Hark, and he took the surname Lay. After his freedom, he chose the name

---

39. "To These Our Grandparents, James Hale and Lucy Clements," *Family Search*, image 8/19, https://www.familysearch.org/memories/memory/25331474,

40. "The Fatal Avalanche," *Salt Lake Herald-Republican*, February 25, 1882, page 16, https://newspapers.lib.utah.edu/details?id=10630135&q=Fatal+Avalanche+&year_start=1882&year_end=1882, <accessed 15 March 2024>

41. Amy Thiriot Tanner, *Slavery in Zion*, 143-144

42. "Green Flake Passes Away," *Deseret Evening News*, October 22, 1903, page 1, https://newspapers.lib.utah.edu/details?id=2040253&q=Green+Flake&sort=rel&year_start=1903&year_end=1904, <accessed 15 March 2024>

Wales.[43] Hark was possibly baptized a member of The Church of Jesus Christ of Latter-day Saints around the same time as Sytha in 1844, but no baptismal record exists for him. The best evidence suggesting he was a member of the church comes from a document created by Charles C. Rich showing the names of those who consented to follow his and Amasa Lyman's counsel during their time in San Bernardino. Hark's name appears on the list under the name Hark Crosby instead of Lay. Those who did not belong to the church were noted with the term "not member."[44]

Sytha and William Lay sent Hark west with Brigham Young's vanguard wagon train, and he was one of the first to enter the valley with the advance group. After he arrived in the Salt Lake Valley, the task previously given him by his enslavers was to prepare for their future arrival by building a house and planting crops for food.[45] As noted previously, Hark Lay was forced to leave his wife and move to California. When Brigham Young called the settlers in San Bernardino to come back to Utah, Hark stayed in Southern California. He was now free. His freedom allowed him to register to vote in California. He lived in San Timoteo, roughly five miles southeast of San Bernardino. He remained in Southern California until about 1875, when he moved back to Utah Territory. It is not known if he ever reunited with the family he was torn from in 1851.[46] Upon his return to Utah Territory, he lived with Lucinda Stevens, Green and Martha Flake's daughter, in Union Fort. Like Green Flake, Hark

---

43. Megan Weiss, "Biography, Hark Wales," *Century of Black Mormons*, J. Willard Marriott Library Digital Exhibitions, https://exhibits.lib.utah.edu/s/century-of-black-mormons/page/wales-hark#?c=&m=&s=&cv=&xywh=-1383%2C-68%2C3550%2C1358, <accessed 16 March 2024>

44. Charles C. Rich collection, 1832-1908; Papers, 1832-1908; California papers, 1851-1856; Church History Library, https://catalog.churchofjesuschrist.org/assets/ce36fd4c-5107-468d-8ed6-48d773b49223/0/1?lang=eng, <accessed 16 March 2024>

45. Amy Tanner Thiriot, "Guest Post: Hark (Lay) Wales: A Slave in Zion," *The Keepapti-chinin*, unpaginated, https://keepapitchinin.org/2012/07/24/guest-post-hark-lay-wales-a-slave-in-zion/, <accessed 16 March 2024>

46. Megan Weiss, "Biography, Hark Wales," *Century of Black Mormons*

invested in the mining operations in Cottonwood Canyon. Hark died sometime in the 1880s and is buried in the Union Cemetery.[47]

Hark came into this world under the bondage of slavery, but he married, fathered children, traveled thousands of miles from one end of the country to the other, obtained freedom, and registered to vote in California. Yet, something pulled him back to friends and family in the community of Fort Union. Because of the absence of records for those who were enslaved, we may never know the real reason he left California and returned to Utah. Hark exemplifies the chasm that exists between the founding ideals of the United States and the reality of intolerance within society.[48] Although Hark is not as well known as Green Flake, his legacy stands alongside Green as one who brought about the advantages we now enjoy. He built dwellings for others. He planted crops for others. He helped settle two separate locations. And, like other enslaved individuals, he accomplished his work with the added oppression of enslavement. Hark's efforts, like the work of other well-known pioneers, should never be forgotten.

OSCAR (CROSBY) SMITH

Oscar (Crosby) Smith's granddaughter recalled that he was born in Mississippi as an enslaved person in about 1815. Following the death of John Crosby, he became the property of William Crosby. One can appreciate the never-ending thirst for freedom he must have felt as an enslaved person. The impulse became so strong he tried to escape from his enslavers. The following short account paints a graphic image of his attempt to escape through a fence: "His head was through the rails, and he could not get his body through as he was a large man. He was caught and beaten. He went through life with his head twisted to one side."[49] As noted earlier, Oscar traveled in Brigham Young's wagon train and was among the first to enter the Salt Lake Valley. He

---

47. Amy Thiriot Tanner, *Slavery in Zion,* 234-235
48. Megan Weiss, "Biography, Hark Wales," *Century of Black Mormons*
49. Amy Thiriot Tanner, *Slavery in Zion,* 203

was present when Brigham Young stood and severely rebuked everyone in the company on 29 May 1847 near Chimney Rock, Nebraska. Young had observed cursing, gambling, card playing, and other vices of the time until he became fed up. In typical Young style, his remarks were blunt. His scolding lasted several minutes, and the impact on those traveling in the wagon train was instantaneous. They all committed to "turn to the Lord and serve Him and acknowledge and honor His name."[50] Some of the words used during the reprimand would be considered discriminatory today.

After arriving in the Salt Lake Valley, Oscar obeyed the direction of his enslavers to build a home and plant crops for their arrival in 1848. One can understand the advantage of having an enslaved man make these preparations for your arrival the following year. The lofty mountains Oscar and the other two enslaved men woke up to each morning would dash any hope of escaping to freedom. The loneliness he must have felt would be crushing. How often he dreamed of being free can only be surmised from a view 177 years later. Oscar appears on the 1850 federal census slave schedule for Utah County, Deseret, as a thirty-five-year-old male. According to that document, William Crosby enslaved ten men and women. The youngest was a one-year-old male named George, while the oldest was a fifty-three-year-old man named Toby.[51] As noted in chapter nine, William Crosby next compelled Oscar to settle in San Bernardino along with the other enslaved men and women. Like Hark Smith, Oscar signed the document from Charles C. Rich saying that he would follow the direction of Rich and Amasa Lyman.[52] Once Oscar was freed, he chose to remain in Southern California.

---

50. William Clayton, *William Clayton's Journal*, (Salt Lake City: Claton Family Association, 1921), 189-198, https://archive.org/details/williamclaytonsj00clayy/page/198/mode/2up, <accessed 19 March 2024>

51. "United States Census (Slave Schedule), 1850," *FamilySearch*, https://www.family search.org/ark:/61903/1:1:MVHW-RZ4, <accessed 19 March 2024>

52. Charles C. Rich collection, 1832-1908; Papers, 1832-1908; California papers, 1851-1856; Church History Library, images 1-3/18, https://catalog.churchofjesuschrist.org/assets/ce36fd4c-5107-468d-8ed6-48d773b49223/0/0?lang=eng, <accessed 19 March 2024>

In 1856, after gaining his freedom, Oscar moved from San Bernardino to Los Angeles, where he was involved with both politics and religion.[53] The 1860 federal census finds Oscar Smith living in Los Angeles with a gentleman named Juan José. Both men worked as laborers. Oscar claimed Virginia as his birthplace, while Juan declared California as his birthplace. Both men indicated they could neither read nor write, and they both indicated they were married. The professions held by their neighbors included attorney, farmer, confectioner, ship caulker, mariner, blacksmith, silversmith, and porter. Of the forty residents on the page where Oscar appears, twenty-eight stated their birthplace was California, and eight stated they were of Black ancestry.[54] The 1870 census shows him still living in Los Angeles. He was then living next door to Charles and Elizabeth Rowen, who were also formerly enslaved in San Bernardino. At that point, he was sixty years old and indicated his occupation was as a bootblack.[55] Oscar collaborated with Biddy Mason to help found the first African Methodist Episcopal Church of Los Angeles (A.M.E.). Both Oscar and Biddy Mason were recognized for their fifty-dollar donation to the A.M.E. Church in 1869.[56] Although he was politically active, he never voted. He died in 1872 before he was able to exercise this right of freedom.[57] Oscar enjoyed the sweet taste of freedom during the last few years of his life, and he made the most of his opportunities.

---

53. Amy Thiriot Tanner, *Slavery in Zion,* 203
54. Oscar Smith Household, Ancestry.com. *1860 United States Federal Census* [database on-line]. Lehi, UT, USA: Ancestry.com Operations, Inc., 2009. Images reproduced by FamilySearch. https://www.ancestry.com/imageviewer/collections/7667/images/4211318_00367?treeid=&personid=&rc=&queryId=31a38647-f082-4cc4-a422-778073619bca&usePUB=true&_phsrc=EUI112&_phstart=successSource&pId=2666147, <accessed 19 March 2024>
55. Oscar Smith Household, "United States Census, 1870", *FamilySearch* (https://www.familysearch.org/ark:/61903/1:1:MN6J-62H, <accessed 19 March 2024>
56. "Letter From Bishop Ward," *The Elevator,* Volume V, Number 22, 3 September 1869, page 2, https://cdnc.ucr.edu/?a=d&d=EL18690903.2.13&e=-------186-en--20-EL-261--txt-txIN-The+Elevator-------, <accessed 20 March 2024>
57. Amy Thiriot Tanner, *Slavery in Zion,* 203-204

12

RECALLING THE LIVES OF ENSLAVED MEMBERS OF THE MISSISSIPPI COMPANY AND FOUR OTHERS

BIDDY MASON

The story of Biddy Mason's rise from enslavement to one of the wealthiest landowners in Los Angeles, California, constitutes one of the most powerful stories of a person overcoming hopeless conditions. Descendants of Biddy Mason noted she was born in Georgia between 1818 and 1825. Robert and Rebecca Smith enslaved Biddy while they lived in Franklin County, Mississippi. At the time of her enslavement, she had two children. The Smiths joined The Church of Jesus Christ of Latter-day Saints and, like other church members, determined to move west. The Smiths traveled with the people they enslaved and briefly settled in the Salt Lake Valley. By the time the Smiths headed west, Biddy had three "young daughters."[1] She traveled with the Willard Richards Company in 1848, which left Winter Quarters on 3 July 1848 and arrived at the Salt Lake Valley between 10 and 19 October 1848.[2]

---

1. Ibid, 275
2. Willard Richards Pioneer Company (1848), *Church History Library Biographical Database,* https://history.churchofjesuschrist.org/chd/organization/pioneer-company/

Biddy appears on the 1850 slave schedule with ten other enslaved individuals. She was the second oldest of the enslaved, while the youngest was only one year old at the time of the census.[3] Biddy went to San Bernardino in 1851 when Robert and Rebecca Smith left the Salt Lake Valley. The Smiths and the group of enslaved persons lived in San Bernardino until 1854, when Smith determined to take his family and the enslaved individuals to Texas. They began the journey by traveling through Los Angeles County, near Santa Monica, where they camped for a few days. During the short stay, word came that Smith was attempting to leave California and take the enslaved persons with him. Fortunately, the Sheriff of Los Angeles County, Frank Dewitt, located the Smith family and issued a writ against Robert, which prevented him from taking the enslaved group to Texas.[4] The *Writ of Habeas Corpus,* or the Freedom Papers of "Hannah, Biddy, and others," was finalized by Judge Benjamin Hayes of California's First District Court in January 1856.[5] Biddy's Freedom Papers record that she was thirty-eight years old at the time Judge Hayes declared her, her children, and all those enslaved by Robert Smith free.[6] After almost four decades of enslavement, Biddy and her children experienced a new feeling of freedom.

Biddy made the most of her freedom, and during the remainder of her life, she never forgot those who suffered. During her years in enslavement, she learned the skills of nursing and delivered babies as a midwife. She soon moved to Los Angeles and, for a time, lived in the home of wealthy Black businessperson and livery stable owner Robert

---

willard-richards-company-1848?lang=eng&timelineTabs=allTabs, <accessed 22 March 2024>

3. "United States Census (Slave Schedule), 1850," *FamilySearch,*

4. Deliliah L. Beasley, *The Negro Trail Blazers of California,* (New York: Negro Universities Press, 1919), 90, "Family Search online," https://www.familysearch.org/library/books/viewer/231510/?offset=#page=85&viewer=picture&o=search&n=0&q=Biddy%20Mason, <accessed 22 March 2024>

5. Ibid, 90;,,

6. *Freedom Papers of Biddy Mason, given to her in 1860 (photographed 1930-1989),* unpaginated, https://digital.library.ucla.edu/catalog/ark:/21198/z1vh76cw <accessed 22 March 2024>

Owens and his wife, Winnie. As a former slave, this nineteenth-century woman faced challenges faced by few others. Yet, with undaunted courage, she made use of her medical skills by working as a nurse for Dr. John S. Griffin at the rate of $2.50 a day.[7] Ironically, this same Dr. Griffin was a former slaveholder.[8] Although unable to read and write due to her decades-long enslavement, she became one of the most influential women in Southern California. Her work as a nurse and midwife allowed her to save money, which she used to purchase property located in what is now downtown Los Angeles. She helped organize the First A.M.E. church in the city and paid the church's taxes. She donated to multiple charities, helped feed the poor, and visited prisoners.[9] During floods in the early 1880s, "she gave an open order to a little grocery store, which was located on Fourth and Spring streets. By the terms of this order, all families made homeless by the flood were to be supplied with groceries while Biddy Mason paid the bill."[10]

A memorial in her honor in downtown LA makes clear the impact Biddy Mason had on her family and the citizens of early Los Angeles. The Biddy Mason Memorial Park is located at 333 South Spring Street in Los Angeles. Katherine Spitz and Pamela Burton designed the "mini park," and Sheila Levrent de Bretteville created an eighty-foot-long "poured concrete wall" artwork entitled *Biddy Mason Time*

---

7. Delilah L. Beasley, *The Negro Trail Blazers of California*, (New York Public Library, 1919), 108, "Internet Archive," https://archive.org/details/negrotrailblazer00beas/page/108/mode/2up?q=Biddy+Mason, <accessed 23 March 2024>

8. Sarah Barringer Gordon, project director, *The Long Road to Freedom: Biddy Mason and the Making of Black Los Angeles*,7, " Funded by the National Endowment of the Humanities," https://www.neh.gov/sites/default/files/inline-files/The-Long-Road-To-Free dom-Biddy-Mason-And-The-Making-Of-Black-Los-Angeles.pdf, <accessed 23 March 2024>

9. Delilah L. Beasley, *The Negro Trail Blazers of California*, (New York Public Library, 1919), 109

10. Kate Bradley Stovall, "The Negro Woman in Los Angeles and Vicinity—Some Notable Characters," *The Los Angeles Times*, February 12, 1919, Page 4, column 1, https://www.newspapers.com/image/380264141/?match=1, <accessed 23 March 2024>

and Place.[11] The declaration of "Biddy Mason Day" on November 16, 1989, gives further confirmation of Biddy's impact. Mason was inducted into the "California Social Work Hall of Distinction" in 2002, which was accompanied by a statement reading, in part, "Despite all her wealth, she continues to serve the community, treating anyone in need, Black or White, as well as those no one else wanted to help, such as prisoners. She gave shelter to the homeless and fed the hungry."[12]

Biddy's astonishing climb to financial independence began in 1866, ten years after her freedom. She purchased lots from William M. Buffurn and James F. Burns, located on Spring Street between Third and Fourth Streets. Two years later, she bought another lot on Olive Street for $375. In 1875, she sold the northern half of the Spring Street lot for $1,500. Biddy sold a portion of the Olive Street land for $2,000 in 1884. At her death, her investments were valued at $300,000, which equals $10,296,659.34 in 2024 dollars. She died in her home at 331 South Spring Street in Los Angeles. Her obituary noted, "She was a consistent Christian and a member of the Fourth Street A.M.E. Church."[13] Los Angeles Mayor Tom Bradley ceremoniously marked Biddy Mason's grave with a gravestone on March 27, 1988. The church Biddy helped found in 1872 first met in her home until a church was built. Over 100 years later, she was honored by the mayor of Los Angeles for her efforts. Cecil Murray, the current pastor of the First African Methodist Episcopal Church in Los Angeles, declared, "We must enshrine that which is noble in our midst, or we miss the landmark that leads us to tomorrow. Biddy Mason's head-

---

11. Biddy Mason Memorial Park, *Los Angeles Conservancy*, https://www.laconservancy.org/learn/historic-places/biddy-mason-memorial-park/ <accessed 23 March 2024>

12. Biddy Mason, *California Social Work Hall of Distinction 2002*, https://biddymason.info/biddy-mason, <accessed 23 March 2024>

13. Jorge Munoz and Dawn Amber Dennis (Department of History, Cal State Los Angeles, 2023), *Biddy Mason, The Making of Black Los Angeles*, unpaginated, https://storymaps.arcgis.com/stories/daf20ded50f144138b56ec19f59f0dbc, <accessed 23 March 2024>

stone thus becomes our heart-stone."[14] Biddy Mason left a remarkable legacy.

BETSY BROWN FLUELLEN AND JOHN FLUELLEN

The success of Biddy Mason following her release from enslavement was not the outcome experienced by most other freed enslaved men and women. Betsy Brown Fluellen's life began as an enslaved person and concluded with her death while locked in the Utah State Insane Asylum in Provo, Utah.[15] Sandwiched between these two dreadful life events, she found a few years of relative peace—even a few brief periods of happiness. After obtaining her freedom, she married a barber named John Fluellen while living in Corrine, Utah Territory. John might have served in the Civil War. Betsy bore three children from this marriage. However, two died as infants.[16] How John Brown and his wife Betsy Crosby Brown enslaved Betsy is unknown. An account written many years after the enslavement comes from John Brown. He wrote that "Betsy Crosby Brown Flewellen was the colored servant of Elizabeth Crosby Brown. In 1848, when she was a little girl, she was brought from the Crosby Plantation in Monroe County, Mississippi, to Utah by Mrs. Elizabeth Crosby Brown. She was a servant in the Brown home from 1848 until the slaves gained freedom during the war between the states."[17]

John Brown brought Betsy to Utah in 1848 when she was only eleven years old. Betsy appears in the 1850 Federal Census Slave Schedule as fourteen years of age.[18] If Betsy did indeed travel from

---

14. Ibid.
15. Julia Huddleson, "Betsy Brown Fluellen," *A Century of Black Mormons*, https://exhibits.lib.utah.edu/s/century-of-black-mormons/page/fluellen-betsy-brown#?c=&m=&s=&cv=&xywh=-848%2C-18%2C2224%2C802, <accessed 25 March 2024>
16. Amy Thiriot Tanner, *Slavery in Zion*, 186
17. John Zimmerman Brown, Autobiography of Pioneer John Brown, 1820-1896, 145
18. Utah Territorial census, 1851; CENSUS RETURNS (ORIGINAL); Great Salt Lake County, schedules 2-6; Church History Library, https://catalog.churchofjesuschrist.org/assets/eadde8a9-1f07-4f12-a10b-7175c5969887/0/14?lang=eng, <accessed 25 March 2024>

Monroe County to Winter Quarters and then from Winter Quarters to the Salt Lake Valley in 1848, she walked over 2,000 miles before reaching the valley. Did this young enslaved girl ever get to know her mother, father, or siblings before she was compelled to leave?[19] What was her workload as a young enslaved girl or as she grew older? John Brown first settled in Cottonwood, then built a home in Salt Lake City, a little later moved to Lehi, and finally settled in Pleasant Grove. He also married two additional wives during the 1850s, which undoubtedly added to Betsy's workload. The first years in the Salt Lake Valley challenged everyone. Betsy's responsibilities likely included helping with planting crops and harvesting. Preparing meals and making cheese, butter, candles, soap, and basic everyday needs to survive would have filled Betsy's days with never-ending tasks. She, along with others in the home, contributed to the well-being of the family. The difference between Betsy and others in the home—her enslavement.

The Church of Jesus Christ of Latter-day Saints instituted an initiative during the years 1856 and 1857, hoping to heighten and improve the spirituality of church members. Since the exodus from Nauvoo in 1846, the Saints had crossed oceans, walked thousands of miles across the frontiers of America, and strived to establish an ideal society. In addition, many church leaders came from a Puritan background, which demanded a constant struggle for perfection. Principals in the church felt the spirituality of members was fading, and they determined the time was right for a recommitment. The so-called Mormon Reformation began at a conference in Kaysville, Utah Territory, on 13 September 1856 under the direction of Jedidiah M. Grant, who was a member of the ruling First Presidency. During that weekend, 500 people renewed their commitments through rebaptism. From this first meeting, the Reformation spread throughout the

---

19. Camp of Israel schedules and reports, 1845-1849; John Brown's company of 10, report, 1848 June; Church History Library, https://catalog.churchofjesuschrist.org/assets/82b3a69e-d5ec-4752-a52f-e9816e27c554/0/0, <accessed 25 March 2024>

church.[20] This Reformation impacted Betsy's life while she was still enslaved. Evidence indicates she was first baptized in 1855 and rebaptized on 12 April 1857—by John Brown himself.[21] The autobiography of John Brown contains no mention of Betsy's baptism, but he does note that he consecrated and deeded to Brigham Young and the church his real estate and personal property. He included Betsy as property and valued her at $1,000, while his land and improvements totaled $775. John did not mention Betsy by name.[22]

In the summer of 1862, Congress abolished slavery in the United States, including both the territories and the states.[23] At the time Congress enacted the law freeing slaves, John Brown was in Omaha, Nebraska, returning from a mission and helping emigrants prepare for their march to Utah Territory. He reached the territory on the night of 16 September 1862. How John found out about Abolition and when or how he told Betsy is not known. However, at some point, she did receive her freedom from her enslavement and was able to breathe in the fresh air of freedom. Betsy lived in a boarding house in Corinne, Utah Territory, during the 1870 federal census, and she worked as a domestic servant.[24] By 1880, her husband had died, and Betsy was living with her one surviving daughter. She was then thirty-five years old and listed her employment as a washerwoman.[25] During the first years of her freedom, Betsy lost her husband and two children.[26] But more significant challenges were yet to come.

Betsy's life following the 1880 census remained a mystery until March 1893, when a small announcement appeared in *The Salt Lake*

---

20. B. H. Roberts, *A Comprehensive History of the Church of Jesus Christ of Latter-Day Saints,* 6 volumes (Salt Lake City: Deseret Book, 1950) 4: 124-125
21. Julia Huddleson, "Betsy Brown Fluellen," *A Century of Black Mormons*
22. John Zimmerman Brown, Autobiography of Pioneer John Brown, 1820-1896, 144
23. Paul Finkelman, "The Revolutionary Summer of 1862," *Prologue Magazine,* National Archives, unpaginated, https://www.archives.gov/publications/prologue/2017/winter/summer-of-1862, <accessed 25 March 2024>
24. Betsy Brown, "United States Census, 1870," *Family Search,* https://www.familysearch.org/tree/person/sources/GS2D-FH7, <accessed 25 March 2024>
25. Betsy Fluellen, "United States Census, 1880," *Family Search,* https://www.familysearch.org/tree/person/sources/GS2D-FH7, <accessed 25 March 2024>
26. Julia Huddleson, "Betsy Brown Fluellen," *A Century of Black Mormons*

Tribune newspaper. Almost hidden on page five of the 2 March 1893 edition appears a small notice, "A warrant is out for the arrest of Betsey Fluella, an aged colored woman at the County Poorhouse. She will be examined for insanity today."[27] The next day, sandwiched between a report about one Officer Lind improving after a leg operation and a regional weather report, the following one-sentence notice appears in the newspaper: "Betsey Fluella, an aged woman from the infirmary, was adjudged insane by Judge Blair yesterday and ordered sent to the asylum."[28] Thus, after years of enslavement, the loss of her husband, and the deaths of two children, Betsy now faced the remainder of her life in an insane asylum. Insanity was a mystery at the time. For example, on 2 March 1893, Judge Blair ordered a young man to the same asylum in Provo. A young man named W. F. Aldrich was determined by the judge to be insane because of his "propensity for forging checks."[29] Betsy's incarceration at the Territorial Insane Asylum in Provo became a life sentence. Her life, filled with tragedy from birth to death, mercifully ended at the age of sixty-six after nine years at the asylum. She was buried in an unmarked grave at the pauper's field in the Provo City Cemetery.[30] Her grit stands as a testament to the human spirit.

MARINDA REDD BANKHEAD

A quaint adobe house in Spanish Fork, Utah Territory, where Marinda and her husband, Alex, lived in the latter part of the nineteenth century and early twentieth century, shone a misleading light onto the challenges both she and her husband faced during their years

---

27. "Another Case," *The Salt Lake Tribune*, 2 March 1893, page 5, column 3, file:///C:/Users/Owner/Downloads/Salt-Lake-Tribune-Mar-02-1893-p-5.pdf, <accessed 27 March 2024> This is a paid subscription site.
28. Unreadable Title, *The Salt Lake Tribune*, 3 March 1893, page 8, column 1, file:///C:/Users/Owner/Downloads/Salt-Lake-Tribune-Mar-03-1893-p-8.pdf, <accessed 25 March 2024> Paid subscription site
29. "Another Case," *The Salt Lake Tribune*, 2 March 1893
30. Julia Huddleson, "Betsy Brown Fluellen," *A Century of Black Mormons*

under enslavement.[31] Marinda appears on the 1851 Utah Territorial Census Slave Schedule as a fifteen-year-old enslaved female.[32] Depending on the accuracy of the information, this would place her date of birth into enslavement between 1835 and 1836. Her skin color is listed as "yellow," a common practice used to describe enslaved men and women with lighter-colored skin. Her enslaver, Elizabeth Redd, brought Marinda west with her husband, John H. Redd, in the James Pace Company in 1850. This pioneer company left Kanesville, Iowa, on 11 June 1850 and arrived in the Salt Lake Valley between 20 and 23 September of that year.[33]

As noted above, the Redds left Tennessee and headed west with several enslaved people and their children. During their trek west, while passing through Kansas, some of the enslaved people escaped to freedom. Marinda did not. Although her enslavers were baptized before traveling west, Marinda did not accept baptism until 1852. Following their arrival in Utah Territory, the Redds settled south of Salt Lake City and helped found the town of Spanish Fork.[34] Like so many other enslaved men and women, Marinda's experiences during the years before she received her freedom were filled with hardships. Within a couple of years of settling in Spanish Fork, Elizabeth Redd died, along with two teenage children. In early 1856, John H. Redd found a new wife in Mary Lewis, who, at the time of their marriage, was sixteen years old. A family member later noted that the new Mrs. Redd now benefited from the three enslaved women who "did it all— took care of the baby and 'petted' Mary."[35] During the church

---

31. Tonya Reiter and Kaitlyn Benoit, "Biography Marinda Redd Bankhead," *A Century of Black Mormons*

32. Utah Territorial census, 1851; CENSUS RETURNS (ORIGINAL); Great Salt Lake County, schedules 2-6; Church History Library

33. James Pace Pioneer Company, "Church History Biographical Database," *The Church of Jesus Christ of Latter-Day Saints,* https://history.churchofjesuschrist.org/chd/organiza tion/pioneer-company/james-pace-company-1850?lang=eng&timelineTabs=allTabs, <accessed 2 April 2024>

34. Parshall, Ardis E. "Guest Post: Marinda Redd Bankhead: A Slave in Zion." *Keepa-pitchin.org,* 26 Mar 2012, https://keepapitchinin.org/2012/03/26/guest-post-marinda-redd-bankhead-a-slave-in-zion/, <accessed 2 April 2024>

35. Tonya Reiter, "Redd Slave Histories: Family, Race, and Sex in Pioneer Utah, *Utah*

Reformation of the mid-1850s, John H. Redd, as a sign of devotion to the church, consecrated his property to Brigham Young. He did not deed over any of the enslaved living in the family, while John Brown did include his enslaved "girl."[36]

Life during the 1860s was hard for Marinda. She gave birth to two sons out of wedlock due to sexual assaults perpetrated by white members of the church. One son, David, was born in 1863, and the second son, whom she named Edward T. Dennis, was born in 1867. Both fathers were white members of the church. Edward only lived a few months before he died, but David lived to adulthood. When Marinda married Alex Bankhead, he helped raise his new stepson, David, as his own. David moved to Salt Lake City and lived as a white man under the surname of Pace, after his white father.[37] Fortunately, Marinda and Alex Bankhead were able to marry, and they lived out their lives in relative peace. During an interview in 1899, a reporter wrote they both had "a very distinct recollection of the joyful expressions which were upon the faces of all the slaves when they ascertained that they had acquired their freedom through the fortunes of war." The reporter also noted the Bankheads "now own a little home, including twenty acres of land. They are both devout and strict Mormons."[38] Marinda received twenty acres of land following the death of John H. Redd. She received similar portions of property as other members of the Redd family passed. Thus, unlike other enslavers, John H. Redd treated the members of his household—free and enslaved—with a small degree of respect by leaving them land after his death. Miranda Redd Bankhead died of breast cancer in Provo, Utah, in 1907. Her death certificate notes she did not know the names of either of her parents, an all too common result of enslave-

---

Historical Quarterly, 85, (Spring 2017), https://issuu.com/utah10/docs/uhq_volume85_2017_number2/s/164170, <accessed 2 April 2024>

36. Tonya Reiter, "Redd Slave Histories: Family, Race, and Sex in Pioneer Utah

37. Tonya Reiter and Kaitlyn Benoit, "Biography Marinda Redd Bankhead," *A Century of Black Mormons*

38. "Slavery in Utah," *The Broad Ax*, Volume 4, Number 31, 25 March 1899, https://idnc.library.illinois.edu/?a=d&d=TBA18990325.1.1&srpos=23&e=-------en-20-TBA-21--txt-txIN-Slavery+in+Utah---------, <accessed 30 April 2024>

ment. The death certificate states her birth date as 1831.[39] Miranda persevered through enslavement and male violence during many years of her life. However, she lived the latter portion of her life free.

ISAAC MANNING

Isaac Manning, the brother of Jane Manning James, was born on 15 May 1815 in Wilton, Fairfield, Connecticut. Isaac's father, also named Isaac, was a free Black person, so he and the family did not experience enslavement; however, they likely still felt the sting of bigotry toward their Black skin. His father died when young Isaac turned ten, which left his mother, Philles Eliza Mead, a widow. Sometime later, Philles married Cato Treadwell, who had fought for his country during the Revolutionary War. Little is known about Isaac's early years, but by the 1840 census, he had married Lucinda, a free Black woman. The couple lived in Wilton, near his mother and her family.[40] In December 1842, while living in Wilton, Isaac and Lucinda received baptism by Albert Merrill. Evidence indicates that the two were not confirmed members of The Church of Jesus Christ of Latter-day Saints until May 1843 for unknown reasons. His sister, Jane, was baptized before Isaac on 14 October 1842. Jane's baptism sparked the interest of other family members, including Isaac. Their baptisms placed these two young people on two divergent paths.[41] Isaac, who was twenty-seven at the time of his baptism, and Jane continued the rest of their lives living in different locations, but both closed their lives as faithful members of the church they joined in the mid-1840s.

About a year after Isaac's baptism, Jane, Isaac, and several other family members left Wilton for Nauvoo, Illinois. Jane Manning James shared her memories of the journey in 1893. She stated that they trav-

---

39. Marinda Bankhead, "Utah, U.S., Death and Military Death Certificates, 1904-1961," *Family Search online,* https://www.ancestry.com/discoveryui-content/view/8532:9174, <accessed 2 April 2024>
40. W. Paul Reeve, "I Dug the Graves," *Journal of Mormon History,* January 2021, Vol. 47. No. 1 (January 2021), 36
41. W. Paul Reeve, "Biography Isaac Lewis Manning, *A Century of Black Mormons,*

eled by canal, likely the Erie Canal, from Albany to Buffalo, New York. After arriving at Buffalo, the party, which included many white emigrants, tried boarding a ship, but the Black travelers were refused passage. This forced them to walk the 800-plus miles to Nauvoo. Jane described their journey in the following words: "We walked until our shoes were worn out, and our feet became sore and cracked open and bled until you could see the whole print of our feet with blood on the ground." Upon arrival in Peoria, Illinois, the local authorities harassed them for free papers. They eventually were allowed to leave the town and continued ahead, constantly praying and thanking God for His protection until they arrived at Nauvoo. After facing frustrations in Nauvoo, they were eventually directed to Joseph Smith's home, where Joseph and Emma Smith warmly greeted them.[42]

Isaac cooked for Joseph and Emma Smith in the Mansion House for about three years. Later in his life, Isaac related the following about his time with the prophet:

> I was a cook at the prophet's kitchen, and he used to say I was a mighty good cook, too. I cooked the prophet's meals for almost three years when I was servant in the family, and then after he was shot at Carthage, they brought him back home, and I dug the graves.[43]

One of the few recorded accounts directly from Isaac comes from a short interview on 6 November 1903, when he recalled burying the bodies of Joseph and Hyrum Smith. He recalled that he dug two graves: one in the cellar of the prophet's log house and the other in the Nauvoo burying grounds. The bodies were buried at night in the cellar of the log house, while two coffins, which were filled with sand,

---

42. James, Jane Elizabeth Manning, 1812-1908. Jane E. Manning James autobiography typescript , https://catalog.churchofjesuschrist.org/assets/24edbf6c-dc89-4144-96be-9e69ff0c1e1a/0/4?lang=eng, <accessed 5 April 2024>

43. "Was Cook for the Prophet Joseph; Negro at Pioneer Day Fete," *Salt Lake Herald-Republican*, 26 July 1910, page 10, https://newspapers.lib.utah.edu/details?id=10511217&q=Isaac+Manning&sort=rel&year_end=1958, <accessed 6 April 2024>

were interred in the burying grounds.[44] Brigham Young and Emma Smith disagreed regarding the ownership of properties previously controlled by Joseph Smith. Two years after Isaac's efforts, Emma had the bodies relocated. The bodies were moved again in 1928 to their current site near the original location prepared by Isaac.[45]

Unlike Jane, who remained loyal to the church and its leaders until her death, Isaac's life took him down a different path. His devotion to the Prophet Joseph Smith never wavered; however, he did not follow Brigham Young and the Saints west like Jane. He lived in various places in the Midwest and Canada. While living in Canada, he joined the Reorganized Church of Jesus Christ of Latter-day Saints (RLDS) in 1876.[46] Joseph Smith III was a young boy of eleven when Isaac arrived in Nauvoo, and he had fond memories of Isaac as he proudly marched with the Nauvoo Legion while playing his enormous drum. Perhaps the memories of Joseph Smith III's father influenced Isaac to join the RLDS church, which was led by the prophet's son. Isaac was able to meet Joseph Smith III while living in Canada. Evidence indicates Isaac was never ordained to the priesthood during his time in Nauvoo, but priesthood ordination was not universal, even among white members of the church in the nineteenth century. Ordinations occurred to ensure congregations could function adequately. It was not until the early twentieth century that the church enacted a process for all young men to advance through the various priesthood offices.[47]

After forty-five years apart, Isaac and Jane were reunited. Isaac arrived in Salt Lake City sometime in 1892, and the siblings were treated kindly by both church leaders and members—due in large part

44. Manning, Isaac Lewis, 1815-1911. Isaac L. Manning statement, 1903 November 6 , https://catalog.churchofjesuschrist.org/assets/7961af90-bfcf-4347-b8fd-52fd9ee059fd/0/2?lang=eng, <accessed 7 April 2024>
45. W. Paul Reeve, "Biography Isaac Lewis Manning, *A Century of Black Mormons*,
46. Reeve, W. Paul. "'I Dug the Graves': Isaac Lewis Manning, Joseph Smith, and Racial Connections in Two Latter Day Saint Traditions." *Journal of Mormon History*, vol. 47, no. 1, 2021, pp. 29–67. *JSTOR*, https://doi.org/10.5406/jmormhist.47.1.0029 <accessed 9 Apr. 2024>
47. W. Paul Reeve, "Biography Isaac Lewis Manning, *A Century of Black Mormons*

to their association with the Prophet Joseph Smith. E.J.D. Roundy recalled some key elements of Isaac's life. In addition to burying Joseph and Hyrum's bodies, Isaac worked at the stone quarry harvesting rock for the Nauvoo temple and taught dancing at the Nauvoo Masonic Hall. Roundy further related that Isaac left the Midwest following the death of his wife in 1891, and he lived with his sister until her death.[48] For several years after his arrival in Utah Territory, Isaac and Jane had seats reserved for them in the front and center of the tabernacle. Jane made cushions for the two of them to sit on during conferences and special events.[49] Isaac was known for "his kind disposition and generous nature.[50] He died fully hoping "he could meet the prophet and be with him on the other side."[51]

Elijah Able and Samuel Chambers

The most well-known and documented Black priesthood holder of the nineteenth century is Elijah Able, who was ordained an elder in January 1836 and later ordained a member of the Quorum of the Seventy. He participated in washings and anointings in the Kirtland temple and baptisms for the dead in Nauvoo. He served three missions for the church. The last mission came at the age of seventy-three when he accepted a call to serve in Ohio. Elijah died on Christmas Day, 1884, within two weeks of returning from his mission.[52] Although racial restrictions were in place after 1852, Elijah sought to participate in the remainder of the temple ordinances and to be sealed to his wife, who had previously passed away. John Taylor

48. "Funeral of Isaac Manning," *The Deseret Evening News*, 17 April 1911, Page 3, column 1, https://newspapers.lib.utah.edu/details?id=24984376&q=Isaac+Manning&sort=rel&year_start=1910&year_end=1911, <accessed 9 April 2024>
49. Ibid.
50. Isaac Manning Servant of the Prophet Joseph Smith Dies in Salt Lake, *Vernal Express*, 21 April 1911, Page 1, https://newspapers.lib.utah.edu/details?id=21269613&q=Isaac+Manning&sort=rel&year_start=1910&year_end=1911, <accessed 9 April 2024>
51. W. Paul Reeve, "Biography Isaac Lewis Manning, *A Century of Black Mormons*
52. W. Paul Reeve, "Biography of Elijah Able, *Century of Black Mormons*

denied his applications for these blessings in 1879. Interestingly, Elijah had recently spoken to a joint gathering of thirty-three Quorums of the Seventy just a few months earlier.[53] Elijah died as faithful as when he was baptized.

An inspiring story of courage and commitment to The Church of Jesus Christ of Latter-day Saints comes from the lives of Samuel D. Chambers and his wife, Amanda Leggroan. Samuel was born an enslaved baby on 21 May 1831 in Pickens, Alabama. Slave traders split his family by taking away his mother when Samuel was a small boy. Now orphaned, Samuel grew up in Noxubee County, Mississippi, on the eastern side of the state bordering Alabama. In 1844, this obscure, enslaved thirteen-year-old boy heard the preaching of a missionary for The Church of Jesus Christ of Latter-day Saints. He knew almost immediately the words he heard were true. He was baptized at night shortly thereafter. Other people who joined the church could move to Nauvoo or other church centers. As an enslaved person, Samuel could not relocate. For the next twenty-five years, he was completely isolated from the church. He had no contact with missionaries, and he was unable to attend church meetings. During his enslavement, Samuel married, but his first wife either died or was sold to another enslaver following the birth of his son, Peter. On 4 May 1858, Samuel and Amanda Leggroan, an enslaved woman, were married.[54]

Even though Samuel had no contact with the church since his baptism, his hope to live with other members of his chosen faith continued burning in his heart. The conclusion of the Civil War brought about his freedom, and he worked tirelessly over the next four years to save enough money to make the journey to Utah Territory. Regarding the years away from any church fellowship, he once stated, "I was baptized in the year 1844, and after that, I was

----

53. W. Paul Reeve, *Let's Talk About Race and Priesthood*, (Salt Lake City, Utah: Deseret Book, 2023), 75-76

54. William G. Hartley, "Samuel D. Chambers," *New Era*, (June 1974, page(s) 46-50, https://www.churchofjesuschrist.org/study/new-era/1974/06/samuel-d-chambers?lang=eng, <accessed 9 April 2024>

twenty-one years in bondage, during which time I never heard a word of the gospel."[55]

In 1870, Samuel, Amanda, and their son, Peter, along with Amanda's brother and family, finally began the long trek west. Samuel and this faithful band arrived in Salt Lake City on 28 April 1870. Samuel's testimony burned as bright now as when he was baptized in 1844. He served as an assistant deacon—even though he did not hold the priesthood. The responsibilities of deacons in the late 1800s were cleaning buildings, ensuring heat was available in the winter, and making sure windows and doors were open in the summer. In 1875, when deacons were asked to usher during summer meetings at the tabernacle, he was his ward's only volunteer.[56]

This formerly-enslaved man, who never received the priesthood, continued faithfully not only by cleaning churches and ushering at various meetings; he also regularly expressed his deep appreciation for the restored gospel, lifting those around him as well. One man stated he knew that Brother Chambers "spoke by the spirit of God." Another member noted, "Brother Chambers has preached as good a sermon as I ever wished to hear."[57] Here are some words from Samuel Chambers, which are available due to the excellent minutes kept by Thomas C. Jones, a stake deacon's clerk during the 1870s. Without the effort of Thomas Jones, the words spoken by Samuel would be lost forever. On 11 November 1873, Brother Chambers declared the following powerful testimony: "I've been blest [sic] from my youth up, although in bondage for twenty years after receiving the gospel, yet I kept the faith. I thank God that I ever gathered with the Saints. May the Lord bless us and help us to be faithful is my prayer. Amen." On another occasion, he stated, "I did not come to Utah to know the truth of the gospel, but I received it away back where the gospel found

---

55. W. Paul Reeve, *Let's Talk About Race and Priesthood*, 21

56. William G. Hartley, "Samuel D. Chambers," *New Era*,

57. Editor, "Saint Without Priesthood: The Collected Testimonies of Ex-Slave Samuel D. Chambers," *Dialogue of Mormon Thought*, Dialogue 12.2 (Summer 1979): 13-21 https://www.dialoguejournal.com/articles/saint-without-priesthood-the-collected-tes timonies-of-ex-slave-samuel-d-chambers/#pdf-wrap, <accessed 10 April 2024>

me."[58] Amanda Leggroan Chambers died on 2 March 1929 and was buried in the Millcreek Cemetery on 10 March 1929. Samuel Davis Chambers passed away on 13 November 1929 and was also interred at the Millcreek Cemetery.[59] Samuel and Amanda displayed remarkable devotion to each other and the church to the end of their lives.

---

58. Ibid.

59. Amanda Leggroan (K2WC-KX7), and Samuel Davis Chambers (L7K9-GTC), *Family Search online*, https://www.familysearch.org/tree/person/details/K2WC-KX7, and https://www.familysearch.org/tree/person/details/L7K9-GTC, <accessed 10 April 2024>

13

SIX MEN WHO RETURNED TO MISSISSIPPI FROM PUEBLO

The group known as the Mississippi Saints, or Mississippi Company, traveled west before any other members of the church during the 1840s. They headed into the unknown at the request of Brigham Young. This book documented the travels of this small band of believers who left Mississippi and Alabama in April 1846 and, after spending a winter in Fort Pueblo, Colorado, finally arrived in the Salt Lake Valley in July 1847. Over the next few years, several of these groups brought enslaved men, women, and children west. Their situations as enslaved remained virtually unchanged, for several years, with the introduction of a form of enslavement beginning in 1852. The previous chapter of this book was dedicated to telling their stories—not at the exclusion of others—but to grant an equal ground for the accomplishments of Black men and women, both in western settlements and as members of The Church of Jesus Christ of Latter-day Saints. This chapter includes accounts of the lives of six original members of the band who trekked west in 1846 and returned to Mississippi from Pueblo. Like you and I, these people lived imperfect lives and, at times, lost faith, but by and large, they remained loyal to their chosen beliefs. We will begin with John Brown, who was at the center of the entire Mississippi group.

John Brown

Elder George P. Dykes baptized John Brown into The Church of Jesus Christ of Latter-day Saints in July 1841. After being shunned by his peers and losing his job, he quickly departed his home area and traveled to Nauvoo, Illinois, with Robert Crow and a few others. He arrived in Nauvoo in time for a conference, and he was able to meet Joseph Smith and other leaders of the church. While in Nauvoo, he roomed with George Dykes and worked on the Nauvoo House. Hyrum Smith pronounced a Patriarchal Blessing on John 11 October 1841. Hyrum also ordained John an elder on 9 February 1842. Shortly thereafter, he filled a short mission with George Dyke to his home area, which allowed him to visit friends and "preach a few times." After returning to Nauvoo, John was called on a mission to the southern states. He left on his mission on 29 May 1843.[1]

John Brown remained devoted to the church and its leaders throughout his life. He married Elizabeth Coleman Crosby on May 20, 1844, in Monroe County, Mississippi.[2] John lived in the home of Elizabeth's mother for the next four years. John met Elizabeth during his mission on 21 December 1843 while preaching at the home of William Crosby.[3] After arriving in the Salt Lake Valley, John quickly returned to Mississippi to bring his family west. In November 1849, John, under the direction of Parley P. Pratt, explored areas south of the Salt Lake Valley. He served as a captain of fifty, and they traveled as far south as present-day St. George, Utah.[4] The expedition party contained twenty-five wagons, and their travel took them over high mountains with snow over six feet deep. Ropes were constantly used

---

1. John Zimmerman Brown, Autobiography of Pioneer John Brown, 1820-1896, (Stevens & Wallis, Inc. Salt Lake City, Utah 1941), 33-38

2. John Brown, *Family Search*, https://www.familysearch.org/ark:/61903/3:1:3Q9M-C9BJ-ZS56-1?i=242&cc=3477669, <accessed 23 May 2024> Marriage of John Brown to Elizabeth Crosby.

3. John Zimmerman Brown, Autobiography of Pioneer John Brown, 1820-1896, 33-38

4. John Brown, 1820-1896. Autobiographical sketch, undated, images 41-42/65, /https://catalog.churchofjesuschrist.org/assets/6c67a206-04f7-410a-be89-1396d c4a3c26/0/40?lang=eng, <accessed 15 April 2024>

to pull the wagons over mountain slopes. Brown described the geography during one portion of the journey as "a dreary waste of table mountains and barren hills destitute of timber, soil, or grass nothing to be seen but rocks clay and sand."[5] After traveling hundreds of miles, suffering hunger, thirst, and fatigue, John Brown reached home on 1 February 1850.[6]

John Brown was selected as one of the directors of the Perpetual Emigration Fund, which was organized to assist church members in leaving their homelands and traveling to Utah Territory. He left Salt Lake City in the spring of 1851 with $5,000 of gold in hand to lead a group of Saints from present-day Council Bluffs to Utah Territory.[7] They departed with fifty wagons on 7 July 1851 and arrived in the Salt Lake Valley on 29 September 1851.[8] John was elected to the Territorial Legislative Assembly in 1851 and served in the first Territorial Legislature in January 1852. In August of that year, John received a mission call to New Orleans, Louisiana. He and a large group of missionaries left Salt Lake City for their assigned missions on 15 September 1852. Upon arrival in New Orleans, John organized a small branch there. He received an assignment to meet a group of Saints in New Orleans who had sailed from Liverpool and take them up the Mississippi River to the town of Keokuk, Iowa. John wrote that these Saints had "never seen a yoke of cattle in their lives. It made a hard summer's work for me."[9] He led this company of roughly 303 inexperienced pioneers from Keokuk on 1 July 1853 and arrived in the valley between 13 and 17 October of that year.[10]

John purchased a farm and moved his family to Lehi, Utah

---

5. Ibid, 42-43

6. Ibid, 51

7. Ibid.

8. John Brown Company, *Church History Biographical Database,* https://history.chur chofjesuschrist.org/chd/organization/pioneer-company/john-brown-company-1851? lang=eng&timelineTab=allTabs, <accessed 16 April 2024>

9. Brown, John, 1820-1896. Autobiographical sketch, 52-53

10. John Brown company, *Church History Biographical Database,* https://history.churchof jesuschrist.org/chd/organization/pioneer-company/john-brown-company-1853? lang=eng&timelineTab=allTabs, <accessed 16 April 2924>

Territory, in 1855. In the spring of 1857, he traveled with Brigham Young and a group of men to Fort Lemhi on the Salmon River. That fall, he was involved, with others, in harassing the United States Military during the Utah War. He traveled as far as Fort Bridger. Two years later, he was elected again to the legislature, this time from Utah County. His seemingly non-stop service to his church continued with another mission call. This time, he served in the British Isles. He departed from Salt Lake City with other missionaries, arriving in Liverpool on 27 July 1860. He served in England until he received a letter releasing him from this assignment. He left for home on 1 March 1862. He was sent in advance of that year's emigration to arrange passage from New York City to Florence, Nebraska Territory. He served in that capacity throughout the summer, and after leaving Florence for Salt Lake City, he arrived home on 16 September 1862.[11]

John Brown's resolute service to the church he joined in 1841, continued to the end of his life. Soon after his arrival back home, he was ordained a Seventy and directed to organize the 68th Quorum of Seventy and preside as "senior president." At this time, a "seventy" within the church served in various leadership capacities within local congregations. In January 1863, John received a letter from George A. Smith (a member of the church's First Presidency) requesting him to come to Salt Lake City, where he would be called as bishop of the Pleasant Grove Ward. John Brown was ordained a bishop 3 February 1863 by Brigham Young himself. John served as a bishop for the next twenty-nine years until his failing health forced him to seek a release from this calling.[12] A bishop's responsibilities are weighty and require a tremendous commitment of time and emotional involvement. A bishop's role is to watch over or shepherd hundreds of individuals within a certain geographic area. Church members look to a bishop for spiritual and emotional guidance. A bishop can have a powerful influence for good on the people under his leadership.

---

11. John Brown, 1820-1896. Autobiographical sketch, 53-55
12. Ibid, 52-56

JOHN DANIEL HOLLADAY

John Daniel Holladay began his life on 22 June 1826 in northeastern Alabama. His parents farmed and raised livestock. John joined The Church of Jesus Christ of Latter-day Saints in June 1844. In March 1845, he traveled north to Nauvoo, where he quarried stone for both the temple and Nauvoo House. He returned home in December 1845 to help his parents and family prepare for a move west in the spring of 1846. John Holladay traveled west with John Brown in April 1846 with the original group of Saints from Mississippi and Alabama. He returned to Alabama with John Brown after spending a few weeks in Pueblo, reaching home in the fall of 1846. During his time in Alabama, he settled his father's business affairs before going west again—this time to the Salt Lake Valley.[13] He remained in the South until 1848, when he started west for Winter Quarters. He arrived there on 23 May 1848 and departed for Utah Territory in the Willard Richards Company on 3 July 1848. This massive company of 526 individuals arrived in the Salt Lake Valley on 10 October 1848.[14]

Upon arriving in the Salt Lake Valley, John married Mahalia Ann Rebecca Mathews. They had traveled together and married shortly after arriving in the valley. As noted in an earlier chapter, his father, John D. Holladay Sr., settled on Big Cottonwood Creek, which is where the two newlyweds decided to live. John Sr. provided the newly married couple a wedding gift consisting of a wagon, a yoke of oxen, a cow, a stewing pot, a frying pan, two knives and forks, two tin plates, and an iron spoon. In addition, the couple also received a log cabin, a bedstead, and provisions.[15] John and Mahalia remained in the area now known as Holladay until 1851 when John traveled to Southern

---

13. Orson F. Whitney, *History of Utah*, (Salt Lake City, Utah, George Q. Cannon & Sons, 1904) 401, https://archive.org/details/historyofutahcom04whit/page/n1/mode/2up?view=theater&q=Holladay, <accessed 1 May 2024>
14. Willard Richards Company (1948), *Church History Biographical Database*, https://history.churchofjesuschrist.org/chd/organization/pioneer-company/willard-richards-company-1848?lang=eng&timelineTab=allTabs, <accessed 1 May 2024>
15. Orson F. Whitney, *History of Utah*, 401

California to help create San Bernardino. There, John served as County Sheriff and additionally functioned as the Marshall for San Bernardino for several years. John and the family left San Bernardino on 15 December 1857 and resided in Beaver for one year before moving to Santaquin, where he lived until his death on 15 September 1909 at the age of eighty-three years.[16]

Following his settlement in Santaquin, John continued living a life filled with service. He spent most of his life farming, but he involved himself in many civic activities. In 1858, he explored a portion of the Colorado River below Grand Falls, near present-day Flagstaff, Arizona. During his early years in Santaquin, he served as a captain of the local militia company. John worked as a school trustee for several years and continued as a deputy sheriff for Utah County. John attended the state constitutional convention in 1895 and was one of the signers of the State Constitution.[17] John married two additional women after marrying Mahalia. He married Johana Blake on 12 October 1867 in Salt Lake City, and he wedded Sarah Elizabeth Holladay on 16 February 1887.[18] In addition to farming, John formed a partnership with his brother, David Holladay, and Norman Taylor for a lumber business. He served a mission to the southern states from the spring of 1868 to 1870. John also served for a period as a guard at the Utah Penitentiary. In 1866, John captained a down-and-back wagon train to the Missouri River to pick up emigrants from Europe and take them, their supplies and needed freight to Utah.[19]

The church used down-and-back wagon trains from 1861 to 1868.

---

16. "Timeline of the Life of John Daniel Holliday, jr. (1826-1909), *Family Search.org*, <KWPN-PNH> unpaginated, https://www.familysearch.org/tree/person/memories/ KWV4-JY5, Contributed by Janeen Christensen, found in the Memories of Robert Crow, <accessed 13 May 2024>

17. S. L. Peterson, "Delegates to the Constitutional Convention, *Salt Lake Herald-Republican*, (28 March 1895, Page 3), https://newspapers.lib.utah.edu/details?id=11334374& q=John+D.+Holladay&sort=rel&year_start=1850&year_end=1910,   <accessed   13 March 2024>

18. *Family Search.org*, Wedding dates for Johana Blake and Sarah Elizabeth Holladay to John D. Holladay, https://www.familysearch.org/tree/person/details/KWNP-PNH, <accessed 13 May 2024>

19. Orson F. Whitney, *History of Utah*, 402

Trains started east in the spring of the year, traveled to the Missouri River, and returned to Utah the same year. John Holladay's down-and-back train departed from Utah Territory for a town named Wyoming, on the west banks of the Missouri River, about forty miles south of Omaha, Nebraska. His company consisted of 350 individuals and sixty-nine wagons, and the group left Wyoming on 16-18 July 1866, arriving in Salt Lake City on 25 September 1866.[20] The organization of the down-and-back trains consisted of a captain, either oxen or mules and high-quality wagons. Teams were organized into companies of fifty men each. As the captain, Holladay held responsibility for the safety and welfare of all involved. Four mounted men took charge of the livestock when they were not in the yoke. The teamsters carried responsibility for the teams, wagons, and any property placed in their possession; the church assumed no liability for such property.[21]

Charles Denny traveled as a passenger on Holladay's down-and-back wagon train. In later years, he wrote about his experiences traveling west. He recalled six people died on the trek. One sister died on the trail after just two weeks, and following a brief burial service, the wagon train continued the march west "as though nothing had happened." Charles noted the wagons leaving the village of Wyoming also carried freight for the church. One wagon carried coal oil for the old tabernacle and for the theater. In addition to the freight carried by the wagons, each emigrant's possessions remained in the wagons. Denny wrote about bathing while on the trail, saying, "I would go into the water with it [a shirt] on, then after I had splashed abut a while, and rubbed my shirt I would lay it on the bank to dry while I went into the water again, so you see I was clean myself and had a clean

---

20. John D. Holladay Company (1866), *Church History Biographical Database*, https://history.churchofjesuschrist.org/chd/organization/pioneer-company/john-d-holladay-company-1866?lang=eng&timelineTab=allTabs, <accessed 13 May 2024>
21. Erick L. Wadsworth, *The Last Outfitting Station on the Missouri River, 1864-1866: Wyoming, NT and the Nebraska City Cut-off Trail*, (Nampa, Idaho, Trail Publishing, 2019), 120

shirt to put on."[22] As Captain Holladay guided the wagon train under his charge toward Utah Territory he met Arza Hinckley's rescue wagon train coming from Salt Lake City. Arza departed the city in late July 1866 and met Holladay's wagon train after traveling east thirty-one days. Hinckley's rescue train deposited needed flour, hobbles to restrain the oxen, and grain for livestock with Holladay's wagon train. Hinckley's rescue wagon train assisted several other wagon trains heading west in 1866.[23] From the time John Holladay joined the church to the end of his long life, he served others with distinction and dignity.

WILLIAM HARVEY LAY

John Vincent Lay and Rhoda Ann Baker welcomed William (Billy) Harvey Lay into their family on 25 July 1817 at Union, South Carolina. His family eventually consisted of four brothers and four sisters.[24] William met Sytha Crosby, sister of William Crosby, during a trip to northeastern Mississippi. One account of their meeting states that when Billy visited the town of Aberdeen (a town near the Crosby plantation), he "noticed a lovely young woman tying the reins of her horse to the long hitching post that extended the full length of the building. He watched her, captivated, for she moved with such grace."[25] According to this account, Sytha's beauty completely over-whelmed William, and following a short courtship, they married in December 1841. Indeed, Monroe County authorized William Lay and Sytha Crosby to seek "any regular Ordained Minister of the Gospel,

22. Charles Denney reminiscences and diary, 1875 January-1883 April; Diary, 1875 January - 1883 April; Church History Library, https://catalog.churchofjesuschrist.org/assets/8bc656db-f945-4035-b8ba-3422349a6669/0/0?lang=eng, <accessed 13 May 2024>

23. Wadsworth, *The Last Outfitting Station on the Missouri River, 172*

24. William Harvey Lay LLQF-Y3B, *Family Search.org*, https://www.familysearch.org/tree/person/details/LLQF-Y3B, <accessed 14 May 2024>

25. Charmaine Lay Kohler, *Southern Grace A Story of the Mississippi Saints*, (Boise, Idaho, Beagle Press, 1995), 39

Judge, Judge of the Police Court, or acting judge" in the county to "join them together as Man and Wife in the holy estate of wedlock."[26]

The newlywed's hope for a future living in their beloved South dramatically changed following Sytha's baptism into The Church of Jesus Christ of Latter-day Saints on 18 June 1844 by John Brown.[27] For reasons still unknown, William Lay never joined the church. However, he walked thousands of miles back and forth across the country and moved multiple times to support his wife's faith before dying in the high desert of Santa Clara in Utah Territory—a land completely different from his treasured South. To show his commitment to Sytha's faith, William left Mississippi in 1846, looking for a home for her and the family in the West. As noted earlier, this group stopped in Pueblo for the winter of 1846-1847. William walked back from Pueblo to his Mississippi home, where he reconnected with his wife and children. Just two years later, William traveled to Utah Territory with his wife and family.[28] In 1851, the family moved again, this time to San Bernardino. William and Sytha's final move took them back to Utah Territory to settle in Santa Clara, located at the southern tip of the territory.[29]

The constant moves made by William, Sytha, and their family reduced their ability to improve financially. Evidence gleaned from federal census records of 1860 and 1870 provides insight into the challenges the family faced. During the 1860 census, William and the family lived in Santa Clara, and the value of their real estate totaled $180, while his property value totaled $900. At this time, Sytha and their seven children lived in the home. The youngest child, Daniel, was recorded as three years of age, while the eldest, John, appeared on the census as seventeen. Of the seven children, two were born in

---

26. "Mississippi Marriages, 1800-1911," *Family Search.org*, image 162/534m https://www.familysearch.org/ark:/61903/3:1:3Q9M-C9BJ-ZS5G-V?i=161&cc=3477669, <accessed 14 May 2024>
27. Brown, John, 1820-1896. Autobiographical sketch, undated, 42
28. Ibid, 70, 96,
29. Washington Chapter DUP's, (Panguitch, Utah, Garfield County News, 1950), 154-155

California, two in Utah Territory, two in Mississippi, and one in Missouri.[30] Ten years later, the value of his real estate climbed to $250, but the worth of his holdings plummeted to $600—a loss of about one-third of his previous net worth. Four of Billy and Sytha's children remained in the home.[31] The 1880 census found William and Sytha living next door to their son, John, his wife, and four children. Sytha passed away on 25 October 1881, and William died on 17 March 1886.[32]

William Lay demonstrated his allegiance to his wife and her faith through his constant moves with her and the family. Like so many other pioneers, Sytha's contribution to her beliefs and family stands as an inspiration for those who followed. One account of her accomplishments during her demanding life follows:

Sytha Crosby Lay died at the age of sixty-three on October 25, 1881. During her lifetime, she accomplished miracles, creating comfortable homes for her family in five different locations—pioneering in four of them. She had helped build houses, even fireplaces and chimneys. She had cut wild hay along river bottoms and stacked it for winter feed. She had grubbed brush, hauled manure to fertilize the land, sheared sheep, and planted and made irrigation ditches. All of this, besides her own 'woman's work.' She had raised eight children and lost three to death. She sacrificed the wealth and luxuries of this life for something of a far greater value, never losing faith in her God or her husband."[33]

In remembering the efforts of Sytha and other pioneers who demonstrated their faith by settling the West, one should also recall

---

30. "United States Census, 1860," *Family Search,* https://www.familysearch.org/ark:/61903/1:1:MH2W-8ZN, <accessed 15 May 2024>
31. "United States Census, 1870," *Family Search,* https://www.familysearch.org/ark:/61903/1:1:MNCB-QM9, <accessed 15 May 2024>
32. Sytha Solena Crosby, *Family Search,* https://www.familysearch.org/tree/person/details/LLQF-Y3B, <accessed 15 May 2024>
33. Cathleen Valentine Sanberg, "Sytha Solena Crosby Lay (Edited version of original) *Family Search,* <KWVP-8S4> unpaginated, https://www.familysearch.org/tree/person/memories/LLQF-Y3B, <accessed 15 May 2024>

the efforts of the Black men and women who accompanied the Mississippi Saints west and worked side-by-side with them to overcome the challenging environment of Utah Territory.

William Crosby

William Crosby, the son of John Jeter Crosby and Elizabeth Glenn Coleman, began his life on 19 September 1808 in Knox, Indiana Territory.[34] Indiana Territory allowed slavery during the late 1700s and early 1800s even though the Northwest Ordinance declared that "neither slavery nor involuntary servitude should exist in the northwest territory otherwise than a punishment of crime."[35] William's parents were enslavers, and following the tragic death of John Crosby in 1840, his will directed that his widow and the children would inherit enslaved persons. The family relocated to Monroe County and were viewed as a well-to-do family. They owned extensive plantations and many enslaved men and women.[36] William married Sarah Jane Harmon on 4 March 1832 at Monroe, Mississippi.[37] The future of William Crosby, his mother, and his siblings dramatically changed following their baptisms into the church. Missionaries baptized Elizabeth and all her children except her daughter, Susan. The spacious Crosby home provided the location for church services.[38] At the time missionary John Brown entered Monroe County in late 1843, William Crosby was serving as the presiding authority in the small local branch. Brown baptized other members of the Crosby family within a few weeks of his arrival.[39]

After arriving in Utah, William settled in the area now known as

---

34. William Crosby, *Family Search*, <KWV7-BJY> https://www.familysearch.org/tree/person/details/KWV7-BJY, <accessed 17 May 2024>

35. University of Illinois Urbana-Champaign, *The Laws of Indiana Territory, 1809-1816,* p. 20, https://archive.org/details/lawsofindianater00indi/page/20/mode/2up?q=slavery, <accessed 17 May 2024>

36. John Brown, 1820-1896. Autobiographical sketch, undated, 49

37. William Crosby, *Family Search*

38. Ibid, 50

39. Ibid, 44

Holladay. In 1851, he and his family moved to San Bernardino under the direction of Amasa Lyman and Charles C. Rich. He willingly served in several community and religious capacities while living there. William left San Bernardino when Brigham Young directed the Saints living in that area to return to Utah Territory.[40] Shortly before leaving for Southern California, by request of William Lay, William Crosby sent a letter to Brigham Young with concerns about how to manage the separation of enslaved Hark Lay from his wife, who was enslaved by George Bankhead. Crosby wrote that William Lay could not pay the cash needed to allow Hark's wife to accompany him to Southern California. Crosby also included in the letter his strong feelings about enslaved Green Flake. He wrote in part, "I will speak of Green the Boy, that came with hark to see you. he is a mean dirty I sarvace [savage] Lying disaffected Saucy to Brother Flakes wife."[41] Brigham Young replied to William's letter by counseling that separating a man and his wife "would not be wisdom." He concluded his response to Crosby by advising him not to take many of the enslaved with them to Southern California because they "would all go free as soon as they arrive in California."[42]

Following his time in San Bernardino, William continued serving his church and community in a variety of ways. He arrived at Santa Clara at the same time as his brother-in-law, William Lay, in the spring of 1858.[43] Like his brother-in-law, William Crosby and the family never reached any type of financial independence like he had enjoyed in Monroe County. The census of 1860 and 1870 tell the story of his financial struggles. In 1860, William lived in Pine Valley, Utah Territory. The enumerator valued William's real estate at $100,

---

40. Jacob H. Crosby mission papers, 1902-1951; William Crosby biography; Church History Library, image 5/13, https://catalog.churchofjesuschrist.org/assets/73f061d8-0471-4f8f-a6ef-7234b8fb0aa4/0/4?lang=eng, <accessed 17 May 2024>
41. Brigham Young office files, 1832-1878 (bulk 1844-1877); General Correspondence, Incoming, 1840-1877; General Letters, 1840- 1877; Co-F, 1851; William Crosby letter; Church History Library, https://catalog.churchofjesuschrist.org/assets/65e7d3bf-9027-4fa1-a451-5e8674022af2/0/0?lang=eng, <accessed 18 May 2024>
42. Ibid.
43. Washington Chapter DUP's, 154-155

and his "personal estate" stood at $1,565.[44] Ten years later, the 1870 census placed the value of his real estate at $500 dollars, but his "personal estate" dropped to $500. At the time of the 1879 census, both William and Sarah were now sixty-two years old.[45] Shortly after arriving in southern Utah, William served as the first postmaster in the first post office for Santa Clara. A weekly mail route from Cedar City to Santa Clara opened 1 July 1862. The route ran by way of Harmony, Tocqueville, Washington, and St. George.[46] William served on the Agriculture, Trade, and Manufacturing Committee with Edwin D. Woolley, Ezra T. Benson, and George Peacock during the legislative session of 1860.[47] In 1862, he represented Washington County at the unsuccessful State Convention for the establishment of a state government. He served with John M. Moody and George A. Smith.[48] William continued to serve the public throughout the remainder of his life.

During his tenure in southern Utah Territory, William involved himself heavily in growing cotton. He developed a strong relationship with Brigham Young, as can be seen in a letter he wrote to Brigham Young 29 April 1860. Young had previously written a letter asking Bishop Judd and William Crosby to sell or rent the farm Young owned on the Virgin River. William's efforts were unsuccessful when he wrote the letter. He also reported the progress of the settlements in the area to President Young. He and Jacob Hamlin toured each of the

---

44. United States Census, 1860," *Family Search,* https://www.familysearch.org/ark:/61903/1:1:MH2W-8QL, <accessed 18 May 2024>

45. "United States Census, 1870: *Family Search,* https://www.familysearch.org/tree/person/sources/KWV7-BJY, <accessed 18 May 2024>

46. "Tabernacle," *Deseret News,* 16 December 1860, https://newspapers.lib.utah.edu/search?q=William+Crosby&sort=rel&year_start=1860&year_end=1860&month_t=%22december%22, <accessed 18 May 2024>

47. "Legislative Proceedings," *Deseret News,* 19 December 1860, https://newspapers.lib.utah.edu/details?id=2585837&q=William+Crosby&sort=rel&year_start=1860&year_end=1860&month_t=%22december%22, <accessed 18 May 2024>

48. "Organization of the Convention for The Establishment of a State Government," *Deseret News,* 22 January 1862, https://newspapers.lib.utah.edu/details?id=2591039&page=5&q=William+Crosby&sort=rel&year_start=1850&year_end=1888,   <accessed 18 May 2024>

settlements in southern Utah. During each stop, Crosby asked for a report regarding their progress. Bishop Tinney from Grafton reported 1,000 acres of good land to grow cotton was available but only seven families were living in the community. The bishop felt twenty more families could live at Grafton. William felt the communities could accept "one thousand more men" to fill up current towns, with more land available further south in Washington County.[49] William Crosby died in Kanab, Utah Territory, 5 October 1880. His life of faithful service to others in the West allowed him and his family to escape the horrors of the Civil War. The area in Mississippi where they lived suffered 500 battles.[50] He lived a life of commitment to his family and faith.

Daniel Monroe Thomas

Henry and Esther Thomas welcomed Daniel Monroe Thomas into the world 27 December 1809 in Rockingham, Richmond, North Carolina.[51] Daniel was the oldest of seven boys and three girls. The family remained in Richmond County, North Carolina, until 1833, the year his mother died.[52] William collaborated with his father on the plantation until he turned twenty-one. He then attended school with his brother, Preston, where he studied science for two years. His next venture lasted three years and found him dealing in general merchandise sales. He moved to Mississippi and built a store, where he worked as a clerk for the next four years. He then moved near his family, who were living in Noxubee, Mississippi, and collaborated with his dad for two years before teaching school for an additional

---

49. Brigham Young office files, 1832-1878 (bulk 1844-1877); General Correspondence, Incoming, 1840-1877; General Letters, 1840- 1877; Co-D, 1860; William Crosby letter; Church History Library, https://catalog.churchofjesuschrist.org/assets/ab580dd2-3a6d-4663-bb80-ac40bcca8a91/0/0?lang=eng, <accessed 18 May 2024>
50. Jacob H. Crosby mission papers, 1902-1951.
51. "Daniel Monroe Thomas," *Family Search*, <KWVP-8S3>, https://www.familysearch.org/tree/person/details/KWVP-8S3 , <accessed 19 May 2024>
52. "Elijah Thomas Sr." *Family Search*, <KWJ8-9W2>, https://www.familysearch.org/tree/person/memories/KWJ8-9W2, <accessed 19 May 2024>

three years.[53] The year 1844 brought significant changes to Daniel's life.

A hand-written account penned years later indicated Daniel fell in love with a Jane Love, but she passed away."[54] No indication is provided regarding a possible marriage between the two. Daniel joined The Church of Jesus Christ of Latter-day Saints on 4 January 1844. He married Ann Crosby, daughter of John and Elizabeth Crosby, on 17 March 1845.[55] Daniel worked on the Crosby plantation as an overseer for about one year.[56] His next move involved the trek west in 1846 with the Mississippi Saints. On his way back from Pueblo to Mississippi, Daniel met his younger brother, Elijah Thomas, who was a member of the Mormon Battalion. This remarkable event took place on 12 September 1846 in southwest Kansas at a crossing of the Arkansas River.[57] As noted in chapter nine, Daniel involved himself heavily in both public and church service during his time in San Bernardino. In 1858, he moved the family to Beaver, Utah, after leaving San Bernardino. During his time in Beaver, he served as a probate judge and postmaster. His postmaster service came during the Civil War.[58] Daniel and Ann were the parents of two girls and three boys, and all but the youngest son began their lives in Mississippi. The youngest, John Thomas, was born in Utah Territory.[59]

The 1860 census provides a glimpse into the financial status of Daniel Thomas. He now lived in Beaver with Ann, a daughter, Mary, and a Nineon Miller from Scotland. The census revealed $450 value

---

53. William Thomas, 1871-1895. Historical sketch and genealogy, 1888-1895.,image 21/154, https://catalog.churchofjesuschrist.org/assets/31f91996-ae0b-4915-a168-6c5efb647b56/0/20?lang=eng, <accessed 19 May 2024>
54. Thomas, William, 1871-1895. Historical sketch and genealogy, 1888-1895, image 22/154
55. "Mississippi Marriages, 1800-1911," *Family Search.org*, image 286/534
56. Daniel Monroe Thomas," *Family Search*.
57. "Elijah Thomas and my Moment of Pain and Suffering," *Family Search*, https://www.familysearch.org/tree/person/memories/KWJ8-9W2, <accessed 20 May 2024>
58. Ibid, image 23/154
59. Daniel Monroe Thomas," *Family Search*.

in real estate and $500 of personal estate. This census also revealed that Daniel lived next to William W. Willis, a former member of the Mormon Battalion.[60] Willis took the last group of Mormon Battalion members to Pueblo during the winter of 1846-1847. The 1870 census found Daniel living in the Rio Virgin, Utah Territory. He lives with Ann and a fellow from Scotland. Daniel's financial standing improved slightly from ten years earlier. His real estate increased to $800, and his estate rose to $800. Following his years in Beaver, Daniel helped settlements on the Muddy River in Nevada. When those settlements failed, he moved to St. George, where he lived until he passed away.[61]

By 1880, Daniel lived in St. George, and he now lived alone. Ann Crosby Thomas died two years earlier on 14 July 1878.[62] Ann and Daniel passed through many challenges during their lives together. Many of the difficulties centered on living the faith they both bound themselves with many years earlier. The loneliness he felt following the death of his first wife created a need to remarry. He married Mary Ann Chandler 19 May 1881 at St. George. Moses Chandler and Matilda Johnson brought Mary Ann into the world 17 February 1835, and she was the third of seven children.[63] Tragically, Mary Ann Chandler Thomas died while confined at the Utah State Insane Asylum in Provo 19 February 1904. The 1900 census indicated she was a widow and sixty-five years old.[64] During the years Daniel lived in St. George, he served faithfully in the new temple. He assisted in performing baptisms, endowments, and marriage sealings for 400

---

60. United States Census, 1860," *Family Search*, https://www.familysearch.org/ark:/61903/3:1:33SQ-GBS8-9GSK?view=index&action=view, <accessed 20 May 2024>
61. "Obituary Notes," *Desert Evening News*, 29 March 1894, https://newspapers.lib.utah.edu/details?id=1616949&month_t=%22march%22&q=Obituary+notes&sort=rel&year_start=1894&year_end=1894, <accessed 20 May 2024>
62. "Ann Crosby," *Family Search*, <KWVP-8S9>, https://www.familysearch.org/tree/person/details/KWVP-8S9, <accessed 20 May 2024>
63. "Mary Ann Chandler," *Family Search*, <LCRW-FQQ>, https://www.familysearch.org/tree/person/details/LCRW-FQQ, <accessed 20 May 2024>
64. "Mary A. Thomas," 1900 United States Federal Census, *Ancestry*, https://www.ancestry.com/discoveryui-content/view/61805172:7602?tid=&pid=&queryId=a5fb75fe-0bc2-4658-93ab-4932ee7ca616&_phsrc=EUI191&_phstart=successSource, <accessed 20 May 2024>

members of his family and friends. Daniel died 21 March 1894 at the age of eighty-four years.[65] Daniel lived a long, productive life.

GEORGE WASHINGTON BANKHEAD

Evidence indicates George Washington Bankhead married Jane (last name unknown) in 1844 or 1845 in Alabama. Little is known about her. Her surname, family history, and background remain a mystery. She received baptism along with George Bankhead, and one account lists Tennessee as her birthplace.[66] George began his life on 13 February 1819, most likely in Alabama. With the exception of the 1850 federal census, he consistently stated that he was born in Alabama.[67] Following George's walk back to Alabama from Pueblo in 1846, he chose to remain home until 1848, when he left Alabama with his wife and young children in the Heber C. Kimball company. The group of 662 individuals departed Winter Quarters on 7 June 1848 and arrived in the Salt Lake Valley on 24 September 1848.[68] By 1850, George, Jane, and their children, James, age five; Samuel, age two; and Jane, who was one month old, lived together in the greater Salt Lake area.[69]

---

65. "Obituary Notes," *Desert Evening News,* 29 March 1894

66. Heather Hardy, compiler, "LDS in the Antebellum South.pdf." image 19/209, file:///
C:/Users/Owner/OneDrive/Documents/Mississippi%20Company/Mississippi%
20Saints%20Company%20Participants/Slavery/Hardy%20LDS%20in%20the%20Ante
bellum%20South.pdf,

67. George Washington Bankhead, Federal Census Records of 1850, 1860, 1870, and
1880 located at *Ancestry.com,* https://www.ancestry.com/search/categories/35/?name=
George+Washington_Bankhead&birth=1819_Franklin-Alabama-United+States&
death=1898_Salt+Lake+City-Salt+Lake-Utah-United+States&child=
James_Bankhead,Samuel_Bankhead,Jane&father=John+Black_Bankhead&gender=m&
marriage=1844_Alabama-United+States&mother=Jane+Watson_McCurdy&
spouse=Jane, <accessed 24 May 2024>

68. "Heber C. Kimball Company (1848), *Church History Biographical Database,* https://his
tory.churchofjesuschrist.org/chd/organization/pioneer-company/heber-c-kimball-
company-1848?lang=eng&timelineTab=allTabs, <accessed 24 May 2024>

69. George Bankhead Family, "United States Federal Census, 1850" *Family Search,*
<K27B-VDT>,   https://www.familysearch.org/tree/person/sources/K27B-VDT,
<accessed 24 May 2024>

Ten years later, George was living alone. Little is known about what happened to his wife and children. No Utah death records for Jane or the three children are known to exist. So, it is possible she and George were divorced, or she left Utah Territory with the children. George married again, to Sarah Jane Swinden, in late 1862 or early 1863. Sarah Jane emigrated to the United States in 1861 on the ship *Underwriter.* The ship left Liverpool on 23 April 1861 and arrived in New York on 21 May 1861, carrying 672 passengers.[70] Sarah listed the spelling of her last name as Swindon on the ship manifest, and she traveled under the designation "Spinster," or an unmarried woman, during the voyage. She listed her age as twenty-eight years old, and she noted the address of her home as Sheffield, England. Like most other LDS emigrants during that time, she sailed in steerage.[71] She did not travel to the Utah Territory until 1862. She traveled on the John R. Murdock down-and-back wagon train, which departed Florence on 24 July 1862 and arrived on 27 September 1862. When the wagon train started west, 700 individuals with sixty-five wagons constituted the company.[72] Interestingly, Captain John Murdock led five down-and-back wagon trains during the time that system was used by the church. In total, Mr. Murdock completed eleven round trips, and he likely brought more church members across the plains than any other person.[73]

Like many of the Southern Saints, George Bankhead first settled in Holladay, but he moved to Draper shortly after. He settled on South Willow Creek in 1852, and according to a manuscript detailing the

---

70. *Underwriter,* "Saints By Sea, Latter-Day Saint Immigration to America," https://saintsbysea.lib.byu.edu/search/?keywords=underwriter&mii=on&europe=on&netherlands=on&scandinavia=on&sweden=on, <accessed 24 May 2024>

71. Sarah Swindon, "Saints By Sea, Latter-Day Saint Immigration to American," https://saintsbysea.lib.byu.edu/mii/passenger/55197?keywords=underwriter&mii=on&europe=on&netherlands=on&scandinavia=on&sweden=on, <accessed 24 May 2024>

72. John Riggs Murdock Company (1862) *Church History Biographical Database,* https://history.churchofjesuschrist.org/chd/organization/pioneer-company/john-riggs-murdock-company-1862?lang=eng&timelineTabs=all-events, <accessed 24 May 2024>

73. Erick L. Wadsworth, *The Last Outfitting Station on the Missouri River,* 70

Draper Ward, "several negroes belonged to his household." In other words, George still enslaved several Black individuals. By the end of 1853, the settlement of Draper stood at 222. The winters of 1854 to 1856 found most of the settlers in Draper choosing to live inside a fort recently built to protect against the Indigenous people who lived in the area.[74] George likely lived inside the fort with the rest of the town. George's mannerisms were gracious and kind to those around him, and he served in positions of trust for the church and in civic responsibilities. Tragically, Sarah died in childbirth in 1863, which left George alone again.[75]

The 1870 federal census shows George still living in Draper, but he was then living with three other individuals, each of whom came from Denmark. Like others who left their plantations behind after joining the church, George's financial standing suffered. He then worked as a "day laborer" and showed real estate holdings valued at $750 and a personal estate value of $250.[76] The three people he lived with at the time were Hannah Jensen, age forty-eight; Mary A. Jensen, age twenty-four; and Martin Jordanson, age nine.[77] George lived through a possible divorce—or abandonment—from his first wife and the death of his second wife. Evidence indicates that George participated in raising his own children for only a few years. However, according to one account, "His was a hospitable home and many youths were befriended by this fine man."[78] George Washington

---

74. Draper Ward manuscript history and historical reports, 1849-1935; Ward historical record, 1849-1935; Church History Library, image 33/172, https://catalog.churchofje suschrist.org/assets/274cac07-6cc3-4a7b-b993-29563e3297f2/0/32?lang=eng, <accessed 25 May 2024>

75. George Washington Bankhead, "Find A Grave," *Ancestry*, Posting by RaNae Rock Anderson correcting errors found a "Find A Grave," https://www.findagrave.com/ memorial/10473348/george-washington-bankhead, <accessed 25 May 2024>

76. George Bankhead, "United States Federal Census, 1870," *Ancestry*, https://www. ancestry.com/discoveryui-content/view/14636078:7163?tid=&pid=&queryId= 33a05a04-8af5-41e7-a4ee-8e6eacba0638&_phsrc=EUI315&_phstart=successSource, <accessed 25 May 22024>

77. Ibid.

78. Kate B. Carter, compiler, "Our Pioneer Heritage," (Salt Lake City, Utah, Daughters of Utah Pioneers, 1959) 467, Vol. 2

Bankhead passed away 9 April 1898 in Draper.[79] He died in full faith and fellowship in the church he had accepted over fifty years earlier in faraway Alabama.

JAMES ALBERT SMITHSON

James Albert Smithson departed Pueblo in September 1846 to walk back to his home in Mississippi. He chose not to return and travel west again. James began his life on 10 June 1825 and was born in Gattman, Monroe, Mississippi. He claimed the honor of being the youngest child of James Barlett Smithson and Sarah Blanks Weatherford. James spent the remainder of his life in Mississippi, passing away in Monroe County on 11 March 1892.[80] James married three times during his lifetime. His first wife, Mary Adaline Thomerson, married James in 1846. Sadly, she died in 1852. James married Sarah Thomason in 1854. They raised seven children together until she died in 1874. His final marriage took place on 14 September 1874 to Liza Melvina Welch. Together, they raised four children.[81] Liza outlived James, passing away on 24 May 1906.[82]

Census enumerators in the 1860 census noted James worked as an "overseer." At that time, he lived with his second wife and her children. This accounting took place just before the Civil War. During the years slavery was allowed in the South, an overseer supervised the work of enslaved men and women in the fields, and often their tactics were brutal. The record also noted James lived next to his mother, Sarah Smithson. Her combined real estate value equaled $2,400 and personal estate worth totaled $8,750, for a combined total of $11,150, while James declared zero value to both his real estate and his

---

79. George Washington Bankhead, *Family Search,* <K27B-VDT>, https://www.family search.org/tree/person/details/K27B-VDT, <accessed 25 May 2024>
80. James Albert Smithson, *Family Search,* <LC8N-7WP>, https://www.familysearch. org/tree/person/details/LC8N-7WP, <accessed 27 May 2024>
81. Ibid.
82. Liza Melvinia Welch, *Family Search,* <L7T7-L5S>, https://www.familysearch.org/ tree/person/details/L7T7-L5S, <accessed 27 May 2024>

personal estate. Interestingly, two other land owners on the same page as James and his mother declared personal estate assessments of $13,000 and $9,186.[83] James's mother reported in the 1850 federal census that she enslaved three Black women ages seventeen to fifty and one Black child, age three.[84] A slave schedule for Monroe County during the year 1860 could not be located, so there is no confirmation that James worked for his mother as the overseer on her property.

One wonders how much James missed his friends and family who traveled west to Utah so many years earlier. His friend, John Brown, returned as a missionary to Mississippi in 1867. The two old friends met once again. Of the visit, Brown wrote, "March 19th. Nice weather. The farmers are planting. Preach trees are in full bloom. Preached in the evening at James A. Smithson's. Had some liberty. Lodged at Smithson's." Years after Brown's visit with his old friend, a tragedy struck James, his second wife, Sarah, and their family in February 1873. James's young son wanted to go bird hunting with some neighbors near the family home, which stood close to Mormon Springs in Monroe County. The son had loaded his gun the previous day and wanted to discharge the load by shooting at a small tree near the house. The young man leveled the gun and pointed at the tree. Just as he discharged the weapon, his little sister came running around the house and ran right into the path of the volley. A total of twenty-five shot slammed into her little body, from which she died later that night. She was buried the following day.[85] Although James Smithson chose to remain in Monroe County, his trek of several thousand miles

---

83. James Smithson Family, "United States Federal Census, 1860," *Family Search*, https://www.familysearch.org/ark:/61903/3:1:33SQ-GBS7-XB5?view=index&action=view, <accessed 28 May 2024>

84. "1850 U. S. Federal Census, Slave Schedules for Sarah Smithson," *Ancestry*, https://www.ancestry.com/discoveryui-content/view/91126115:8055?tid=&pid=&queryId=b67af7a0-7c49-44fc-941b-93ebf471fed6&_phsrc=EUI410&_phstart=successSource, <accessed 28 May 2024>

85. Heart-rending Account, *Ancestry*, https://www.ancestry.com/mediaui-viewer/collection/1030/tree/18340126/person/18000835289/media/0b86215b-56a1-4816-816a-f537e9bf642a?queryId=c8976ab1-7c2b-43d6-8e2b-37a0932824ea&_phsrc=EUI400&_phstart=successSource, <accessed 27 May 2024>

during the spring and fall of 1846 demonstrate his love and devotion to his family and friends of the Mississippi Company.

ABSALOM PORTER DOWDLE

Absalom Porter Dowdle was born to wealthy parents on 1 June 1819 in Franklin County, Alabama. Absalom described where he took his first breath by writing, "They bought a wonderful plantation in Franklin County, Alabama, the old home where I was born. It was a beautiful old colonial mansion, one of the garden spots in the south." This beautiful home and plantation were built on the backs of the enslaved men and women who worked the land. Absalom's parents belonged to the Baptist Church and attended church services every Sunday.[86] He described his life on the plantation, writing, "We did not know anything but just to go to bed at night and get up in the morning and go through the same: eat, sleep, and go riding, come home and take care of my dogs and train them."[87] Absalom constantly rode his horse. The two would ride for miles at a time. At the age of twenty-one, he "heard a young man preaching on the streets," who he learned represented the "Latter-day Saints" from Missouri. Absalom rode daily to hear his preaching, and he quickly "was converted, so I made arrangements to be baptized in The Church of Jesus Christ of Latter-day Saints."[88] Absalom received the ordinance of baptism on 18 October 1844, and he was confirmed a member of the church the same day.[89]

When Absalom told his father about his baptism, he was immediately kicked out of his plantation home. Absalom wrote, "He never said a word, he just pointed his finger at the door for me to leave. He

---

86. Dowdle, Absalom Porter, 1819-1897. Absalom P. Dowdle autobiography, image 3/51, https://catalog.churchofjesuschrist.org/assets/4bd7e829-80dd-4098-b5d9-d2443e7b4cdb/0/2?lang=eng, <accessed 2 July 2024>
87. Ibid, 15/51
88. Ibid, 15-16/51
89. Absalom Porter Dowdle, "Ordinances," *Family Search*, https://www.familysearch.org/tree/person/ordinances/LRZ4-5LT, <accessed 3 July 2024>

held a rod of iron in his finger and his heart." As Absalom hugged his mother goodbye on the porch, his father said, "Get what you want and don't ever let me see your face again."[90] In an instant, Absalom's life changed from affluent to penniless. His commitment to his new religion would demand a lifetime of allegiance. Following his baptism, introduction to John Holladay, and marriage to Sarah Ann Holladay 6 September 1845 at Marion, Alabama, Absalom went west. As noted in an earlier chapter, Absalom was appointed the presiding elder at Pueblo. After arriving in the Salt Lake Valley in 1847, Absalom's active life continued. He attended one of the first sacrament meetings held in the valley 8 August 1847. Fellow Mississippi Company members joined him, including Benjamin Mathews, William C. Ritter, Allen Smithson, and William D. Kartchner.[91]

Dowdle noted in his autobiography that he was called to settle in Provo Valley in 1848, and the family remained there until 1849. He wrote about boiling a black crow and eating it. The family boiled the meat for twenty-four hours before anyone attempted to eat it. The family's next stop took them further north to the town of Coalville.[92] On 28 August 1852, Absalom received a call to serve a full-time mission to Australia. A report in the *Deseret News* of 18 September 1852 noted a total of nine missionaries serving full-time in the Australia Mission. At the same time, missionaries were serving in such diverse locales as Norway, Gibraltar, England, Wales, Siam, and China, to name a few.[93] Absalom served as a counselor in the mission presidency until President August Farnham departed for home in May 1856, at which point he assumed the role of mission president.[94] During the time Absalom served in Australia, Sarah and their four

---

90. Ibid, 17/51

91. "Sacrament Meeting, Great Basin, Aug 8, 1847," *Family Search,* https://www.family search.org/tree/person/memories/LRZ4-5LT, <accessed 3 July 2024>

92. Dowdle, Absalom Porter, 1819-1897. Absalom P. Dowdle autobiography,, image 46/51

93. No Title, *Deseret News,* https://newspapers.lib.utah.edu/search?page=3&mon th_t=%22september%22&year_start=1852&year_end=1852, <accessed 4 July 2024>

94. Australasian Mission manuscript history and historical reports, 1840-1897; Volume 1, 1840-1899; Part 1, 1840-1859; Church History Library, https://catalog.churchofje

children remained behind in Utah Territory. The children ranged in age from under a year to twelve.[95] Raising four young children without the support of a husband must have been extremely difficult for Sarah.

During Absalom's time in Australia, and without Sarah's knowledge, he married another woman, reportedly to live the "orders of polygamy." He had three children with his new wife, but there was no possibility for her to leave Australia. Absalom knew Sarah "did not believe in polygamy" and hoped Sarah would not find out about his marriage in Australia, but she did. The couple continued to live together for the next several years, and Sarah even bore four more children with Absalom. Their final child came in 1868. Eventually, the situation with his wife deteriorated to the point where he either left or Sarah requested that he leave. Absalom wrote about the separation:

> I got up out of my wagon and washed and cleaned up and went to the house and told my wife that I was going away. She did not answer, so I took Louise and Johnny by the hand and took them down to a small store and bought them candy and knelt down and took my boy on my knee.[96]

Absalom and his wife never got back together, and he passed away 5 June 1897 in Weber, Utah. His burial took place at Greenville, Beaver, Utah.[97] Sarah Ann Holladay died 2 February 1915 at Ogden, Weber, Utah, and her burial took place 5 February 1915 at Santaquin, Utah.[98]

---

suschrist.org/assets/d6c83a2f-b2de-458b-b5de-58e96eb52152/0/384, <accessed 4 July 2024>

95. Absalom Porter Dowdle, *Family Search*, <LRZ4-5LT>, https://www.familysearch.org/tree/person/details/LRZ4-5LT, <accessed 4 July 2024>

96. Dowdle, Absalom Porter, 1819-1897. Absalom P. Dowdle autobiography, images 49, 50/51

97. Absalom Porter Dowdle, *Family Search*, https://www.familysearch.org/tree/person/details/LRZ4-5LT, <accessed 4 July 2024>

98. Sarah Ann Holladay, *Family Search*, <KWJL-WBG>, *https://www.familysearch.org/tree/person/details/KWJL-WBG* , <accessed 4 July 2024>

14

ADDITIONAL MISSISSIPPI SAINTS

WILLIAM CHRISTOPHER RITTER

William Christopher Ritter came into the world 19 February 1824 at Marion, Alabama. His parents were Isaac Anderson D. Ritter and Phebe Douglas Young. William entered the Salt Lake Valley with great anticipation for the future 29 July 1847. Tragically, he perished from an avalanche while working at the Prince of Wales Mine 19 January 1875. Ritter, along with several other miners were "snaking," or hauling ore from the mine down the mountain on "rawhides." Two men were able to dig themselves out of the deep snow and survived. However, William and six others could not be rescued from the thirty feet of snow. The slide traveled roughly three-quarters of a mile down Big Cottonwood Canyon and measured 200 yards wide.[1] William married his first wife, Sarah Ann Lowry, 17 March 1845, only a year before the couple went west with the

---

1. Latest News up to 12:30 this Morning," *Salt Lake Herald Republican*, 21 January 1875, https://newspapers.lib.utah.edu/details?id=11670903&month_t=%22january%22&q= Prince+of+Wales+Mine&sort=rel&year_start=1875&year_end=1875, <accessed 1 July 2024>

Mississippi group.[2] William and Sarah Ann divorced in 1869. At the time of their divorce, four children lived with the couple.[3] William married Jeanette Freeland Bland 18 October 1862, and they brought six children into the world. On 18 April 1868, he married Margaret Ann Bailey, to whom one child was born.[4]

Unlike many of the Mississippi Company, William remained in Utah Territory until his premature death. He entered the valley at forty-three and died when he was only fifty-one.[5] He lived in Salt Lake County during the 1850 census. Sarah and two children, a four-year-old little boy and a one-year-old girl, lived in the dwelling with William. He declared his occupation as a farmer, and his real estate value stood at $100. Ephraim Hanks, who was later famous for his efforts in helping to rescue the stranded pioneers of the Martin and Willie handcart companies, lived near William and Sarah's family. One interesting note made by the census enumerator about one of his neighbors was unexpected. The census taker wrote that this person was "convicted of stealing oxen."[6] No record of an 1860 census appears for William. However, by 1870 he was working as a miner. He lived with his new wife, Jeanette, and seven children ranging in age from one to thirteen years old. His current real estate value stood at $100 and his personal assets totaled $150.[7] One reason for the low real estate value was his divorce from Sarah, about which he wrote:

----

2. Monroe Marriage Records, *Family Search*, https://www.familysearch.org/ark:/61903/3:1:3Q9M-C9BJ-ZS57-1?view=index&personArk=%2Fark%3A%2F61903%2F1%3A1%3AZ249-G73Z&action=view, <accessed 1 July 2024>
3. William Christopher Ritter, "Gallery," *Ancestry.com*, https://www.ancestry.com/family-tree/person/tree/31465726/person/18048954722/gallery?galleryPage=1&tab=0, <accessed 2 July 2024>
4. William Christopher Ritter, *Family Search*, <LH2W-5PY>, https://www.familysearch.org/tree/person/details/LH2W-5PY, <accessed 1 July 2024>
5. William Christopher Ritter, *Family Search* <LH2W-5PY>
6. United States Federal Census, 1850, *Ancestry.com*, https://www.ancestry.com/discoveryui-content/view/1098235:8054?tid=&pid=&queryId=dcc36cad-93a6-4f15-ac91-6404856bc70c&_phsrc=EUI881&_phstart=successSource, <accessed 2 July 2024>
7. United States Federal Census, 1870, *Ancestry.com*, https://www.ancestry.com/discoveryui-content/view/14631769:7163?tid=&pid=&queryId=c5a45519-e162-4c6b-b3ca-dfa68b8b0ced&_phsrc=EUI883&_phstart=successSource, <accessed 2 July 2024>

> This is to certify in the beginning of 1869 when I gave a bill of divorce
> to Sarah Ann Lowry I gave to her for the good of her four children the
> following property viz. a parcel of land of about nine acres enclose all
> around with a house of two rooms and one cow and a heifer.[8]

The cause of William's divorce from Sarah remains unknown. His offer of land and livestock was an act of thoughtfulness to his former spouse. Divorce is a part of life, but acting respectfully to a former spouse offers insight into his integrity.

William received a patriarchal blessing 5 August 1849 in Salt Lake City. The Church Patriarch John Smith pronounced the blessing.[9] He served in the Nauvoo Legion during the battles against the Indigenous people living in the area. He also served as part of the Cottonwood Military District, assigned to Company B, and was commanded by Captain William Casper. William owned a rifle, while many others in the company owned muskets. The muster date on the enrollment document is 4 July 1855.[10] Issues between the thousands of pioneers who settled the Utah Territory and the Indians who first lived on the land began almost immediately after the first members of the church arrived in the Salt Lake Valley. The disagreements between the new settlers and the Natives resulted in several armed conflicts during the 1840s, 1850s, and 1860s.[11]

8. "William C. Ritter Divorce," *Ancestry.com, Gallery,* https://www.ancestry.com/family-tree/person/tree/31465726/person/18048954722/gallery?galleryPage=1&tab=0, <accessed 2 July 2024>

9. William Christopher Ritter, *Family Search,* <LH2W-5PY>, "Utah Family Search, Early Church Information File, 1830-1900, https://www.familysearch.org/ark:/61903/1:1:QPC8-WH7L, <accessed 2 July 2024>

10. William Ritter, "Cottonwood Military Records, Muster Rolls, Militia Records," *Family Search,* https://www.familysearch.org/ark:/61903/3:1:33SQ-G5XQ-1ZQ?view=index&action=view, <accessed 2 July 2024>

11. Robert S. McPherson, "A History of Utah's American Indians, Chapter 1, *History to Go,"* https://historytogo.utah.gov/uhg-history-american-indians-ch-1/, <accessed 2 July 2024>

ALLEN FREEMAN SMITHSON

Bartley Smithson and his wife, Sarah Weatherford Smithson, welcomed a new baby boy into their home in the year 1816, just forty years after the Declaration of Independence instigated the Revolutionary War. Shortly after his birth, this new baby boy, known as Allen Freeman Smithson, moved with the family to Marian, Alabama, in the northwest portion of the state. Allen married Lettisha Hollis Holladay 9 April 1840 in Marion, Alabama. Lettisha was the oldest living daughter of John Daniel Holladay and Catherine Beasley Higgins. Allen Freeman accepted baptism 8 January 1841.[12] Evidence indicates Lettisha followed her family's lead and received her baptism 8 January 1841.[13] Soon after their marriage, the couple moved to Fayette County, Missouri. Two children were born during their time there. By March of 1846, the family returned to Marion County. Lettisha bore another child shortly before leaving with her husband and the couple's other small children for their hoped-for Zion in the West.[14]

On 29 July 1847, Allen and Lettisha arrived in the Salt Lake Valley with their four children: John Barkley, Cathrine, James D., and Mary Emma.[15] The family spent the winter of 1847 to 1848 at the Salt Lake Fort. In the spring of 1848, they relocated to a new community further south known then as Big Cottonwood and later as Holladay. This allowed the family to settle close to family and other members of

---

12. Allen Freeman Smithson, *Family Search*, <L5R3-PBF>, https://www.familysearch. org/tree/person/details/L5R3-PBF, <accessed 27 May 2024>

13. Lettisha Hollis Holladay, "Public Member Photos & Scanned Documents," *Ancestry*, https://www.ancestry.com/mediaui-viewer/collection/1030/tree/176266741/person/ 412541237370/media/0c4d4c0c-45d9-4429-b74b-962b9d8572a1?queryId=124eea1b- b928-4104-beef-bae558bd3018&_phsrc=EUI345&_phstart=successSource, <accessed 27 May 2024>

14. "A Short History of Allen Freeman Smithson, Lettisha Holladay, Jennette Burton Taylor, James Daniel Smith, Elizabeth Dorrity" image 3/27, https://www.familysearch. org/tree/person/memories/L5R3-PBF, <accessed 27 May 2024>

15. Names of Pueblo soldiers and Mississippi brethren , https://catalog.churchofje suschrist.org/assets/ab774142-989d-4df6-a024-1f3a90e5bbd3/0/1?lang=eng. <accessed 28 May 2024>

the Mississippi Company. Tragedy struck the family with the death of Lettisha 16 August 1849—just over two years since their arrival in the valley. She was buried the same day in the Salt Lake City Cemetery. In accordance with the LDS doctrine of eternal marriage, Brigham Young sealed Lettisha and Allen 27 February 1851 in the Council House in Salt Lake City. Allen now faced raising five children ages one year to eight. He married Jennette Burton Taylor four months after his first wife's death 16 December 1849. Allen was thirty-three and Jennette was twenty-two when they married.[16] One can understand his desire to remarry so soon after his first wife's death. Life on the frontier could be brutal, and sharing that burden with another person eased the day-to-day survival mode most settlers in the West experienced.

Jennette Burton Taylor Smithson was born in South Carolina 2 May 1826, and her family later moved to Mississippi, where she learned about the LDS church. Before joining the church, she prayed one evening for "a sign if the Church is true." Of the experience, she wrote, "A light came into the room and in that light was a personage. He said, 'Yes, the Church is true, but it is wrong to ask for signs.'" The visitor instructed Jennette to join the church and go west with the Saints. If she chose to not go west now, the opportunity would not happen again. Jennette joined the church and traveled west to Utah Territory, arriving in 1848. Jennette and Allen settled in Cottonwood until 1851, when the family moved to San Bernardino. In 1857, they left California and settled in Beaver, Utah, for a short time before moving to the Cotton Mission.[17] Jennette bore fourteen children and raised them along with Allen's five kids from his previous marriage. She also raised two granddaughters.[18] Jennette accomplished all this

---

16. "Biography of Lettisha Hollis Holladay Smithson," *Family Search*, <KWV9-VHW> https://www.familysearch.org/tree/person/memories/KWV9-VHW, <accessed 28 May 2024>

17. Cora B. Smithson Ransom, "Jenette Burton Taylor Smithson," *Family Search*, <LKVB-95V>, unpaginated, https://www.familysearch.org/tree/person/memories/ LKVB-95V, <accessed 29 May 2024>

18. Ibid.

while moving from one location to another—hundreds of miles apart by wagon—always at the direction of their church leaders.

Allen Freeman Smithson lived in Beaver only a short time before moving to Harmony, Utah Territory. Allen remained in Harmony until 1872, when he received a letter from Erastus Snow to establish a settlement in Pareah, Utah.[19] The settlement, a waystation, was meant to help those traveling to Arizona. The location where the town once sat is on the Paria River in the Grand Staircase-Escalante National Park in Kane County. Settlers remained in this town from 1870 to 1929, but it was first settled by Peter Shirts and a small group in 1865. Following the conclusion of the Black Hawk War in 1867, people settled the area at an increasing rate. Allen received the call of bishop after settling the area and held that leadership position until his death. In August 1877, Allen and Jennette traveled to the new St. George Temple to perform ordinance work for their ancestors, but on the return trip to Pareah, Allen was stricken with typhoid fever, from which he never recovered. A daughter wrote, "He was the most free hearted man I ever knew. He would take his coat off and give it to the other fellow if he needed it. I have seen him do it."[20]

WILLIAM COX SMITHSON

William Cox Smithson entered this world 30 March 1804 in Pendleton, Anderson, South Carolina. He married Lucinda Wilson 16 February 1831 in Pendleton District, South Carolina. He died 2 March 1889 in southern Utah Territory. William and Lucinda were sealed 3 March 1851 in the office of Brigham Young.[21] His death occurred 2,000 miles from his home in Monroe County. He and his

---

19. "Died," *Deseret News,* https://newspapers.lib.utah.edu/details?id=2628583&q=Allen+Freeman+Smithson&sort=rel&year_start=1877&year_end=1877, <accessed 29 May 2024>

20. "A Short History of Allen Freeman Smithson, Lettisha Holladay, Jennette Burton Taylor, James Daniel Smith, Elizabeth Dorrity," *Family Search,* image 20/27, https://www.familysearch.org/tree/person/memories/L5R3-PBF, <accessed 30 May 2024>

21. Willliam Cox Smithson, *Family Search,* https://www.familysearch.org/tree/person/details/K2HF-WCJ, <accessed 30 May 2024>

brother, Allen, traveled almost 3,300 miles in their quest to follow directives from church leaders to settle unique areas in the West. The vast majority of those miles were completed walking side-by-side with oxen at a rate of two-and-a-half miles per hour. William received his baptism in 1843, and James Brown ordained him a deacon that same year. Brown also ordained William a High Priest in 1851.[22] Like Allen, William settled in Holladay before heading to San Bernardino in 1851. He returned to Utah Territory in 1857 at the request of Brigham Young.

Following the call to leave San Bernardino, William settled in Washington, Utah Territory. The following account demonstrates William's resolve:

> During the winter of 1857-1858 abut fifty families from the abandoned San Bernardino colony made Washington their temporary quarters; and in the spring they all left except William Smithson, properly known as "Buck" and "Bucky." He found kindred souls at Washington, for Buck was himself a southerner, and he soon became the most enthusiastic and successful cotton farmer there. By a persistent trial and error process the knowledge and experience necessary to produce cotton in this new country was obtained by settlers.[23]

With the constant moving from Mississippi to Pueblo, Salt Lake City, San Bernardino, and finally Washington County, William found his efforts to gain any financial independence seriously jeopardized. The 1850 census indicated his personal assets totaled $300. Ten years later, when he lived in southern Utah, he declared no value for either real estate or personal assets. The 1870 census revealed some growth

---

22. William Cox Smithson, "William Cox Smithson in the Membership of the Church of Jesus Christ of Latter-Day Saints, 1830-1848," *Ancestry*, https://www.ancestry.com/discoveryui-content/view/84020:5333?tid=&pid=&queryId=b5a50b79-0aae-4b31-b1bf-42ac996bb6dd&_phsrc=EUI459&_phstart=successSource, <accessed 30 May 2024>
23. Hazel Bradshaw, editor, *Under Dixie Sun*, (Panguitch, Utah: Washington County Chapter Daughters Utah Pioneer, 1950), 236

for William, with real estate valued at $500 and his personal assets at $500.[24] Like other faithful members of the church from the Mississippi Company, William did not focus on gaining personal wealth.

Life was challenging for the early settlers in Washington County. They suffered "chills and fever" to an extent greater than other locations in southern Utah Territory. During William's time in Washington County, the December 1860 term of the Washington County Court levied a poll tax of "three days labor on all males over thirteen years." A fine would be levied for anyone without a justifiable excuse. If the court determined the person missed work for a valid reason, Washington County would pay the expense. Since there was little currency available, the assessor and collectors were authorized to accept wheat and shelled corn for a value of $1.50 per bushel, clean and washed wool at forty-five per pound, and good quality molasses at two dollars per gallon.[25] Settlers had been moving to southern Utah Territory for seven years, yet the population remained small. By the middle of 1861, those who remained in Washington County totaled only twenty families. To create a better road between Salt Lake City and Washington County, the Utah Territory Legislature appropriated $200 for road improvement.[26]

William and Lucinda spent almost three decades together in southern Utah Territory. Lucinda bore ten children during their time together. Six girls and one son came into the family before they left Mississippi. The other three children were born in San Bernardino. All but one of their children lived to adulthood and married. One son, born in San Bernardino in 1851, died before 1860.[27] Lucinda Wilson

---

24. William Cox Smithson, *Family Search*, <K2HF-WCJ>, https://www.familysearch. org/tree/person/details/K2HF-WCJ, accessed 30 May 2024>, Under memories for William Cox Smithson the census records are available for 1850, 1860, 1870, and 1880.
25. Annals of the Southern Utah Mission, circa 1903-1906; 1847-1869 (Book A); Church History Library, image 86-87/162, https://catalog.churchofjesuschrist.org/ assets/3faee6c9-545e-42fd-9c67-41745a5e3622/0/86?lang=eng, <accessed 30 May 2024>
26. Ibid. 88-89
27. William Cox Smithson, *Family Search*, <K2HF-WCJ>, Searching the names and

was born 13 March 1813 at Tennessee River, Jackson, Alabama, and she accepted baptism 6 September 1844.[28] The couple traveled great distances together during their fifty-eight-year marriage. She stood side-by-side with him during the winter of 1846 to 1847 at Pueblo. She lived for a short time in Utah Territory before leaving with her husband and children for San Bernardino. She bore staggering challenges as she and the family walked the challenging trail from Salt Lake City to the Cajon Pass while she was pregnant with her child, Nicholas. She bore two more children and suffered through the death of Nicholas while living in San Bernardino. She endured the trials of settling in southern Utah Territory—including the marriage of her husband to a plural wife at St. George in 1857.[29] Lucinda stands tall as one who remained faithful to her husband, children, and the church she believed in.

WILLIAM D. KARTCHNER

John Kartchner Sr. and Prudence Wilcox welcomed William Decator Kartchner into the world 4 May 1820 at Montgomery, Pennsylvania. William's family eventually consisted of six siblings. Sadly, John Sr. died in 1826, leaving Prudence a widow with five children to support. Consequently, William bounced from one home to another during the next several years. He found employment in a cotton factory for two dollars a week and fifty cents spending money, which he used to purchase tobacco. He continued working in the cotton factory until he reached the age of twelve, when an accident caused him to miss six weeks of work. After he sufficiently recovered, his mother told him to either go back to the cotton factory or learn a trade because she could

---

birthdates of the children of William and Lucinda at *Family Search* provide the information stated above.

28. Lucinda Wilson, "Lucinda Wilson in the Membership of the Church of Jesus Christ of Latter-Day Saints, 1830-1848," *Ancestry*, https://www.ancestry.com/discoveryui-content/view/99135:5333?tid=&pid=&queryId=85b1175f-9c6d-4137-a0a6-dcf3d9187805&_phsrc=EUI476&_phstart=successSource, <accessed 31 May 2024>
29. William Cox Smithson, *Family Search* <K2HF-WCJ>

not support him. He chose to learn blacksmithing, a trade that bene-fited him throughout his life. After learning the blacksmithing trade, he lived with his brothers Peter and John in a house Peter purchased in the summer of 1842. Two missionaries from the LDS church taught William the message of the restored gospel, which he readily accepted. He was baptized May 1843. His baptism into the church infuriated his brother John, so William moved out within a month and relocated to Nauvoo.[30]

A few months after his baptism, William married his first wife, Margaret Jane Casteel, 21 March 1844 at Nauvoo. Margaret was born 1 September 1825 in Cooper, Missouri, to Jacob Israel Casteel and Sarah Jane Nowlin.[31] Following their marriage, the couple lived with Margaret's parents near Nauvoo. William moved his blacksmithing tools and belongings into his in-laws' home. He worked on the temple and as a guard against the increasing mob activity in and around Nauvoo, standing many hours in the rain, snow, and sleet. William later wrote this exposure to the elements caused his rheumatism, which plagued him throughout the remainder of his life. Until they headed west with the Mississippi Company in 1846, William and Margaret suffered through the abuse of another member of the church during a failed migration through Iowa. However, the couple eventually escaped from their confined situation and located William's brother, John, who they lived with until they joined the group from the South in Independence.[32]

Aspects of William's time in Pueblo, Holladay, and San Bernardino are contained in earlier chapters, so the following accounts of his life begin with his arrival in Beaver, Utah Territory, March 1858. A few years after arriving in Beaver, he married a plural wife by the name of

---

30. Connie Mikesell Hale, 1946-. William D. Kartchner memoirs, undated., images 4-9/74, https://catalog.churchofjesuschrist.org/assets/3d2b6c1f-2a28-42c3-a9a8-93c04ba38108/0/8?lang=eng, <accessed 3 June 2024>
31. Margaret Jane Casteel, *Family Search,* https://www.familysearch.org/tree/person/details/KWJ6-WGG, <accessed 3 June 2024>
32. Connie Mikesell Hale, 1946-. William D. Kartchner memoirs, undated., images 9-13/74

Elizabeth Gale. Elizabeth was born in Sydney, Australia, 20 January 1845, and her family emigrated to Beaver following their baptism into the church. They were married 5 December 1862 in Salt Lake City, and she bore ten children during their time together.[33] In 1865, William received a directive from George Albert Smith to fill a mission to the Muddy River. Within two weeks, he was on the road with Elizabeth. He left his first wife in Beaver with the children, but Margaret and the children joined the family within a few months. The family found it necessary to move to a new location every six months. In 1869, the entire family moved to Overton, a part of the Muddy Mission, now in the state of Nevada. In 1870, settlers of the Muddy Mission relocated to other parts of Utah.[34]

The 1860 census shows William and Margaret living in Beaver with six children. His real estate value stood at $250, and his personal estate value totaled $450. He worked as a farmer, and he lived next to John D. Lee and only two houses away from his future wife.[35] By the 1870 census, William, his two wives, and his children lived in Overton, Nevada, and were still part of the Muddy Mission. His real estate value now stood at $300, and his personal estate value rose dramatically to $1,500. Margaret lived in the same dwelling as William, while Elizabeth lived next door with her two children.[36] William served as the secretary on the board of a newly organized and short-lived United Order. The organization began in December 1874, and within just a few months, thirty of the thirty-nine members (including W. D. Kartchner) withdrew—the order died a quick death.[37] During a general conference in St. George, William and his

---

33. Elizabeth Gale, *Family Search*, <KWNV-G3F0> https://www.familysearch.org/tree/person/details/KWNV-G3F, <accessed 4 June 2024>

34. Connie Mikesell Hale, 1946-. William D. Kartchner memoirs, undated., 19-20/74

35. "United States Census, 1860" *Family Search*, https://www.familysearch.org/ark:/61903/3:1:33SQ-GBS8-9LTY?view=index&action=view, <accessed 4 June 2024>

36. "United States Census, 1870," *Family Search*, https://www.familysearch.org/ark:/61903/3:1:S3HY-6DCS-Q9K?view=index&action=view, <accessed 4 June 2024>

37. Connie Mikesell Hale, 1946-. William D. Kartchner memoirs, undated., image 20/74

family received a call to help settle a part of Arizona that later became known as Snowflake.

The 1880 census shows them living in Snowflake. His two wives and children lived in the same household. William then listed his occupation as a blacksmith, but he also deals with dropsy.[38] Margaret passed away 11 August 1881 while living in Snowflake. Elizabeth lived until 9 March 1928.[39] Following William's death, Elizabeth supported the children by constantly taking in washing work. She washed laundry all day for fifty cents. She still worked the farm, kept a garden, and raised grain with the help of the children. The family raised pigs, cows, and chickens. One daughter noted she did not remember ever being hungry.[40] William's life ended 14 May 1892 in Snowflake.[41] So ended the lives of two original members of the Mississippi Company who remained faithful to their beliefs throughout their lives. Multiple moves, extreme living conditions, and a struggle for survival constituted their lives. Elizabeth did not cross the plains, but she did cross an ocean to settle in Utah. She, like William and Margaret, sacrificed all to follow their convictions.

GEORGE WASHINGTON GIBSON

As noted in chapter seven, George Washington Gibson likely remained in Pueblo for a period and did not enter the Salt Lake Valley with the other members of the Mississippi Company. His arrival date is currently unknown, but he did settle in the Holladay area with

38. "United States Census, 1880," *Family Search,* https://www.familysearch.org/ark:/61903/3:1:33S7-9YY1-9GG7?view=index&personArk=%2Fark%3A%2F61903%2F1%3A1%3AMH24-2F2&action=view, <accessed 4 June 2024>

39. William Decator Kartchner, *Family Search,* <KWNV-G3N>, https://www.family search.org/tree/person/details/KWNV-G3N, <accessed 4 June 2024>

40. "Zina Kartchner Perkins 1964 Interview with Keith Perkins," *Family Search,* <KWNF-G3F>, https://www.familysearch.org/tree/person/memories/KWNV-G3F, <accessed 4 June 2024>

41. "Death of W. D. Kartchner," *Deseret Weekly,*" 11 June 1892, page 32, https://newspa pers.lib.utah.edu/details?id=2691776&q=Kartchner&sort=rel&year_start=1892&year_end=1892, <accessed 4 June 2024>

many others from the Southern United States. According to his High Priest Quorum record, he remained in that area until leaving for the Cotton Mission in 1862. George was born to Robert and Mary Williams Gibson at Union District, South Carolina, on 17 June 1800, and he accepted baptism in December 1843.[42] George and Mary Ann Sparks married 15 March 1822 while living in South Carolina. Mary Ann was the daughter of Josiah Sparks and Lydia Tollison. The couple experienced the birth of four of their eleven children in South Carolina. They moved to Monroe County sometime before the birth of their fourth child, Francis Abigail, in 1832. [43] There is some evidence that indicates the Gibsons lived on a plantation and possibly enslaved fifteen Black men, women, and children while living in South Carolina before their move to Mississippi.[44]

After arriving in the Salt Lake Valley, George built a small cabin for the family in Holladay.[45] During the first years in the area, the family experienced many challenges. Shortly after arriving in the valley, Mary Ann contracted an unknown illness, and she required special assistance from other family members. George and the children succeeded in obtaining sufficient nourishment for the family, which now included ten children. He was able to find rabbits and pine hens, and the nearby stream provided ample fish. Due to the expense of flour, the family survived on "Johnny Cake" and Sego roots. After a time, their garden began to provide vegetables such as beans, peas, carrots, beets, and turnips. For a sweetener, the family made molasses from sugar beets. However, the constant use of molasses for meals

---

42. George Washington Gibson, "George W. Gibson High Priest Quorum Record," *Family Search*, https://www.familysearch.org/memories/memory/117506672, <accessed 7 June 2024>

43. Mary Ann Sparks, *Family Search*, <KWJ1-44R>, https://www.familysearch.org/tree/person/details/KWJ1-44R, <accessed 7 June 2024>

44. Mary Ann Sparks Gibson, "Mary Ann Sparks Gibson (10 June 1802-7 September 1871) *Family Search*, <KWJ1-44R> https://www.familysearch.org/tree/person/memories/KWJ1-44R, <accessed 7 June 2024>

45. C.R. Savage Co., photographer. Gibson log cabin , https://catalog.churchofjesuschrist.org/assets/adb9f75d-072e-4429-a95a-538821584df4/0/1?lang=eng, note on the back of the photograph reads, "Gibson Home in Cottonwood built in 1854," <accessed 7 June 2024>

created a distaste for it. As sugar became more affordable, molasses use declined significantly. During an interview in 1936, Manomas Gibson Andrus stated, "And a really delectable cake, such as is often on their table these days, was quite unheard of then." Lighting for the cabin came from the fireplace or by using tallow dip in a saucer. Mary Ann made a dress for Manomas and her sisters from a piece of cloth similar to unbleached muslin. They dyed the cloth bright brown by using dock root. The clothing lasted throughout the week, which meant Mary Ann washed and pressed the dresses Saturday night to prepare for Sunday services. The family understood their situation, and they hoped "for the time when we would have more food and clothing, and better homes."[46]

George filled his time in South Cottonwood supporting his family, helping on community projects, and serving in the church. He helped dig the irrigation ditch that flowed into the communities of Holladay and Big Cottonwood. This ditch supplied lifesaving water to the two communities. He served as a counselor in the bishopric of the South Cottonwood Ward during the latter part of the 1850s. As his children grew to maturity, they began to marry. His daughter, Frances, married Alvin General Green November 1850. George, Mary Ann, and other members of their family traveled to the Endowment House 6 November 1855, where they were sealed. At the same time, Francis and Alvin participated in the eternal marriage sealing ordinance—as did Robert P. and Lucinda Wakefield. The Endowment House, located in downtown Salt Lake City, served as a temporary location for temple ordinances as the temples were being built.[47] Mary Ann Sparks supported George throughout their marriage. She bore eleven children, nursed him during his sickness in Pueblo, and helped as best

---

46. George Washington Gibson, "Manomas Lavina Gibson Andrus," *Family Search,* Image 2-4/9, file:///C:/Users/Owner/OneDrive/Documents/Mississippi%20Company/Mississippi%20Saints%20Company%20Participants/George%20Washington%20Gibson%20KWJ1-43B/Mohana%20Gibson%20Andrus%20interview%201936.pdf, <accessed 7 June 2024>

47. George Washington Gibson, "George Washington Gibson & Mary Ann Sparks," *Family Search,* p. 46-47, https://www.familysearch.org/tree/person/memories/KWJ1-43B, <accessed 7 June 2024>

she could during the challenging years in the valley. Her greatest test came when George chose to live in polygamy and married another woman. He married Elizabeth Ann Newman 15 March 1856, and they had six children together.[48] Mary Ann now shared her husband with another woman. She continued to support George, his new wife, and their children.

Following the move to the Cotton Mission in southern Utah, George, Mary Ann, and Ann faced many difficult situations. The 1860 census, taken while the family lived in Holladay, disclosed the value of George's real estate at $600, and the worth of his personal estate equaled $600.[49] The 1870 census, taken as the family lived in Duncan's Retreat, indicated his real estate value dropped to $100, while his personal estate rose to a value of $1,000. George's son Joseph and his wife, Ruth, also lived in Duncan's Retreat. In addition, George's daughter, Lydia Hunt, widow of former Mormon Battalion member Gilbert Hunt, lived in the same location with her four children.[50] Her husband Gilbert died in 1858 under suspicious circumstances. Gilbert had contracted to guide a large group of wagons to California at a cost of $10 per wagon. His lifeless body was found the morning of the scheduled departure, and the money had been lifted.[51] After exhausting battles against the flooding Virgin River, issues with the restless Indigenous people, and the consistently inadequate food supply, George Washington Gibson and Mary Ann both passed away within a few days of each other. George died 17 August 1871 at age

---

48. Ann Elizabeth Newman, *Family Search,* https://www.familysearch.org/tree/person/details/LLQ6-2FQ, <accessed 7 June 2024>

49. "United States Census, 1860, *Family Search,* https://www.familysearch.org/ark:/61903/3:1:33SQ-GBSF-9ZHZ?view=index&personArk=%2Fark%3A%2F61903%2F1%3A1%3AMH2W-LCY&action=view, <accessed 8 June 2024>

50. "United States Census, 1870, *Family Search,* https://www.familysearch.org/ark:/61903/3:1:S3HY-XHRQ-TJV?view=index&personArk=%2Fark%3A%2F61903%2F1%3A1%3AMNCT-ZRX&action=view, <accessed 8 June 2024>

51. Gilbert Hunt, "From Mormon Battalion Official Facebook Page," *Family Search,* unpaginated, https://www.familysearch.org/tree/person/memories/KWVS-NSJ, <accessed 8 June 2024>

seventy-one, and Mary Ann passed away 6 September 1871.[52] Elizabeth Ann Newman passed away 9 February 1875 at Salt Lake City while on a visit to see her parents. She was only thirty-four years old when she died. She had remarried following George's death to a Samuel Bradshaw.[53] Two Mississippi Company members and a young girl from England faced life's difficulties with unrelenting courage, and each died committed to their beliefs.

John Daniel Holladay

Of all the Mississippi Company that traveled west in 1846, John Daniel Holladay may have sacrificed the most financially. He was born 10 March 1798 in Kershaw, Camden District, South Carolina.[54] Evidence indicates his parents owned a plantation in that state. On 16 April 1822, John married Catherine Beesley Higgins. She was previously married to a Benjamin Jones, with whom she had two children. Catherine sent the two children to live with their grandparents in South Carolina so they could inherit a "vast estate at the appropriate time." South Carolina soil began wearing out, causing poor harvests, so in 1826, John, Catherine, and their family moved to Alabama in search of better ground. Upon arriving in northwestern Alabama, the family found the better topsoil they had hoped to find, so John purchased and operated a large plantation. John, his family, and the enslaved people grew corn, cotton, and tobacco.[55] The family's lives changed dramatically following their baptism into the church. Absolom Porter Dowdle, the young missionary who baptized John and married his daughter, discloses a small insight into Holladay's

---

52. George Washington Gibson, "George Washington Gibson & Mary Ann Sparks," Page 50.

53. "Died," *Deseret News*, 24 March 1875, page 16, https://newspapers.lib.utah.edu/ark:/ 87278/s6126n30/2615541, <accessed 8 June 2024>

54. John Daniel Holladay, *Family Search*, https://www.familysearch.org/tree/person/ details/LH7M-SYW, <accessed 11 June 2024>

55. "History of John Daniel Holladay, Sr from Ancestry.com, Feb 2011," *Family Search*, https://www.familysearch.org/tree/person/memories/LH7M-SYW, <accessed 11 June 2024>

disposition and temperament—both before and after John Holladay joined The Church of Jesus Christ of Latter-day Saints.

Absolom Dowdle and his companion were repairing cracks in a log cabin church near Holladay's plantation when Dowdle first encountered his soon-to-be father-in-law. During the repairs, Absolom smashed his thumb and middle finger badly. Later that day, a man entered who was "real drunk," a condition this person was in regularly before his baptism. That man was the well-to-do plantation owner John D. Holladay. Although he was behaving poorly, Holladay handed the stunned Dowdle ten dollars, a substantial amount of money in the mid-1840s. Dowdle described his new acquaintance as about forty-five years of age and noted he wore "regular old cowboy boots," a large white hat, and a shirt that was "open to the neck." Holladay possessed a booming voice, which he often utilized, particularly when he arrived at his plantation. He was kind to "poor people and was very good to his slaves when he was sober."[56] He possessed a sense of humor, came across as a likable man, was street smart, and took charge of things when necessary. At times, he could also be prone to periods of despondency, and during his periods of drinking, he was mean to those around him.[57] John, Catherine, and several children accepted baptism into The Church of Jesus Christ of Latter-day Saints in June 1844.[58] The couple never wavered from this initial commitment.

John and Catherine felt the sting of death while the family lived in Holladay, when their daughter Lettisha Holladay Smithson passed

---

56. Dowdle, Absalom Porter, 1819-1897. Absalom P. Dowdle autobiography, images 25-26/51, https://catalog.churchofjesuschrist.org/assets/4bd7e829-80dd-4098-b5d9-d2443e7b4cdb/0/25?lang=eng, <accessed 18 June 2024>

57. Jay M. Todd, "Physical Size, Personality, and Character of John D. Holladay for Whom the City of Holladay is Named," unpaginated, In the fall of 2004 Jay Todd received a phone call from a sculptor who wanted to propose a statue of Holladay for that city. Todd's conclusions on Holladay's characteristics come from his review of Absolom Dowdle's written account found in fn 45.

58. "A Short History of the Life of John Holladay," *Family Search*, <LH7M-SYW>, https://www.familysearch.org/tree/person/memories/LH7M-SYW, <accessed 18 June 2024>

away 16 August 1849 at twenty-six years of age. Lettisha was the first wife of Allen Freeman Smithson. John Holladay traveled to San Bernardino in 1851 and lived there until returning to Utah Territory.[59] During his time in Southern California, he and his wife suffered through the death of two daughters. Leanora died on a Sunday afternoon 20 February 1853 of typhoid fever, and Keziah Donnell Holladay Boyle passed away 29 November 1853 at the age of nineteen years. At the time of her passing, she was married to Henry Boyle.[60] John Holladay served two missions during his time in San Bernardino. Both focused on obtaining funds for San Bernardino and encouraging Saints to gather there. One mission, in the summer of 1855, took John to the Northern California gold fields, where he and his companion, David M. Stuart, visited members to seek needed funds. John and David worked from 29 July to 22 September "preaching and converting… all the old Mormon[s] we could find."[61] John served another mission with William D. Kartchner. Their field of labor included Santa Barbara, in Southern California. During this mission, Kartchner wrote that he found "Bro. Holladay down-hearted and lonesome." Nevertheless, the two missionaries continued in their service until returning home in September 1856.[62]

The Holladay family followed the direction of Brigham Young and left San Bernardino for Utah Territory. The 1860 federal census found sixty-two-year-old John Holladay living in the small town of Santaquin with Catherine and two grandchildren. His real estate

---

59. " "Biography of Lettisha Hollis Holladay Smithson," *Family Search*, <KWV9-VHW> https://www.familysearch.org/tree/person/memories/KWV9-VHW, <accessed 18 June 2024>

60. "Died" *Deseret News*, 16 March 1854, page 3, https://newspapers.lib.utah.edu/details?id=2582259&q=Died&sort=rel&year_start=1854&year_end=1854&month_t=%22march%22, <accessed 18 June 2024>

61. J. Kenneth Davies and Lorin K. Hansen, *Mormon Gold Mormons in the California God Rush*, (North Salt Lake City, Utah; Granite Mountain Publishing Company, 2010), 273-274

62. Connie Mikesell Hale, 1946-. William D. Kartchner memoirs, undated., images 18-19/74, https://catalog.churchofjesuschrist.org/assets/3d2b6c1f-2a28-42c3-a9a8-93c04ba38108/0/18?lang=eng, <accessed 18 June 2024>

value totaled $150, and the value of his personal estate totaled $450.[63] He had left behind his beloved plantation in lush, green northwestern Alabama fourteen years earlier to live in a small town in the high desert of Utah Territory. Since leaving Alabama, John, Catherine, and their family lived in Pueblo, Salt Lake City, Holladay, San Bernardino, and Santaquin. The longest John and the family lived in any location since leaving Alabama was the six years in San Bernardino. John died 31 December 1864 in Holladay and is buried at the Santaquin City Cemetery.[64] Unlike many others from the South, John Holladay did not bring his enslaved people west. He chose to not live in polygamy. Upon the death of their daughter, Donnell Holladay Boyle, in San Bernardino, John and Catherine took her children into their home. He remained committed to his chosen religion to the end of his life. He helped found a city that now carries his name. John Holladay grew spiritually from the impetuous men of his early years to a rock-solid man of character later in life.[65]

JAMES ALBERT CHESNEY

Information about James Albert Chesney is limited. He was born 20 September 1824 at Cooper County, Missouri. His parents, Robert Chesney and Winifred, welcomed their new son on the borders of the frontier. The Chesney family included three sons, one older than James and one younger.[66] Records indicate James was baptized and confirmed 1 August 1847, and he received his endowment 14

---

63. United States Federal Census, 1860, *Ancestry.com,* https://www.ancestry.com/dis coveryui-content/view/34793036:7667?tid=&pid=&queryId=8fe2b1b2-1160-4653-847b-43989efd9fe2&_phsrc=EUI513&_phstart=successSource, <accessed 18 June 2024>
64. John D. Holladay, *Find A Grave,* https://www.findagrave.com/memorial/43300361/john-holladay, <accessed 18 June 2024>
65. Jay M. Todd, "Physical Size, Personality, and Character of John D. Holladay for Whom the City of Holladay is Named," unpaginated.
66. James Albert Chesney, *Family Search,* <K2WC-PY4> https://www.familysearch.org/tree/person/details/K2WC-PY4, <accessed 4 July 2024>

February 1852 in the Endowment House.[67] Whether this baptism was a rebaptism or his first is not clear. Two years after arriving in the Salt Lake Valley, James lived with the family of Samuel and Celestina Marble and their two young children. At the time of the census, James lived in Manti, Utah Territory. His house companions, Samuel and Celestina, both hailed from New York and their two children were born in Utah Territory when it was still known as Deseret. Samuel farmed and showed a real estate value of $150. James did not declare an occupation for the census.[68] Isaac Morley, a prominent early church member, established the city of Manti. He had led a group of 224 individuals made up of 124 men and 100 women. The company arrived 22 November 1849 and immediately began establishing rudimentary accommodations.[69] Although neither of the names Marble or Chesney appears on the list of original founders of Manti, they lived in the area less than a year after the settlement of the town.[70]

James married Jane Findley 29 September 1853 at Salt Lake City. James Chesney was born to this union about two years later.[71] Jane began her life 17 June 1817 at Louder, Ayrshire, Scotland.[72] She emigrated with her family in the James Chauncy Snow company in 1852. The company contained 250 people and fifty-five wagons. They used Kanesville, Iowa, as their outfitting post. They arrived at the Salt

---

67. James Albert Chesney, <K2WC-PY4>, *Family Search*, "Ordinances," https://www.familysearch.org/tree/person/ordinances/K2WC-PY4, <accessed 4 July 2024>

68. United States Federal Census, 1850, *Family Search*, https://www.familysearch.org/ark:/61903/3:1:S3HY-DRBW-MT3?view=index&personArk=%2Fark%3A%2F61903%2F1%3A1%3AMCSX-3PF&action=view, <accessed 4 July 2024>

69. Historical Department journal history of the Church, 1830-2008; 1840-1849; 1849 July-December; Church History Library, https://catalog.churchofjesuschrist.org/assets/27c27cf1-1319-4c97-b505-06ca11485a7b/0/596?lang=eng, <accessed 4 July 2024>

70. Adelia B. Cox Sidwell, *Reminiscences [sic] of the Early Days in Manti*, pages 1-3, https://www.familysearch.org/library/books/records/default?search=Manti%20Utah&sort=_score&perpage=10&page=1&fulltext=1&&refine[AccessLevel][]=Full+Permission&r&&refine[AccessLevel][]=Public&r&&refine[AccessLevel][]=Limited+Permission&r&&offset=, <accessed 4 July 2024>

71. James Albert Chesney, *Family Search* <K2WC-PY4>

72. Jane Findlay, *Family Search*, https://www.familysearch.org/tree/person/details/LHV7-K2S, <accessed 4 July 2024>

Lake Valley 9-10 October 1852.[73] The 1860 federal census recorded James lived in Salt Lake City, but the records indicate he lived alone. His real estate value totaled $50, and his personal estate value came to $150. He worked as a laborer.[74] James received a call to serve as a counselor to Joseph Harker in the priest's quorum in Salt Lake City in March 1849. He received a call to settle in southern Utah Territory in 1861, specifically in Meadow Valley.[75] James Chesney died 8 October 1869 in Salt Lake City, and he was interred at the Salt Lake Cemetery. He died of cancer, and the records show no attending physician and no undertaker.[76]

MARY ANN REER

Of all the participants in the Mississippi Company, Mary Ann Reer and her four children—Perril E., age twelve; James, age five; Sally Ann, age four; and Josephine, age three—have the smallest amount of recorded information. Mary Ann and her children spent the winter of 1846 and 1847 in Pueblo, and they suffered the same privations as others in the group. This brave mother and her children departed Pueblo in the spring of 1847 and entered the Salt Lake Valley 29 July 1847 along with the others who traveled with James Brown of the Mormon Battalion.[77] Mary Ann Reer was baptized 8 August 1847 by Addison Everett and confirmed by George Albert Smith and Albert

73. James C. Snow Company (1852), "Church History Biographical Database," https://history.churchofjesuschrist.org/chd/organization/pioneer-company/james-c-snow-company-1852?timelineTab=allTabs&lang=eng, <accessed 4 July 2024>

74. United States Federal Census, 1860, *Family Search*, https://www.familysearch.org/tree/person/sources/K2WC-PY4, <accessed 4 July 2024>

75. James Albert Chesney, "Brief Life History," *Family Search*, <K2WC-PY4> https://www.familysearch.org/tree/person/details/K2WC-PY4, <accessed 4 July 2024>

76. James Albert Chesney, "Burial Records," *Family Search*, <K2WC-PY4> https://www.familysearch.org/ark:/61903/3:1:3QS7-89CR-BSW4?view=index&action=view, <accessed 4 July 2024>

77. Names of Pueblo soldiers and Mississippi brethren , https://catalog.churchofjesuschrist.org/assets/ab774142-989d-4df6-a024-1f3a90e5bbd3/0/1, <accessed 4 July 2024>

Carrington.[78] The names of Mary Ann and the four children appear in the "Utah Gazetteer and Directory of Logan, Ogden, Provo, and Salt Lake Cities for 1884."[79] No names of the Reer family appear under the residential entries for the four named cities, though they were recorded entering the Salt Lake Valley in 1847. Unfortunately, the lives of Mary Ann and her children seem to conclude with their entrance into the Salt Lake Valley. Mary Ann and her children deserve to have their story told.

---

78. Historian's Office rebaptism records, 1848-1876; Rebaptism record, 1850-1863; Church History Library, https://catalog.churchofjesuschrist.org/assets/5222873a-795c-4922-b7f5-41a01a1e7a38/0/41?lang=eng, <accessed 10 July 2024>

79. Robert W. Sloan, editor, "Utah Gazetteer and Directory of Logan, Ogden, Provo and Salt Lake Cities for 1884," *Ancestry.com*, image 132/351, https://www.ancestry.com/discoveryui-content/view/1197956632:2469?tid=&pid=&queryId=98faa9b2-e4ea-4886-bd1c-44026b999bed&_phsrc=EUI961&_phstart=successSource, <accessed 5 July 2024>

15

MISSISSIPPI SAINTS WHO LIVED AND WORKED IN CALIFORNIA

JAMES HARMON

James Harmon, son of Stephen A. Harmon and Lucinda Joslin Harmon, was born at Boonesborough, Lincoln, Kentucky, on 29 September 1801 as the second of nine children. One account noted that James knew and admired Daniel Boone during his youth in Boonesborough.[1] How much he interacted with the noted explorer is a matter of conjecture since Boone lived in Missouri after 1799.[2] It is possible Daniel Boone occasionally visited the town that bears his name even after settling in Missouri. James married Mary Ann Blanks Smithson in 1828 at Pendleton, Anderson, South Carolina. Their marriage produced six children—four boys and two girls. Each of the six children lived to adulthood, and they all outlived their father.[3] The Harmon family relocated to northeastern Mississippi before July

---

1. Mary Ann Carter, compiler, "Our Pioneer Heritage," (Salt Lake City, Utah, Daughters of Utah Pioneers, 1959), 449, Volume 2

2. Editors of Encyclopedia Britanica, "Daniel Boon American Frontiersman," *Britanica,* https://www.britannica.com/biography/Daniel-Boone, <accessed 20 June 2024>

3. James Harmon, *Family Search,* https://www.familysearch.org/tree/person/details/KWVQ-NCM, <accessed 19 June 2024>

1835.[4] Nine years later, in August 1844, both James and Mary Ann accepted baptism into the church.[5] James only lived seven more years before his sudden death, but during those short years, he traveled extensively within the United States and into Central America.

James Harmon worked as a blacksmith, which greatly aided him and his family during their travels to Pueblo and the Salt Lake Valley.[6] As noted in a previous chapter, his knowledge of blacksmithing helped him find work at Bent's Fort while in Pueblo. Shortly after arriving in the Salt Lake Valley, he opened a blacksmith shop in partnership with Dimick Huntington. James, along with many others from the Mississippi Company, settled at Big Cottonwood. By 1848, James headed to the gold fields of California.[7] Brigham Young publicly denounced gold mining; however, he also promoted the mining of gold—under his direction. Knowing the allure of gold to the cash-strapped, starving Saints living in Utah Territory, his public oratory constantly told the Saints to stay put, but he also knew of the dire need for money to support the growth of the church. Thus, he called many men on missions to the gold fields of California. Over $80,000 in gold went through the "Mormon mint" between 1848 and 1851. Without the infusion of gold into the coffers of the fledgling Salt Lake Valley economy, the results might have been catastrophic.[8] It is not known if James received a call to fill a gold mission or if he went independently.

The Harmon family journeyed to California and first settled in the

---

4. Ibid, the Harmon's daughter Paralee America Harmon was born at Aberdeen, Monroe, Mississippi July, 1835.

5. Heather Hardy, compiler, "Remembered and Known: Latter-day Saints in the Antebellum South," unpublished manuscript, image 59/209, file:///C:/Users/Owner/One Drive/Documents/Mississippi%20Company/Mississippi%20Saints%20Company% 20Participants/Mississippi%20background/Hardy%20LDS%20in%20the%20Antebel lum%20South.pdf, <accessed 20 June 2024>

6. James Harmon, *Family Search*, <KWVQ-NCM>, https://www.familysearch.org/tree/ person/details/KWVQ-NCM, <accessed 19 June 2024>

7. Mary Ann Carter, compiler, "Our Pioneer Heritage," 450, Vol. 2

8. J. Kenneth Davies, Lorin K. Hansen, *Mormon Gold Mormons in the California Gold Rush*, (North Salt Lake City, Utah; Granite Mountain Publishing Company, 2010), xvii-xix

Sacramento area. They later relocated up the American River, likely near Long Valley or Mormon Ravine, near current-day Auburn. During their time in the gold fields, James worked in Placer Mining, and Mary Ann ran a hotel known as the Homestead House. This hotel became a stop-over point for missionaries as they proselyted in the area or passed through on their way to their assigned missions.[9] Apostles Amasa Lyman and Charles C. Rich toured the gold mining area of California to collect tithes from church members living in the area. On one occasion, August 11-12, 1850, Rich and his companion stayed for two days with the Harmons, likely in the Homestead Hotel.[10] There is no mention of any tithes or offerings being collected during this visit. However, during a later visit to the Harmons, Rich noted he received "substantial tithing from both Harmon and [Benjamin F.]" Mathews. In 1851, James determined to bring west a daughter who had remained in Mississippi. During this effort to reunite with his daughter, he contracted a fever as he crossed the Isthmus of Panama.[11] James died in Auburn, California, on 14 September 1851 and is buried there.[12]

Following the premature death of her husband in 1851, Mary Ann lived another forty-six years. She filled those widowed years with a determination worth emulating. A letter written by a daughter, Josephine Smithson Harmon Evans, on 12 July 1926, offers a glimpse into Mary Ann's life in California. In part, her letter noted:

After staying there [Salt Lake Valley] for two years, we left for California in the spring of 1849 [other accounts indicate 1848 as the year]. Lived in Auburn, California, for eight years. My parents ran a hotel, and it was a gathering place for the Latter-day Saint missionar-

---

9. Ibid, 137

10. Charles C. Rich diaries, 1833-1862; Volume 8, 1849 October 8-1851 September 22; Church History Library, image 43/90, https://catalog.churchofjesuschrist.org/assets/5f6b8c06-4a3f-4763-a75f-b80d973d5324/0/60?lang=eng, <accessed 20 June 2024>

11. J. Kenneth Davies, Lorin K. Hansen, *Mormon Gold Mormons in the California Gold Rush*, 137

12. James Harmon, *Family Search,*

ies. I remember as many as fifteen Elders being there at one time, and for eight years, we housed and entertained as many as came there. My parents done well in their hotel.[13]

Mary Ann purchased a large cattle ranch at Carson City, Nevada, after the death of her husband and lived there until 1859, when she returned to Utah Territory with three children: James, John, and Josephine. One daughter remained in Nevada, and another continued living in California. Mary Ann selected Centerville as her home, and she remained there until her death. She taught her daughters the art of spinning and weaving, allowing them to make clothing from cotton, linen, and wool.

Mary Ann served as the first Relief Society President of the Centerville Ward. She always enjoyed traveling and made several trips to Nevada and California to see her children. On a trip to California in 1872, she ordered twelve walnut trees, twelve almond trees, two fig trees, twelve quince trees, and multiple grape vines to be planted in Centerville. Five of the walnut trees were still standing as of 1934. She stayed active until suffering a stroke on 15 January 1897 during a visit to her son in Salt Lake City. She died on 25 January 1897 at eighty-nine years of age.[14] Mary Ann faced life on the frontier with an indomitable spirit. She remained faithful to the church she and James joined while living in Mississippi. Following her husband's death, she chose not to remarry. Although James experienced an early death, he lived a life full of adventure. Before leaving for the West, he made several trips to Nauvoo, where he helped build the temple and worked on the Nauvoo House. He knew gunsmithing, was an excellent hunter, and was superb on a horse.[15] Both Mary Ann and James completed their life journey with honor. They embraced a new reli-

---

13. Mary Ann Carter, compiler, "Our Pioneer Heritage," 451

14. Mary Ann Carter, compiler, "Our Pioneer Heritage," 450-451

15. Mary Ann Blanks Smithson, "Biography of Mary Ann Blanks Smithson from http://cannariatoferrell.tripod.com'id87.htm, *Family Search*, https://www.familysearch.org/tree/person/memories/KWVQ-NH1, <accessed 20 June 2024>

gion, traveled thousands of miles in support of their convictions, and raised their six children.

ROBERT AND ELIZABETH CROW

Robert Crow joined the Mississippi Saints at Independence and continued with them to Pueblo and then to the Salt Lake Valley in 1847. He holds the distinction of being the oldest member of the company at fifty-two when this group of believers trekked west. He was born on 22 June 1794 in Greenville, Greene, Tennessee. His parents, Benjamin Crow and Nancy Ann Gregg raised eleven children together, and Robert was the seventh child born to the family. In 1802, Benjamin and Nancy moved their family (including married children) to a district known as St. Genevieve, next to the Mississippi River in the southeast corner of present-day Missouri. At the time of the move, Spain owned the area, but this small enclave spoke French.[16] Robert Crow married Elizabeth Brown Crow on 5 September 1817. Elizabeth Brown took her first breath on 1 April 1795 in Abbieville District, South Carolina. The newlyweds initially lived near his parents at St. Genevieve, but they eventually moved to Perry County, Illinois, to be near her father, Benjamin Brown.[17]

Elizabeth Brown was a cousin to pioneer John Brown, one of the key organizers of the Mississippi Saints of 1846.[18] Robert and Elizabeth accepted baptism on or before 1841. Five years later, the Crow family, William D. Kartchner's family, and the George W. Threlkel family departed from Perry County, Illinois, to travel west for their anticipated rendezvous with members of the church from

---

16. Robert Crow, " Benjamin & Ann Gragg Crow Family," *Family Search,* <KWV4-JY5>, Contains excerpts from "Robert Crow—Pioneer of 1847" by Darline Chaffin Law, https://www.familysearch.org/tree/person/memories/KWV4-JY5, <accessed 21 June 2024>

17. Robert Crow, "Story #1, Robert & Elizabeth Crow," *Family Search* <KWV4-JY5>

18. John Zimmerman Brown, "Autobiography of pioneer John Brown, 1820-1896, arraigned and published by his son, John Zimmerman Brown, (Salt Lake City, Utah, Press of Stevens & Walls, inc. 1941), 439, https://archive.org/details/autobiographyof p00brow/page/438/mode/2up?q=Robert+Crow, <accessed 21 June 2024>

Nauvoo. The group departed on 17 May 1846.[19] As noted in an earlier chapter, Robert Crow and those traveling with him left Pueblo before the others who lived there and arrived in the valley before most of the others. In the spring of 1848, Robert moved north, settling near the "junction of the Ogden and Weber rivers." He and his sons built cabins and farmed. During the years 1848 to 1849, Robert and his family raised vegetables, watermelons, and grain.[20] Captain James Brown of the Mormon Battalion purchased the land settled on by the Crow family from Miles Goodyear in 1847. He paid $3,000 for all the land that now encompasses Weber County. Brown and Crow knew each other during their time in Pueblo during the winter of 1846-1847. When Brown purchased the land in 1847, it was part of Mexico, so the sale documents were written in Spanish.[21]

Knowing others had been selected for the gold fields in California, Robert Crow sent a petition to Brigham Young and the council of church leaders seeking permission to go there. Robert and the seven others who signed the petition desired sanction from church leaders for their relocation. During a meeting held Saturday 24 March 1849, Brigham Young responded to the request by asserting, "Most of those who have been to the gold mines, had made use of the gold to oppress their brethren, and they certainly would do nothing for their benefit, nor anybody's else, but would spend most of their time in idleness, drunkenness, or riding horses to death."[22] The next Sunday, during a speech in the bowery, President Young delivered a stinging rebuke regarding those who desired to go to California, saying, "I advise the corrupt and all that want, to go to California and not come back, for I

---

19. Robert Crow, "Story #3, Conversion to Mormonism," *Family Search*

20. Robert Crow, "Story #8, Family Moves to Weber County and Plant Crops, *Family Search*

21. "Utah-Weber County," *The National Society of the Sons of the Utah Pioneers*, unpaginated, https://www.sup1847.com/utah-weber-county, <accessed 22 June 2024>

22. Historical Department journal history of the Church, 1830-2008; 1840-1849; 1849 January-July; Church History Library, image 139/624, https://catalog.churchofje suschrist.org/assets/1f1cca14-5bb5-4574-90f4-5dcf07f230b8/0/138, <accessed 22 June 2024>

will not fellowship them. I came here to serve the Lord."[23] It is possible Robert Crow, his family, and the others who traveled with him went to California without the desired authorization. However, Robert kept a close relationship with Apostle Amasa Lyman, which allowed a continued connection to the church in Utah Territory.[24]

On 30 July 1850, he authorized his friend Amasa Lyman to be his "only lawful agent" to dispose of all his assets in Utah Territory." [25] Robert wanted to make California his permanent home. The 1850 federal census found fifty-six-year-old Robert Crow and Elizabeth living near Sacramento. Robert declared he worked as a wood chopper, a part of the timber industry. Other family members lived either in the same dwelling as Robert or right next door. The males, who ranged in age from eighteen to fifty, declared their occupations as wood choppers as well.[26] George Threlkel, his wife, Jane Crow Threlkel, William Crow, and Lewis B. Myers all lived within the same area as Robert and Elizabeth following their move to California. The 1852 California state census noted Robert now worked as an innkeeper, and both he and Elizabeth were fifty-eight years old.[27] The 1870 federal census listed Robert as a farmer. He declared no monetary value for either real estate or personal assets on either the 1850 or 1870 federal census records.[28] One important detail to gain from the federal and state census records is that he did not settle in California to seek gold. Each of the census records indicates his involvement with other pursuits.

Robert, Elizabeth, and his brother-in-law operated a hotel called

---

23. Ibid, image 143/624

24. J. Kenneth Davies, Lorin K. Hansen, *Mormon Gold Mormons in the California Gold Rush*, 116

25. Ibid, 136

26. United States Federal Census, 1850, *Family Search*, https://www.familysearch.org/tree/person/sources/KWV4-JY5, <accessed 22 June 2024>

27. California, U. S. State Census, 1852, "Robert Crow," *Ancestry*, https://www.ancestry.com/discoveryui-content/view/164222:1767?tid=&pid=&queryId=e20909cd-43d1-4f65-ae2b-fd40e02bd151&_phsrc=EUI546&_phstart=successSource, <accessed 22 June 2024>

28. United States Federal Census, 1870, *Family Search* <accessed 22 June 2024>

The Long Valley House. Like the Harmons' tavern, missionaries and other church leaders used The Long Valley House to rest from their travels. A fire destroyed the hotel in 1856, but rebuilding took a high priority. Once restored, the roadhouse continued to function. On 13 January 1857, missionary Henry G. Boyle preached at the Odd Fellows Hall near present-day Auburn. The next day, he met with Hamilton Crow and wrote, "This is a good family may the Lord bless them. I enjoyed myself here better than usual." On 15 January 1857, Robert Crow received a visit from Henry. Of that visit, Boyle wrote, "I like Father Crow, and I think his daughter Araminda is a good girl, and also Mr. Timkill's [Threlkel's] wife, one of his daughters."[29] Robert Crow and many of his family returned to Utah Territory in November 1857. He and his family settled in Santa Clara, building a home near Pinto Creek. Robert's beloved wife, Elizabeth Brown Crow, died on 25 May 1870 at Pinto Creek.[30] Robert Crow passed away on 29 May 1876 at Long Valley, Placer, California, and is buried in the Threlkel Family Cemetery at Long Valley.[31] Robert and Elizabeth Crow embraced religion in the early 1840s and continued faithful to the end of their lives—even after traveling thousands of miles, settling in various locations, and never attaining the financial status they enjoyed before joining the church.

George Washington Threlkel

George Washington Threlkel began his life on 26 January 1820 at Peoria, Peoria, Illinois. His future wife, Matilda Jane Crow, sister of Robert Crow, was born at Perry, Pike, Illinois, in June 1824.[32] George's father, William Harwood Threlkel, actively participated in

29. Henry Green Boyle, vol. 03, 1857, *BYU Library Digital Collections*, page 5, https://con tentdm.lib.byu.edu/digital/collection/MMD/id/34939/rec/5, <accessed 22 June 2024>
30. Robert Crow, "Story #12, The Crow Family Return to Utah," *Family Search*
31. Robert Crow, *Family Search*, https://www.familysearch.org/tree/person/details/ KWV4-JY5, <accessed 22 June 2024>
32. Geroge Washington Threlkel, *Family Search*, https://www.familysearch.org/tree/ person/details/KG3J-J19, <accessed 24 June 2024>

local government during the early years of Perry County, Illinois. He served as one of the first county commissioners. He began his term on 2 March 1829. William also functioned as a justice of the peace and on a standing grand jury.[33] George married Matilda on 29 December 1842 at Perry, Illinois. An authorized minister of the "gospel of Christ," Eli Short, performed the wedding.[34] The baptism of George and Matilda likely took place around the time of Matilda Jane's brother, Robert Crow, in 1841 or 1842. As noted in chapter five, George and Matilda Jane left Illinois with her brother's family and met the Mississippi Saints in Independence, Missouri. A short account concerning the tragic death of their son three days after reaching the Salt Lake Valley and the birth of their daughter Harriet Ann four days following his death is also contained in that chapter.

After remaining in Utah Territory for two years, George traveled with the Robert Crow group to the gold fields of California. George, Matilda, and their children settled in California for the balance of their lives. His impact on those around him was significant, and he lived a life filled with helping his family and others. Following their move to California, Matilda and George experienced the birth of two more children. George Louis Threlkel was born in 1850, shortly after the family arrived in California, while Mary Elizabeth came into the world in 1852.[35] The first place the family settled was in Louisville, El Dorado, California. They lived with their four living children and a twenty-year-old miner from New York in 1850. George mined gold during his first years in the state.[36] By 1860, George lived in

---

33. Unknown author, "The combined History of Randolph, Monroe and Perry Counties, Illinois, *Family Search*, https://www.familysearch.org/library/books/records/item/288583-combined-history-of-randolph-monroe-and-perry-counties-illinois-and-biographical-sketches-of-some-of-their-prominent-men-and-pioneers?offset=, <accessed 24 June 2024>

34. George Washington Threlkel, *Family Search*, <KG3J-J19> https://www.familysearch.org/tree/person/sources/KG3J-J19, accessed 24 June 2024> Information taken from Illinois County marriages located in sources.

35. George Washington Threlkel, *Family Search*, <KG3J-J19>

36. United States Federal Census, 1850. *Ancstry.com*, https://www.ancestry.com/discoveryui-content/view/18029907:8054?tid=&pid=&queryId=9156fa52-2c18-4ed2-a6f5-54b719475d09&_phsrc=EUI636&_phstart=successSource, <accessed 24 June 2024>

Township No. 3, Placer County, California. George was then farming, probably after discovering the lack of mineable gold. His property was valued at $1,000, and his assets were $2,000. His children, his brother, and a miner lived with George and Matilda. Matilda was thirty-five years old, and George was forty years old.[37] By 1870, George's real estate value came to $2,000, and his assets were $5,000.[38]

George registered to vote in several elections.[39] He was noted as "one of the first American settlers of California." He first landed at Mormon Island. In 1851, he relocated to the Auburn area, where he built a guesthouse on the Auburn and Sacramento wagon road that became a favorite resting place for travelers and teamsters. George was also known as an expert fruit grower, and his orchards were the envy of his neighbors. He possessed a reserved personality and used his words carefully until he became acquainted with a person. He died on a Wednesday evening at home on 3 January 1900. George had suffered from heart issues for several years, and his younger brother had passed away only a few months earlier. His services were held in the family home, and he was interred on the farm he tended for many years. The following two sentences from his obituary express what George meant to his friends and his children: "His home and orchard bear witness to his thrift, care, and ceaseless industry…. To his children, he leaves the priceless legacy of a good man."[40]

George and Matilda celebrated their fiftieth wedding anniversary on 28 December 1892 at their homestead. Surrounded by family and friends, the couple enjoyed an "elegant wedding dinner," received many gifts, and enjoyed the evening surrounded by those they loved. The couple was also remembered for being the first to bring fruit

---

37. United States Federal Census, 1860, *Ancestry.com*

38. United States Federal Census, 1870, *Ancestry.com*

39. George Washington Threlkel, "California Great Registers, 1850-1920," *Family Search,* <KG3J-J19> https://www.familysearch.org/tree/person/sources/KG3J-J19, <accessed 24 June 2024>

40. "Gone to His Rest," *Ancestry.com,* https://www.ancestry.com/family-tree/person/tree/142676/person/-2114315973/gallery?galleryPage=1&tab=0, Obituary located in the "Gallery" for George Washington Threlkel. <accessed 24 June 2024>

trees to the valley, which created an industry for which Placer became famous.[41] Following George's death, his son, George Louis Threlkel, served as the administrator for his father's will. The total value of his real estate and personal assets equaled $4,099.58. After all outstanding debts were satisfied, George's will provided $3,864.60 to his wife, Matilda Jane.[42] Six months following George's death, Matilda was living in Long Valley with her daughter, Harriett, on the family farm. Matilda was then seventy-three years old, and George's death had occurred only six months earlier.[43] Matilda Jane Crow Threlkel died at the age of eighty-six years on 6 April 1906 at the family farm in Long Valley, California. Her obituary noted she died of complications due to pneumonia and had likely lived in Placer County longer than any other woman. Her obituary stated, "She was a woman of many noble and lovable traits of character."[44] Thus, the lives of two members of the Mississippi Saints ended. George and Matilda lived their lives nobly, and as can be seen from their obituaries, each of them influenced their family, friends, and community most positively.

George Washington Sparks

George Washington Sparks entered life on 27 May 1819 at Athens,

<hr>

41. Anniversary Notices, "Their Golden Wedding," *Ancestry.com*, Public Member Stories, https://www.ancestry.com/mediaui-viewer/collection/1030/tree/142676/person/-2114315973/media/5bad65d2-dc1a-44cc-84af-856c14e356fa?queryId=b4400931-ce04-4b85-a8dc-a667ae945052&_phsrc=EUI668&_phstart=successSource, <accessed 25 June 2024>

Document needs to be downloaded before reading.

42. George Threlkel, "California, U.S., Wills and Probate Records, 1850-1953, for G W Threlkel," *Ancestry.com*, https://www.ancestry.com/discoveryui-content/view/358039:8639?tid=&pid=&queryId=06d55b3b-3cd5-400a-aafa-a5a6df60b900&_phsrc=EUI673&_phstart=successSource, <accessed 25 June 2024>>

43. United States Federal Census, 1900, *Ancestry.com*, https://www.ancestry.com/discoveryui-content/view/36495176:7602?tid=&pid=&queryId=a339e677-a9b1-42cc-b3ca-ef0908ab87f9&_phsrc=EUI677&_phstart=successSource, <accessed 25 June 2024>

44. Matilda Jane Crow, Obituary, *Ancestry.com*, https://www.ancestry.com/family-tree/person/tree/36517651/person/18947282295/gallery?galleryPage=1, <accessed 25 June 2024>

Blount, Alabama. He was born to Mary Ann Sparks Gibson and Amon Sparks. George's future wife, Lusianna "Luana" Roberds, came into the world on 11 December 1818 in Marengo, Alabama. They were married on 26 August 1841 in Monroe County. Eight children came into this union within a span of eighteen years. When George and Luana started west in 1846, they brought along a three-year-old son and a newborn baby girl. One can only imagine the difficulty of feeding a newborn, watching a three-year-old boy, cooking, washing, and the never-ending tasks involved in walking from northeastern Mississippi to the mountains of Utah by way of winter in Pueblo, Colorado. Amazingly, the family settled in several different locations in California, including Diamond Springs, Sonoma, San Bernardino, and Anaheim. Following their arrival in Utah Territory, another son arrived in 1848. The other five children were born in California.[45]

George did not spend much time in the Utah Territory. By 1850, he and his family were living in Diamond Springs, California. He worked as a merchant and operated a boarding house. He moved the family to Suisun Valley for about two years. Their next stop was just west of the Sacramento River in Mendocino County. He then moved the family near the Russian River, where they lived, until they moved to San Bernardino in 1857, where George farmed.[46] Three years after moving to the area, he achieved a real estate value of $4,000 and a personal assets value of $4,100. He and his wife were then forty years old, and they lived with their five children and a sixteen-year-old female named Hannah VanLeunen.[47] Twenty years later, George still resided in San Bernardino. He was then sixty years old and lived with his wife and three sons on 8th Street. The three sons were all over the

---

45. George Washington Sparks, *Family Search*, <KWV7-RMD> https://www.family search.org/tree/person/details/KWV7-RMD, <accessed 25 June 2024>

46. J. Kenneth Davies, Lorin K. Hansen, *Mormon Gold Mormons in the California Gold Rush*, 138

47. United States Federal Census, 1860, George W. Sparks, *Ancestry.com*, https://www. ancestry.com/discoveryui-content/view/2674151:7667?tid=&pid=&queryId=8cab d1ea-f2c8-47df-a2d4-df2ad319bbd4&_phsrc=EUI754&_phstart=successSource, <accessed 27 June 2024>

age of nineteen and worked on George's farm. A detail of interest from the 1880 census is the fact that Luanna could not write.[48]

After moving to San Bernardino in June of 1857, George purchased 168 acres of land in partnership with one James M. West. He later added forty acres to that parcel. He also purchased eight sections (5,120 acres) of land in San Diego County, where he raised cattle, horses, wheat, and barley. His sons worked the ranch in San Diego County.[49] George experienced much success during his time in Southern California. The 1900 census noted that eighty-one-year-old George now lived in Anaheim Township, Orange County, California, and owned his home and farms. Sadly, Luanna passed away before the census, so George lived with a son, a daughter-in-law, Lizzi, and two boarders.[50] She died on 17 October 1895 in Anaheim at the age of seventy-five years.[51] Her commitment to her children, her husband, and their nomadic lifestyle after joining the church stands as a remarkable illustration of her character and an example of a life well-lived. She faced life's challenges head-on and seemed to always keep moving forward. Like the others from the Mississippi Saints, Luanna, her husband, and their descendants profoundly impacted western expansion during the mid-nineteenth century.

Through the diary kept by missionary Henry G. Boyle, we gain an intimate view of the relationship George and his family maintained with church headquarters in Utah Territory during the mid-1850s. During a conference, which began in San Bernardino on 23 June 1855, Charles C. Rich and Amasa Lyman discussed the impending need to pay for the land they had purchased in San Bernardino. Henry Boyle received and accepted a call to "preach and raise money to pay for the ranch." Before he left for Northern California, one John Hill

---

48. United States Federal Census, 1880, Geroge W. Sparks, *Ancestry.com*

49. Unknown author, *An Illustrated History of Southern California,* (Chicago: The Lewis Publishing Company, 1890), 717, https://archive.org/details/illustratedhistofsc00lewi/page/716/mode/2up?q=Sparkes , <accessed 27 June 2024>

50. United States Federal Census, 1900, George W. Sparks, *Ancestry.com,*

51. Lusianna "Luanna" Roberds," *Family Search,* <2HMS-VPJ>, https://www.family search.org/tree/person/details/2HMS-VPJ, <accessed 27 June 2024>

handed him five dollars to help with the expenses of the mission. Henry and the other missionaries who were headed north were set apart (blessed) for their mission. They began their journey with a four-horse team, which needed provisions and horses for several of the men.[52] On Wednesday, 1 August 1855, Boyle noted he traveled over rough country, got lost, found his way again, and found "Brother Sparks and his family all well and doing well. They are glad to see us and use us kindly. The family feel[s] better than any I have seen in this part of the country."[53] Boyle explained to George the need to help pay for the land in San Bernardino, to which George replied that he would help if he could sell his farm. Just a few days later, George Sparks was baptized and confirmed a member of the church, though this may have been a rebaptism.[54]

Henry developed such a personal relationship with George that he helped with branding young cattle, working "at his milk house," and driving his pigs to where they could be sold.[55] During this time together, George warned Henry that some of the people living in town were talking about hanging the missionaries.[56] Fortunately, nothing happened. To fulfill his promise to provide money for the ranch in San Bernardino, George paid Henry $200.[57] George's wife, Luanna, received baptism on 16 September 1855.[58] Whatever hard feelings might have existed between the Sparks family and the church softened during this time in 1855. When Brigham Young called for the evacuation of San Bernardino, George and the family elected to stay, and he and Luanna participated in the Reorganized Latter-Day Church.[59] George passed away on 18 October 1906 in Anaheim and

---

52. Henry Green Boyle, vol. 03, 1857, *BYU Library Digital Collections*, 141-144

53. Ibid, 180

54. Ibid, 185

55. Ibid, 196, 202, 206

56. Ibid, 197

57. Ibid, 225

58. Ibid, 226

59. J. Kenneth Davies, Lorin K. Hansen, *Mormon Gold Mormons in the California Gold Rush*, 138

was buried at the Anaheim Cemetery.[60] Thus, another good man from the Mississippi Company died. Both George and Luanna left a lasting legacy for their descendants, friends, and those who were privileged to learn about their lives.

JOHN ROBERDS

John Roberds and George Washington Sparks were brothers-in-law due to George marrying John's half sister, Luanna.[61] They left Mississippi together in 1846 and maintained a close relationship throughout their lives.[62] They often lived close to each other at the multiple locations where they settled. Richard T. Roberds wrote an account of his mother and father for a history of Southern California. His mother, Martha T. Roberds, was born in Madison, Alabama, on 16 May 1817. His father, John Roberds, was born in Franklin County, Georgia, in August 1800. Richard recalled leaving Mississippi at nine years of age with his parents and his six siblings.[63] The oldest child was eleven years old, while the youngest was about four months.[64] Martha faced the challenges of her cross-country migration with seven small children. Richard wrote about his mother, "I will say here, if there ever was a pioneer woman, my mother is one, for she almost raised her family on the road traveling."[65] John and Martha traveled with the Mississippi Company in 1846 and stayed the winter in Pueblo with the others. Rather than leaving with the other members of the group, the Roberds family stayed in the Pueblo area until the

---

60. Geroge Washington Sparks, "George Washington Sparkes in the U.S., Find a Grave Index, 1600s-Current," Ancestry.com, https://www.ancestry.com/discoveryui-content/view/96251316:60525, <accessed 27 June 2024>

61. Anna Nix, *Family Search*, <LCVF-BCW>, https://www.familysearch.org/tree/person/details/LCVF-BCW, <accessed 27 June 2024>

62. Monroe County Book Committee, *A History of Monroe County, Mississippi, Vol. 1*, (Curtis Media Corporation, 1988), 767, 976.2975.H2

63. Unknown author, *An Illustrated History of Southern California*, 553

64. John Roberds, *Family Search*, https://www.familysearch.org/tree/person/details/LDFF-WTS, <accessed 27 June 2024>

65. Unknown author, *An Illustrated History of Southern California*, 555

next spring, when they lived about ten miles below the town for a short time before moving back. The family lived in both Hardscrabble and another fort where they could see Pike's Peak. In the spring of 1848, the family left the area and settled in the Salt Lake Valley for a short time.[66]

In the spring of 1850, the family left the valley on the northern route to California. They arrived at Diamond Springs, California, in July 1850 after a long, wearisome journey. Like the Sparks family, the Roberds family relocated to the Suisun Valley, then to near the Sacramento River, next to the Russian River, and finally to San Bernardino in 1857.[67] In the year 1855, while living in the gold fields of Northern California, Elder Henry G. Boyle visited the family and wrote, "Today we are resting, however we go and visit John Roberts [Roberds]. They have no very great feelings for Mormonism, although they are friendly enough."[68] Three days later, Elder Boyle visited again, and during this visit, he simply wrote, "This evening we visit Brother John Roberts [Roberds] they use (treat) us kindly."[69] During a visit in March 1857, he wrote, "We also had [a] prayer meeting at Bro Roberts [Roberds] by candlelight. We had a lively time and enjoyed ourselves very well."[70] Elder Boyle showed tenderness toward the Roberds family.

John Roberds captained a group of twenty-three persons who left Northern California for San Bernardino in mid-May 1857.[71] Their journey took them through areas where the game was plentiful, and the travelers harvested the needed game to supply their food stocks. After traveling for a little over five weeks, the pioneer group arrived

---

66. Ibid, 554-555

67. Ibid, 555

68. Henry Green Boyle, vol. 1, 1855, *BYU Digital Library Collections*, page 181, https://contentdm.lib.byu.edu/digital/collection/MMD/id/34387/rec/4, <accessed 28 June 2024>

69. Ibid, 184

70. Henry Green Boyle, vol. 3, 1857, *BYU Digital Collections*, page 30, https://contentdm.lib.byu.edu/digital/collection/MMD/id/34964/rec/6, <accessed 28 June 2024>

71. Ibid, 46

in San Bernardino on 25 June 1857.[72] John, Martha, and their family spent the remainder of their lives in Southern California. John reported during the 1860 federal census that he worked as a farmer, his real estate value totaled $400, and his assets came to $725. He lived in the San Salvador Township in San Bernardino County. Five children lived in the home with John and Martha, ranging in age from one year old to fourteen, and all but the youngest attended school. John and Martha's ages were fifty-seven and forty-four, respectively.[73] The 1870 census inaccurately noted John was seventy years old, and Martha had reached the age of fifty-four. John still farmed, and four children now lived at home.[74] Concerning the family's impact on the San Bernardino area, a newspaper report from 1938 stated, "The family became prominent in the development of this city."[75] The Roberds, Bemis, and Hancock families continued holding family reunions in the Southland through 1938. Lovice Angeline Roberds Ashcraft was the only surviving child of the Roberds in that year.[76]

John Roberds joined the Reorganized Church of Jesus Christ of Latter-day Saints in the mid-1860s, and he served as one of six elders in the San Francisco branch.[77] John listed his occupation as a farmer on the census records. John owned a "fine ranch of about one hundred acres on Ninth Street, one and one-half miles northwest of San Bernardino, and has been very successful as a farmer and stock

---

72. Unknown author, *An Illustrated History of Southern California*, 555

73. United States Federal Census, 1860, *Ancestry.com*, https://www.ancestry.com/dis coveryui-content/view/2673784:7667?tid=&pid=&queryId=9d726f78-2e51-4203- 9718-b77e32481f34&_phsrc=EUI791&_phstart=successSource, <accessed 28 June 2024>

74. United States Federal Census, 1870, *Ancestry.com*, https://www.ancestry.com/dis coveryui-content/view/140968:7163, <accessed 28 June 2024>

75. Covered Wagon Families, "Family of John Roberds, 1857 Settler, Among the City's Largest." *Family Search*, https://www.familysearch.org/tree/person/memories/LDFF- WTS, <accessed 28 June 2024>

76. Manuscript histories of the Church in the United States, circa 1910-1971; Manuscript history of Church activities in San Bernadino, California, 1850-1860; Church History Library, https://catalog.churchofjesuschrist.org/assets/2eeb16d3- 7205-4aad-add3-2d4d123db880/0/218?lang=eng, <accessed 28 June 2024>

77. J. Kenneth Davies, Lorin K. Hansen, *Mormon Gold Mormons in the California Gold Rush*, 138

dealer. He has seen a good deal of the world and is one of the pioneers of the valley."[78] There is a discrepancy about John's death date. The 1880 federal census, which was taken on 3 June 1880, shows Martha as a widow. However, the death date on his tombstone is inscribed as 21 October 1880. The date on the tombstone is likely incorrect.[79] The newspaper article referred to above noted John's death as 15 October 1878.[80] There is a possibility that neither date is correct. Martha died on 5 December 1897 and is buried in San Bernardino.[81] John, Martha, and their children traveled from coast to coast to establish a permanent home. They finally found that home in San Bernardino, California.

BENJAMIN FRANKLIN MATHEWS

Benjamin Franklin Mathews lived a life filled with accomplishment and misfortune. Benjamin was born in Pendleton, Anderson, South Carolina, on 16 April 1819. He was the son of Thomas Mathews and Jane McDavid.[82] His first wife, Temperance Weeks, entered life on 19 April 1817 at Franklin, Tennessee. Her parents were Jeptha Weeks and Sarah "Sally" Jones.[83] Benjamin's parents moved to Marion, Alabama, when he was one year old. At twenty years of age, he married Temperance, and together they raised eight children—six girls and two boys.[84] They moved to Monroe County in 1840 and

---

78. Unknown author, *An Illustrated History of Southern California*, 555-556

79. John Roberds, "Find a Grave," *Ancestry,* https://www.findagrave.com/memorial/29616244/john-roberds, accessed 28 June 2024>

80. Covered Wagon Families, "Family of John Roberds, 1857 Settler, Among the City's Largest."

81. Martha Tucker Walpole, *Family Search,* <MJH5-R9H> https://www.familysearch.org/tree/person/details/MJH5-R9H, <accessed 28 June 2024>

82. Benjamin Franklin Weeks, *Family Search,* <KLQ9-T75> https://www.familysearch.org/tree/person/details/KLQ9-T75, <accessed 30 June 2024>

83. Temperance Weeks, *Family Search,* <K2F5-ZWR> https://www.familysearch.org/tree/person/details/K2F5-ZWR , <accessed 30 June 2024>

84. Rockwell D. Hunt, editor, *California and Californians, Vol. 4,* (Los Angeles, The Lewis Publishing Company, 1926), 72, https://www.familysearch.org/library/books/viewer/427007/?offset=&return=1#page=87&viewer=picture&o=info&n=0&q=, <access 30 June 2024> Family search contains book online at the above link.

joined the church while living there. Benjamin, Temperance, and their three children departed Monroe County with the other Southerners bound for the West.[85] Benjamin and Temperance entered the Salt Lake Valley on 29 July 1847. Thomas Bullock's list noted an addition to their three children; the Matthews began the trek with a newborn noted as "a babe four weeks old." Bullock wrote the title "elder" next to Benjamin's name.[86]

The Matthews family remained in Utah Territory until 1850, when they left for the gold fields of California. The company departed early March 1850 and traveled the northern route to California, taking them through the deserts of northern Nevada and across the Sierra Nevada. After crossing the Sierras into California, Benjamin split from the main group to travel to Sacramento for supplies. He settled on the North Fork of the American River, built a hotel, and met with success by provisioning the gold seekers.[87] After a year, Benjamin sold the hotel and moved to near Auburn and Sacramento. During his short time there, he managed a hotel. Cholera ravaged this area, so he moved his family to San Bernardino in 1852. He left in 1854 for his home in Mississippi and returned to San Bernardino two years later, arriving on 7 November 1856.[88] Benjamin elected to stay in San Bernardino rather than return to Utah Territory in 1857. Sadly, Temperance died on 19 April 1859 in San Bernardino.[89] She was buried in the Pioneer Memorial Cemetery in that town. Unfortunately, her grave marker is no longer at the burial site. Evidence suggests she may have been one of the bodies exhumed years later during excavation for a new ballpark.[90] Benjamin married

---

85. Ibid.

86. Names of Pueblo soldiers and Mississippi brethren , https://catalog.churchofje suschrist.org/assets/ab774142-989d-4df6-a024-1f3a90e5bbd3/0/1, <accessed 30 June 2024>

87. Rockwell D. Hunt, editor, *California and Californians, Vol. 4,* 73-74

88. Ibid, 74

89. Temperance Weeks, *Family Search,* <K2F5-ZWR> https://www.familysearch.org/tree/person/details/K2F5-ZWR, <accessed 1 July 2024>

90. Ibid.

Mahala Ann Whiteman on 20 May 1866, and they had five children together. Her first husband, George Williams, died in 1865.[91]

Benjamin Franklin Matthews captained a wagon train from Mississippi all the way to San Bernardino. As noted earlier, he traveled back to Mississippi and stayed for about two years. In 1856, he brought a small contingent of about twenty pioneers west. This small pioneer company arrived in the Salt Lake Valley on July 19, 1856.[92] A seemingly harmless incident happened on the trail that caused a death and brought condemnation from Salt Lake Valley residents. The small contingent left Mississippi with few difficulties until they approached the Green River in Wyoming. As the wagons lumbered along, a young boy of about six fell out of his wagon, was run over, and became seriously injured. Shortly thereafter, a fellow traveler on the wagon train found a "large bead, stuffed with cotton, and gave it to the little boy."[93] The little boy's aunt picked out the cotton and handed the seemingly harmless article to him to play with. The boy was sick with a fever for about five days later. After they arrived in Utah Territory, the source of the fever became clear when he broke out with the dreaded smallpox. Benjamin believed the "bait" came from a wagon train traveling ahead of his and was directed at "the inhabitants of Utah."[94]

Benjamin lived in San Bernardino until his death. His election as Sheriff of San Bernardino County in 1863 brought him face-to-face with danger, and the arrest of the wrong man brought unwanted criticism. Those who lived in San Bernardino emigrated from both the Northern and Southern portions of the country, so the county contained both Confederate loyalists and Unionists. The feelings were so strong that five other men held the office of sheriff during the Civil War. In 1864, Sheriff Matthews and his deputy, W. W. Rubottom,

---

91. "Mahala Ann Whiteman, *Family Search,* <27SW-BVX> https://www.familysearch. org/tree/person/details/27SW-BVX, <accessed 1 July 2024>

92. "Arrivals," *Deseret News,* https://newspapers.lib.utah.edu/ark:/87278/s6xp809v/ 2573403, <accessed 1 July 2024>

93. B. F. Matthews "Disclaimer," *Deseret News,* https://newspapers.lib.utah.edu/ark:/ 87278/s66x05fk/2576162, <accessed 1 July 2024>

94. Ibid.

tracked an alleged horse thief for miles throughout Southern California. They eventually located a fellow who fit the description of the horse thief, arrested him, handcuffed him, and brought him back to San Bernardino—only to find out they had arrested the wrong person. The misidentified man received a payment from the county for $127.46 for unlawful arrest. Benjamin lost his reelection bid but remained in the area. He opened a grist mill in Colton and operated a mill called Matthews Mill in San Bernardino.[95] Before he was elected sheriff, Benjamin allegedly shot Richard Allen in the abdomen on 27 July 1858. According to one account, witnesses at the trial included his wife, Temperance, and his daughter, Sarah Jane. The verdict of the shooting trial is unknown.[96] Benjamin's life ended tragically when a falling tree crushed him on 21 August 1888 at Devil Canyon.[97] Like most of us, Benjamin lived a life filled with a little success, pierced with suffering. He traveled thousands of miles back and forth across the country. He took the challenges of leadership, and he lived life to the fullest until its conclusion.

The members of the company that left Mississippi in 1846 settled throughout Utah Territory, Southern California, and Northern California. The Saints left Monroe County with high hopes for their future. They crossed an unforgiving country, experiencing starvation and often failure. In addition, the enslaved who traveled with them to both the Utah Territory and San Bernardino also faced the challenge of crossing the plains and felt the sting of starvation while experiencing the unthinkable pain of enslavement. Most of the Mississippi Company remained faithful to their beliefs. Many served in leadership positions during their time in the West. Several families experienced a loss of faith and joined other denominations, including the

---

95. "Civil War Tensions put the Squeeze on County Sheriffs," *Sab Bernardino Sun,* 28 June 1987, *Family Search, Memories,* https://www.familysearch.org/tree/person/memo ries/KLQ9-T75, <accessed 1 July 2024>

96. "Life History of Richard Allen—Shot by Benjamin Mathews," *Family Search, Memories,* https://www.familysearch.org/tree/person/memories/KLQ9-T75, <accessed 1 July 2024>

97. "Civil War Tensions put the Squeeze on County Sheriffs,"

Reorganized Church of Jesus Christ of Latter-day Saints. All of those who left their homes with such high hopes lived lives worthy of our respect. This book offers a glimpse into the lives and struggles of these amazing men, women, and children from the South—both Black and white—and their impact on the church and western settlement.

AFTERWORD

JOSEPH SMALLS

Interview of Joseph Smalls conducted by the author 25 October 2024, recordings and notes from the interview in possession of Erick Wadsworth; account used by permission of Joseph Smalls.

Meeting a man named Joseph Smalls constitutes one of the sweet privileges of my life. He and his wife Karen live in Nampa, Idaho. My wife Marilyn and I first met them several years ago through a church assignment. We visited this delightful couple once a month, and over time, we learned more about Joe and his background in the church. You see, Joe is a Black member of The Church of Jesus Christ of Latter-Day Saints, and as a Black member, he experienced the unilateral priesthood ban on Black men, denying them the opportunity to receive the priesthood. The ban deprived Joseph of the chance to serve in any leadership capacity within the church, participate in most temple ordinances, and kept him in an almost subservient position as a church member. Yet, while stationed in Alaska, Joe accepted baptism into the church. What follows is a short synopsis of Joseph's life.

Joe was born 23 November 1950 at Edisto Island, South Carolina. Edisto Island lies about forty-two miles west of Charleston, South Carolina. He was born in his grandparents' home, and a midwife performed the delivery. He began working on a small farm his grand-parents owned at the age of ten or twelve years. He helped his family plant and harvest green beans, potatoes, and tomatoes. His grandparents did not own a tractor, so a plow horse completed the work of preparing the fields for planting. Joe spent most of his childhood with his grandparents, whom he loved deeply. Joe believed he "had one of the best childhoods that anyone could have." He lived with his mother during his sophomore year in high school and graduated from high school in May 1969. Joe enlisted in the United States Air Force in April 1970. He served thirty years in the Air Force, achieved the rank of Chief Master Sergeant, and retired in 2000. During his time in the Air Force, he met his wife, and together they raised four children.

Joe met his wife, Karen Killpack, after being transferred to Mountain Home Air Force Base in Mountain Home, Idaho. During the early 1970s, Air Force Bases operated Service Clubs. These clubs provided an opportunity for low-ranking service members to play games, watch TV, play music, and make new friends. The clubs also sponsored dances, which were attended by young women from local colleges and business schools. Karen, who attended Links Business School, attended one of the dances in the fall of 1971. She and Joe met, they danced together, and soon fell in love. They were engaged in March 1972, and married at the Mountain Air Base Chapel in June 1972. A little over two years later, Joe received transfer orders to Alaska. While living in Alaska, Joe became acquainted with The Church of Jesus Christ of Latter-day Saints. Joe knew nothing about the church, but due to his Baptist background, he held a strong belief in Jesus Christ.

After transferring to Alaska, Joe's mother-in-law contacted the bishop of the Anchorage, Alaska 1st ward, and told them Joe was not a member of the church. Soon, two full-time missionaries, one from Burley, Idaho, and another from Spanish Fork, began teaching Joe the discussions (an explanation of church beliefs). Following one of the discussions, Joe accepted baptism into the church, and he was baptized 8 May 1976. As a Black member of the church, Joe could not participate in many church activities. However, all that changed when

President Spencer W. Kimball announced a revelation removing the priesthood ban for Black men who were members of the church. Joe describes the impact the revelation had on his life.

I was happy, overjoyed, and unsure of what would happen next. My spirituality received a huge boost. I also felt like I was going to be a whole member of the church. Before that, young twelve-year-old-boys held more priesthood than I did. Something that still haunts me was that I was unable to bless my first three children, but I would get the opportunity to bless my last child in 1981, my daughter Naire.

Joe received the Melchizedek priesthood 11 June 1978 in the Plainview, New York Stake. Joe and his wife were sealed together, as husband and wife, in the Washington, D. C. temple 18 August 1978. He was ordained a High Priest 20 June 1986 in Kaiserslautern, Germany. Since receiving the priesthood, Joe has served in many leadership positions all over the world. He helped lead church groups in Italy, Turkey, New York, Washington, North Dakota, and Idaho.

Joe has experienced discrimination throughout his life. His wife, who is white, was taught at an early age to avoid Black men and women. Her instructions also included directives to cross the street if she saw a Black person walking toward her. However, Karen met a Black classmate at school, and they became great friends. This allowed her to recognize that what she was being told was incorrect. Joe believes "no child is born a racist." He believes a person learns racism by the environment he or she is raised in. Family, schools, religion and government either help eliminate racist attitudes or reinforce bigoted views. Joseph, Karen and their family represent the best of our nation's potential. Joe harbors no ill will concerning past prejudice regarding Black men and women. Both Joe and his wife look forward to a brighter day when all can be accepted as equal in the eyes of God.

APPENDIX

BIRTHS, MARRIAGES, AND DEATHS IN PUEBLO DURING THE WINTER OF 1846-1847

BIRTHS

- Sarah Ann Kartchner: November 1846; first known Caucasian baby born in Colorado
- Sarah Catherine Dowdle: November 1846
- John Taylor Harmon: 6 April 1847
- Wealthy Matilda Higgins: 2 May 1847
- Betsy Prescinda Huntington: 21 October 1846
- Malinda Catherine Kelley: 7 February 1847
- Sarah Ellen Sharp: 28 November 1846
- Margaret Elizabeth Shupe: 2 March 1847 (page 7 Diary of Andrew Jackson Shupe FS; daughter of James W. Shupe)
- Phoebe Isabell Williams: 15 January 1847

MARRIAGES

- Gilbert Hunt to Lydia Gibson: 23 April 1847
- John Chase to Almira Higgins: 12 February 1847
- Abner Chase to Mary Brand:????
- Bill New to Mary Gibson: ca. 1847

DEATHS

- Marvin Blanchard: 10 April 1847
- Eli Dodson: 21 March 1847
- Prescinda Huntington: 9 November 1846
- Milton Kelley: 4 November 1846
- Melcher Oyler: 25 February 1847
- John Perkins: 19 January 1847
- Alva Phelps: 15 November 1846
- Joseph Richards: 21 November 1846
- James Scott: 5 February 1847
- Arnold Stevens: 26 March 1847
- Parley Hunt: 1 January 1847

CAPTAIN JAMES BROWN

Allred, James	*Clark, Albert
Allred, Reuben	*Cummings, George
Blanchard, Marvin	*Glazier, Luther
Caulkins, James	*Hanks, Ebenezer
Garner, David	*Hess, John
Glines, James	*Hopkins, Charles
Holden, Elijah	*Jacobs, Bailey
Hulett, Schuyler	*Karren, Thomas
Jackson, Charles	*Miller, Daniel
Lake, Barnabas	*Park, William
Oyler, Melchior	*Pugmire, Jonathan

Richards, Joseph
Rowe, Caratat
Sessions, John
Clifford, John
Allen, Franklin
Bingham, Erastus
Bird, William
Chase, John
Garner, Phillip
Luddington, Elam
Pierson, Harmon
Stevens, Lyman
Stillman, Dexter
Walker, William
*Whiting, Almon
*Whiting, Edmond
*Williams, Thomas

*Stephens, Yes
Adams, Orson
Beckstead, William
Brown, Alexander
Brown, James
Brown, Jesse
Calvert, John
Carpenter, Isaac
Carpenter, William
Durphee, Francillo
Gould, John
Gould, Samuel
Johnson, Jarvis
Larson, Thurston
Nowlin, Jabez
Perkins, David
Perkins, John
Pierson, Judson

Shupe, Andrew
Shupe, James
Smith, Milton
Smith, Richard
Terrell, Joel
Tindell, Solomon
Wilkin, David
Abbott, Joshua
Averett, Jeduthan
Castro, William
Chase, Abner
Davis, James
Douglas, Ralph
Gifford, William
Gribble, William
Hirons, James

Kenney, Loren
Lamb, Lisbon
Laughlin, David
Messick, Peter
Oakley, James
Roberts, Benjamin
Rowe, William
Sanderson, Henry
Sargent, Abel
Sharp, Albert
Smith, John
Steele, John
Stephens, Arnold
Stillman, Clark
Tanner, Myron

CAPTAIN NELSON HIGGINS SOLDIERS

Hunt, Gilbert
Shelton, Sebert
Hendrickson, James
Mowrey, Harley
Brown, James
Button, Montgomery
Higgins, Nelson
Huntington, Dimick
Sharp, Norman

JOHN BROWN'S COMPANY OF 10, REPORT JUNE 1848 (WILLARD RICHARDS COMPANY 1848)

Family	**#Wagons**	**Enslaved**	**Age of Enslaved**
John Brown	2	Betty	11 years
Elizabeth Brown			
William Crosby	5	Violet	50
Sarah Crosby		Rose	15
		Grief	32
		Nelson	13
		Henderson	11
Elizabeth Crosby	2	Tobe	48
		Edy	21
		Mary	18
William Lay	3	Harriet	21
Sytha Lay		Lucy	12

Family	#Wagons	Enslaved	Age of Enslaved
Robert Smith	4	Rande	26
Rebecca Smith		Biddy	28
		Ellen	10
		Hannah	26
		Harriet	8 months
		Ann	11
		Lawrence	5
		Nat	3
		Jane	4 months[1]

JOHN AND GEORGE BANKHEAD AND THE UNNAMED ENSLAVED THEY BROUGHT WEST IN 1848

Family	#Wagons	Livestock	Unnamed Enslaved
John Bankhead	3	59	"4 Black servants"
Nancy Bankhead			"2 female servants"
George Bankhead	2	12	"3 male Blacks"
			"2 female Blacks"[2]

---

1. Camp of Israel schedules and reports, 1845-1849; John Brown's company of 10, report, 1848 June; Church History Library, https://catalog.churchofjesuschrist.org/assets/82b3a69e-d5ec-4752-a52f-e9816e27c554/0/1, <accessed 16 July 2024>

2. Nauvoo (Illinois); City Court. Nauvoo City Court docket book, 1844 February-1845 May , image 64/380, https://catalog.churchofjesuschrist.org/assets/faa87b6f-3343-4486-927a-a5347ebae3c5/0/64?lang=eng, <accessed 16 July 2024>

KNOWN IMAGES OF THE MISSISSIPPI COMPANY

John Brown and Elizabeth Crosby Brown Family

Family Search, https://www.familysearch.org/tree/person/memories/KWJC-KNF

Betsy Brown Fluellen, *100 Century of Black Mormons*

https://exhibits.lib.utah.edu/s/century-of-Black-mormons/page/fluellen-betsy-brown#?

#documents&xywh=-333%2C21%2C1195%2C410

John Daniel Holladay

Family Search, https://www.familysearch.org/tree/person/memories/KWNP-PNH

Mahalia Ann Rebecca Mathews Holladay

Family Search, https://www.familysearch.org/tree/person/memories/KWJ6-MHT

ca. 1848, George Washington Gibson

Cabin Built by George Washington Gibson

https://www.familysearch.org/tree/person/details/KWJ1-43B

Mary Ann Sparks Gibson

Family Search, https://www.familysearch.org/tree/person/memories/KWJ1-44R

Lt. William W. Willis Soldiers

Bevan, James
Calkins, Alva
Coleman, George
Curtis, Josiah
Dodson, Eli
Earl, James
Frederick, David
Hewitt, Eli
Maxwell, Maxie
Willis, William
Woodworth, Lysa
Clifford, Isaac
Bingham, Thomas
Bybee, John
Camp, James
Carter, Richard
Church, Hayden
Clark, George
Eastman, Marcus
Freeman, Elijah
Hinckley, Arza
Whitney, Francis
Babcock, Lorenzo
Blackburn, Abner
Brimhall, John
Burt, William
Dalton, Edward
Dalton, Henry "Harry"
Dunn, James
Green, John

Johnstun, Jesse

Richmond, Benjamin
Rust, William
Shipley, Joseph
Squires, William
Thomas, Nathan
Welch, James
Boring, Boring
Badham, Samuel
Buchanan, John
Compton, Allen
Higgins, Alfred
Hoagland, Lucas
Mecham, Erastus
Stewart, Benjamin
Stewart, James
Hayward, Thomas
Tippets, John
Tubbs, William
Brazier, Richard
Brown, Daniel
Burns, Thomas
Cazier, James
Cazier, John
McCelland, William
Richardson, Thomas
Scott, James
Skeen, Joseph
Wilson, George

MEMBERS OF THE ORIGINAL 1846 MISSISSIPPI COMPANY

The following list indicates those who traveled in the original Mississippi group and the names of those who wintered in Pueblo, Colorado, during the winter of 1846 to 1847.

Returned to Mississippi 1 September 1846

John Brown (1820-1896)
John D. Holladay (1826-1909)
William Harvey Lay (1817-1886)
George Washington Bankhead (1819-1898)
William Crosby (1808-1880)
Daniel Monroe Thomas (1809-1894)
James Albert Smithson (1825-1892)

Remained at Pueblo During the Winter of 1846-1847

Allen Freeman Smithson (1816-1877)
Wife: Letitia Holladay (1824-1849)
Children: John Bartley, Sarah Catherine, James Davis, Mary Emma

George Washington Gibson (1800-1871)
Wife: Mary Ann Sparks (1802-1871)
Children: Mary Densia, Lydia A., Robert Pulaski, Francis Abigail, William, Laura Altha, Moses, Manomas, Joseph

James Harmon (1801-1851)
Wife: Mary Ann Blanks Smithson (1808-1897)
Children: James Bartlett, Sarah Elizabeth, Paralee American, Josephine Smithson, John Taylor (born in Pueblo)

William Cox Smithson (1804-1889)
Wife: Lucinda Wilson Smithson (1813-1899)
Children: Sarah Elizabeth, William Bartley, Martha, Almira

George Washington Sparks (1819 - 1906)
Wife: Lusianna "Luanna" Roberds (1818-1895)
Children: William Thomas, Mary Ann

Benjamin Mathews (1819-1888)
Wife: Temperance Weeks (1817-1859)
Children: Mary Elizabeth, Sarah Jane, Sally

Absolom Porter Dowdle (1819-1897
Wife: Sarah Ann Holladay (1828-1915)
Child: Sarah Catherine

William D. Kartchner (1820-1892)
Wife: Margaret Jane Casteel (1825-1881)
Children: Emma (born in Pueblo)

Mary Ann Reer (unknown birth and death dates)
Children: Perril E., James, Sally Ann, Josephine

William Ritter (1824-1875)
Wife: Sarah Ann Lawery (1825-1876)
Child: Anderson Taylor

John Roberds (1800-1880)
Martha Tucker Walpole (1817-1897)
Children: Lodesky Ann, Richard Thomas, Mary "Belle," Harriet
Liuanna, Francis, William Brown

PICTORIAL JOURNEY OF MISSISSIPPI SAINTS AND MORMON BATTALION; 1846 - 1847

Mississippi Springs, Mississippi

Mississippi Springs monument

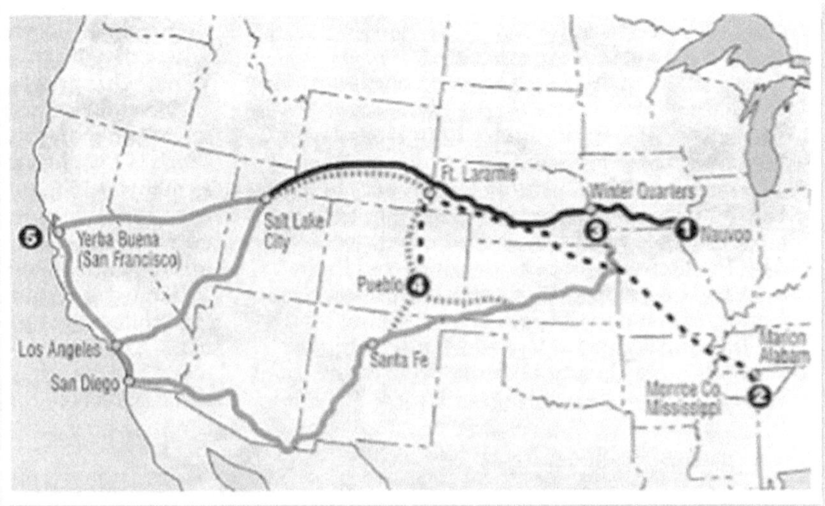

Trails of the Scattered Saints, 1846-47. (1) Main body of Saints (Mormon Pioneer Trail), left Nauvoo on 4 February 1846. (2) Mississippi Company, left Marion County, Alabama, in March 1846 and Monroe County, Mississippi, in April. Spent winter of 1846-47 in Pueblo. (3) Mormon Battalion, left Winter quarters in July 1846. (4) Mormon Battalion Sick Detachments, spent winter of 1846-47 in Pueblo. (5) Saints on the Ship *Brooklyn,* left New York on 4 February 1846 and arrived at Yerba Buena on 31 July 1846.

Reconstructed Fort El Pueblo, at Pueblo, Colorado

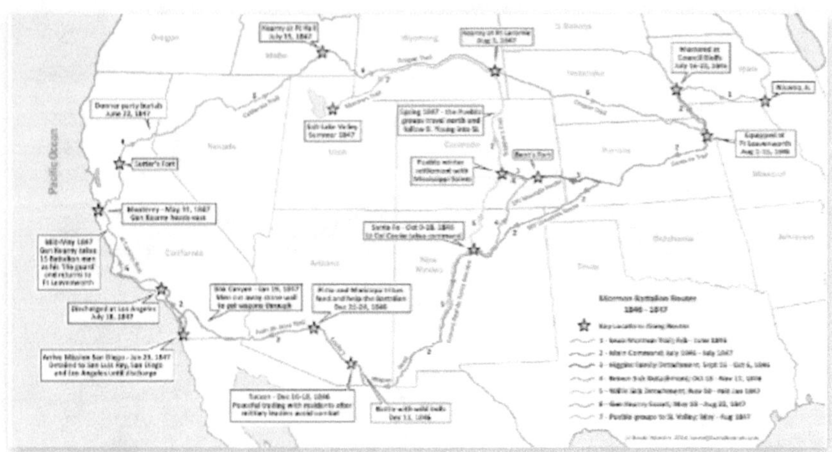

Mormon Battalion Routes, 1846-1847

Reconstructed Replica of Bent's Fort

Possible Hill location of cemetary during the winter of 1846-1847

Mormon Battalion Monument in Pueblo, Colorado

President George Albert Smith Visiting the Mormon Battalion Monument — July 11, 1946

This is the Place, July 1847

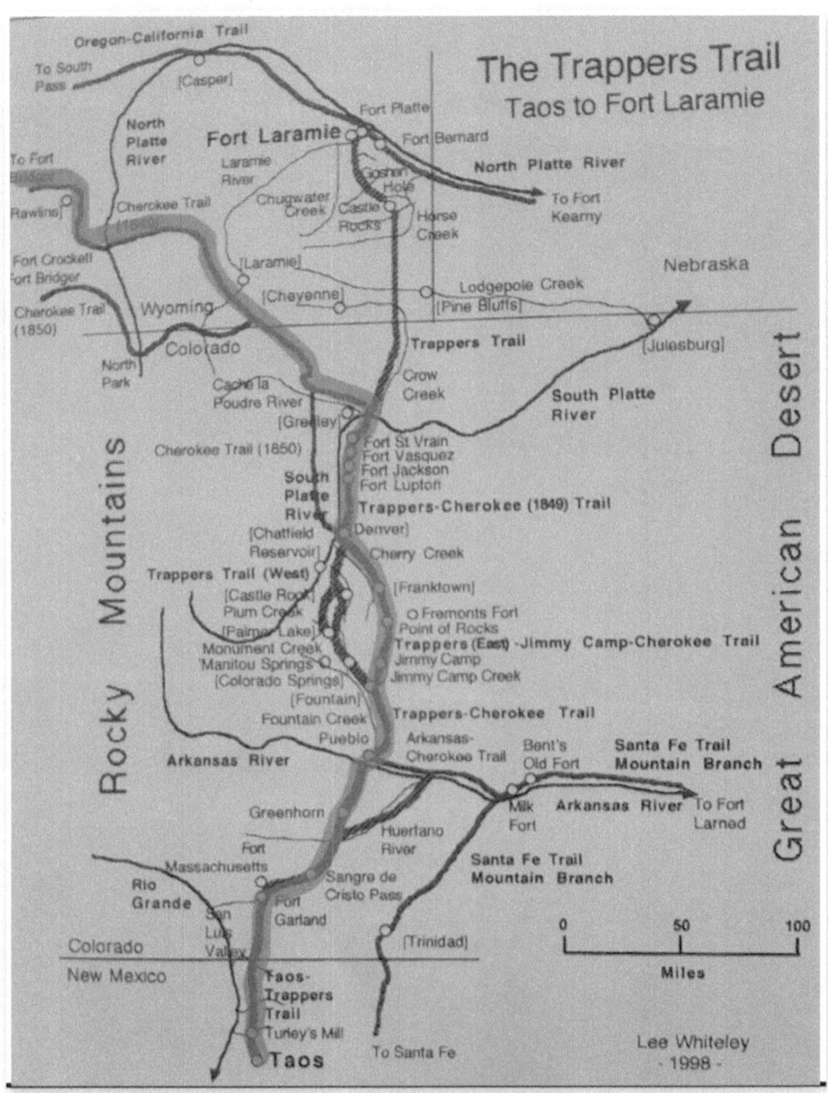

Likely trail taken by the Mississippi Saints, and several members of the Mormon Battalion after leaving Pueblo for Fort Laramie.

G

H

J

Jesus Christ, 2
Jesus Christ, Church of, 7, 11, 15, 25-26, 34, 42, 46, 61, 69, 82, 85, 98, 111, 126, 130, 147, 196, 206, 210, 214, 219, 224, 226, 228, 231-232, 235, 239, 245, 252, 271, 298-300
Jesus Christ, Church of Reorganized, 226, 291, 294, 299
Jimmy's Camp, 115
Johnson, Alice Rowen, 174
Johnson, Charles, 31
Johnson, Jarvis, 305
Johnson, Matlida, 246
Johnstun, Jesse, 311
Jones, Benjamin, 270
Jones, Daniel Webster, 84-85
Jones, Sarah "Sally", 294
Jones, Thomas C., 229
Jordanson, Martin, 249
José, Juan, 213
Judd (Bishop), 243

K

Kansas, 50, 222, 245
Kansas, Alcove Springs, 71
Kansas/Nebraska, Little Blue River, 62
Karren, Thomas, 304
Kartchner, Elizabeth Gale, 266-267
Kartchner, Emma, 315
Kartchner, John Jr. , 265
Kartchner, John Sr., 264
Kartchner, Peter, 265
Kartchner, Prudence Wilcox, 264
Kartchner, Sarah Ann, 303
Kartchner, William D. , 54, 69, 87-88, 102, 139-140, 142, 151-152, 171, 176, 253, 263-265, 272, 281, 313

L

N

P, Q

R

S

U

Y

ABOUT THE AUTHOR

Erick Wadsworth took his love of history to new heights when he wrote the history for the company that he worked for, *Franklin Building Supply: 40 Years and Counting,* which was published in 2016. He enrolled at Brigham Young University (BYU) in 1969, taking a sabbatical until he reentered BYU's online program in 2004, graduating in 2010. He went on to  earn his Master's of History at the University of Nebraska at Kearney (UNK). His thesis earned the "Outstanding Thesis Award" for 2013 – 2014 from the College of Natural and Social Sciences. While attending UNK, Erick was accepted into Phi Alpha Theta. He presented at three regional conferences and one national conference while attending UNK.

Erick loved working at the Family History Center and spending time with his beautiful wife, Marilyn, and his children and grandchildren until his passing in 2025.

www.ingramcontent.com/pod-product-compliance
Lightning Source LLC
Chambersburg PA
CBHW032039050726
47590CB00001B/54